LIVING TOGETHER

LIVING TOGETHER

Rationality, Sociality, and Obligation

Margaret Gilbert

ROWMAN & LITTLEFIELD PUBLISHERS, INC.
Lanham • Boulder • New York • London

ROWMAN & LITTLEFIELD PUBLISHERS, INC.

Published in the United States of America
by Rowman & Littlefield Publishers, Inc.
4720 Boston Way, Lanham, Maryland 20706

3 Henrietta Street
London WC2E 8LU, England

Copyright © 1996 by Rowman & Littlefield Publishers, Inc.

British Cataloging in Publication Information Available

Library of Congress Cataloging-in-Publication Data
Gilbert, Margaret.
Living together : rationality, sociality, and obligation / by
Margaret Gilbert.
p.   cm.
Includes bibliographical references and index.
1. Social groups.   2. Social action.   3. Collective behavior.
4. Political obligation.   I. Title.
HM131.G435   1996   305—dc20   96-12280   CIP

ISBN 0-8476-8150-5 (cloth: alk. paper)
ISBN 0-8476-8151-3 (pbk.: alk. paper)

Printed in the United States of America

∞ ™ The paper used in this publication meets the minimum requirements of
American National Standard for Information Sciences—Permanence of Paper
for Printed Library Materials, ANSI Z39.48–1984.

For Peter Gilbert

Contents

Preface

In my book *On Social Facts* I argued that in order to understand the social dimension of human life one must go beyond the prevailing picture of people acting as independent individuals. People regularly form what I refer to as *plural subjects* and operate as members of the plural subjects that they help to constitute.

The present book, *Living Together*, extends and deepens the discussion in *On Social Facts*. Its subtitle, *Rationality, Sociality, and Obligation*, indicates its main themes. On the one hand, it is concerned with the capacities and limitations of rational agents operating as individuals. On the other hand, it continues the investigation of our sociality, clarifying and probing further the nature of plural subjects. In particular, the idea that membership in a plural subject involves obligations and rights is precisely explained.

Each chapter of *Living Together* is a relatively self-contained essay. The essays refer to one another to some degree but can generally be read independently of one another. A prior reading of *On Social Facts* is not presupposed.

On Social Facts is a long book, with lengthy chapters. Some of the essays included here are more compact or focused presentations of important material in that book. *Living Together* can therefore serve as an introduction to the earlier book as well as an extension and elaboration of its arguments.

I hope and expect that *Living Together* will lead readers who are not familiar with *On Social Facts* to read it for related discussions and a variety of supporting arguments (many pertinent references can be found in the notes). These works complement each other. My proposals concerning the nature of plural subjects and their centrality to human life can best be judged in the light of both. I should stress that I

ix

continue to refine these proposals and see these works as determining the outlines of a theory as opposed to completing its articulation.

Though I have arranged the sections and chapters in a particular sequence—from those focusing on rational individuals to those concerned with sociality and obligation, and within the latter group from earlier to later material—readers are encouraged to start where their interests take them, something made possible by the relative independence of each chapter.

This collection includes both previously unpublished and published material. I have kept changes in previously published essays to a minimum. Any change in substance is indicated in the notes. The introduction addresses the concerns and themes of the book as a whole. A summary precedes each of the book's three sections.

Acknowledgments

In addition to the many individuals and institutions thanked in connection with specific chapters, I should like to thank John Greenwood, Gilbert Harman, Virginia Held, and Frank Stewart for support and encouragement in relation to this book. Saul Kripke is thanked in many places throughout the book, so it seems right to single him out for special thanks here. It has been a great privilege as well as a great pleasure to be able to discuss my ideas with him at many different stages. I should also like to express my admiration and gratitude to David Lewis for encouraging me to publish criticisms of his work on convention, as well as for that work itself.

Keya Maitra read through the whole manuscript and provided thoughtful feedback on a number of editorial and organizational matters. James Phelps, Stowe Teti, Richard Lewis, Miriam Gilbert, Kathleen Roberts, and David Gilbert helped in the preparation of the manuscript. My grateful thanks to all of these, and also to Jennifer Ruark, with whom it has been a pleasure to work.

Work on the manuscript was completed while I was a Visiting Professor at King's College London, on leave from the University of Connecticut, Storrs.

The interest and enthusiasm of colleagues in many disciplines and places have been of invaluable support, as has the love—and patience—of my friends and family. Special thanks in connection with this book go to Cindy Niedoroda and Betty and Paul Kane in New York, and to Maria Bassi and Jane Goldman in Connecticut.

I dedicate this book to the memory of my father, Peter Gilbert, a wise and wonderful man.

*   *   *

I gratefully acknowledge permission to reprint the following chapters.

Chapter 1, "Rationality and Salience," previously appeared in *Phil-*

osophical Studies 57, 1989: 61–77. Reprinted with permission of Kluwer Academic Publishers.

Chapter 2, "Rationality, Coordination, and Convention," previously appeared in *Synthese* 84, 1990: 1–21. © 1990 Kluwer Academic Publishers. Reprinted by permission of Kluwer Academic Publishers.

Chapter 3, "Notes on the Concept of a Social Convention," previously appeared in *New Literary History* xiv, 1982–1983: 225–251. Reprinted with permission.

Chapter 4, "On Language and Convention," originally published as "Agreements, Conventions, and Language," *Synthese* 54, 1983: 375–407. © 1983 by D. Reidel Publishing Co., Dordrecht, Holland, and Boston, U.S.A. Reprinted by permission of Kluwer Academic Publishers.

Chapter 5, "Game Theory and *Convention*," previously appeared in *Synthese* 46, 1981: 41–93. © 1981 by D. Reidel Publishing Co., Dordrecht, Holland, and Boston, U.S.A. Reprinted by permission of Kluwer Academic Publishers.

Chapter 6, "Walking Together: A Paradigmatic Social Phenomenon," previously appeared in *MidWest Studies in Philosophy*, vol. xv, *The Philosophy of the Human Sciences*, eds. P. A. French, T. E. Uehling, Jr., and H. K. Wettstein, University of Notre Dame Press; Notre Dame, 1990: 1–14. Reprinted with permission.

Chapter 7, "Modeling Collective Belief," previously appeared in *Synthese* 73, 1987: 185–204. © 1987 by D. Reidel Publishing Company. Reprinted by permission of Kluwer Academic Publishers.

Chapter 8, "Fusion: Sketch of a 'Contractual' Model," previously appeared in *Perspectives on the Family*, eds. R. C. L. Moffat, J. Grcic, and M. Bayles, Edwin Mellen Press; Lewiston, 1990: 65–78. Reprinted with permission of The Edwin Mellen Press.

Chapter 9, "On the Question Whether Language Has a Social Nature: Some Aspects of Winch and Others on Wittgenstein," previously appeared in *Synthese* 56, 1983: 301–318. © 1983 by D. Reidel Publishing Co., Dordrecht, Holland, and Boston, U.S.A. Reprinted by permission of Kluwer Academic Publishers.

Chapter 11, "More on Social Facts," originally appeared as "The Author Responds: More on Social Facts," *Social Epistemology* 5, 1991: 233–44. Reprinted with permission.

Chapter 12, "Agreements, Coercion, and Obligation," previously appeared in *Ethics* 103, 1993: 679–706. © 1993 by the University of Chicago. All rights reserved. Reprinted with permission.

Chapter 13, "Is an Agreement an Exchange of Promises?" previously appeared in *The Journal of Philosophy* 90, 1993: 627–49. Reprinted with permission.

Chapter 15, "Group Membership and Political Obligation," previously appeared in *The Monist* 76, 1993: 119–31. © *The Monist*, La Salle, Illinois. Reprinted with permission.

Chapter 16, "On Feeling Guilt for What One's Group Has Done," is a shorter version of "Group Wrongs and Guilt Feelings," which will appear in the *Journal of Ethics* in 1997. Reprinted with permission.

Introduction

Two Standpoints—The Personal and the Collective

I. Social Individuals

We are social individuals: beings both independent and interdependent, units that are unified into larger wholes. Living together, we live our lives in terms of two distinct standpoints: the personal standpoint and the collective standpoint.

Each of us has personal goals, such as finding a job or writing a book. Sometimes we see ourselves primarily as pursuing such goals, and doing so in the context of others who do the same. This personal standpoint is to some extent captured within the mathematical theory of games, a theory that has been influential among social scientists and others who seek to understand the nature of social processes.

We have personal goals, but we also participate in group efforts, such as beating the opposing team or increasing the department's output. We then see ourselves as pursuing a goal that is "ours." We take a collective standpoint.

This collective standpoint permeates human life at every level, from that of friends and family to that of nations. What does it amount to? Under what conditions is one justified in adopting it? How is it related to the personal standpoint? Is one of these standpoints the more basic one? In what ways are we helped or hampered by the fact that we have these two standpoints open to us?

The essays in this book address these fundamental issues. In so doing they continue the defense and development of a particular interpretation of the collective standpoint. This was introduced in my book *On Social Facts*.

1

I argue there along the following lines. Quite standardly, when people think and act in terms of what they see as "our goal," for instance, they understand themselves to be members of what I call a *plural subject*. They see themselves, more precisely, as members of a plural subject of the goal in question. People think and talk not only of "our goals" but also of "our beliefs," "our values," "our principles of action," "our language," "our canons of reasoning," and so on. Here, too, quite standardly, they employ the concept of plural subject.

To speak of the goal of a plural subject, in the sense I have in mind, is not *ipso facto* to speak of a goal that each of its individual members has personally, a "shared goal" in what we may call a *summative* sense. The same goes for "our belief" and so on. I argue that whether or not we sometimes use such phrases as "our goal" in a summative sense (and we probably do), we regularly use them in a quite different sense, the plural subject sense.

A plural subject in my sense is founded on what I call a *joint commitment*. Two or more people constitute the plural subject of a goal, for instance, if they are jointly committed to accepting that goal together, or, as I have preferred to put it, *as a body*. Two or more people can accept a goal as a body without each one individually having it as a goal of his or her own. For example, we may, as a body, accept the goal of improving our department's status in the university, without each of us having the improvement of our department's status as a personal goal. (Some of us may think that we personally have little to offer in that regard.)

The fundamental concept of joint commitment is more fully explored in this book. In particular there is a detailed filling out of the claim that joint commitment carries with it *obligations* and *rights* of a special kind. The theory of plural subjects has direct relevance to central debates in ethics and political philosophy by reason of this normative aspect of joint commitment.

One notable aspect of the concept of a joint commitment is what may be called its *holism*. (Traditionally opposed to *individualism*, this might more helpfully be spelled *wholism*.) A joint commitment is the commitment *of two or more individuals considered as a unit or whole*.

I say more about this later, but it is worth mentioning at the outset since it helps to show the special nature of the concept of a plural subject. Not only does the concept of the plural subject of a goal, for instance, not break down into the concept of a set of personal goals. The concept of a joint commitment that lies at its core does not break down into the concept of a set of personal commitments.

The main positive thrust of my argument both here and in *On Social Facts*, then, has to do with the plural subject interpretation of the collective standpoint. When we speak of our goals, beliefs, and the like, we standardly speak as the members of particular plural subjects. This plural subject perspective pervades our lives, private and public. It is radically distinct from the personal standpoint. It is rich and consequential. If we wish to live together in full consciousness of what we are doing, we need to understand the nature and implications of plural subjecthood as best we can.

I discuss the concept of a plural subject in more depth shortly. First I say something by way of introduction to the game-theoretical approach to human interaction, the focus of the first part of this book.

II. The Theory of Games and the Personal Standpoint

If we are interested in the scope and limits of the personal standpoint, the theory of games is a significant tool. An important question is whether and how, if at all, the theory of games can illuminate the nature and functioning of the collective standpoint.

The theory of games is a theory of rational choice: it considers when and why a person has reason to act in one way rather than another in a variety of situations of a specific kind.

The following is typical of the kind of situation considered. Alice and Naomi must both choose, independently, to perform one out of several specified actions, such as going to Cafe Paradis or going to White's Cafe. Naomi ranks the possible combinations of choices her way, and Alice ranks them her (Alice's) way. Thus Naomi may prefer their both going to Cafe Paradis to their both going to White's, and so on. The operative idea here is not that these rankings are in any objectionable way "selfish" but that they are purely personal rankings.

Naomi and Alice are both "rational": each will understand and do what (if anything) reason dictates that she should do, in the light of a concern to do as well as possible according to her ranking of the outcomes, and the facts as so far stated.[1] Further, each person knows of the rationality and rankings of both—these are out in the open between them.[2]

The game theorist asks, of situations like this: Does reason dictate a choice for either party? Can either be sure of achieving the outcome she most prefers? How well can each agent expect to do, according to his or her personal ranking of the outcomes?

Some philosophers assume that whenever all of the agents most want the same outcome, and this fact, and their rationality, is out in the open, reason will dictate to each one that she does her part in that outcome—and hence each will get what she most wants. In Chapter 2, focusing on a case I call "The Guest's Dilemma," I argue that this is not so. Other discussions in Chapters 2 and 5 make it clear that reasoning on the basis of the agents' preferences and rationality is not as powerful a tool as is often assumed.

In Chapter 1, I argue that the existence of a "focal point" or "salient" outcome is not the help it is often assumed to be. In Chapter 2, I argue similarly regarding the existence of a successful precedent, that is, one or more preceding situations in which each party achieved the best possible result for him or herself. In short, the discussion in these essays helps to show that many situations that have been thought tractable for rational agents acting independently are actually problematic.

One way in which the theory of games can throw light on the collective standpoint is by virtue of what it can show of the limitations of the contrasting personal standpoint. One can argue for the importance of plural subjects by looking at some of the ways in which rational agents acting in terms of their personal preference rankings and personal principles of action are liable to be frustrated. In at least some cases, the formation of a plural subject of a relevant kind can alleviate the problem. This is argued in the last three sections of Chapter 2.

III. Game Theory and Social Processes

It is important to see that for people operating roughly like the agents of game theory, rationality has severely limited power. Those who are inclined to deny this are inclined, I think, to see our own situation as largely realizable in game-theoretical terms. Can a satisfactory account of our sociality be given in such terms?

Inspired by proposals of the economist Thomas Schelling, the philosopher David Lewis argued in his well-known book *Convention* that, in effect, the everyday concept of a social convention could be analyzed in game-theoretical terms, without bringing in any holistic concepts.

Lewis's treatment of convention has been rightly admired. It has influenced discussion in many disciplines, including philosophy, economics, and jurisprudence. My own work on rationality and sociality has been spurred by questions raised by Lewis's discussion, and by his impressive attempt to bring precision and clarity into the analysis of social process concepts. Some important *problems* in Lewis's use of game theory are detailed in Chapter 5.

According to Lewis, a convention exists if and only if (roughly) members of a certain population regularly conform to a certain pattern of action, this conformity achieves a generally desired coordination of actions, members expect it to continue, and this gives them reason to continue to conform themselves. For example, members of a population of drivers may regularly drive on the right side of the road, thereby avoiding collisions. Everyone may expect everyone else to go on driving on the right, which gives them reason to go on doing so themselves. The important thing for everybody is not which side is chosen, but that the same side is chosen by all.

This account of convention raises a number of important questions. Among these are its relationship to rationality, and its relationship to sociality and the collective standpoint.

We tend to see ourselves as beings who guide our lives by reference to reasons. Many have found Lewis's account of convention attractive because it seemed that after one or more lucky coincidences, conventions in Lewis's sense would arise and be perpetuated by purely rational processes. Nor does anything resembling an agreement between the parties have to play a role. It turns out, however, that Lewis's model of convention is not "rationality-driven" in the relevant sense. The arguments of Chapters 1 and 2 concerning salience in general, and precedent in particular, make this clear.

Suppose it is allowed that, in order to generate Lewisian conventions, people may need to go beyond reasoning, making use of certain "blind tendencies," such as the tendency to follow a successful precedent. This could still seem to be an attractively "minimalist" picture. It could look as if the movement from individuality to sociality is very smooth—hardly a movement at all. Given successful precedent, social conventions, paradigmatic social phenomena, arise out of the operation of personal psychological tendencies and reasoning capacities. No agreement need be entered into. No *sui generis* synthesis of distinct persons is required.[3] No "real unity" is made of a plurality of individuals.[4]

Have we in fact entered the realm of social processes and phenomena when we arrive at Lewisian conventions? One way of approaching this question is to consider whether Lewis's account of social conventions captures our everyday concept of a social convention, as he hoped. For on the face of it the concept of a social convention is the concept of a social phenomenon: if there is a social convention, there is sociality *par excellence*, or so one might think.

I argue in Chapter 3 that Lewis does not capture the everyday concept of a social convention. None of his conditions on convention appear to be necessary from this point of view. In that chapter I also develop an alternative account, according to which social conventions are "norms of quasi-agreement." I do not now think we can rest with this account. As I indicate at the end of Chapter 2, I believe that a wholly adequate account will characterize the concept of a social convention as a plural subject concept.

What of the sociality of conventions in Lewis's sense? I focus on sociality as such in Chapter 11, presenting a case for a relatively narrow characterization in terms of plural subjecthood. According to this characterization, those who arrive at Lewisian conventions have not thereby arrived at sociality.

Certainly we cannot fully understand human sociality if we do not come to grips with the concept of a plural subject. This—in my view—is inherent in a family of everyday concepts including the concept of a social convention. Only when we understand the nature of plural subjecthood do we understand the collective standpoint, and without understanding that standpoint, we cannot understand human sociality.

IV. Social Processes and Language

Though he has made an important contribution to philosophical social theory, Lewis himself was not especially concerned with the nature of sociality or the collective standpoint. He was concerned, rather, with language. He hoped that his account of convention would help to explicate the platitude that "language is ruled by convention." Such explication was, indeed, the avowed aim of *Convention*.

I argue in Chapter 4 that we should not try to explicate the nature of language as such in terms of *social conventions* either as Lewis construes these or in any plausible sense. The question of the allegedly *social nature* of language as such is approached from a different angle in Chapter 9, where I critically explore certain arguments inspired by Wittgenstein for the thesis that language as such has a social nature.

Even if language *as such* does not necessarily have a social nature, it is clear that groups have languages, and the question of what it is for a group to have a language is extremely important. Most of us, most of the time, use the language of a group. I see the concept of a group's language (or "group language") as a rich one. A key aspect of group languages is discussed in Chapter 10. Group languages are argued to require *outward criteria*, in a Wittgensteinian sense, for sensation and other mental process terms. The concept of a group language adumbrated here is a plural subject concept.

V. Plural Subjects: A Developing Theory

I now say more about plural subjects. The essays in this book that relate to plural subjects were written at different points between 1986 (when *On Social Facts* was completed) and 1995. In what follows I explain some of the developments in my ideas and formulations during this period.

Those unfamiliar with *On Social Facts* may wish to read some of the essays before proceeding with this section, starting perhaps with Chapters 6 and 7. The essays connect plural subject theory with one or another aspect of everyday thought and experience—doing things together, for instance, or feeling guilt over what one's group has done. Most incorporate some account of plural subjecthood, relating it to the matter at hand. What follows should help further to illuminate the most fundamental matters touched on in the essays.

i. Formulations: toward an emphasis on joint commitment

I have gradually settled on a particular way of characterizing plural subjects. This stresses the pivotal role of joint commitment. When I began to explicate the plural subject concepts in *On Social Facts*, I experimented with a number of different characterizations.[5]

a. Group belief, "joint acceptance," and joint commitment

Regarding a plural subject of belief, one characterization I have proposed runs roughly as follows: Two or more people constitute a plural subject of belief if and only if they jointly accept some proposition (for instance, the proposition that it is now snowing in Vermont). In order *jointly to accept* a proposition people must express to one another their personal willingness jointly to accept that proposition.

The joint acceptance of a proposition carries with it a set of obligations and entitlements.

My use of the phrase "joint acceptance," as opposed to "joint belief," was not intended to make any particular point. There is, I take it, a sense of the term "acceptance" in which it is a synonym of "belief." "Acceptance" and cognate terms should be interpreted in this sense in my account of a plural subject of belief.[6]

The joint acceptance account as articulated thus far is fine as far as it goes. One does better, however, explicitly to incorporate a reference to joint commitment. One does best to put things this way: in order to constitute the plural subject of a belief, or, equivalently, jointly to accept a certain proposition, two or more people must be jointly committed to accept the relevant proposition jointly. Or, as I prefer: they must be jointly committed to accept the proposition *as a body* (*as a unit, as one*).

An expression of willingness jointly to accept a proposition can now be explained as an expression of willingness to be jointly committed with others to accept that proposition as a body. This helps to clarify my reiterated claim to the effect that the relevant individual *expressions of willingness* are closely related to *commitment—reach toward commitment*, if you like. For a joint commitment is formed on the basis of such expressions, no one of which has the power, on its own, to bring it or even part of it about.[7]

In Chapter 7 of this book the elements of the account of a plural subject of belief I prefer are all present. The connection between joint commitment (there "commitment as a body") and joint acceptance is implied rather than spelled out. Chapter 14, which elaborates on a number of important aspects of the account in Chapter 7, and was written some years later, explicitly proceeds on the basis of the recommended formulation.

b. A general schema

A plural subject of belief is, of course, just one example of a plural subject. I referred earlier to the plural subject of a goal, discussed in Chapter 6 in relation to walking together. My preferred account of this is of the same form. Generalizing: for any set of people, $P1, \ldots Pn$, and any psychological attribute A, $P1, \ldots Pn$ form the plural subject of A-ing if and only if they are jointly committed to A-ing as a body.

This general schema makes it clear that the plural subject concepts can be characterized as psychological concepts in more than one sense. First, plural subject concepts apply only when certain individual people are in specific psychological states, that is, only when they are jointly committed with certain others in some way. Second, one cannot employ a particular plural subject concept without employing the concept of the relevant psychological attribute *A*—such as belief, having such-and-such as a goal, and endorsing such-and-such a principle.

When people speak about *our* belief, *our* goal, and so on, they use a very familiar form of words. I argue in *On Social Facts*, Chapter 4, that the first person plural pronoun "we" is standardly used in what may be termed the *plural subject sense*. That is, in this use the people referred to by the pronoun are presumed to constitute some kind of plural subject—in the sense defined here.

To be the member of a plural subject is to be part, with certain others, of the subject of certain psychological attributes. This may sound quite mysterious—as may the idea of what *we* believe as opposed to what you and I both believe, and so on. But when unpacked it should not mystify. To be part of the subject of a psychological attribute with certain others is to participate in a joint commitment with the appropriate content.

Further aspects of the general schema just proposed are addressed in Chapter 14.

c. Pooled wills and joint commitment

In describing the constitution of plural subjects in *On Social Facts*, I often use the phrase "a pool of wills" and related expressions. (See also Chapter 6 here.) I do not find these expressions inappropriate. The terminology of joint commitment, however, is more helpful. I now tend to use it exclusively, saying that in forming plural subjects people form joint commitments, rather than that they pool their wills.

The difference does not reside in the familiarity of the notion of joint commitment. Though I argue that it is a fundamental part of our everyday conceptual scheme, it is not a standard part of social theory or philosophy. But it can be made relatively precise, and, if the notion of a pool of wills can be criticized as vague or metaphorical, the notion of a joint commitment is not open to such criticism.

As I explain below, once the reference to joint commitment is incorporated explicitly in the account of plural subjects, the idea that those who form a plural subject have a corresponding set of obligations and rights is more easily grasped. This is a compelling reason for making the presence of joint commitment explicit in any account of a plural subject concept.

ii. Plural subjects, joint commitment, and obligation

Joint commitment is introduced in Chapter 4 of *On Social Facts*. Important aspects of the notion are noted at different points through the rest of the book.[8] A more unified treatment is found in several of the essays here. Among other things, this allows one clearly to perceive the sense in which joint commitment—and hence plural subjecthood—involves obligations and rights.

Such involvement was emphasized rather than explained in *On Social Facts*. Several of the essays here elaborate upon it in different contexts and in varying ways. I regard this as a crucial part of the theory of plural subjects.

As noted earlier, the general idea of a joint commitment is the idea of the commitment of two or more individuals considered as a unit. This rather stark description may not be obviously fruitful. But consider the following.

Suppose that a commitment is not yours, or mine, nor a composite of a commitment of yours and a commitment of mine, but rather the commitment of the two of us. Who, if anyone, is in a position to rescind or abrogate the commitment? Presumably neither you alone, nor I alone, but the two of us, together.

What may be called the *joint abrogation constraint* goes very naturally with the root idea of the commitment of two or more individuals considered as a unit, whether or not that idea straightforwardly implies it. In any case I take the concept of joint commitment that (in my view) underlies much of our everyday life to incorporate that constraint: A joint commitment cannot be rescinded unilaterally by any individual party to it. The parties must rescind it together.[9]

What, someone may ask, of my *part* of a joint commitment to which I am a party? Can I not at least rescind *that*? As I understand it, the answer is negative. One way of putting things is to say that one cannot rescind one's part of a joint commitment. Another, better way, is to say that a joint commitment does not, in the relevant sense, *have* parts. A joint commitment is not a *sum* or *aggregate* of commitments such that each of those committed through it "holds sway" over his or her part of that sum, and is in a position to rescind it.

This is not to say, of course, that a joint commitment does not commit the parties to it. It serves as a constraint on the behavior of each. But it is not composed of something of mine and something of yours, for instance. It is "ours," period, and only we can rescind it.[10]

Given only the foregoing considerations, the question of how and in what sense obligations and rights are involved in joint commitment can be answered. What follows gives the gist of the answer I have in mind. More is said about this in Chapter 12.

Like a personal decision, a joint commitment in which I participate serves as a constraint on my behavior. There is a sense in which I now have reason to act in a particular way—in conformity to the commitment. In the case of a joint commitment, as opposed to a personal decision, *I need the concurrence of certain others* (as they need mine) *both to impose the constraint and to lift it*. In other words, the joint commitment *ties me to the other participants* with respect to what I have reason to do: together we control both the genesis and the demise of the reason in question. A very natural way to put this is as follows: I have an *obligation* to conform to the joint commitment.

I conjecture that much of our talk of obligations, and correlative rights, as well as much of our talk about "ties" and "bonds" between people, actually comes from our understanding that there is a joint commitment in the relevant place. I believe, for instance, that our talk of the obligations of everyday agreements and promises, such central and such common features of everyday life, has this source. If we are to understand agreements and promises and the hold they have upon us, we must understand the nature and structure of joint commitment. I argue for this in Chapters 12 and 13.

It should now be clear that the obligations and rights involved in a joint commitment are of a special kind. From a technical point of view, they may best be referred to as "obligations of joint commitment."

The relationship between the obligations of joint commitment and *moral* obligations is worth pursuing. This matter is given an initial treatment in Chapter 12.

iii. On being committed (and obligated) through a joint commitment

Though it is not clearly appropriate to speak of the *parts* of a joint commitment, each of the parties to a joint commitment is committed through it. It is therefore tempting to refer to the parties' "individual commitments."

This could seem to be the way to reduce the concept of joint commitment to something less holistic. Such a reductive aim must ultimately fail, however, for the—quite special—logic of these so-called individual commitments is driven by the holistic concept of a joint commitment, a commitment that is the commitment of two or more people considered as a unit or whole. It is this concept in terms of which the parties to a joint commitment themselves operate.

If one does speak of "individual commitments" here, one must bear in mind that these so-called individual commitments have quite special properties. First, there is what may be called the *no unilateral abrogation property*. Two or more people are required in order to abrogate the joint commitment on which each party's individual commitment depends. The only way of "abrogating" one of these individual commitments is by abrogating the joint commitment, which a given committed party is not in a position to do.

Second, there is what one might call the *non-independence property*. The so-called individual commitment of a given party to a joint commitment cannot exist independently of all other such commitments.

The minimum number of people who can be subject to a joint commitment is two. It is therefore impossible for anyone to be committed—or obligated—through a joint commitment unless at least one other person is. More precisely, if someone is subject to a joint commitment, the correlative individual commitment of that person is such that it cannot exist unless at least one other person, with whom the first person is jointly committed, also has a correlative individual commitment.

In many of my discussions I have had occasion to focus on a case of joint commitment involving just two persons. In this kind of case the lack of independence of the "individual commitments" of the parties is especially clear.

Suppose that Hetta and Netta are the sole participants in a joint commitment. They are jointly committed to believe as a body that Jason will soon return. All else being equal, if Hetta were no longer committed through their joint commitment, Netta could no longer be committed through it either. Netta must lose her commitment through the joint commitment as soon as Hetta does, since it is impossible for just one person to be committed through a joint commitment. Here, then, the individual commitments of the parties are *interdependent* in the following strong sense: *they cannot exist without each other*.

This comes out in an important way in another context. Suppose Hetta and Netta are not, initially, jointly committed to believe as a body that Jason will come soon. Netta then indicates to Hetta that she is ready to be jointly committed in this way. She has done—let us assume—all that need be done on her part in order to participate in such a joint commitment. She is still not committed through the relevant joint commitment. In order for Netta to be committed through the joint commitment, Hetta must indicate *her* readiness to be so committed. When and only when Hetta responds appropriately, will either one be committed. Then both will be committed—simultaneously.

Not only are the "individual commitments" inherent in Hetta and Netta's joint commitment interdependent in the strong sense noted, and (hence) arrived at simultaneously. So are the obligations inherent in that commitment. Hetta cannot be obligated through the commitment if Netta is not.

The two person case is clearly somewhat special, if only because it is the minimal case of joint commitment. It is best to discuss the variety of cases involving more than two people on their own terms.[11]

For now, suffice it to say that, quite generally, the type of "individual commitment" that I automatically have through a joint commitment is not a type of commitment that I can have on my own. The individual commitments of those who are jointly committed are always interdependent in the broad sense that *they cannot exist without fellows of their own kind.*

One who lives in isolation, away from other people, can come by no new individual commitments through a joint commitment: he or she would need to engage with someone else in order to do so. So much is obvious, given that a joint commitment requires more than one person in order to exist. It is worth stressing, however, because *it is not obvious that there is a type of "individual commitment" such that one cannot be subject to a commitment of that type unless someone else is subject to one as well.*

iv. On what it takes to escape from a joint commitment— and some related matters

It is of some interest to consider whether and how someone can lose or escape from a joint commitment that has not been abrogated.

One simple method involves a particular type of joint commitment. This is not so much a commitment between people insofar as they are those particular individuals, but rather a commitment between people insofar as they have some feature or other, such as living on a certain island or being members of a certain university department.

Presumably when you cease to have the feature in question you cease to be subject to the commitment. This would not need the intervention of any other parties, but would accord with the understanding of all.

What, it may be asked, of *default*? There are certain cases which suggest that—in those cases at least—one person's defaulting on their obligations through the commitment in effect destroys the commitment and gets everyone out of it. A plausible candidate case here is that of one side's willful default on a joint commitment between two persons, where each has effectively just one thing to do in order to fulfill the commitment. For instance, we jointly commit together to accept the plan that you will come to the beach with me today and I will go to the movies with you tomorrow.

One can look at it this way: the person who defaults has nullified his or her own obligation under the commitment. But that is to nullify the joint commitment as a whole. Hence that commitment no longer exists to affect the other party.

For more complex cases, the idea that one default of one person necessarily explodes the whole thing may seem less plausible. As I discuss in Chapter 16, default *in general* may function as follows: one person's default renders the joint commitment not so much *void* as *voidable* at the pleasure of the other parties (to use legal terminology).

In the two person case, there is only one other party, so that the joint commitment would now be voidable at that person's pleasure. This would mean that person was now in a position unilaterally to void the joint commitment and so be free of it. But this means that already the party who has not defaulted is not obligated as before, for to be obligated in the relevant sense is to be subject to a commitment that one is not in a position to remove on one's own.

This way of looking at things, then—in terms of voidability—may be a promising way of tying different cases together, retaining the intuition that in certain cases one person's default amounts to the end of the joint commitment.

At this point a brief note on the fragility or otherwise of joint commitments is in order. If one person can destroy a joint commitment by defaulting on it (albeit in a special case) does this not mean that a joint commitment is to begin with so fragile (at least in this case) as to be useless?

The answer (even for this case) is that much depends on the parties' needs and attitudes. If what both most need is to pin the other (or both of them) down, then neither will have an incentive to default. For if I default, I remove the original constraints of the joint commitment from *you*.

Clearly, people do default on their joint commitments as these are understood here: there is a sense in which most of the time they *have that power*. In the middle of a conversation, I *can* abruptly turn away without the slightest preliminary communication or explanation. And so on. On the other hand, by jointly committing ourselves, we understand ourselves to affect our situation in a variety of ways. Apart from affecting what we now have reason to do, in a way we cannot unilaterally change, we grant others a special standing in relation to us. We make our business *their* business. Among other things, we give them a mutually understood, and known to be mutually understood, basis for upbraiding us if we default on the commitment, a basis equally for demanding recompense. The knowledge that all this is so can serve as a powerful incentive not to default. It is a standing potential incentive in all cases of joint commitment.

The discussion here and in the previous section makes it clear that there can be significantly different types of plural subject, types of which importantly different things can be said. Precisely which kinds are different from others and in what ways I take to be an important question, if we are to understand the plural subject concepts fully. Among the types I discuss in this book are those formed by a group of people in a context where all are present together (the walkers in Chapter 6, the discussion group of Chapter 7, the couples in Chapter 8, the parents talking in the privacy of their own room in Chapter 14). At the other end of the spectrum are the plural subjects involving many people who may not know of each other personally, who may never have seen most of the rest, and so on. If nations, for instance, are ever plural subjects, they will be plural subjects of this kind. The conditions of the coming to be and the persistence of such plural subjects clearly needs careful consideration. (I say something about such groups in a number of places including Chapter 15.)

My understanding of the plural subject concepts, both as a family and as individuals, continues to evolve. The essays included here advance the discussion considerably beyond *On Social Facts*.

VI. The Explanatory Power of Plural Subject Theory

An understanding of joint commitment and its attendant obligations suggests solutions to many problems in moral and political philosophy as well as social theory. Several such problems are addressed in this book.

i. "Social pressure"

In Chapter 14, I focus on a puzzling phenomenon that has to do with the expression of opinions. There are many occasions on which someone expresses an opinion and one or more listeners rebukes the speaker in a special way, a way that suggests the speaker has somehow *offended against them*. In explanation, I propose an underlying collective belief construed as the belief of the plural subject the listeners and the speaker form.

Another type of situation in which "offended rebukes" occur is when people are doing things together—something that happens in practically every realm of human life. People run countries and companies together, build roads and houses together, eat together and go walking together, to cite a range of examples. The simple example of walking together is one I have focused on in more than one place, in large part because of its simplicity (see Chapter 6, and, more briefly, Chapter 15).

When walking together one party may rebuke another who is, say, lagging behind. I argue in Chapter 6 that a range of initially plausible analyses of acting together does not provide a satisfactory explanation of what goes on here. A plural subject account in terms of a jointly accepted goal—that is, the goal of a plural subject formed by the participants—appears to do so.

Given the points made in the last three paragraphs, we have a new way of construing a phrase common in social theory, namely, "social pressure." We can understand social pressure as, roughly, pressure exerted by virtue of common membership in a plural subject. Whatever we call them, we have a new way of understanding the basis of the pressures we put on one another through offended rebukes and more stringently punitive actions in a variety of contexts.[12]

ii. Agreements and contracts in social and political theory

Another example of the explanatory power of plural subject theory concerns the perennial attraction that talk of "agreements" and "contracts" have for those who theorize about human society. Many philosophers and social theorists refer to "tacit" agreements or "implicit" contracts in describing the social world. But before we can make much use of such references we need to know what an *explicit* agreement amounts to.

In *On Social Facts* I at one point briefly sketched a novel interpretation of explicit agreements: underlying any such agreement is a joint commitment of a specific kind, one that constitutes a *joint decision*. This idea is developed and defended in detail here (see Chapters 13 and 14).

One consequence of my account is that agreements involve the same underlying structure of commitment as many other social phenomena, including social conventions (as I understand these) and collective beliefs. The proneness of social and political philosophers to talk of agreement as the core of human association thus becomes understandable. Explicit agreement is not a good candidate for this role, and certain ideas of what a tacit or implicit agreement amounts to make that, too, an implausible candidate. Joint commitment is a far more plausible one.

Feminist philosophers among others have argued against a "contractual" model of personal relationships or societies. How one assesses this position depends, of course, on how "contract" is understood. However that may be, my arguments suggest that if we focus on what everyday agreements *achieve* (a particular form of joint commitment, which itself constitutes an interpersonal *bond* or *tie*) we will be more sympathetic at least to the proposal that something *agreement-like* is fundamental to our personal relationships and social being. Understanding the core of an agreement to be a joint commitment, I argue in Chapter 7 that love itself, in one guise at least, may have a "contractual" base.

Moving from the small to the large, in Chapter 15 I sketch an account of political obligation which could be referred to as the *plural subject account*. It has affinities with traditional "actual contract" accounts but diverges from the existing accounts in significant ways. Philosophers have puzzled over the sense many people have that they have "political bonds" (A. John Simmons). My argument for the connection of joint commitment with obligation plays a crucial role in my explanation of the sense in question.

iii. Group wrongs and guilt feelings

A common feeling that has been argued to go "beyond conception" (Karl Jaspers) seems, on the contrary, to be explicable in terms of joint commitment and plural subjecthood. This is a feeling of guilt for what one's group—perhaps one's country—has done, irrespective of one's own role in the group's action. I argue for such an explanation in Chapter 16. My argument suggests that many commonly accepted claims about what it is to feel guilt must be rejected.

iv. Observations and images of human society

The special structure of the plural subject concepts makes sense of many observations and images that have been put forward since the beginning of reflection on the human condition by philosophers, sociologists, and psychologists. Among these are Plato's thought that people could (to a large extent) operate in terms not of "mine" and "thine" but of "ours," Durkheim's stress on the *constraining power* of what he referred to as "social facts," the frequent idea that society is something *organic*, Simmel's view that it is of the essence of marriage that it harbor conflict, his related (and important) claim that the human individual is both inside and outside the community of which he or she is a member (on both see Chapter 8), and Maslow's sense that the marital couple is indeed a true unit (see Chapter 8).

The explanatory power of the plural subject concepts may not be limitless, but I want forcefully to stress how many questions seem to be answerable or at least illuminated by reference to them and their special structure.

VII. Summary

The essays in this collection approach the complex condition of social individuals from a variety of angles. They continue my attempt to illuminate the special character of the collective standpoint that pervades our living together, distinct and separate individuals though we may be.

The gist of my understanding of the collective standpoint is this: joint commitment, a commitment of a special, "holistic" kind, lies at its core. Joint commitment obligates us, one to the other. It makes—to some extent—unified wholes out of disparate, unified parts. There is a sacrifice of personal freedom in group life, and a risk of great personal frustration (on these see in particular Chapter 8 and Chapter 14). There are also the compensations of a joining of forces, including the creation of fund of concern for our singular selves (on which see Chapter 8).

A joint commitment is not a matter of feeling or emotion, and its positive effects are by no means limited to emotional ones—important as these are. An example that ties together the different strands in these essays concerns rational agents who are regularly faced with a particular coordination problem. They will be well served by jointly accepted standards of conduct, for the underlying joint commitment provides a crucial stabilizing force that even common personal desires or common personal principles of action cannot supply. (I argue this in Chapter 2.) In addition, the joint commitment provides an intelligible basis for the imposition of pressure that all parties can be expected to acknowledge simply by virtue of their acknowledgement of the commitment itself, pressure that can act to keep the participants on track.

My claim is that the plural subject concepts, concepts of joint commitment, are "everyday" concepts, concepts at work all the time as human beings live their lives in one another's company. These are concepts in terms of which we both create and make sense of our experience. It is to be expected that many phenomena can be better understood theoretically, once we are armed with explicit analyses of these concepts.

The concept of a plural subject is both descriptively and explanatorily fruitful, and, at the same time subtle and special. Its continuing investigation is an important task.

Notes

1. Sometimes additional factors—such as a successful precedent—are allowed in, sometimes one or another is subtracted. Note that "rational" is given a specific interpretation here. In effect, *reason is given a restricted mandate*: "Work out how I (the reasoner) can do as well as possible according to my ranking of the outcomes."

2. Here I write of something's being "out in the open." In a game-theoretical discussion it would be said, rather, to be "common knowledge" between the parties. On "common knowledge," see Chapter 1, note 4, Chapter 3, and elsewhere. Though common knowledge of rationality is the usual assumption, there has been some discussion of the effects of removing that assumption.

3. Cf. Durkheim (1895/1982).

4. Cf. Hobbes (1651/1982), cited in Chapter 6.

5. See *On Social Facts*, Chapter 7, especially pp. 408–10, where, summarizing the argument of the book, I give three possible schemas for analyzing the plural subject concepts, prefer the third, and articulate the third in

terms of "jointly committed wills," that is, in terms of what I call "joint commitment." The latter phrase was introduced in *On Social Facts* at p. 198. In "Modeling Collective Belief," 1987 (Chapter 7 here), I wrote of being "committed as a body."

6. This is discussed further in Chapter 14.

7. In *On Social Facts* and elsewhere I have sometimes written, in this context, of people expressing a "conditional commitment." This is probably not the most appropriate phrase, though it may be the most appropriate of the phrases in common usage. See Chapter 12 here, note 25.

8. Central passages include p. 198 (the special type of mutual expression that leads up to a joint commitment; there are ensuing entitlements and obligations), pp. 209–10 (dependence on some kind of continuous mental activity of the parties), pp. 212–21 (cases involving many people who do not know each other personally or know of each other as individuals; possibilities of misunderstanding; communication and plural subject formation; adding members; changing content; multiple memberships), p. 382 (the exchange of "conditional commitments" leads to the parties becoming bound to act in certain ways simultaneously and interdependently), and pp. 412–14 (possibilities of exit; the meaning of default; agreement).

9. There may be ways of getting around this constraint, in practice, but these ways of getting around it will be driven by the understanding that it is there. I have sometimes referred to this constraint as the "mutual rescension" constraint, but the label I give it here is preferable.

10. In *On Social Facts* I sometimes write of a "sum of wills" as well as of a "pool of wills," and at one place, in response to a question from Jerry Shaffer, I rejected the idea that "pool" was intended to imply that the wills in question somehow merged together to become indistinguishable, as drops of water might merge in a pool of water. (I stressed, at the same time, that the wills in the pool were "dedicated *as one*.") I would now prefer not to use the word "sum," and would not be so ready to dismiss the analogy with the "component drops" of a pool of water. As indicated in the text above, I now prefer not to talk of a pool of wills but rather of a joint commitment. It is crucial to an understanding of joint commitment that such a commitment is understood not to be constituted by "parts" each of which can meaningfully be ascribed to one of the parties as "his" or "hers."

11. I have rewritten passages in some of the later essays for this book in the light of a concern not to describe the general case in more detail than I do here. All revised passages are signaled in the notes.

12. I bring this point of view to bear on social rules in (1995ms) and (forthcoming c).

Part I

Rationality, Coordination, and Convention

Essays 1 and 2 argue for some important limitations of rationality in the context of the common type of situation that has come to be known as a *coordination problem*. The essays dispute the efficacy of certain proposed solutions. Among other things, it is argued that success is not guaranteed by the existence of a salient solution, a combination of actions preferred by all, or a combination of actions that succeeded earlier.

Coordination problems became the subject of philosophical focus through an influential account of *social conventions*. According to David Lewis, coordination problems underlie conventions—by definition. Essays 3, 4, and 5 approach Lewis's account critically, from different angles: as an account of the everyday concept of a social convention, in relation to the platitude "language is ruled by convention," and in terms of its use of the mathematical theory of games. An alternative account—conventions as "norms of quasi-agreement"—is explored in essays 3 and 4.

The account of social conventions that the author currently prefers—conventions as group *fiats*—is sketched in essay 2. It is argued that conventions in this sense can help to overcome some of our difficulties in coordination problems.

1

Rationality and Salience

It turns out that sophisticated subjects in an experimental setting can often do very well—much better than chance—at solving novel coordination problems without communicating. They try for a coordination equilibrium that is somehow *salient:* one that stands out from the rest by its uniqueness in some conspicuous respect. It does not have to be uniquely *good,* indeed, it could be uniquely bad. It merely has to be unique in some way the subjects will notice, expect each other to notice, and so on. [Lewis (1969), p. 35; Lewis is reporting experimental findings of Schelling; see Schelling (1960)]

A number of authors have envisaged a model of the generation of action in coordination problems in which salience plays a crucial role. (Apart from Schelling and Lewis, I have in mind later work by Schiffer, Ullman-Margalit, and others.) As the above quotation indicates, appeal to salience accords with experimental results: empirical studies suggest that human subjects are likely to try for the salient combination of actions in situations of the relevant type. This tendency to choose the salient seems all to the good. If everybody chooses the salient, a fortunate result is obtained. There remains an important question in the theoretical understanding of action: how precisely does salience facilitate the successful coordination of actions in a coordination problem? Some have thought that rationality dictates that one do one's part in the salient solution. That this is so may even seem obvious: failing any other reason for action, surely one has reason to do one's part in the salient combination of actions? In this essay I shall argue that one does not. If human beings are—happily—guided by salience, it appears that this is not a consequence of their rationality. It looks as if it may be said: When we do our parts in the salient combination, we do not reason. We act blindly.[1]

23

I. Preliminaries

Some preliminary clarification of terms is in order. A standard example of a *coordination problem* is the telephone case: a telephone call is cut off, and each party has to decide what to do, whether to call back or to wait. Both want the call restored. The situation may be represented by the following payoff matrix.

I shall not attempt to settle on a formal definition of a coordination problem here.[2] For present purposes, the following general features may be assumed. First, the value of the outcome of any one person's action to that person will depend on what the other does. (In the telephone case, if and only if only one waits, and only one calls back, will the call be reconnected.) Second, the agents' rankings of the various possible combinations of agents' actions are identical. Hence, were it possible for the agents to make an agreement as to who would do what, there would be nothing very problematic about the situation. Third, where it is not possible for the parties to make an agreement

	Call Back	*Wait*
Wait	1 1	0 0
Call Back	0 0	1 1

Fig. 1.1   Payoff Matrix

(The cells of the matrix represent combinations of the agents' actions. A given cell represents the combination of the action described at the top of the relevant column, together with the action described at the side of the relevant row. The numbers in the lower left-hand corner of each cell represent the payoff to the player whose available choices of action are described at the side of the rows, the numbers in the upper right represent the other player's payoffs, and the actions referred to at the top of the columns represent his[3] available choices.)

about who will do what, or otherwise to communicate their intentions, and there is no special background knowledge, the parties have a genuine problem: Should each make a random choice of action, the chances of achieving the desired coordination of actions are not good.

Our question can be put thus: will agents who are rational in the sense of the mathematical theory of games find a reason for action in mere salience? In the context of game theory the attributes of *rational agents* are implicitly held to include the following: (a) They are perfect reasoners, in particular, given the information available they will make no mistaken inferences. They will, moreover, utilize all relevant information that is available. (b) Each one is out to do as well as possible according to his/her individual ranking of the outcomes. (c) Each will act on the balance of reasons, if the balance of reasons dictates a particular course of action (which it may not do). In what follows, when I refer to "rational" agents, I should be understood to be referring to agents with the features just mentioned.

In game theoretic discussions of problems of coordination (and other problems) among rational agents, it has always been assumed that each agent's rationality, and each agent's preferences over the outcomes, are entirely out in the open between them. Thus each can assume that the other will reason appropriately, and that the other will assume that he will reason appropriately, and so on. In what follows I shall take it that, when discussing the situation of rational agents, we are discussing agents whose rationality and preferences are out in the open in this way. Following David Lewis, and, later, Robert Aumann in economics, it is now standard to write of "common knowledge" in this connection.[4]

There is an issue as to whether and to what extent human beings are game theoretically rational. I shall not enter into that question here, but what I have to say will have an obvious bearing on it, given the reported experimental data.

Following what seems to be the general understanding, I shall take it that a particular combination of actions is *salient* if and only if it is entirely out in the open among the agents concerned that this combination is "the odd man out" or "stands out from the rest" for all.[5] Given that a certain combination of actions is salient in a certain situation each agent can assume that the premise that *the combination in question stands out for all* will be recoverable from his reasoning by the others. In other words, he can take it for granted in his reasoning, while relying on the others being able to figure out that he does, and to figure out that he relies on this, and so on.

II. Does Salience Generate Reasons for Acting?

Salience in general may be a psychological matter, in the sense that what is salient depends on who is involved. Whether or not this is so, there remains the question whether salience, once it is present, will generate a reason for action for rational agents as such, other things being equal.

In the literature we find partisans of both sides on the question of reason-generation. David Lewis, who appeals to salience in presenting a model of the genesis of conventions, appears to assume that salience is *not* in itself reason-generating.[6] Meanwhile, others assume that it is. Indeed, as far as I can tell this has become a standard assumption among writers influenced by Lewis's account of conventions.[7] Possibly Lewis's use of a broadly game theoretical framework has misled some people. It is quite easy to fall into the assumption that he has presented a flawless "rationality-driven" model of a convention's origins.

Jane Heal argues for reason-generation explicitly against Lewis. Many others simply take it for granted. In this essay I shall, in effect, be presenting considerations in favor of Lewis's (unargued) position, and against that of Heal and others.

Is salience sufficient, ceteris paribus, to solve a coordination problem for all rational agents? To provide a focus for discussion, here is an example of a coordination problem containing a combination of actions which would (presumably) be salient at least in a population of Western academicians.[8]

Suppose that Sally Brown and Joe Smith, strangers to each other, have been kidnapped and put in separate cells. They have no means of communicating with each other. The kidnapper has given both of them a board with four colored squares (red, blue, yellow, and purple) and a button by each square. The boards are connected to a central unit that records who has pressed which button. Neither Sally nor Joe can see the other's colored board. At noon, the kidnapper makes the following announcement over a loudspeaker that can plainly be heard by both of them. "At 12:15 P.M. precisely I want each of you to press a button on your color board. If, without communication, you both press the button for the same color, you will both go free. If you are not unanimous, or someone fails to press a button, you will both die. It matters not at all which color you choose. The only thing that matters is that you choose the same color." He pauses, then begins to speak again. "To afford you some distraction before 12:15 P.M., my secretary will turn on the radio for five minutes and play it over the loudspeaker. Have a good day!'' After a moment the radio comes on. There is some music at first and then the announcer says: "Today is our president's birthday. His wife is giving a party for him using red as the theme color. Red is the president's favorite color. There will be red tablecloths on the tables, the waiters will wear red jackets and ties, the president's wife will wear a red dress, red stockings, and red shoes, and the food eaten will all be red: gazpacho soup, sole in a tomato sauce, and a strawberry dessert.'' At this point the radio clicks off. Let us take it that when, a few minutes later, Sally and Joe look at their color boards, the combination of actions constituted by each one's choosing red will "stand out" for each one, and this will be entirely out in the open. In other words, this will be the salient combination of actions as far as they are concerned.

Now suppose that Sally and Joe are rational agents according to the characterization given above, and suppose that the following facts are entirely out in the open: (1) They are both rational. (2) Each wants to live. (3) Combination of actions C (choosing red) stands out for both. (4) *There are no other relevant facts bearing on the decision as to what is to be done.* Is each one now in a position to figure out what to do? This should be so, if, ceteris paribus, salience is a reason for action in an otherwise recalcitrant coordination problem. In my view, it is not. No reason for acting can be directly inferred at this point. This can be argued quite briefly, as follows.[9]

Given that C is salient, Sally can argue as follows: "C stands out for us both. Clearly, I should do my part in C if Joe does. But will he?'' How can Sally figure out what Joe will do? Suppose she tries to look at things from Joe's point of view, that is, to figure out how Joe will reason. By hypothesis, she will see that Joe also knows that C stands out for both. She will also see that he is faced with the question whether to do his part in C. He will see that he should do his part if Sally does hers, and he will ask himself whether he has reason to think she will do her part. But it is clear that he will find no such reason; in particular, an attempt to replicate Sally's reasoning will get him nowhere.

Someone might wonder whether it would help matters if we stipulated that it was common knowledge that Sally and Joe were out to maximize *expected utility*. This would not seem to make any difference. The expected utility of a given action of Sally's will depend on the probabilities associated with the different actions open to Joe. But why should she assign a higher probability to his doing his part in C? The original argument arises again in terms of probability rather than proof.[10] Someone may suggest that Sally could rely on induction, knowing that people like herself and Joe tend to rely on the salient, and thus assign a higher probability to his doing the salient thing than to his doing the nonsalient thing. But we are not supposing that there is any such background knowledge. We are considering precisely what Sally and Joe might figure out given only the salience of one combination of actions, plus common knowledge of rationality, as defined, and of the matrix. One reason for so doing is precisely to see whether a "tendency" of the kind referred to might just be, in effect, the result of the exercise of reason alone in a pared-down context of the kind in question. My argument is that any such tendency cannot be seen as having such a genesis.

It should now be apparent that if anything is going to give Sally or Joe a reason for action in the presence of salience, it is going to be some new background belief such as the belief that the other person will in fact do his part in the salient combination. It may help to reinforce the idea that salience does not itself provide a reason for action to consider a case that involves the introduction of a belief providing a reason *against* choosing the salient. Assume that, after his statement about the president's birthday, the announcer had presented the following news item: "Sally Brown, who has been kidnapped along with Joe Smith, is said by her husband to be salience-shy. In other words, in a coordination problem with a salient combination of actions, Sally may be expected not do her part in the salient combination: she will do her part in some other combination." Whether or not Sally is indeed salience-shy, Joe now has reason to believe that she is, and Sally knows that he has this reason. In brief, each now has reason to avoid the salient option, and, surely, will be rational to choose some other option. Though we could think this while allowing that salience always provides a prima facie reason to choose the salient, it may well be judged in this case that it is not as if an existing prima facie reason for action has been overridden or outweighed by another reason.[11]

A rather special type of case may suggest this even more clearly. Suppose that Sally and Joe hear a single radio announcement, as follows: "It is well known that Joe Smith and Sally Brown are phobic with respect to the color red. Each will avoid choosing something red at any cost." Presumably when they have heard this the combination of actions consisting in their both choosing red will be the salient combination of actions: it will definitely be the "odd man out" and "stand out" more than any of the other action combinations. But here the fact that makes choosing red salient is the fact that red *will not be chosen.* It seems hard to credit the idea that salience so derived could provide even a prima facie reason for action. And, if it does not, then it is false that salience in general provides such a reason.

Whatever one's immediate reactions to these cases, the argument I have given above seems to me conclusive against the idea that salience as such provides a reason for action. Let me now consider a counter-argument, from Jane Heal. "Both *A* and *B* have good reason for choosing the salient simply in virtue of the fact that, clearly, doing so is the only (or the easiest and most reliable) way of coordinating."[12]

This argument is used *"contra* Lewis": "we do not have to suppose as a last resort that *A* thinks that *B* has a tendency to choose the salient so that *A* himself has a reason for choosing the salient." In other words, Heal supposes that nothing other than (valid) reasoning directly from the fact of salience need be "resorted to," to explain why agents choose the salient.

As stated here, this argument does not seem to work. If both agents were to do their parts in any acceptable combination of actions, surely this would be an equally good "way of coordinating." So each agent has an equally good reason for doing his part in any one of the other acceptable combinations of actions. In other words, no special reason is available to support doing one's part in the salient combination.

Heal's suggestion that choice of the salient is the "most reliable" way of coordinating may suggest that she implicitly assumes that a significant empirical premise about human behavioral tendencies will be common knowledge to the participants. I have in mind the premise that human beings tend to do their parts in a salient solution. The rest of Heal's discussion goes against this interpretation, however, for she explicitly claims that there is no need for the agents to appeal to anyone's "tendency to choose the salient."

Prior to the passage quoted above, Heal writes at greater length on the issue. Though I do not think her argumentation here is more successful, it has points of contact with that of other authors (in particular Stephen Schiffer) and is worth examination.

Heal suggests that (1) the agents in a color matching case "know that they can co-ordinate their choices only if they can single out one colour from the rest, by some feature" (ibid.).[13] She goes on: (2) "*A* and *B* know that by choosing a colour which does stand out for them, and *only* by doing this, can they hope to coordinate" (ibid.). She continues: (3) "This provides a reason for each to make the choice of the outstanding colour, which is reinforced by knowledge that the other has that reason" (ibid.).

These remarks suggest the following points, with which one can easily agree. First, the situation when there is only common knowledge of rationality, the matrix of preferences, and the actions available to them is truly problematic. Assuming that, when rational agents with a color matching problem individually lack a reason to choose a particular color, they will then choose at random, their chances of coordinating their choices is not good: the more colors that are involved, the worse their chances become. Second, given this initial situation, it will be both necessary and sufficient for the successful coordination of action that for each agent one and the same color is "singled out," in the sense that, for each agent, there is a reason to choose that color. For, if each has such a reason, and, rationally, acts on it, their choices will be coordinated in the desired fashion. What have these indisputable points to do with salience? Something, indeed, but not enough for Heal's argument to go through. If the situation is otherwise unchanged but one acceptable combination of actions is salient, one and the same color is now, indeed, "singled out" for each agent, in the sense that it appears as the "odd man out"—this is so by the definition of salience. Thus, as Heal suggests, granted that it is common knowledge that no further facts that could aid their reasoning are available, it seems that the agents know this: if anything can help them, it must be salience.

At this point, however, we seem to have gone as far as we legitimately can down the path Heal traces. *Can* salience do the trick? Does it, that is, provide each agent with a reason for choosing the salient? If the argument I have given is correct, it does not. Mere salience is *not* enough to provide rational agents with a reason for action (though it would obviously be nice, from the point of view of rational agency, if it did). We may grant that salience is the only thing that *could* provide a reason here. We must conclude, however, that it fails to do so.

Nothing I have said here is intended to deny that salience may allow agents with instincts or psychological propensities of the right type unfailingly to solve otherwise recalcitrant coordination problems. For agents endowed with the appropriate psychological features, salience may presumably serve as a "clue" sufficient for the achievement of coordination. What I have argued is that salience gets us nowhere within the pared-down framework of game theory. In order to ensure that a rational agent moves in a particular direction we need to give him knowledge that he *has a reason* to move in that direction rather than another. I have argued that salience as defined here does not provide what is needed.

It looks as if hidden equivocations may sometimes lie behind the sense that salience can conquer all. What is in fact necessary for a solution of the problem is that each agent single out one and the same combination of actions *as the one he personally has reason to do his part in.* Any other sort of "singling out" is not enough. Each must "notice" that a given combination is *the one he should do his part in.* Each must see that a given combination is (obviously) *the one he should do his part in.* Unfortunately, participation in common knowledge that a certain combination is "uniquely conspicuous" or (perhaps most ambiguously and treacherously) "obvious" does not lead to the right kind of "singling out" or "noticing." It will not help matters to redefine salience in a reason-providing manner. For salience is supposed to provide a mechanism by reference to which the question "How might rational agents discover what they ought to do?" may be answered. Clearly it is pointless to answer: "By finding that some particular combination of actions is *obviously the one they should do their parts in.*" How are they supposed to find *that* out?[14]

A point about the general notion of salience as defined here may now be noted. Presumably the notion is at least sometimes properly applied to a combination of actions that rationality dictates one should do one's part in quite independently of salience considerations. In such cases the intersection of required strategies could be called "salient," from the point of view of the general concept of salience. But even though this is so, the fact that this combination is (or may be) salient *will not affect anyone's reasoning,* since independently of the salience, reason already dictates what each is to do, and being rational they will do that thing. A reference to the salience of a particular combination in this context, then, is theoretically pointless, albeit conceptually proper. But it could also be misleading. Since the salient combination is also the one each ought to do his part in (by hypothesis), the important conceptual distinction between combinations of these two types in general could become blurred. That it is an important conceptual distinction has been the burden of my discussion of salience here. To use a phrase of John Mackie's, I have argued that salience in the sense at issue here is not *intrinsically action-guiding.* This is one good reason for not talking about salience in the kind of context in question.[15]

Of course, one might point out, as Thomas Schelling does in effect, that if we were all to follow the maxim "ceteris paribus, do your part in the uniquely salient solution" we would solve more problems than we would otherwise.[16] Pointing such things out can be helpful. But it is the main burden of this essay that this maxim will not necessarily be followed by all rational agents as such.

A similar response is appropriate, I suggest, to an idea of David Gauthier's. Gauthier argues that salience "does enable persons (in a coordination problem) to coordinate their actions" (1975, p. 210). Though this is his overall view, his position is complex. He first argues that, insofar as salience as such does not alter the payoff structure, it cannot be taken as in itself providing a reason for acting by "rational maximizers of utility." Hence "salience does not in general allow rational persons to generate mutually supporting expectations which converge on the salient equilibrium." Nonetheless he insists that salience does enable persons to coordinate their actions. He argues that salience enables persons to "substitute, for their original conception of the situation, a more restricted conception," given which the situation is no longer problematic. In this new conception of the situation, each person has to choose between two options: (1) go for the salient point; (2) randomly choose, with equal probabilities to each, among all the available strategies. Gauthier then argues "coordination is easily achieved" once the parties so reconceive the situation, which has its own, derived payoff matrix.

In his explicit reasoning Gauthier appeals to the idea that the reconceived situation has "but one best equilibrium." And he takes it that when this is so, successful coordination is achieved by acting in accordance with what he calls the "principle of coordination."[17] I have argued against this principle as a general principle elsewhere.[18] But for present purposes we can waive Gauthier's own general characterization of how reconceiving the situation helps, noting that in at least some cases the reconceived situation allows for a straightforward argument as to what one should do, which makes appeals only to the payoff numbers. (Indeed, each party may now have a dominant strategy.) Let us ask whether this shows that at least these cases are solvable for all rational agents in the way Gauthier suggests.

The logical structure of Gauthier's suggestion seems to be as follows. In certain circumstances, a rational agent can reason starting thus: "If each of us reconceives the situation in such-and-such a way (and his having done so is out in the open), then it will be obvious to each of us that he should do his part in the salient combination of actions, and then we will coordinate (more or less) as desired." From this it is presumably supposed to follow that each *should* reconceive the situation in the relevant way. Given that each one does so, and this is obvious to all, coordination at the salient point will be achieved. But this form of argument is open to the very type of objection that, I have argued, can be made to a direct or ground-level appeal to salience in the first place. It begins with a *conditional* about what will happen (a good outcome) if each player does a certain thing. But you only have reason to play your own part here if you have reason to think the other players will. But what reason can this be? Each of them is in the same position as you.

Once again, then, we can agree that in certain cases it would be *good* if *all* rational agents as such would do a certain thing (in this case reconceive their situation in a certain way). All rational agents can recognize this, without that generating any confidence in a given rational agent that his rational opposite number will act accordingly on this or any other occasion. (Note what might be referred to as the *influence-independence* of the participants. The fact that a good outcome would be reached if *both* did something cannot by itself be a reason for either one individually why he should do it. For his doing it cannot itself ensure that the other does it.)

Someone might defend Gauthier as presenting an account of how salience *could* work (if everyone decided to abide by a certain policy) or an implicit psychological account as to how it is salience often seems to be *used*. (People may tend to reconceive the situation as suggested.) His own discussion is perhaps slightly ambiguous on this score. But he does imply that "successful coordination" which "depends on conceiving a situation" in a certain way, is a "matter . . . of reason." In any case, in the context of a discussion of game theoretic rationality as characterized here, I think we must conclude that his idea does not show that rational agents as such will derive a reason for acting directly from the fact that one solution is salient.

A final point. The psychological nature of salience, and so perhaps the non-reason-providing nature of salience, might be queried for some cases. For instance, in a color-matching case in which there are more than two colors it may seem that if one color has been mentioned over a loudspeaker just before the choice had to be made, choosing that color now would be the salient choice *for all rational agents*. (Contrast here the case where each party only has two choices. Then whereas one color can be singled out as being the color that has just been mentioned, the other can be singled out as being the color that has *not* just been mentioned.) The psychological nature of salience may seem even more open to question for a type of case noted by Schelling, in which the matrix itself contains an observable asymmetry. It may be, for instance, that one of the more preferred outcomes is the worst, several tie for best.[19] Possibly in such a case the worst of these points will, *for all rational agents,* "stand out from the rest by its uniqueness in some conspicuous respect" (Lewis).

Even if this point is well taken—it may be—it leaves the crucial question whether in these cases there is a reason for doing one's part in the salient combination of actions. Given that rationality does not in general dictate that one do one's part in a solution by virtue of its salience, it is hard to see how it can do so here.

I conclude that rational agents as such cannot be expected to do their parts in a salient solution in a coordination problem. This point is worth stressing, and not just because we could run into rational beings who are not equipped with human psychologies. For one thing, it is clear from the literature in this area that it is tempting to deny it. (I was myself quite surprised when I first saw it was true.) Meanwhile, it is important to understand the scope and limits of rationality. This is so for more than one reason. We may prefer that our lives be structured as far as possible by the exercise of reason. Then we need to understand which are the situations in which reason can indeed move us. We may also want to know how we actually work. As my opening quotation suggests, it seems that human agents tend to do their parts in a salient combination of action in an otherwise intractable coordination problem. According to the argument of this essay, this tendency cannot be explained as an expression of each agent's knowledge that, if a combination obviously stands out for all, then *ipso facto* each one has reason to do his part in it.

III. Salience and Instinct

What, then, might explain it? There are various possibilities. In this concluding section I focus on one general idea of what goes on—an idea contemplated by David Lewis—and two possible developments from it. In my kidnapping case, perhaps we would choose red under those conditions because we are made that way. That is, because each of us feels pulled toward a combination of actions that obviously stands out for all.[20] Evidently it is useful to be made that way, if all one's fellows are. So there could be some evolutionary explanation of how this tendency developed.

There is more than one way things could develop given the seed of an instinctive pull, on the part of each, to choose the salient. Suppose that each of us feels an instinctive pull or tendency to choose red.

Given an understanding that others are made the same way, this will not be a pull there is any obvious reason to resist. Indeed, there is every reason to go along with it. Hence, from the seed of common instinct, a mutually acceptable pattern of behavior could emerge.

Lewis points out that it would be enough for each agent in a coordination problem simply to ascribe to the others a tendency to choose the salient "as a last resort, when they have no stronger ground for choice," and hence choose the salient himself.[21] In this case it is not necessary that anyone in fact has a tendency to choose the salient as a last resort. All that is necessary is that each one believes the others have such a tendency, and that in this case each of the others is so placed he will act on this tendency. Each will then have sufficient reason to do his part in the salient combination of actions. In the event, each could be acting purely on the basis of reasons in choosing the salient.

There is clearly something disturbing about such a state of affairs. For one thing, everyone is wrong about everybody else. (Everyone in fact acts on the basis of reasons, rather than on the basis of his unreasoned tendency, but everyone thinks that everyone else will act on his unreasoned tendency.) Again, everyone regards his own situation as unique; he is acting on the basis of reasons, the others are not.

I do not say that some people may not sometimes operate in such terms. (I can report that one participant in an informal experiment I conducted explained his choice of the salient combination in terms of *everyone else's* "suggestibility.") However, in the model I am now considering the main force operating in each case is not the agent's reasoning (about others or anything else) but his own unreasoned impulse. Reasonably ascribing a similar impulse to others (either through observation of their actions or simply through knowledge that they are the same kind of creature) he sees no reason to struggle against this tendency. As Lewis in effect points out, if he does ascribe a similar impulse to others, this will provide a strong prima facie reason to do his part, irrespective of his own impulse. However, it seems plausible to suggest that generally the process starts with the inclination of the agent in the face of salience, and proceeds with reason allowing inclination to take its course.

Another way things could develop from the seed of impulse is suggested by the ease with which many have felt salience considerations could be fitted within the framework of game theory. Not only do we in fact tend to choose the salient, but apparently the combination of actions that obviously stands out for all may come to seem *the thing*

one should (obviously) do one's part in. Given the natural impulse
model under consideration, a Humean (and also Wittgensteinian) idea
comes to mind. Recall how Hume famously talks of the human mind's
tendency to expect that a *B* will follow an *A*, once *B*s have followed *A*s
in the past, and suggests that it is this tendency in us that produces our
(dubious) belief in some kind of necessary connection between *A*s and
*B*s: we project the tendency of our minds on to objects "out there"
(and then attempt to justify our tendency by appeal to the [perceived]
nature of things). Recall also how, according to Wittgenstein, in
"obeying a rule" for the use of a word we actually act "blindly,"
"without reasons."[22] Meanwhile there is an evident temptation to
suppose (wrongly) that we are relying on some knowledge that *justifies*
our going on as we do. In other words, we are tempted to suppose that
we do what we do for a reason.

   We may or may not accept the "debunking" arguments of Hume
and Wittgenstein on the matters that concerned them. In particular,
we may not be convinced that the proposed justification of the practice
in question is indeed unavailable.[23] Meanwhile, in the salience case, if
we insist that the salient combination is what *should* be chosen, it
seems that we may well be involved in the projection of an unreasoned
compulsion on to reason. If this makes it easier for each of us to
choose the salient, then perhaps it is just as well, as a matter of
practice, if not of theory.[24]

Notes

   1. "Blindly": here I echo Wittgenstein (1953), part I, section 219. I say
some more about the relation of my concerns in this essay to Wittgenstein's in
the final section.
   2. For notice of some problems with David Lewis's game theoretic definition of "coordination problem" see Chapter 5.
   3. In all such contexts "his" is to be read as "his or her," and so on.
   4. Doing so is somewhat complicated by the fact that more than one
technical definition of "common knowledge" has been given. The commonest
definition in philosophy and economics is as follows: For any two agents *A*
and *B*, *it is common knowledge between A and B that p* if and only if *A* knows
that *p*, *B* knows that *p*, *A* knows that *B* knows that *p*, *B* knows that *A* knows
that *p*, and so on. Several alternatives to this definition have also been
contemplated. See Lewis (1969 and 1975), Schiffer (1972), Aumann (1976).
Also see Heal (1978). I discuss the issue of definition further in *On Social*

Facts, pp. 188–95, and elsewhere. See also Chapter 4, section 3, this volume. The details of this issue need not concern us here.

5. In the passage quoted above, Lewis (1969) writes of "standing out from the rest by its uniqueness in some conspicuous respect": he also uses a characterization which seems considerably weaker, in terms of "being unique in some way everyone will notice, expect the others to notice, and so on." It is not clear that several different combinations of actions could not be salient in this sense. The definition of salience in this context should, evidently, be such that there can only be a single salient combination of actions in a given occurrence of a coordination problem.

6. See Lewis (1969), p. 35. On the presence of nonrational factors in Lewis's model of the origin of conventions, see Chapter 2 and *On Social Facts*, Chapter 6. See also section III below.

7. See for instance Ullman-Margalit (1977) (p. 112); Schiffer (1972), pp. 145–47. See also G. Postema (1982), p. 174.

8. This example resembles the case on which Heal (1978) focuses. In her case salience is a result of a previously successful precedent. I deliberately eschew examples in which precedent gives rise to salience here, since precedent involves special features and we are concerned with salience as such and in general. I discuss the case of precedent separately in Chapter 2. See also *On Social Facts*, Chapter 6.

9. The following way of arguing regarding salience is an application of a type of argument I have used in discussion of successful precedent as such, and other facts common knowledge of which some have deemed to give rational agents a reason for action. See Chapter 5, and, with the focus on precedent, Chapter 2. See also *On Social Facts,* Chapter 6, and my discussion of Gauthier, below.

10. Sally might simply assign a high prior probability to Joe doing his part, but, if one does not engage in circular reasoning here, she might just as well assign a high prior to one of Joe's other actions. Actually, it seems to me that any assumption of the assignment of such arbitrary priors to particular actions, rather than of the deduction of probabilities from the assumed rationality of the other agents, is dubious in a discussion of purely rational agents with common knowledge of rationality. This position conforms with that of classical game theory. (See Aumann [1987], p. 1236, "Headnote.") I shall not attempt to debate this issue here.

11. I am indebted to an anonymous referee whose comments suggested this line of argument. Thanks also to Simon Blackburn for an example that suggested to me the next case in the text.

12. Heal (1978), p. 129, footnote.

13. This is very similar to Schiffer (1972), p. 146. See also Postema, loc. cit.

14. I do not deny that there could be a use in a different context for a conception of the salient as that which one is "obviously" called upon to do. Cf. McDowell (1979), p. 335. I thank Joel Kupperman for the reference.

15. See for instance, in Gauthier (1975), pp. 207–9, Gauthier's first example of a way in which one of the best equilibria in a situation may be salient. (It is not clear that we need to bring consideration of expected utility and expected indifference into play here, as Gauthier does. We can appeal to the rationality of maximizing one's security level, ceteris paribus. Cf. Schelling (1960), p. 297. See also Kuflik (1982).

16. "Ceteris paribus" is to rule out any cases where there is somehow a conflict between the salient solution and what rationality dictates given the payoff matrix. Cf. Gauthier (1975), p. 209, note 11.

17. Gauthier presents this principle on p. 201.

18. Gilbert (1983ms). See Chapter 2, this volume.

19. See Schelling (1960), pp. 295–96.

20. Cf. Lewis (1969), p. 35.

21. See Lewis (1969), pp. 35–36.

22. "Without reasons": Wittgenstein (1953), section 211.

23. There is a skeptical discussion of Wittgenstein in *On Social Facts,* Chapter 3.

24. I presented a version of this material to the Philosophy Department, the University of Connecticut, Storrs, 9 October 1985. I am grateful for the comments I received. Thanks also to Simon Blackburn, Peter Hammond, Saul Kripke, and John Troyer for comments on written material. I completed this version while a Visiting Fellow in the Philosophy Department, Princeton University.

2

Rationality, Coordination, and Convention

Introduction

In what contexts can rational agents rely on a favorable outcome in their dealings with others? In this essay I contest some common assumptions relating to this question. Assuming that each agent is rational in a certain sense, less is possible for them than might be thought. But my discussion is not wholly lacking in comfort for rational agents.

I. Assumptions

My discussion uses certain standard assumptions of the theory of games. Thus I shall consider situations initially assumed to satisfy the following ("ideal") conditions: (i) Two or more agents are involved, and each one has to choose one of a number of actions that are open to him (or her). (ii) Each agent has ranked the possible combinations of the different agents' actions on a personal scale of preferences. (These preferences need not be derived only from "selfish" considerations.) (iii) Each of the agents is rational. In particular: (a) he is a perfect reasoner, and will take all relevant known facts into account in reasoning about what to do; (b) he is out to do as well as possible in the circumstances, according to his preference ranking. (iv) In the absence of reasons sufficient to determine what he should do, a given agent will act freely in the following sense: no probability will be (rationally) assignable to his choosing one action over another.[1]

(v) There is common knowledge among the agents of the rationality of each agent, of the actions available to each, and of the payoff matrix, that is, of the way the outcomes are ranked by each agent. These things are known to everyone, each one knows that they are known to everyone, and so on.[2]

In consequence of these assumptions, the agents are empowered to replicate each other's reasoning. Moreover, each one's reason-replication can take into account that the other agent knows of his rationality and can replicate *his* reasoning. Finally, (vi), no one has any further information bearing on their decision problem beyond that already noted, and this is common knowledge.

Within this general framework, in what contexts can we confidently say "In such a situation, a rational agent will do such-and-such"? In particular, when can we predict that a rational agent will reach his most preferred outcome?

II. The Unreachable Peak

Let us call a combination of actions that each agent ranks higher than any other a *unique best point*. Many philosophers have expressed the view that if there is a unique best point then rational agents will do their parts in it.[3] This view may hardly seem to need arguing, given that plainly it will be common knowledge that if each agent does his part in such a point, everyone will get what he most wants. Nonetheless I believe this view is false. I argue this in relation to an imaginary case which I call the "Guest's Dilemma."[4]

Consider the situation of two people—call them David and Joshua—who have been invited to dinner by a mutual friend. Each has to decide whether or not to bring a present of wine or some such offering to the dinner. It is common knowledge between them that they have both been invited, and that each is considering whether to bring a present. They have no way to communicate with each other before the dinner.

Let us suppose that since giving a present is expensive, and both are strapped for money, each would prefer not to bring a present than to bring one, all things being equal. However, the very worst possible outcome for each is if he fails to bring a present and the other brings one. He will then feel ashamed, uncomfortable, ungenerous, and so on. This is one outcome he intensely wishes to avoid. Meanwhile, these are people who do not wish to see each other discomfited. While his own embarrassment is the very worst thing he can imagine, he does not particularly want the other to be shown up. He would, then, rather be joined in giving a present than be the sole present-giver. The preference rankings in this case can be represented as in Figure 2.1 (including a representation of degree of preference). A given cell of the matrix represents the combination of the action indicated at the left of its row (David's option) and the action at the head of its column (Joshua's option). David's payoffs are represented in the lower left corner of a cell, Joshua's at the upper right. There is common knowledge of the preference rankings.

Suppose we look at the case at an intuitive level first. What would you advise David to do? I know that I would suggest that he take a present. It seems to be too much to risk the acute embarrassment he will feel if he alone fails to bring a present. It could be, however, that there is an overriding argument for the unique best point strategy—that is, not taking a present— that such advice overlooks. I do not believe that there is, but this view evidently needs arguing. Let us consider by what argument each agent could reach the conclusion that he should do his part in the unique best point.

Let us first ask what seems to follow for a rational agent from the fact that he is in a situation in which there is a unique best point, this is common knowledge, and there is common knowledge that all the agents involved are rational. What, in particular, might David and Joshua conclude when these are the materials they use to construct an argument?

By virtue of what a unique best point is, the following premise is

	No Present	Present
No Present	2 2	0 -10
Present	-10 0	1 1

Fig. 2.1

available to each: If the other does his part in the unique best point, then I should do mine. This premise is conditional, however. In order to generate the conclusion that "I should do my part in the unique best point," it evidently requires, in addition: the other will do his part in the unique best point. Let us consider whether there is any way each can each add this premise to his stock.

Let us look at how reason-replication might work, imagining how David might proceed. "Let me put myself in Joshua's shoes. Like me, he will know that if I refrain from taking a present, then he should too, and we will then both get our most preferred outcome—saving money without embarrassment. Knowing this, he may try to figure out what I will in fact do. He will be hoping to discover that I will not give a present. So let me see how Joshua will get on if he tries to replicate my reasoning: will he find out that I will not give a present?"

At this point, David should begin to smell a rat. How could it be that Joshua will find that he, David, will not give a present, if David's decision not to do so is contingent on his knowledge of Joshua's, and Joshua's decision remains to be determined by David's? The basis for a decision in either case cannot, it seems, be forthcoming.

It is now clear that, in the context at issue, reason-replication is an indefinite and useless process.

It is of course trivially true that if and only if I do my part in a unique best point can I possibly get my maximum payoff. Perhaps, then, that can count as a reason for doing my part. Clearly, however, it is not a reason of a type to settle the matter.[5] It is not in the same class as: I definitely will get my maximum payoff provided that I do my part. Given that a unique best point does not provide, by its mere existence in a situation, a conclusive reason for doing one's part in it, a rational agent must look at the other details of any payoff matrix containing such a point.

Returning to the Guest's Dilemma, note first that the situation of the agents is entirely symmetrical. So let us arbitrarily consider the matter from David's viewpoint. I have already noted, in effect, that David has available to him a "maximin" strategy: a strategy that minimizes his possible loss. Choice of this strategy will, in this case, guarantee that he will obtain a relatively good payoff, and that he will avoid the very bad worst outcome. There is, then, something to be said for his adopting this strategy, given that he has no basis for any rational expectation about what Joshua will do. Perhaps there is also something to be said for his adopting the best point strategy, namely, that only by doing so can he get his top-ranked outcome. However, what he will actually get depends on what Joshua will do. And unless Joshua chooses his unique best point strategy, he stands to do very badly.

In the absence of some helpful information about Joshua, then, it can surely not be argued that the balance of reasons favors the best point strategy. Let us ask, finally, what happens if David has recourse to reason-replication now taking into account the nature of the matrix as a whole?

Presumably, if the situation of the agents is entirely symmetrical, as in the Guest's Dilemma case, it will be impossible for a given agent to use reason-replication to derive reasons for thinking the others will do their parts in a unique best point if he does not already have independent reasons himself for doing so, reasons that outweigh any reasons pointing in the other direction. If he does seem to have sufficient independent reasons, even fairly weak ones, for doing his part in such a point, then reason-replication can presumably only amplify the force of these reasons. In such a case, then, reason-replication may have some point in confirming the suggested strategy. However, if we consider a situation like the Guest's Dilemma, which appears unclear from the viewpoint of the agent wondering what independent reasons he has for acting one way rather than the other, it seems that reason-replication can only amplify his doubts. In such a case it is hard to see how it could be argued that rationality dictates that one do one's part in the unique best point.

Someone might suppose that the unique best point will be the salient combination of actions—that it will be common knowledge that it will "stand out for all."[6] He might infer that each agent, being rational, will do his part in the unique best point. The premise may seem plausible, though it is not obviously true for any rational agent as such. (The risk averse might find the intersection of maximim strategies salient.) Even if we grant the premise, however, the conclusion does not follow. We can argue in a vein similar to that used in the case of the unique best point as such. From the premise, "Our both refraining from bringing a present is the salient combination of actions," David cannot infer that he personally should refrain from bringing a present. Once again, it is true that (in this case) if Joshua does his part in the salient combination of actions, David should then do his, but that is all. I have argued at greater length elsewhere for the uselessness of salience from the point of view of rationality.[7]

III. Unique Equilibria

At one point in his paper "Coordination" David Gauthier makes a claim which entails that rational agents will do their parts in a unique best point that is also the unique equilibrium in the situation.[8] (By definition, an equilibrium combination of actions is such that if everyone else does his part in it, no one can improve his own position by doing otherwise.)

We cannot show that this consequence of Gauthier's claim is false by using the Guest's Dilemma, since there is more than one equilibrium in that case. (Each giving a present, and neither giving a present, are both equilibria.) But we can devise a matrix with a unique equilibrium that enables us to show that it is false, using similar reasoning. See Figure 2.2. Here, again, each agent has a unique best point strategy (doing his part in the combination of actions yielding each one the payoff "5"), which could in principle deliver his (relatively very bad) worst possible outcome. Meanwhile he has an alternative strategy that necessarily avoids his worst outcome. This seems to provide a counterweight to any argumentation on behalf of the unique best point strategy.

	5	−50	4
5		−50	2
	−50	4	3
−50		2	4
	4	3	3
4		3	3

Fig. 2.2

The preceding does not only show that a certain special type of unique best point fails to generate an unproblematic situation. It also shows, of course, that unique equilibria in general fail to do so, a point that has not generally been acknowledged.[9] See also the discussion of "coordination" equilibria, below.

I now address two pertinent ideas suggested by some of Gauthier's other remarks. Gauthier makes one claim that entails that rational agents will always do their parts in *any* unique best point (p. 201, cited in note 2 here). Given a later reference (p. 201) to "the principle on which we must act to resolve the coordination problem," he may also be read as suggesting that it is part of the proper characterization of a rational agent that such an agent has in effect adopted and always will act on the principle: "Do your part in any unique best point." Now, given that rationality is initially characterized in terms of maximizing utility and perfect reasoning, and adding in the common knowledge assumption also, the reasoning in this essay shows that in some cases the principle just stated will not necessarily be conformed to by a rational agent when confronted with another such. Since this is so, it is hard to see how one could argue that it is part of the proper characterization of a rational agent that it adopt the principle under discussion.

We can of course devise a new "richer" concept of rationality such that rational agents will always act on principles such that, if they are universally adopted by other agents, the outcome will be more agreeable to all than any other. But it is important to be clear what the implications of any given concept are, and to be clear when a shift between concepts is being made. It is important to be clear that if we are dealing with beings rational in the game theoretical sense specified in this essay, we cannot rely on their acting on such principles. If this makes game-theoretically rational agents look a little limited, so be it: evidently, they are a little limited.

The second pertinent aspect of Gauthier's discussion that I wish to take up is this. Discussing a particular case involving two equilibria, one of which is a unique best point, Gauthier writes: "Given this mutuality of knowledge and—as far as the equilibria are concerned—of interest, and the mutuality of knowledge of interest, each of us may treat the situation as if his decision were a common decision" ("Coordination," p. 200).

There are various ways one might explain what it is for me to act as if my decision is a common one. This could mean that I act as if I am able to legislate for the others, as if what I decide will *ipso facto* be their decision also. Or it may mean that I make a decision not with respect to myself as an individual, but rather in terms of what is most preferred taking everyone into account. Or perhaps the idea is that I act according to the agreement the set of us would have made, had we been able explicitly to agree on what each one should do. Now it could appear that when there is a unique best point in a situation, an agent will be justified in acting in any of these terms. It is certainly true that in such cases there is no question as to what is most preferred taking everyone into account. It is obvious what agreement would have been made, and if everyone legislates from his own selfish point of view everyone will be satisfied. Moreover, all these perspectives lead to the same choice of strategy. However, in the context at issue here none of these standpoints is mandatory, and none can be assumed by a given agent to characterize the other agents involved, albeit he knows they are rational in the sense at issue. It is obviously important to see this.[10]

IV. Unique Coordination Equilibria

A crucial assumption in Lewis's argumentation toward an account of conventions in *Convention* concerns what he calls "coordination" equilibria: combinations of actions in which "no one would have been better off had any one agent acted otherwise, either himself or someone else" (p. 14).

Lewis asserts that:

> If there is no considerable conflict of interest, the task of reaching a unique coordination equilibrium is more or less trivial. It will be reached if the nature of the situation is clear enough so that everybody makes the best choice given his expectations, everybody expects everybody else to make the best choice given his expectations, and so on. [p. 16]

According to Lewis, these conditions will "ensure coordination" (p. 16). Many of Lewis's readers have assumed that the claim is correct that rational agents will do their parts in unique coordination equilibria, given no considerable conflict of interest. (See, for instance, Schiffer 1972, p. 143.) The previous matrix in this essay, however, shows that this is not so. There is "predominant coincidence of interest," according to Lewis's technical account of this feature (see *Convention*, p. 14). The unique best point is *a fortiori* a coordination equilibrium. It is also, being a unique equilibrium, *a fortiori* a unique coordination equilibrium. Meanwhile, according to my argumentation in this essay, rationality does not dictate that rational agents do their parts in the unique best point.

Lewis in the above quotation sketches an argument for the triviality of situations with a unique coordination equilibrium. This involves "making the best choice given his expectations" and so on. But it is not clear that any "expectation" about others can be generated from the mere existence of such an equilibrium; according to my previous discussion, it seems that reason-replication, in particular, cannot infallibly lead to such expectations.

If it is not obvious to rational agents what they should do in some cases where there is a unique coordination equilibrium, then the situation will not be trivial for them: at least I assume that Lewis would say this. But Lewis's eventual definition of convention is apparently dependent on the assumption that situations with a unique coordination equilibrium will be trivial. (See Lewis 1969, especially pp. 8–24. See also Chapter 5, this volume.) The refutation of that assumption, then, has clear implications for the soundness of the game theoretical foundation of Lewis's account of convention.

V. The Impotence of Precedent

I come now to rather a different kind of limitation of rationality. This involves the inability to use experience in a certain way. Reading Lewis on convention, one might come to assume that there is no such limitation.

According to Lewis, a convention is

> a self-perpetuating system of preferences, expectations, and actions capable of persisting indefinitely. As long as uniform conformity is a [proper] coordination equilibrium, so that each wants to conform conditionally upon conformity by the others, *conforming action produces expectation of conforming action,* and expectation of conforming action produces conforming action. [p. 42, my stress; "proper" was added in the revised edition]

Lewis's definition of "proper coordination equilibrium" is ambiguous (see Gilbert 1981). For present purposes we can take his point to concern (coordination) equilibria that are also "proper"; by his definition, a proper equilibrium is an equilibrium such that each agent is better off doing his part in it, if everyone else does.

On reading Lewis, it is easy to fall into thinking that rational agents will do their parts in any proper equilibrium, given that each has done so last time, and hence a self-perpetuating pattern of action will evolve. This would imply that no unique best point situations will be problematic as long as, perhaps by luck, each agent has previously done his part in that point, and this is common knowledge. Its implications are wider than this, since you can have a proper equilibrium in other types of situations, including some involving multiple best points, and some where one proper equilibrium is inferior to another. Thus one reviewer of Lewis writes:

> In fact . . . if the players should at some point choose . . . [an inferior proper coordination equilibrium] it would be rational to persist in these choices . . . even though the payoff is less for both players than it would be with other choices. [Richard Grandy, review of Lewis, p. 131]

Now, in my view common knowledge of precedent as such will not by itself automatically generate expectation of conformity or conformity on the part of rational agents in situations of the type at issue. I shall first argue this, then return to Grandy's discussion.

Rather than presupposing the correctness of my results in the previous sections, I shall henceforth focus on a simple and indisputably problematic matrix, representative of many real-life situations (see Figure 2.3). We can think of it as the case of an interrupted telephone call, where each agent has the option of calling back or

Fig. 2.3

waiting to be called, and a favorable outcome will be reached if and only if they choose different options.

We initially assume that all the agents have to go on is common knowledge of rationality and of the matrix. We next allow them common knowledge of a certain successful precedent. Previously, whoever was the original caller has called back. Will rationality now dictate that precedent be followed?

Consider how Betty, a rational agent, might reason concerning precedent.

1. Previously when Sue and I were in this situation whoever was the original caller has called back, and our problem was solved. The question is, what to do NOW? It does not seem obvious that I—the original caller in this case—should call back this time, just because the original caller has called back in previous cases. It is obvious, however, that:

2. I should conform to precedent now, if Sue does. So my next question is: will Sue conform to precedent? Let me try to replicate her reasoning.

3. Sue will realize, as I do, that though it is not obvious that she should wait now, just because previously the person called waited, it is obvious that she should conform to precedent if I do. Only if so, it seems, will she have reason to conform to precedent herself.

4. She will, therefore, ask: Will Betty conform to precedent?

5. If Sue starts reviewing my reasoning she will soon see that reason-replication will get her no further than it gets me.

I believe that we have now exhausted what a rational agent might figure out about what to do on the basis of precedent as such, under our other assumptions.

Someone might claim that a precedent will make one particular course of action salient. (Compare Lewis, *Convention*, pp. 35–36.) I have already argued that the salience of a particular preferred combination does not constitute a reason for doing one's part in it, in which case this claim is irrelevant. In any case, in the instant situation, at least, the claim that the precedented case will be salient appears to depend on psychological assumptions that may not be true of rational agents as such. If calling back when the original caller is distinguished by being the precedented case, then, from a purely formal point of view, not calling back when one is the original caller is distinguished by being the unprecedented case. In a society of highly nonconformist, or countersuggestible, or determinedly creative people, that something had been done in the past would make the other option the more attractive one for everyone, and so perhaps the one that everyone would notice, expect the others to notice, and so on. Were one faced with a rational Martian, one would hardly know, on the basis of known rationality, what kind of psychological set one was dealing with. We can conclude that in general it is not the case that salience of the precedented combination of actions is generated by knowledge of successful precedent, given common knowledge of rationality.

What of the following contention?

> If e.g. by chance, they should on some round of the game end with a coordination choice, it is reasonable to expect that they will persist in that choice in all future rounds. This requires no communication—only the recognition that neither of them can unilaterally improve his position. [Grandy, review of Lewis, p. 131]

Let us consider the idea that "neither can unilaterally improve his position." This is really irrelevant to *future* cases. That is, by definition, if two agents do their part in any equilibrium, then neither could have improved his position unilaterally. Any other choice one alone could have made could not have made him better off. However, the fact that two agents have in the past done their part in an equilibrium so far says nothing about what either one will do in the future. So of course it remains true that if my opposite number will do his part in this particular equilibrium then I should do my part (or I might as well). But this has no logical consequences for what I should in fact actually do, or expect him to do, failing some further assumptions about our natures. I conclude that Grandy has not provided any argument to show that rationality dictates that one conform to precedent as such under the conditions stated.

Lewis's own view of the import of precedent for rational agents as such is not made entirely clear. For instance, at one point he writes that "we are entitled to expect that agents . . . will succeed in achieving coordination by following precedent" (p. 41). This is the kind of remark that may have influenced Grandy and others. Earlier, however, Lewis suggested that successful precedents may in the event be followed as a result of "tendencies" or "expectations of tendencies" to follow successful precedent (pp. 36–37). He does not at this juncture suggest that rational agents as such will have such tendencies or will presume each other to have them. Nor would the assumptions of the present discussion allow for acceptance of this suggestion.

VI. Patterns of Action among Rational Agents: The Personal Principle Model

Lewis's reference to "tendencies to follow successful precedent" raises an important question. Can we provide an explanatory model of a regularity in successful action that maintains the view of the agents as free from subjection to, and as seeing themselves as free from subjection to, "blind" tendencies to conform to successful precedent? In particular, can this desirable state of affairs come about without an explicit agreement, as it can when instinctive tendencies play a crucial role?

In this section I sketch what I shall label the "Personal Principle model." This uses the notion of deliberate adoption of a principle of action, as opposed to the notion of being "possessed by" a tendency to act in certain ways.[11]

In a "one-off" telephone case rationality evidently allows each agent to call back or to wait. That is, each may make an arbitrary choice of action. I take it that, *pari ratione,* each may arbitrarily adopt one of a variety of general principles of action, for instance the principle: all else being equal, whenever your telephone call is interrupted, call back if you are the original caller, but never do so otherwise.

Let us assume that the following is true of a rational agent who has adopted a principle of the above form. First, it will characterize him in the future, unless he decides to give it up. Until then, it will continue to be his principle. Second, if he has not given it up, and there is no reason for acting against it, he will conform to principle. Granted only this much, we can derive a model of the regular conformity to successful precedent among rational agents.

Suppose that two such agents, Jan and Jo, encounter the telephone problem for the first time. Neither has any reason to opt for one course of action rather than another. As luck would have it, each decides, there and then, to adopt the principle "all else being equal, whenever your telephone call is interrupted, call back if you are the original caller, but not otherwise." This is quite consistent with her rational nature. Given her principle, rationality dictates that she conform in this instance. Jan and Jo thus reconnect their call. Each has acted quite consistently with her rational nature up till now. What of the next occurrence of the telephone problem?

Absent special new considerations, it seems that, for each agent, past successful precedent can hardly argue against her acting in conformity with her principle. *A fortiori,* it cannot argue against her maintaining the principle. Thus it will be perfectly rational for her to maintain her principle, and assuming that she does, rationality will dictate that she conform to it. Consider that, as far as the evidence goes, her opposite number may have adopted the same principle. It can hardly be irrational to act in conformity with her principle when, according to the evidence available to both, both may have adopted it, and general conformity gives results which are the best possible for all. Generalizing, it seems that in the absence of relevant new information, it will be perfectly conformable to the rationality of the parties that, in all subsequent occurrences of the telephone problem, each maintains the principle she adopted for the very first case, and (hence) conforms to it.

Thus it seems that a pattern of action, the population-wide regular conformity to a certain strategy, need not be the result of blind built-in tendencies to follow successful precedent or of the ascription of such tendencies to others. Nor need it be the result of agreement. Nor need it be the result of a sequence of independent lucky choices, with no underlying explanatory factor. It may result, rather, from an initial free choice of personal principles of action, principles maintained in conformity with rationality, and conformed to on each occasion according to rationality's dictates. In short, the agents may exemplify the Personal Principle model of regular conformity to successful precedent.

VII. Remarks on the Personal Principle Model

It is important to understand what the above reasoning does and what it does not achieve. My claim is that it is perfectly consistent with rationality to adopt a principle of action covering all situations of a certain kind, and, if there is no reason not to do so, it is perfectly consistent with rationality to maintain that principle. I have not claimed, nor do I mean to claim, that it is a requirement of rationality that one adopt a principle rather than simply deciding anew each time. It seems hard to argue this for rational agents as such. Nor do I claim that everyone else's past regular "conformity" to a certain principle shows that each has adopted the relevant principle. Each one could equally well be deciding anew each time, and choosing an action that just happens to conform to the principle.

The following should also be noted.[12] Suppose for the sake of argument that Jo knows that when they first encountered the telephone problem Jan chose to adopt a particular principle, *P*. Jo also knows that in all subsequent instances of the telephone problem Jan has followed *P* and this has so far proved fruitful in conjunction with Jo's actions. Given a certain plausible assumption, it can be argued that Jo has no reason to suppose that Jan will conform to *P* in the future. The assumption is that if one has adopted a principle without positive reason for doing so (as is so by hypothesis here) rationality allows one to give up one's principle at will, all else being equal. If this is so, it appears that Jo has no reason to suppose that Jan will not give *P* up before acting in a new instance of the telephone case, and either make a new one-shot choice or adopt and act on a different principle. But then her knowledge of Jan's previous adoption of and conformity to *P* gives her no reason to suppose Jan will conform to *P* in a new case.

If we are dealing with human beings who have certain psychological properties such as inertia or laziness, we can perhaps feel relatively confident that principles that have been adopted will not be changed unless there is positive reason to force a change. But here we are considering rational agents as such. In the original version of this essay (1983ms) I used the assumption that once a rational agent has adopted a given principle, it will characterize him in the future. This now seems too strong. In any case it is important to see what happens if we make the weaker assumption now under discussion.

Suppose Jo asks: what would allow me to figure out that Jan will act in conformity with principle *P*? She could do this, if she knew Jan knew that she, Jo, had not given up or changed a complementary principle of her own. For if Jo has such a principle it is incumbent upon her, all else being equal, to act upon it. But how can Jan have this certainty? As Jan knows, absent special considerations, Jo is free to give up her principle. Evidently, even common knowledge of previously adopted complementary principles of action does not give either person a basis for inferring that the other will act in conformity with the principle at issue.

It is arguable, then, that the best I can say about the future behavior of other rational agents who have regularly been doing their parts in a certain proper coordination equilibrium, is that they may have adopted, and may not have changed, a principle that complements my own. This appears to allow me to keep my own principle without irrationality. But it does not pin me down in any way. For, as far as I know, each of the others has just abandoned his principle and is about to make an arbitrary choice. Thus I can rationally do that too.

In sum, the Personal Principle model can be argued to lack inherent stability for rational agents as such. Given the permissibility of giving up a principle, all else being equal, even common knowledge that everyone in one's population has previously adopted and conformed to a given fruitful principle gives one no positive argument for maintaining one's own principle, and hence conforming to it, in a new case.

VIII. From Personal Principles to Group Principle: Social Convention

Is there some plausible model of social rules that would give them more inherent stability than a set of identical personal principles among rational agents? In this section I briefly sketch such a model. I shall call it the Group Principle model. It involves what I have elsewhere referred to as *joint acceptance* of a principle. (For further discussion of joint acceptance phenomena and related matters see Gilbert 1987 and 1989.)

Consider first the following example involving the telephone case. We start with the usual initial assumptions about the agents, Kate and Coe. We then suppose that, over a period of time, when one of their calls has been interrupted, Kate has called back when and only when she has been the original caller, and Coe has done the same. One day Kate calls Coe, the call is interrupted, and both Coe and Kate call back. Each gets a busy signal. Eventually they reconnect the call. Let us now imagine that the following dialogue ensues. Kate says, a little irritably, "Why did you call me back? I made the call." Coe says, "Oh, I'm sorry, I must have forgotten who called whom." In this interchange, one chides the other for not conforming to a certain principle; the other accepts the criticism, apologizing for her behavior.

Now, such criticism and acquiescence in criticism could not be justified on the basis of the background we have assumed: common knowledge of rationality, the payoff matrix, and a sequence of successful precedents. In particular, assuming the validity of my argument in the previous sections, neither can fault the other for having given her a basis for rational expectations of continued conformity. But suppose that Kate and Coe choose to speak in the way imagined. (Kate's criticism could be intentionally *tendentious,* and Coe may decide to acquiesce.) By reason of this interchange they would, I suggest, have laid the foundations for such rational expectations. For by speaking as they do, albeit without justification in what has gone before, they indicate that they are willing to regard the principle in question in a certain special way. As I shall put it, each is willing to regard the principle "call back if and only if you are the original caller" as a principle they *jointly accept,* or, to put it another way, as "our" principle. In my view, the concept of the joint acceptance of a principle is an important part of our everyday conceptual scheme.

To regard something as "our principle" in the relevant sense is radically different from regarding something as a principle each of us personally accepts. If a principle is "our principle," then, first, each of us has reason to follow it, all else being equal. Second, and most important for present purposes, neither is entitled unilaterally to give it up without the acquiescence of the other. Thus interchanges of the type in the example become intelligible. Interestingly enough, the structure of reasons envisaged here is of the type generated by an explicit agreement. Note, however, that there has not been any explicit agreement on a principle in this case.

When does a principle become "our principle" as opposed to a principle each of us personally holds? I take it that it is not enough for each of us to regard it as such. We must have expressed to each other our willingness so to regard it. When this has taken place, in conditions of common knowledge, we are entitled forthwith to regard the principle as "our principle." More succinctly, it is our principle.

It may look as if this process has to involve some sort of verbal interchange. However, this is surely not so. One might show one's sense of things by gestures, frowns, grunts, and so on, as well as words. Thus, a stranger entering a town "improperly" dressed may gain an immediate sense of the town's dress code, from the looks that greet him, even if he does not know the language. The process of joint acceptance of a principle, then, may be *tacit* in the sense of *nonverbal.* Certainly it does not require the use of *an agreed-upon* language. Thus, a group's language can be founded on the basis of a process of precisely this type. (On group languages see Chapter 10. See also *On Social Facts,* Chapter 3.)

Assumption of the general adoption of a particular *personal* principle could in actual cases lead human agents to see a covering principle as "our principle." But, as I have argued, rational agents in general will not necessarily believe that "this is our principle" in such circumstances. In theory, an agent could be rational but unwilling to accept the domination from outside himself that is inherent in a jointly accepted principle. He or she may be a "rugged individualist." Even someone who talks on the telephone with another (which we may assume involves thinking of the parties as "us") could in principle be unwilling to go so far as joint acceptance of a principle governing the interaction.

Contrary to David Lewis, I do not think that social conventions are regularities in behavior, according to our everyday concept, nor do I think that they must cover problems of interpersonal coordination. I argue for my position on these points in Chapter 3. In *On Social Facts* I propose that according to our everyday notion, a social convention is a jointly accepted fiat, a rule of the fiat form that is properly seen as "ours" by the members of some population: a "group principle" (Chapter 6, especially section 8).[13] The foregoing example indicates one way in which social conventions in this sense may arise out of problems of coordination. If I am right, a given set of rational agents, though capable of observation of conforming behavior, may be unable to reach this desirable state of affairs. In order to reach it, they do not need to make an explicit agreement on a principle. As long as they somehow express to one another their willingness jointly to accept a certain principle, that is enough.[14] Once the parties jointly accept a principle of the right sort, they will finally have positive grounds for expecting future conformity.[15]

Notes

1. This assumption may seem contrary to the Bayesian approach to probability. It is, however, implicit in classical game theory. See Aumann, 1987, headnote. This is not the place to discuss this matter further.

2. "Common knowledge" is a technical term from David Lewis, 1969. (It was introduced into the literature of economics with a similar definition, independently, by Robert Aumann, 1979.) Exactly how this term is best defined is somewhat moot. For present purposes the account in the text may suffice. For further discussion see Schiffer 1972, Heal 1978, Gilbert 1989.

3. See, for instance, Ullman-Margalit, 1977, who writes: "in the situations depicted . . . there is . . . no genuine problem of co-ordination: in both there is just one state of affairs most preferred by both participants . . . and once they both aim at it . . . . it is achieved without further ado" (p. 80). The matrices in question are indeed such that rational agents will do their parts in, and hence reach, the unique best point. This is not, however, because it is the unique state "most preferred by both participants," as the text suggests.

In one of these matrices both agents have a dominant choice. In the other one has a dominant strategy so the other player can rely on his pursuing this, and will then clearly be justified in pursuing the strategy that leads to the unique best point. (I assume here that, in spite of the disappointing outcome in the famous Prisoner's Dilemma, a rational agent may be relied on to pursue his dominant strategy, at least when the given round of the game is considered in isolation.) See also p. 34, second paragraph, which concerns a situation with a structure similar to my Guest's Dilemma (below). (Partial quotation: " . . . since each stands to gain from remaining as long as the other remains, there is reason to assume that the choice of both . . . will fall on the" strategy that leads to the unique best point.)

In his paper "Coordination" David Gauthier implies that rational agents will always do their parts in a unique best point. Thus Gauthier: " . . . in a situation with one and only one outcome which is both optimal and a best equilibrium, if each person takes every person to be rational and to share a common conception of the situation, it is rational for each person to perform that action which has the best equilibrium as one of its possible outcomes" (p. 201). By "optimal" Gauthier means "Pareto-optimal," that is, an optimal outcome is such that there is no other outcome which is both better for at least one player and at least as good for all the other players. A "best" equilibrium is defined by Gauthier as such that "it affords each person in the situation at least as great a utility as any other equilibrium" (p. 201). Now if there is a unique best point, it will be the unique optimal outcome: it will be such that, for any other outcome, it will afford each player a better payoff, so no other outcome can be optimal. It will also be a unique best equilibrium—since it will afford a greater utility to each person than any other point, equilibrium or otherwise. Hence anything which is true for the unique outcome which is "both optimal and a best equilibrium" will be true for a unique best point.

In addition to published references, several philosophers have in conversation expressed the view that rational agents will inevitably do their parts in any unique best point.

4. The payoff matrix for this case has the structure Amartya Sen has called the "Assurance Game" (see Sen 1974). Ullman-Margalit's "discipline matrix" has the same structure (p. 33, op. cit). See the previous note.

5. Someone might possibly try arguing thus: Rational agents are by definition utility maximizers. They must therefore do their parts in any unique best point: for this is the only possible way they can maximize utility. This argument uses the term "utility-maximizer" in a quite untoward sense. From the standard game theoretical assumption that each agent is out to do as well as he can in the circumstances, given his preference ranking, it does not follow that he is a "utility maximizer" in the sense that he will infallibly select that strategy which contains as a possible outcome his highest payoff. Indeed, my argument in this section shows that rational agents as I characterize them need not "maximize utility" in that untoward sense.

6. At one point, Lewis, 1969, characterizes a "salient" combination as one such that everyone will notice it, everyone will know that everyone will notice it, and so on. As it stands this seems to allow that more than one

combination may be salient in a given group. This is clearly not the notion needed here.

7. See *On Social Facts,* and Chapter 1 of this volume.

8. See Gauthier, p. 200: "In a situation in which but one outcome is in equilibrium, the problem of coordination is easily solved. Provided this equilibrium is optimal, and provided every person takes every person to be rational and to be aware of the unique equilibrium, then it is rational for each person to perform that action which has the equilibrium as one of its possible outcomes. Every person being rational every person will act on this principle, and successful coordination will result." By "optimal" Gauthier here means "Pareto-optimal." Clearly a unique best point is an equilibrium, and is Pareto-optimal, since no one's position can, by definition, be improved.

9. As I found from Aumann 1987, Harsanyi 1977 gives an example of a unique equilibrium point that he suggests players should not do their parts in. The example here differs from Harsanyi's in several ways. Here the unique equilibrium is a *strong* equilibrium point and is *profitable,* in Harsanyi's terminology. (Harsanyi's "strong" equilibrium is equivalent to Lewis's "proper" equilibrium; see my section V below.) Also, it is an equilibrium in pure strategies (there are no mixed strategy equilibria in this matrix). I thank Harold Kuhn for proving on my behalf that there are no mixed strategy equilibria in this game, using the theory of his paper, Kuhn 1961.

10. Some of the language used in discussing problems in game theoretical contexts is suggestive of a similar perspective to Gauthier's. If people who are not in communication are described as "coordinating" a certain result, for instance, this is suggestive of group agency or at least of an entitlement to act as they would agree to act if making an explicit joint decision. Compare also the way people are commonly said to "cooperate" in a Prisoner's Dilemma.

11. As should be clear enough from the text, in what follows I use the word "principle" in roughly the sense of *general prescription,* and not in the sense of "moral principle" or "ideal." The Personal Principle model may or may not avoid implicit appeal to blind or automatic tendencies of *any* kind. I have in mind Wittgensteinian views about meaning and concept-possession. This is not the place to discuss such issues. But see *On Social Facts,* Chapter 3.

12. Thanks to Saul Kripke and Cristina Bicchieri for comments that have helped to clarify my thoughts on this point.

13. I have thus come to reject the account of conventions as "norms of quasi-agreement" sketched in Chapters 3 and 4. Some problems (and attractions) for that account are discussed in *On Social Facts,* Chapter 6, section 7.

14. We may assume that reason will not dictate the choice of a particular group principle. As with the adoption of personal principles, a *choice* not dictated by reason will then have to be made. Such a choice is, of course, conformable with purely rational natures of the sort that have been in question here, in a way that unwilled tendencies to follow precedent are not. This note responds to a comment from Julia Jack.

15. Early versions of this essay, under the title "Some Limitations of Rationality," were presented at the New Jersey Regional Philosophical Association meetings, spring 1983, and at the American Philosophical Association meetings, December 1983 (see 1983abs, p. 615), and circulated in manuscript. Other versions have been presented at the Institute for Social Choice held at Dalhousie University, Nova Scotia, in 1984, at the University of Connecticut, Duke University, and the Ockham Society, Oxford University. The main changes here are in the last two sections, where the structure of the personal and group principle models are discussed at somewhat greater length than before. I am grateful for comments and discussion of my ideas to Saul Kripke, Harold Kuhn, David K. Lewis, Thomas Scanlon, John Troyer, David Gauthier, Alan Gibbard, and Cristina Bicchieri.

3

Notes on the Concept of a Social Convention

I. Introduction

Most people would surely agree—perhaps after giving the matter some thought—that social conventions are both ubiquitous and important phenomena. What, then, is a social convention? In this essay I shall be concerned, more particularly, with the question: How, if at all, is the everyday concept of a social convention to be analyzed? In his influential book *Convention*, the philosopher David Lewis has proposed an answer to this question which traces its lineage back to David Hume's *Treatise of Human Nature* and through Thomas Schelling's recent work on the mathematical theory of games.[1] According to Lewis social conventions involve regularities in the behavior of members of a group, expectations about that behavior, and the occurrence of what Lewis calls "coordination problems" among members of the group in question. Various modifications of Lewis's account have been suggested in the ensuing literature.[2] Nonetheless, that the threefold account just adumbrated is at least partly right has become the accepted, not to say the conventional, view among philosophers concerned with this topic. In my view, however, the three major features of Lewis's account, just noted, have no place in the analysis of the everyday concept of a social convention.

In what follows, I shall set out in more detail Lewis's account of social conventions; after indicating some of its attractions, I shall explain why I think it is mistaken. Finally, I shall advocate an alternative approach to the concept of a social convention.

II. Social Convention: Some Fixed Points

I begin by noting what I take to be some uncontentious points about social conventions as we ordinarily conceive them. This will help to fix the topic. Moreover, any plausible theory of the everyday concept of a social convention will have to accommodate at least the following points.

We refer to social conventions when we say things like, "There's a convention in my social circle that one send a thank-you note after a dinner party," and "There's a convention in this country that you do not kiss people on greeting them in public, unless you are greeting a close family member," and "We no longer have a convention that poetry use rhyme." A social convention is, to put it generally, a convention of, or possessed by, a society or a smaller social group, like a discussion group. Evidently, such conventions need not only relate to our social lives in a narrow sense, to situations such as dinner parties. There can be social conventions relating to almost every aspect of life: to greeting behavior and eating behavior; to behavior in public places, at work, at school, in political debate; to the behavior of scholars and scientists, writers and artists.

A striking feature of social conventions—one stressed by David Lewis—is that they may be tacit, that is, they can exist among people who have never agreed explicitly to adopt them, nor explicitly referred to them as conventions they have. However tacit they are and however local their field, social conventions are evidently forces to be reckoned with. If I arrive in a country where the convention is that only close family members are to be kissed in public, and I kiss an old college friend on meeting her at a party, I risk being thought outrageous, alien, insane, or all three. Once I know that there is such a convention in the country where I am living, I have an argument for acting in accordance with the convention, though not necessarily one that will finally dictate how I act. The existence of a convention is, in any case, apt to encourage conformity to the convention.

While conventions attract conformity to them, continued conformity does not necessarily have desirable consequences, all things considered, for an individual conformist or for the group with the convention. If there is a convention in my social circle that one never explicitly says that one likes another person, and if I am bad at showing in nonverbal ways that I like someone, sad consequences can be expected from conformity to the convention on my part. Meanwhile, in the arts, for instance, the abandonment by artists in general of certain constraints imposed by convention may be precisely what is needed to prevent stagnation or decay in a given field at a particular point in its history.

Conventions may change within a society, social group, or discipline. A convention that one does such-and-such in this or that manner may be replaced by a convention requiring a different kind of behavior in the same circumstances. Or a point may be reached where "anything goes." There may in fact be a convention in some circles that one does not comment adversely on any form of dress, manner of eating, drinking, speech, and so on: each to his or her own way. On the other hand, social conventions may reach into the heart of a person's private life: there can be conventions about when and on what and for how long and with whom one sleeps, about the degree to which one's home is to be kept tidy, and so on. Evidently, conventions can vary quite widely from one society to another, from one group to another, at a given point in time. Anyone who has spent time as a resident alien somewhere knows that. So much for what is commonplace about social conventions, according to our everyday notion of a social convention. The question remains as to what a social convention is.

III. Lewis on Social Convention

In *Convention* David Lewis presents an intricate proposal concerning the contents of the "common, established concept of convention" (p. 3). Though Lewis does not himself write of "social" conventions, this may be because he sees this simply as a redundant qualification. Conventions of the type with which Lewis is concerned require for their existence a multiplicity of persons, or a population. The concept he is trying to capture appears to be what I have—without idiosyncrasy—referred to as the concept of a social convention. It is from this point of view, at any rate, that Lewis's analysis will be discussed here.

Lewis's account of conventions centers on the idea of a special structure of preferences within a group, a "coordination problem." Lewis gives eleven examples of such problems. One is roughly the following. Two people are talking on the telephone and the line goes dead. Each wants the connection restored, and neither cares who calls back and who waits. What is important is that only one call back and only one wait, since otherwise obviously the connection will not be restored. Assuming that there are no clear guidelines as to what to do when a call is cut off, clearly such a situation presents a problem for the participants. Each has to decide whether to wait or whether to call back, and the structure of the situation gives no clues. Another example involves language: "It matters comparatively little to anyone (in the long run) what language he adopts, so long as he and those around him adopt the same language and can communicate easily" (pp. 7–8).

These examples suggest that we have a coordination problem on our hands when we have a common interest in achieving a particular end result—speaking the same language, restoring a telephone connection, or whatever—and where there are at least two possible combinations of actions that will enable the result to be achieved. Lewis gives his own account of a coordination problem in terms of the mathematical theory of games, reaching a definition at the end of a fairly lengthy and complex piece of game-theoretical argumentation.[3]

It turns out that in Lewis's definition the idea of a shared end for which a variety of means exists is not included explicitly. The definition runs roughly as follows: a *coordination problem* is a situation in which there are two or more people and there are two or more possible combinations of their actions such that each person prefers that, if all but one person do their parts in that action-combination, the remaining person does likewise.[4] (We can see that the telephone case is a coordination problem in this sense.)

Having given this general account of a coordination problem, Lewis leads up to his account of convention by arguing plausibly that the recurrence of one and the same coordination problem is likely to lead to the entrenchment of a specific way of acting in a population. Consider again the case of an interrupted telephone call. Suppose that this has never happened before to the people involved, and they have no clue as to what to do once their call is interrupted. Perhaps the original caller then happens to decide to call back, and the person called, as luck would have it, waits. The parties might at this point agree that if they are ever interrupted again the original caller will call back. It is fairly obvious that such an agreement would lead to the entrenchment of the practice of calling back if and only if one is the original caller. Lewis is concerned to stress, however, that explicit agreement is not the only possible foundation for the entrenchment of a practice in the context of a recurring coordination problem. He argues that another foundation, of major importance, is precedent.

As Lewis points out, the lessons of precedent may be far from clear. It may be, say, that the first interrupted phone call was made by the person who was the tenured member of the department. This person then called back. If on the second occasion the original caller was the nontenured member of the department, the precedent may seem to point in two different directions at once: should the original caller call back, or should the person with tenure call back, whether or not she was the original caller? Nonetheless, precedents will not always seem unclear. Particularly when cases have piled up, various possible interpretations will have been eliminated. One particular interpretation may stand out as the one everyone will make: the precedent will appear to be unambiguous.

Lewis's idea is that when the existence of an unambiguous precedent is well known and obvious to all, then this may be enough to lead the parties in a coordination problem to expect their opposite numbers to conform to precedent. Now clearly, if I expect you, the original caller, to call back, it is in my interest to wait for your call, since only thus will we reestablish our connection. Similarly, if you expect me to wait, you will call back. In a coordination problem, then, precedent can lead, through expectation of conformity to precedent, to regular conformity (pp. 36–42). Then we have "a self-perpetuating system of preferences, expectations, and actions capable of persisting indefinitely" (p. 42). This, Lewis says, is "the phenomenon I call convention" (p. 42). Lewis's final, formal account of conventions (p. 78) is roughly as follows:

> A regularity R in the behavior of members of a population P when they are agents in a recurrent situation S is a convention if and only if, in almost any instance of S among members of P,
>
> (i) almost everyone conforms to R;
> (ii) almost everyone expects almost everyone else to conform to R;
> (iii) almost everyone prefers that any remaining person conform to R if almost everyone conforms to R;
> (iv) there is at least one possible regularity, R', distinct from R, such that almost everyone prefers that any remaining person conform to R' if almost everyone conforms to R'.

A few explanatory notes are in order. First, clauses (iii) and (iv) develop the idea that the situation covered by a convention is a coordination problem, and stipulate that a convention is such that almost everyone prefers that any remaining person conform to it if almost everyone else conforms. Second, for Lewis a convention is, evidently, a "regularity in behavior in a recurrent situation S." We might ask when, precisely, such a regularity is to be taken to exist. Lewis himself does not make this very clear. The impression one gets from his discussion, however, is that in clear cases the situation in question occurs fairly frequently among members of *P*, and, *more or less as often*, a particular type of behavior, *B*, occurs in instances of *S*.[5]

According to Lewis, then, a convention only exists when, roughly, there is a recurring coordination problem in a population and when members of the population regularly behave in some specific way when confronted with the problem. In addition, members of the population must expect the other members to do their parts in the relevant regularity more or less whenever it occurs.

A further condition on convention, according to Lewis, involves the important notion of common knowledge. The simplest account of this notion is given in Lewis's paper "Languages and Language." According to this account, *it is common knowledge in a group G that such-and-such* if and only if: everyone in *G* knows that such-and-such; everyone in *G* knows that everyone in *G* knows that such-and-such; and so on *ad infinitum*. Some have jibbed at such a condition as unrealistic. It may be pointed out, however, that it does not obviously require that anyone at any time consciously entertain an infinite number of propositions, nor that anyone consciously consider some highly complex propositions. For you can properly be said to know that such-and-such (that Aristotle never met Babe Ruth, say) without ever consciously considering the matter.

The situations one wants to capture with a notion of common knowledge are those in which, roughly, not only are some facts open for all to see, but also it is open for all to see that these facts are open for all to see. No one need be deluded about what the others know in such cases. A simple example in which there is common knowledge of some fact would be the case where a group of people are sitting together watching television, and the news that Isaac Bashevis Singer has won the Nobel Prize for Literature has just been announced. It will then be common knowledge in this group that Singer has won the Nobel Prize. I shall not discuss further here how common knowledge may best be defined.[6] Suffice it to say that Lewis requires that, in order for there to be a convention in a population, it must be both true and common knowledge in that population that the other conditions on convention (the conditions on behavior, preferences, and expectations) are fulfilled.

We have now covered Lewis's account of convention in some detail. Indeed, one of the striking things about Lewis's account is how detailed and precise it is. Given the complexity of the account and the relative clarity with which it is presented, the way to check its accuracy as an exposition of the "common, established" notion of a social convention seems clear: consider each of the proposed conditions and ask whether it is in fact necessary that this condition be fulfilled if there is to be a social convention. This is indeed what I shall do. First, however, let me note some considerations in favor of Lewis's account.

We can easily concur with Lewis that social conventions often, at least, cover coordination problems as he defines them. It is easy to imagine, for instance, two friends who have a convention that if their phone conversations are cut off the original caller will call back. Again, it seems plausible to suppose that there are social conventions relating to language use. Thus there might be a convention in a certain American family of Russian origin that Russian be the language spoken at home. And perhaps there is a social convention, widespread across America, that if you can make requests, write letters, and so on in English, then you should do so. Meanwhile, there appears to be something like a coordination problem in Lewis's sense posed by all situations in which communication is a common goal: I want to use words you will interpret as I interpret them. As long as this is my overriding aim, and yours is to interpret my words as I do, then it matters not which words I interpret in a certain way, only that you and I give the same interpretations to the same words. What's in a name, as long as our communicative needs are satisfied? So it seems that social conventions about what language to use may arise out of, and cover, a coordination problem common to all communicators and their audiences.[7]

It is notable that different societies may have different conventions relating to one and the same situation. In some societies men are supposed to wear trousers; in others they are supposed to wear a kind of skirt. Different sets of friends might have different conventions about interrupted telephone calls, and so on. Now, recall that in a coordination problem in Lewis's sense there are at least two combinations of actions such that each person involved prefers that any remaining person does his part in that combination once the rest do theirs. This seems to mean that where there is a recurrent coordination problem, there are at least two possible regularities in behavior that might perpetuate themselves indefinitely. Thus even when the same coordination problems occur in different societies, and people in different societies are equally rational, it is still to be expected that different regularities in behavior will become entrenched in different groups. Different precedents could occur quite accidentally, as people made an initial, unmotivated stab at coordination, and would then give rise to the corresponding different regularities. Were conventions regularities occurring within coordination problem situations, the fact of a *diversity* of conventions across cultures would be easy to explain. Moreover, should conventions inevitably cover coordination problems, and should conformity to them inevitably be such that everyone wishes to conform providing the others involved in the same instance of the problem conform, this could provide an explanation of the relative *stability* of conventions. Conformity to the standing convention will be expected of the others, and it will be in everyone's interest to conform also. So unless there is some reason, and some possibility, for people to get together and decide to act differently, or unless the structure of preferences in the situation changes, one can expect the convention to be stable.

Whatever its logical relation to convention, Lewis's notion of a coordination problem could have its uses. It is possible that as a matter of empirical fact, the stability of many social conventions is to be explained in terms of underlying coordination problems. Thomas Schelling makes a similar suggestion in *The Strategy of Conflict*.[8] My concern here, however, it not with these issues, nor with the assessment of Lewis's claim that conventions as he defines them are a "phenomenon important under any name" (p. 3). My concern is with whether Lewis has brought into clear view, as he claims, the concept expressed by a "name" in common use, the name social convention. Thus we need to ask, for one thing, whether this concept appears to involve that of a coordination problem. If it does not, then the claim that such problems often, or even always, underlie such conventions remains for investigation by students of society. But it will not be settled by definition.[9]

IV. Some Problems for Lewis

I now turn to the difficulties that stand in the way of our accepting Lewis's account of the notion of a social convention. Let us look first at the idea that the very concept of a social convention involves that of a coordination problem as defined by Lewis. An initial question is why one might be inclined to think not just that conventions may cover coordination problems, but that they must do so.

Lewis seems to have based his coordination problem account of convention on an abstract line of argument that he never makes explicit. In what follows I shall not attempt to define the various technical terms, but I will try to give a general idea of the nature of the argument and the problems involved in Lewis's use of it.

The argument starts from the premise that "it is redundant to speak of an arbitrary convention" (p. 70). It is assumed, more specifically, that a convention is—by definition, as it were—an arbitrary regularity in the behavior of members of a population of "rational" agents. More specifically still, it is assumed that a convention is an arbitrary regularity in the behavior of members of a population of rational agents when they are in a situation of "interdependent decision" in which their interests more or less coincide. The argument proceeds roughly as follows: rational agents would not participate in an arbitrary regularity in behavior if they were in a trivial situation, that is, one where it is obvious what each should do. For they would then do the unique thing they should do, and hence would not act arbitrarily. So, the argument concludes, conventions—arbitrary regularities—must spring out of nontrivial situations. It seems to follow from this argument that all one has to do to clarify the concept of a convention is to give a precise characterization of a nontrivial situation of the kind at issue in the argument.

That Lewis was influenced by such an argument is indicated by the fact that, having started out ostensibly seeking a general account of coordination problems as these are exemplified in his eleven cases, he moves to seeking a mathematically precise characterization of a nontrivial situation of interdependent decision among rational agents with more or less coincident interests. He then claims, in effect, that his eventual definition of a coordination problem amounts to a definition of a nontrivial situation of this kind.

Were the abstract argument just adumbrated acceptable, and were Lewis's account of a nontrivial situation correct, it seems that the issue of what social conventions are would be settled. Taking the abstract argument first, however, there are at least two crucial aspects of it which are, at best, not obviously acceptable. First, it is not clear that one should ground a theory of social convention on the assumption that conventions are arbitrary. There are examples of social conventions that would not automatically be thought of as arbitrary: arbitrariness of some definite kind is at least not a strikingly salient characteristic of them. A convention that one send one's hosts a thank-you note after a dinner party, for instance, may be arbitrary in some sense or to some degree or from some point of view, but it is not immediately clear that this is so, or that what arbitrariness this convention has contributes to its being a convention. In short, one of the fundamental premises of the argument is not entirely compelling. Second, the argument assumes that conventions are regularities in behavior, and provides an explanation of why rational agents should participate in such regularities, if they are arbitrary. But it is not obvious that social conventions are normally conceived of as regularities in behavior.[10]

The abstract argument from arbitrary regularities to nontrivial situations is not, then, as it stands, an obvious force to be reckoned with. It turns out, moreover, that Lewis does not in fact effectively define the relevant kind of nontrivial situation with his definition of a coordination problem. He has not, therefore, done what the argument from the arbitrariness of convention requires.[11]

I shall not go into the details of this issue here. But some of the main conclusions that have emerged from my own examination of Lewis's use of game theory are as follows. First, one can construct examples of nontrivial situations of the kind at issue in the above argument that lack the precise structure of preferences required for a coordination problem in Lewis's sense. Second, it is clear that such nontrivial situations could give rise to regularities in behavior among rational agents that would be arbitrary according to the argument. Finally, it is also clear that situations lacking the precise structure of preferences Lewis requires could generate and be covered by social conventions. There is no doubt, in other words, that some modification needs to be made to Lewis's coordination problem account of conventions if this is to capture the everyday notion of a social convention. This would be so even if we were to accept the abstract argument that assumes that conventions are arbitrary regularities and ties arbitrariness to nontrivial situations.

The question I wish to move on to now is whether social conventions always arise within and apply to situations that might naturally be thought of as interpersonal coordination problems (no longer assuming Lewis's precise definition). If this must be so, then at least Lewis's general idea that interpersonal coordination is the key to convention might be accepted.

It will be helpful, first, to distinguish the idea that social conventions are the conventions *of* a social group or, more generally, a population, from the idea that such conventions always *apply to* situations in which a number of people are involved. It is clear that for Lewis, coordination problems always involve at least two people (pp. 5–6). Hence, on Lewis's account of them, conventions always apply to situations involving more than one person. This will be true, it seems, of any account of conventions which has it that they must, by definition, apply to problems of interpersonal coordination of some kind. However, it seems that there are situations involving only one person—so the natural description of the situation would have it—which can be covered by social conventions. There can be and are conventions about what we do when we are alone, or when we, considered as isolated individuals, are in a particular situation.

For instance, there is, I suppose, in some families or larger circles, a convention that one brushes one's teeth before going to bed, or takes a shower every morning. There could be a convention that one sleeps on the floor, or on a tatami rug, or on a sheet of foam rubber, or on a "regular" bed, or on a waterbed, depending on the group in question. There could be a convention in a certain circle that one has a double bed or larger, whether or not one has any immediate prospects of sharing one's bed with anyone. Or consider conventions of dress. I take it that there is a social convention in America that men do not wear skirts. This convention almost certainly is not restricted to what men wear when there are other people present, but applies also to what they wear when they happen to be alone. Or consider the convention that a poet must (or must not, or may) use rhyme. It is at least arguable that the most natural way of taking this is as applying precisely to what poets themselves, taken individually, must or must not or may do. There is no obvious a priori need to construe it as "really" applying to a situation involving more than one person.

I should briefly refer here to some possible responses on behalf of Lewis to the claim that social conventions may apply to situations in which only one person is involved, and hence to situations lacking an essential feature of coordination problems. There are various ways in which ostensibly one-person situations might be construed as involving coordination problems of a sort. Let me take just one here, which invokes the desire to resemble other people in one's society, in one's physical appearance and behavior, as much as possible. Consider a population of people who are primarily motivated by this desire; call them *Conformists*. In such a population, it might be argued, an analogue of a coordination problem will be involved even when people are in ostensibly one-person situations. When Conformists prepare to go to sleep, for instance, they wish to do whatever most other people do before *they* go to sleep, if there is any such thing. Hence every situation is a kind of coordination problem for these people: each wishes to do whatever, if anything, most others in the society do when they are in this situation. Each wants to do, in his or her own private "instance of S," whatever the others do in their own private "instances of S." Now consider some of our own conventions, like the convention that we sleep in "regular" beds: are not such conventions, it may be asked, simply the outcome, on everyone's part, of the desire to resemble others as much as possible? That "regular" beds came to be somewhat widely used might be the result of fortuitous precedent and imitation; then, when the common use of such beds became known, Conformism may have made it all the more widespread, and then perpetuated it. Thus, it may be alleged, Conformism may account for many of our conventions, including at least some applying to ostensibly one-person situations: Conformism would make these, in effect, into multiple-person cases.

This response, and others like it, do not provide any compelling support for a coordination problem analysis of the concept of a social convention. It seems that we can be perfectly clear that there is a convention that people sleep on tatami rugs, or that poets use rhyme, and so on, without it being at all clear whence these conventions come to us, what desires, needs, interests, and so on underlie them. To put it another way, it seems to be an empirical question whether the conventions we have—our conventions of etiquette, dress, artistic expression, or whatever—derive from our need to coordinate our actions in certain ways. With respect to Conformism in particular, it is not clear to me, as a factual claim, that actual social conventions applying to ostensibly one-person situations in fact rest on an underlying Conformism among the parties concerned, and it is certainly not clear that there could not be conventions relating to one-person situations that obtained among persons who were not particularly interested in doing whatever others did. It seems that we can say without contradiction that there is a convention in a certain group that one sleeps on a waterbed, even though, at the same time, everyone would prefer to sleep on a waterbed whatever the others did, even if they all slept on tatami rugs or "regular" beds.

We should not be confused by the fact—noted earlier—that once there is a certain convention in a population, this will encourage conformity to the convention. This does not logically imply that, where there is a convention, parties to the convention must have any desires or preferences that would naturally be called preferences for coordination of action. The existence of a convention in a group could encourage conformity for some reason having nothing to do with silly preferences. For instance, it could be that when there was a convention, then everyone in the group preferred, of any given person, that that person conform to the convention, and to that extent preferred that everyone conform. This would not mean that they must value uniform conformity as such or have any ultimate goal in mind that uniform conformity to the convention serves.

I take it that the idea that the concept of a social convention involves that of a problem of coordination is at best not proven. If we remove this aspect of Lewis's theory, we are left with the question whether conventions are or involve *regularities in behavior* that parties to the convention *expect* to continue. First, then, are conventions regularities in behavior? Must they cover situations that occur fairly frequently and in which parties to the convention almost as frequently conform to the convention? Various considerations militate against the idea. For instance, there could be a convention in a certain academic discipline that very eminent scholars are given Festschrifts at the age of sixty-five. It could also be the case that in this discipline, there are few very eminent scholars, or few reach sixty-five. If this were so, however, it is hard to see how the convention could be identified with, or be said to involve, a situation occurring with fair frequency. Moreover, perhaps when the next eminent scholar reaches sixty-five, no Festschrift is produced.

It does not seem that this takes anything away from the existence of the convention, that there is anything less of a convention because there was no conformity. Yet it would seem that if conventions are regularities or require that something be done regularly in the relevant situation, then there would be that much less of a convention here. Even if one's notion of regularity allows exceptions, it seems to me, first, that each exception individually makes the regularity less of a regularity, but, second, that a given exception may make a convention no less a convention *at all*.[12]

Just because there was no Festschrift for Jones we cannot conclude that the convention concerning Festschrifts has died or is fading away or even exists to a lesser degree. Jones might be known to hate Festschrifts in general, or he may be hated by many colleagues, and so it may have been decided that, *in spite of the convention*, no Festschrift should be produced. Continued and widespread lack of conformity to a convention could, presumably, contribute to the demise of the convention. But this could be a causal rather than a logical contribution.

Consider another example. Say that there is a convention in my social circle that after a formal dinner party one send a thank-you note. Assume that at a certain point in time people do conform to the convention, by and large. But as people get busier and busier, they keep forgetting to send notes until it seems too late; personal letter and note writing in general, let us suppose, go rather out of fashion; people are used to telephonic communication, it seems wrong to type a thank-you note, and one's handwriting is so illegible. So, on the whole, people do not send thank-you notes any longer. Some, with attractive handwriting, time, and stamps, do so regularly. Others do so occasionally. Many think about it but do not actually do it. Does it follow from all this that there is no longer a convention in my social circle that one send a thank-you note after a formal dinner party? I do not think that it does. Of course, in circumstances like those described one might wonder how long a convention could survive. But this could be because conventions, by their nature, do not easily survive in the absence of conformity, not because conventions actually are or involve, as a matter of conceptual necessity, regularities in behavior.

One might perhaps try to modify Lewis's account thus: conventions require, not that people do regularly conform, but just that they would conform, *ceteris paribus*. But in fact, when must people conform to a convention if they may properly be said to have one? Is it provided they know of no reasons for not conforming? But it is not clear that one cannot simply decide not to conform to a convention, for no reason. Conventions seem to be the kind of thing that may not move actual human beings to action, though perhaps they must move ideally rational agents. If everyone were to feel perverse or to act irrationally a few times and not conform to the convention, that would not obviously show there was no convention. But then one seems to be left with the following "regularity" for convention: people who have a convention must conform to it unless, for whatever reason, they do not do so. This also seems to be true for those who do *not* have a convention that one do such-and-such in some situation: *they* will conform unless, for whatever reason, including no reason, they do not. This modified regularity condition is, in other words, quite vacuous. Yet it also seems to be the only clearly acceptable regularity condition on the existence of social conventions.

On the issue of whether there is some nonvacuous regularity condition on the existence of social conventions, once again there must be a verdict of, at best, not proven. Conventions may tend to spring out of, or give rise to, regularities in behavior, to distinctive patterns of action, like the uniform wearing of clothes or speaking of Dutch; but it appears that a convention can exist without the correlative regularity in behavior. It would be satisfying if some positive account of conventions could indicate how conventions were intrinsically independent of regularities in behavior while at the same time tending to be correlative with such regularities. Before adumbrating such an account, let me turn to the interesting issue of expectations and convention. This issue is particularly interesting, in my view, because there is a crucial ambiguity affecting a reader's response to the use of the term "expectation."

What we seem now to be left with out of Lewis's initial, complex account of conventions is the following hypothesis: there is a social convention only if it is true, and common knowledge in a certain population, that almost everyone in the population *expects* almost everyone else to perform an action of a certain type. For instance, the idea is that there will be a convention in my social circle that one does not telephone anyone after 11 P.M. if almost everyone expects almost everyone else to refrain from making phone calls after 11 P.M., and this fact about expectations is common knowledge.

Before noting my assessment of this view, let me explain the ambiguity about "expectation" that I have in mind. Sometimes "I expect that you will come," for instance, means "I believe that you will come." In other words, on one interpretation to expect that such-and-such is to believe that such-and-such will occur at some future time. Lewis's claim that where there are conventions there must be expectations of conformity is most naturally taken in this sense. The whole context of the claim indicates this. So much, then, for the first interpretation. On the second, "I expect you to come" has a normative sense; that is, it may amount to or at least include the idea that I believe that you ought to come (and not just in a sense of "ought" where it means that you *will* come). Let us be clear, then, that in considering Lewis's proposal about expectations, we are concerned with expectations in the first sense. To improve the clarity of the discussion, we might refer to these as *plain* expectations.

There seem to be at least two problems in taking commonly known plain expectations of conformity as definitive of social conventions. First, it is not obvious that there could not be a social convention in the absence of such expectations. Consider again the case of the convention that one send a thank-you note after a dinner party. Let us allow that this might at some point in its history be accompanied by regular conformity. But suppose we have reached the point where conformity has dwindled, and most people no longer conform. There are two possibilities: it may be common knowledge that most people have stopped conforming, or it may not. If it is not, then people may well go on expecting conformity. But it seems possible that there is uncertainty, say, about how many people actually still conform. If people are uncertain about this, then there is no common knowledge of general conformity nor of general nonconformity.

Suppose, then, that there is no common knowledge concerning how many people act in accordance with the convention. Then there may equally be no common knowledge about how many people have plain expectations that most others will conform. People may, at this point, still actually have plain expectations of conformity, by and large. But suppose they do not. Suppose that their views about what others will do are affected by their uncertainty about what others are currently doing. Then, it seems, it may well no longer be true that almost everyone expects almost everyone to conform. Once again, as with the supposition that there is no longer a regularity, one can raise the question: Does this mean that there is no longer a convention? That is, does the supposition that there are no plain expectations of conformity logically entail that there is no longer a convention? If our concept of a social convention was such that social conventions existed only if the corresponding plain expectations of conformity did, we should have a *clear* sense that of course there was no longer a social convention. The present author, at least, has no such clear sense. Consider, for instance, that someone might say, "I know I really should write that note, but this convention seems to be honored in the breach these days. I don't suppose anyone else will write one." The naturalness of such utterances as this suggests that social conventions can exist in the absence of widespread conformity and in the absence of expectations of conformity. What may be true, as is the case where there is no conformity, is that where there is an absence of expectations of conformity, there is now some evidence which suggests that the corresponding convention may no longer exist. But this could be because, social conventions being what they are, and being by their nature distinct and independent from plain expectations, they nonetheless tend as an empirical matter to bring regularities and plain expectations of conformity in their train.

A second problem with analysis of social conventions in terms of commonly known plain expectations is as follows. It seems intuitively clear that if I tell you that, say, there is a convention in our department that people have lunch together in the faculty club on Fridays, then I have told you something that might move you to action. It seems, that is, to provide an obvious reason (though one that may be overridden or ignored) for your participation in the lunch. Now, it is not clear that the idea that someone believes that I will do something provides an obvious reason for me to live up to this plain expectation. To say that there is a social convention that such-and-such seems to imply that the parties to the convention favor conformity to the convention in a relatively strong sense. The case of plain expectations is intuitively different. (The reader may consider whether he or she would like the plain expectation that a lion is about to attack to be fulfilled.) The mere claim, then, that there is a commonly known, generalized plain expectation that people will do their parts in a certain practice does not seem to capture that aspect of social conventions which makes a social convention a "moving force."[13]

The upshot of these considerations on the possibility of analyzing the notion of a social convention in terms of commonly known plain expectations is that, first, it is not obvious that social conventions require the correlative plain expectations of conformity in order to exist, and, second, it is implausible to *equate* social conventions with commonly known, generalized plain expectations. Something other than plain expectations is necessary to explain the relatively powerful moving force of social conventions.

It is worth noting the implausibility of an account of conventions wholly in terms of commonly known plain expectations. Though David Lewis, whose work I have been focusing on, did not give such an account, something very similar has been put forward by at least one writer proposing an alternative to Lewis's account.[14] More than one writer on the subject has assumed, with Lewis, that commonly known, generalized plain expectations are a logically necessary requirement for the existence of a social convention. As I have argued, however, this weaker claim for social conventions is also implausible.

V. Reflections on Social Convention

In what follows, I draw attention to some salient features of social conventions that have not been given prominence in discussions of convention influenced by Lewis. I suggest that these features provide a plausible starting point for an analysis of the concept of a social convention. I then sketch a possible development from this starting point. Finally, I examine the relationship of the tentative account of social convention that I arrive at to Lewis's account of convention. I should stress that the material in this section comes from my own work in progress, and much of what follows is both rough and speculative; nor will there be space to develop or debate particular points in any detail.[15]

I have already noted that according to our common conceptions, social conventions are forces to be reckoned with; I have also suggested that to say that there is a convention in a certain group is to imply that the parties to the convention favor conformity to the convention in a relatively strong way. Some connected points may now be added. Consider how social conventions are manifested—how, in effect, we typically discover that they exist. One way is by reference to a certain sort of nonverbal critical behavior, to certain expressions of approval and disapproval. Thus if people look askance, or uncomfortable, or embarrassed, or doubtful when you do or propose to do something, that is a sign that there may be a convention in the offing (though such things are not conclusive). There are also various linguistic expressions, typically associated with conventions, which are powerful clues to their existence. Where there is a convention, we would expect to come across locutions like the following: "One is supposed to wear one's gown to dinner"; "You really ought to put on a tie for an occasion like this." Parallel with this, the absence of a particular convention may be marked by such comments as "You don't have to use rhyme, you know."

Such considerations suggest that if a group has a convention that such-and-such is done in certain circumstances, then a large or important segment of the group must believe that members of the group ought to do such-and-such in the circumstances in question. Thus consider a case where people regularly take tea at four o'clock, for example. We might immediately feel licensed to talk of a custom or a social habit in this connection. The hypothesis about convention, meanwhile, is this: We would not say that these people had a convention concerning the taking of tea unless they regarded taking tea at four o'clock as, in a certain sense, required, as something that to some extent or to some degree ought to be done. Another way of putting the idea, using a notoriously ambiguous term, is that the concept of a convention is the concept of a type of norm.[16]

Such a view of our everyday notion of convention will find support in texts from a variety of fields. Here, for instance, is a brief passage from Jacques Barzun's *The American University*: "The conventions governing these outside activities are more or less explicit. . . . These norms came out of pre-existing university customs."[17] One might also refer to a classic of sociology, Max Weber's *Economy and Society*;

Weber's account of the "fundamental sociological concept" of convention runs as follows: "The term convention will be employed to designate that part of the custom followed within a given social group which is recognized as 'binding' and protected against violation by sanctions of disapproval."[18]

The hypothesis that social conventions are, of logical necessity, norms—that is, that parties to them must regard certain things as things that ought from some point of view to be done—does not solve all problems, or forestall all queries, about the nature of social conventions. Let us consider a little further how the "ought" of convention seems to function. A few important points may be briefly noted. Consider a case in which you have some simple choice to make, say, whether or not to wear jeans to the theater tonight. Now, you could consider what you yourself would most like to do in the absence of any external constraints. You might find that you would prefer to wear jeans, since you would not have to change clothes. This, then, is what you should do, if your own personal preferences are all that is at issue. The ought of convention, meanwhile, is clearly not one that is seen as dependent on personal preferences of this sort. In the context of a convention we quite naturally and properly say things like: "I know you'd rather just wear jeans, but you really ought to dress up a bit." You might also consider your choice from the point of view of morality; in particular, you might consider whether the wearing of jeans to the theater had any intrinsic moral value or defect. You would probably conclude that it did not. (As a contrast case, you would probably conclude that lying about your decision to a friend had some intrinsic moral disvalue.) Meanwhile, it is clear that use of the ought of convention does not imply a claim about the intrinsic value of what one ought to do. You could quite properly say, in the context of a social convention: "Though (of course) there's nothing intrinsically wrong with wearing jeans to the theater, I obviously ought to wear something more formal." To say, then, in the context of a convention, that a given person ought to do such-and-such is not to imply that their doing such-and-such has intrinsic value, nor that the person in question would prefer to do such-and-such, all other things being equal.

It is natural to assume that the use of "ought" associated with social conventions presupposes the sharing of some features by the majority of members of the group with the convention. As for what those features might be, our previous discussion of Lewis suggests that they will not be anything about the coordinative preferences, or plain expectations, or regular practices of the majority of members of the group. And this seems to be so. Regarding preferences, it would be quite consistent to claim that a group had a convention requiring that everyone dress in sober garb even though, first, no member of the group would currently prefer to dress soberly, if it were up to him; nor, second, is there anyone who, if it were entirely up to him, would currently like most members of the group to dress soberly; finally, there may be no one who, if it was up to him, and he knew that almost everyone else was going to dress soberly, would prefer then at least to do so himself, or would prefer any potential nonconformists to dress with the majority.

The ought of convention could still be properly uttered, it seems, in all these circumstances. This "ought," one must suppose, can be properly uttered whenever there is a convention in the offing; since there can be conventions in the absence of generalized plain expectations of conformity, or regular conformity, this "ought" cannot presuppose the existence of such expectations or conformity, any more than it can presuppose the existence of the pattern of preferences definitive of Lewisian coordination problems or the other patterns of preferences just alluded to.

What more can be said about the ought of convention—and about social conventions themselves? One might at this point draw attention to the striking correspondence that exists between the ought of social convention and that of explicit verbal agreement. There is some possibility that this may lead us to the heart of social conventions.

Consider what happens when there is an explicit verbal agreement. Suppose you and I agree that you will telephone me tomorrow evening and we will have a chat. Once we have agreed and are no longer in contact, each of us will believe that you ought to call me tomorrow, that you are, to some extent and to some degree, bound or required to do so. We will also both believe that I am obliged, to the same extent, to wait for and accept your call. Now, in the context of our agreement, these "oughts" or beliefs that one is bound can be characterized negatively in much the same way as the ought of social convention has been characterized: your calling me need not be presumed to have any intrinsic moral value, and it could well be that, immediately following the agreement, each of us realizes and continues to feel that they do not wish to have the projected chat, since each has work to do, or whatever. The other negative points concerning the ought of convention also hold here: we need have no general practice of calling each other in the evening, or any plain expectations that we will honor our agreement in this case, nor any current preferences for coordinating our actions in this matter. Nonetheless, we have made this agreement, and this in itself supports an ought judgment: we are obliged to do or ought to do such-and-such, insofar as we have agreed to do so.

What, if anything can be made of the observation that the oughts of explicit agreement and of social convention behave in strikingly similar ways? It is natural to suggest that social conventions must involve a species or analogue of agreement, and this idea is worth investigating. In what follows I shall suggest one way in which it might be fleshed out.

Discussion of this idea should start by stressing that although there may indeed be a sense of the term "convention" in which it means something like "verbal agreement" or "joint declaration,"[19] there is clearly no need for—and often no possibility of—an explicit verbal agreement between the parties to a social convention. Further, it seems implausible to suppose that social conventions must involve something which is actually a species of agreement—to suppose that the convention that men wear ties on formal occasions, for instance, involves what is literally speaking an agreement between the members of the society that men shall wear ties on formal occasions. Let us pursue the idea, then, that social conventions involve an analogue, rather than a species, of agreement.

Are there situations in which people will be justified in thinking that "it is, to all intents and purposes, as if we have agreed to do such-and-such"? There is one type of situation in which such a belief would seem to be justified, and that is the following: in a certain social group, people generally make ought judgments with respect to participation in a certain practice, in much the way they would if there had been an explicit agreement between them to participate, except that there has in fact been no such agreement, and they neither allude to one nor believe that one has occurred. Assume, more particularly, that if challenged to explicate their use of *ought* they go at least this far: they characterize it negatively in the various ways referred to above. In addition, the general normative attitude to the practice in question, and the nature of this attitude as specified above, is common knowledge in the group. Let us not immediately inquire into how such a situation might arise. It is in any case surely fitting to describe such a situation as one in which "it is as if they have agreed" to participate in the relevant practice. Let us call such a situation, then, a *quasi agreement*.

What is the relation, if any, between social conventions and quasi agreements as defined above? Let me first note something further about quasi agreements: if there is a quasi agreement, then this fact may itself be perceived as supporting an ought: "We ought to, because it is common knowledge that most people think that we ought to." It may also come to be common knowledge that people think in this way, that they regard their quasi agreement as grounding an ought for them. Let me now note something further about social conventions. It is natural to judge that people would not have a fully fledged social convention unless they were inclined to support their oughts with locutions like, "That's what one is supposed to do." In the light of these considerations, among others, it is tempting to speculate that our conception of a social convention is the conception of a generalized, commonly known ought judgment, which is itself seen as grounded in what I have called a quasi agreement.

The account of convention we have arrived at can be stated, in a somewhat cumbersome fashion, without using the technical term "quasi agreement": roughly, there is a social convention in a group when and only when it is common knowledge in that group that most people think that one ought to do such-and-such in a certain context, and that one ought to do this because it is common knowledge that most people believe that one ought to do this. It is important to note that it is not required by the account of convention that we have arrived at that the parties to a convention must themselves think in terms of agreements or that they must have the thought "it is as if we have agreed." This seems to be a desirable feature of the account, moreover. It seems right, intuitively, to suppose that people could have a social convention without having the concept of an agreement. Nonetheless, if the account we have here is correct, one can reasonably say that conventions do involve an analogue of agreement, on which the ought of full-fledged convention is based.

Let us call the account of convention arrived at here the view of conventions as norms. (A more precise but longer label would be: the view of conventions as norms of quasi agreement.) There is little space to examine this view further here, but it is appropriate to say something about its relation to David Lewis's account of conventions.

At one point, after he has given his complete definition of convention, Lewis argues that given his account of conventions, conventions are "norms: regularities to which we believe one ought to conform" (p. 97). He claims that whenever an action would conform to a regularity of the kind he calls a convention, then there are "presumptive reasons, according to our common opinions, why that action ought to be done" (p. 97). Lewis's idea is that for most individuals in a group with a convention in his sense, their conformity to the convention will, most of the time, answer both to their own and to most other people's current preferences. So according to our common opinions, Lewis says, they ought to conform: we presume that, other things being equal, one should do what answers to one's own and to others' preferences.

This is fine insofar as what Lewis shows is how a regularity satisfying his conditions would in fact become a norm in a society sharing these common opinions on the relevant matters of value. But for one thing, it seems that as far as Lewis's own statements go, societies with other sets of values are conceivable. In such societies, the mere existence of a regularity satisfying Lewis's conditions would not of itself entail that there was a norm that the regularity be conformed to. So it seems that for Lewis it is a matter of contingent fact, rather than a conceptual necessity, that a convention be a norm. Meanwhile it appears that, rather, normativeness is not a purely contingent feature of social conventions. It is hard to see that people who did not think that such-and-such ought to be done could be said to have a convention.

In any case, I have already argued that the ought of convention is not an ought whose grounds are facts about the current personal preferences of the parties to the convention. Lewis's oughts, on the other hand, when they occur, are seen as grounded in the existence or supposition of a certain current structure of preferences in the population. Thus even where conventions, in Lewis's sense, give rise to ought judgments in the way he notes, they do not seem thereby to give rise to the kinds of ought judgments typically associated with conventions as ordinarily conceived.

Finally, Lewis argues for the normative nature of social conventions on the assumption that his coordination problem account of the concept of a social convention is right. I have, in the course of this essay, argued against this assumption in various ways. It is more plausible to claim that it is part of the concept of a social convention that parties to social conventions believe that they ought to do certain things in certain situations: this aspect of the concept seems to be more firmly fixed, and better suited to serve as a foundation for a theory of social convention. If social conventions are not logically required to cover coordination problems, their necessary normative aspect can hardly be explicated in terms of such an underlying structure.

On the view of conventions as norms, conventions are not logically required to cover coordination problems of any kind. One can agree that a convention—a norm of the specified kind—would be well suited to solve a coordination problem of Lewis's type. One difficulty with many such problems is that there is nothing at all to choose between alternative courses of action, say between the original caller's calling back and the person called calling back. In such a situation the existence of a norm would point people in a particular direction, and, if all took heed, the desired coordination would occur. Explicit agreements will be similarly apt to solve coordination problems, when such agreements are feasible. But this cannot mean that explicit agreements, or conventions as norms, are essentially solutions to coordination problems.

Clearly, we might make an explicit agreement on a whim ("Why don't we spend the afternoon picking apples!") where there was no special antecedent desire on anyone's part to coordinate our actions in any way. Once the agreement is made, we each have some degree of obligation to honor it, and believe that this is so. The preference structure thus created, however, insofar as a belief in obligation creates a preference structure of some kind, is not that of Lewis's coordination problems. If we were all neutral about all available combinations of actions before, we may all now feel a positive pull only toward picking apples, and may feel perfectly neutral, still, toward all other combinations of actions. It seems that conventions as norms, similarly, need not involve preferences of the type that Lewis focused on.

On the view of conventions as norms, conventions need not be accompanied by expectations of conformity, or conformity itself. Once there is an existing convention it will clearly be apt to generate conformity, and we should often find expectations of conformity, and conformity, where there are conventions. If we do not, however, it will not prove there was no convention. It is similar, evidently, in the case of agreements. We may have agreed, perfectly sincerely, to meet for lunch at Oscar's on Wednesday; each thus knowingly incurred an obligation to go to Oscar's on Wednesday. Normally, I would expect someone with whom I had made such an agreement to show up. But on this occasion, I may not expect you to show up, in spite of our agreement, since I realize that you are trying to disentangle yourself from our relationship and are likely to see a useful move available to you here. You may not expect me to show up, since you suspect that I know what you are up to. In the event, perhaps, neither of us shows up. This would not prove, however, that we were not both under an obligation to go to Oscar's or that we did not believe that we were, insofar as we had agreed to do so.

I have noted that on the view of conventions as norms, social conventions are not definitionally tied either to coordination problems, or to expectations about future behavior, or to regularity in behavior. I have not discussed the processes by which conventions as norms of the kind specified here might arise. In principle, any process which could result in people's thinking that they ought to do such-and-such, where the ought is not seen as grounded directly in the circumstances, could generate what I have called quasi agreements and, hence, norms of quasi agreement. I take it to be a task for empirical investigations to discover and classify those contexts that in fact tend to generate such norms.

Considering the nature of norms of quasi agreement, as defined, I believe that coordination problems of Lewis's type are indeed apt to generate such norms. At the same time, there seems to be no reason to suppose that such problems alone could generate norms of this type. Durkheim's idea that normlessness in general affects the human spirit adversely suggests that a need on the part of individuals for "directions for living" in general could be productive in this area. Such a need has not obviously, at base, anything to do with the actions of other people. Doubtless there are other factors that also could be involved in the production of norms of quasi agreement. Since it seems quite natural to speak of social conventions in the absence of any obvious coordination problems, this is a point in favor of the view of conventions as norms of quasi agreement.

VI. Conclusions

Analytic philosophers who have most recently been concerned with the analysis of the everyday notion of a social convention—David Lewis in particular—have concentrated on the idea that regularities in behavior, plain expectations about behavior, and coordination problems in something like Lewis's sense are constituents of conventions. I have argued that, on the contrary, none of these elements should be considered part of the concept of a social convention, though they may tend to be connected, as a matter of fact rather than definition, with the social conventions that there are. I have suggested an alternative approach to the analysis of the concept of a social convention: social conventions are, I suggest, to be seen as involving, by definition as it were, beliefs about what ought to be done. In this sense, they are or involve norms. I have observed, further, that the kind of ought used in the context of conventions parallels in a striking way the oughts associated with explicit agreements. Further discussion led to the hypothesis that, as I have put it, social conventions are norms of quasi agreement: roughly, the oughts of social convention are implicitly predicated upon their general endorsement by members of the society in question.

The idea that social conventions are norms is certainly not new, though it is strangely lacking from most recent philosophical writing. It is not an entirely easy idea, since we need to distinguish the oughts of convention from other oughts and to attempt some more positive characterization of their nature. As I have noted, the positive suggestions in this essay come from my own work in progress. Further work in this area is still needed. Meanwhile, I feel quite hopeful that these suggestions are on the right track.

David Lewis has argued that whatever we call them, regularities occurring within coordination problems in his sense are important phenomena. The everyday concept of a social convention draws attention to another such phenomenon: if social conventions are, at least, norms of the kind suggested, it is easy to see why they are as powerful, helpful, and confining in the direction of the ways of our world as they seem, pretheoretically, to be.[20]

Notes

1. Lewis (1969), hereafter cited in text; see also Lewis (1975). For Hume's discussion, to which Lewis alludes, see the *Treatise* (1739/1978), Bk. III, pt. 2, sec. 2, and also the *Enquiry* (1958/1957), app. 3. In the *Enquiry* Hume gives a set of examples of actions performed by convention—for instance: "Thus two men pull the oars of a boat by common convention, for common interest, without any promise or contract; thus gold and silver are made the measures of exchange; thus speech, and words, and language are fixed by human convention and agreement" (p. 123). Some types of practice, he asserts, can only arise as a matter of human convention: "Whatever is advantageous to two or more persons if all perform their part, but what loses all advantage if only one perform, can arise from no other principle" (p. 123). Hume suggests that convention, in this context, is to be understood to be "a sense of common interest, which sense each man feels in his own breast, which he remarks in his fellows, and which carries him, in concurrence with others, into a general plan or system of actions which tends to public utility" (p. 122). There is no space in this essay for detailed discussion of Hume's text, but it will be apparent that Lewis's account can be seen as a development of Hume's suggestions (not necessarily in ways Hume would have approved). On Thomas Schelling's work, see note 3 below.

2. See, e.g., Schiffer (1972), Chapter 5; Burge (1975), pp. 249–55.

3. The mathematical theory of games was invented by John Von Neumann. A standard textbook is Luce and Raiffa (1957). Roughly, the theory is concerned with situations (games) in which there are a number of people (players) who have to decide what to do, and where a given player's "payoff" from a given action will depend, in at least some cases, on what the other players do. One considers what types of strategy an agent should adopt in various types of situations.

Perhaps the most well-known types of situation treated are the "zero-sum" situation, or situation of pure conflict, and the "Prisoner's Dilemma." Schelling (1960) argues for the interest of pure "coordination games," in which all the people involved rank the possible combinations of actions in the same order, and drew attention to cases like the telephone case (see p. 94). Lewis acknowledges the special influence of Schelling (Lewis, p. 3). Meanwhile, Lewis's definition of coordination problem, his game-theoretical argumentation, and his account of conventions are his own.

4. Lewis's definition is in fact ambiguous. I have opted for one of the possible interpretations. Nothing in my discussion here will hang on it. On this issue see Chapter 5.

5. Note that the type of behavior in question may have quite a complex description, e.g., "calling back if and only if one is the original caller."

6. I discuss this further in *On Social Facts*. Lewis discusses common knowledge at (1969) pp. 51–57 and at (1975) p. 6. For further references on the topic see Chapter 1, note 4.

7. For further discussion of conventions, in Lewis's sense, in relation to languages and language use, see Gilbert (1974), and, in this volume, Chapter 4 and Chapter 10, note 4.

8. Schelling (1960) suggests that "the coordination game probably lies behind the stability of institutions and traditions" (p. 91).

9. Those influenced by W. V. O. Quine's arguments that there is no analytic-synthetic distinction will not find the question of what is or is not included in a given concept or in the meaning of a given term an acceptable question. Lewis, however, sets out to give an analysis of the concept of convention, and suggests that it has a number of components. This seems to me to be a claim that makes sense, and which can sensibly be examined for accuracy without any a priori assumptions that it will be false. (In fact, Lewis sometimes seems to suggest that his enterprise may be viewed in more than one way; however that may be, I consider it here as a candidate analysis of a concept, which can therefore be refuted if no contradiction is found in saying certain things are social conventions when, according to Lewis's proposal, they cannot be counted as social conventions.)

10. I return to this issue below.

11. For this and other problems with Lewis's game-theoretical argumentation, see Chapter 5, this volume.

12. Lewis in fact gives a definition of the "degree of conventionality" of a

regularity that implies, among other things, that each instance of nonconformity reduces the degree to which a given regularity is a convention. Intuitively, the degree to which a convention exists does not seem to be reduced. See Lewis (1969), pp. 78–79.

13. It may be suggested that it is in general better to have true beliefs rather than false ones, so that reasonable people will want their beliefs about the future to be true, ceteris paribus. Insofar as something like this is true, it is clear that the desire involved is of a special kind and is going to be very weak; in particular, it seems clear that the parties to a social convention must favor conformity to it in a more serious and stronger way, generally speaking. This would give one who knows of their attitude (and wishes not to displease them) a relatively strong reason for conformity to the convention.

14. See Schiffer (1972), p. 154.

15. I discuss the ideas in question further in Chapter 4. In *On Social Facts*, Chapter 6, I explain why I think this account ultimately fails, and propose an alternative which I currently prefer. See Chapter 2, this volume, for brief discussion of that alternative, according to which a (social) convention is a "jointly accepted fiat."

16. On the variety of uses of norm in one discipline, sociology, see Gibbs (1965), 586–94.

17. Barzun (1968), p. 50.

18. Weber, *The Theory of Social and Economic Organization*, tr. Henderson and Parsons (1964), p. 127 (a translation of Part I of *Economy and Society* [*Wirtschaft und Gesellschaft*]).

19. Some uses of the term "convention" suggest that it can simply mean "agreement," as when we speak of the Geneva Convention, for example. According to Hume (see the Enquiry, Bk. III, pt. 2, sec. 2) the central use of the term "convention" in his day was to refer to a contract or explicit promise.

20. Versions of this essay have been read at colloquia in the philosophy departments at Indiana University, Bloomington (1981), at Cornell University (1982), and at the University of Connecticut, Storrs (1982). I am grateful for comments received then. I must also thank Saul Kripke, David Lewis, and Thomas Scanlon for reading and commenting on earlier versions of this work. They bear no responsibility, of course, for the views presented here.

4

On Language and Convention

I. Introduction

Talk about conventions has for a long time been common in a variety of disciplines, including philosophy, in particular the philosophy of language and the philosophy of social science. However, it has not proved easy to say what a convention is.

In this essay I draw attention to some neglected facts about our use of the term "convention" that seem to me to need explanation in any general theory of convention. These facts have a special relevance to our conception of languages and of language use. I shall discuss the facts in question primarily in relation to David Lewis's theory of convention, since they appear to present difficulties for Lewis's theory. Before turning to them, I explain Lewis's aims and the substance of his theory.[1]

II. Lewis's Project

Lewis's theory was developed in order to elucidate a certain platitude.

> It is a platitude that language is ruled by convention. Words might have been used to mean almost anything. . . . We could perfectly well use these words otherwise—or use different words, as men in foreign countries do. We might change our conventions if we like . . . necessary truths, like geological truths, are conventionally stated in these words rather than those. [*Convention*, pp. 1–2]

Immediately after introducing his platitude, Lewis refers to some earlier discussions of convention which, he asserts, present a challenge

89

to it. According to W.V.O. Quine and Morton White, Lewis writes, "Conventions are agreements" and "the [supposed] conventions of language could not possibly have originated by agreement, since some of them would have been needed to provide the rudimentary language in which the first agreement was made" (p. 2). These authors concluded, Lewis sums up, that "We have no concept of convention which permits language to be conventional; we are inclined to call some features of language conventional, but we cannot say why" (p. 2).[2]

Lewis reacts:

> We may protest, desperately, that there must be *something* to our notion of conventions of language, even if we cannot say what. When we are exposed to the notion we *do* all manage to get the idea, and all of us go on more or less alike in distinguishing between features of language we call conventional and features of language we do not. [p. 3]

Thus Lewis arrives at the project he undertakes in his book: to provide an account of "convention in its full generality, including tacit convention not created by agreement . . . an analysis of our common, established concept of convention" (p. 3).

III. Lewis on Conventions in General

According to Lewis, a convention is, roughly, a regularity in the behavior of members of a population when they are in a recurrent situation involving a specified structure of preferences: the structure he refers to as a "coordination problem." One of his examples of coordination problems concerns language specifically.

> Suppose that with practice we could adopt any language in some wide range. It matters comparatively little to anyone (in the long run) what language he adopts, so long as he and those around him adopt the same language and can communicate easily. Each must choose what language to adopt according to his expectations about his neighbors' language: English among English speakers, Welsh among Welsh speakers. . . . [pp. 7–8]

There is a coordination problem in Lewis's sense when, roughly, there are at least two disjoint combinations of different agents' actions, *C1* and *C2*, such that each agent prefers that if all but one person do their parts in *C1*, then the remaining person does his/her part in *C1*. At the same time, each prefers that the remaining person do his/her part in *C2* if all but one do theirs.[3]

Lewis is not the first to find attractive the idea that something like a coordination problem in his sense underlies conventions.[4] He seems to have taken the specifics of his account to be supported by an abstract game-theoretical argument.[5] This starts from the idea that there is something *arbitrary* about conventions.[6] As I argue elsewhere, whether or not this is so, the argument as a whole does not validate the conclusion that coordination problems as defined by Lewis must underlie conventions.[7]

I now turn to Lewis's conception of conventions as regularities, that aspect of his account of convention that is most relevant here. Precisely when, one may ask, does a "regularity in behavior in a recurrent situation *S*" exist? Lewis does not make the conditions entirely clear, as he leads up to his account of conventions in general. Evidently we have a clear case if situation *S* occurs fairly frequently and, more or less as frequently, a particular type of behavior, *B*, occurs in instances of *S*. I shall take it that it will be a necessary condition on the existence of a regularity of the kind in question that the relevant situation together with the relevant type of behavior on the part of all participants in it *have occurred more than once*. I shall therefore dub regularities of the kind in question "actual regularities."[8]

Lewis discusses how coordination problems in his sense can give rise to actual regularities in behavior in a given population. This can happen, Lewis stresses, without the helping hand of any explicit agreements, by force of precedent.

Lewis's final definition of convention "in its full generality" incorporates his important notion of common knowledge.[9] It is worth repeating the definition here. It runs roughly as follows:

A regularity *R* in the behavior of members of a population *P* when they are agents in a recurrent situation *S* is a convention if and only if, in almost any instance of *S* among members of *P*,

(i) almost everyone conforms to *R*;
(ii) almost everyone expects almost everyone else to conform to *R*;
(iii) almost everyone prefers that any remaining person conform to *R* if almost everyone conforms to *R*;
(iv) there is at least one possible regularity, *R'*, distinct from *R*, such that almost everyone prefers that any remaining person conform to *R'* if almost everyone conforms to *R'*.

Though logically speaking Lewis's definition leaves it open whether there are some conventions which are not "regularities in the behavior of members of a population when they are agents in a recurrent situation," the whole context in which it is presented makes it clear that for Lewis the class of conventions that are regularities of the above kind is the class of conventions, period. Did Lewis not mean to make this claim, he could hardly assert that he had given an analysis of our concept of convention in its full generality.

Lewis's examples of conventions hark back to the examples of coordination problems given earlier. The discussion of the eleventh case, involving language, is fairly lengthy; excerpts follow:

> A population's common use of some one language—Welsh, say—is a convention. The Welshmen in parts of Wales use Welsh; each uses Welsh because he expects his neighbors to, and for the sake of communication he wishes to use whatever language his neighbours use. . . . If using Welsh is to be a convention, it must be a regularity in behavior. . . . I do not want to say that the users of Welsh are conforming to their convention when and only when they are rightly said to be "using Welsh." A man lying in Welsh is using Welsh, but he is violating its convention. . . . In due course we shall see how the convention of a language may be described; here I will say only that it is a regularity restricting one's production of, and one's response to, verbal utterances and inscriptions. [pp. 49-51]

The idea of a regularity *restricting behavior* will, I suppose, best be taken as the notion of regularity such that, if one is to participate in it, one must restrict one's behavior in specific ways.

Lewis's fuller description of the "convention of a language" much later in the same work is this: for possible language L to be the actual language of a population P, there must be, in P, a convention of truthfulness in L. More recently Lewis modified the account: a population's use of a language L is now defined in terms of a convention of truthfulness and trust.[10] Conventions are still seen as actual regularities in behavior.[11]

IV. "One-Shot" Conventions

Examination of a class of examples of our use of the term "convention" in relation to language suggests that the concept of convention in general is not that of an actual regularity in behavior. As will emerge, the situation is quite complex.

Consider the following case, which involves signaling. Suppose that you and I agree that if today's battle is lost you will wave a black flag from the hilltop. We agree, in other words, that you will signal to me that the battle has been lost by waving a black flag. It seems natural here to say that we have, in making this agreement, adopted a certain "signaling convention."[12] We have, in short, adopted a convention. So, I believe, one could quite naturally describe the case, given the conventions governing the use of "convention" in English.

Let us fill in some more detail about the above case. Assume that there will be only one occasion on which you can let me know that this battle has been won or lost. You explicitly say the following to me, and I concur: "I shall only have time to come to the hilltop and signal once. I'll use a black flag to signify that the battle is lost, if it is lost. As for any future signaling of any kind, we'll have to agree later about what to do, when we next meet." In other words, we agree on a signal for use on a single occasion. It would still be perfectly natural to say that we have adopted a certain signaling convention, when the details are so filled in. What will it be to conform to this convention? Presumably, we conform to the convention whenever we use a black flag to signify that the battle in question is lost. In this instance, however, we have evidently adopted the convention for conformity on a single occasion.

Call a convention adopted for conformity on a single occasion a "one-shot" convention.[13] On the basis of this example it seems that there can be one-shot conventions. Assuming that we carry out our plan, there can be conventions conformed to on a single occasion. Moreover, the explicit one-shot nature of the convention does not seem to make it any less of a convention. If conventions are or involve actual regularities in behavior, however, there could not be a convention conformed to on a single occasion.[14]

A distinction that might confuse the issue may be briefly noted here. It concerns the phrase "conventional signal." At one point in *Convention* Lewis writes: "Even the rising of the moon can be a signal—to begin an uprising, say—though it would be a prearranged, one-shot signal, not a conventional one" (p. 129). Now, there does seem to be an accepted sense of "conventional signal" such that the adoption of and conformity to a certain signaling convention need not, in general, involve the adoption of a conventional signal. I shall not try to say here what it is, precisely, for a signal or symbol to be conventional in the relevant sense. The quotation from Lewis could be construed accordingly, however, and in that case, it would have little bearing on the question whether one-shot signaling conventions are possible.

The following example should help to point up the contrast: suppose that Romeo and Juliet agree that Juliet will wave a red scarf from her balcony to signify that all's clear on a certain night. Before they make this agreement, they have never used this signal; moreover, in their society a red flag is the "conventional signal" for danger, not for all's clear. (Perhaps that is why Romeo and Juliet adopt this particular signaling convention on this occasion: they wish to confuse observers from the wider society.) In doing what they do, then, they may correctly be said not to be adopting something that is, already, a "conventional signal" on an accepted interpretation of that phrase. It does not follow, however, that they do not adopt a certain signaling convention, for use on a certain occasion. In a standard sense of "signaling convention" that is, indeed, what they do.

In the cases described so far, there was a verbal agreement on a signal to be used on a single occasion. In each case, the agreement evidently involved the adoption of a convention. It is important to note, however, that an agreement to do an action A on a particular occasion O does not automatically carry with it the adoption of a convention.[15] Perhaps that is obvious. Nonetheless, it will be useful to describe a particular case as a contrast to those described above.

Consider the case of the members of Jane's seminar. At the beginning of the seminar break one afternoon the members of the seminar agree to have tea together in the student cafeteria. There is surely little temptation to say here that the seminar members now have, or have in making this agreement, adopted a convention.[16] It may be true, of course, that their action is influential in producing a chain of actions that leads to the coming into being of a convention. There could, I presume, come to be a convention among the members of the seminar that they have tea together during the seminar break in the student cafeteria. But there is no need to think that this must be so. They might now explicitly agree: "Let's go to the cafeteria for tea *in this break,* deciding next time what to do then." They might abide by this agreement; later, a convention could arise of going to the Pancake Shoppe for tea in the break. In any case it is quite clear that the original agreement does not in itself involve the adoption of a convention.

One problem for a theory of convention, then, is how it can be that people can sometimes be said to have adopted a one-shot convention as an immediate result of an agreement to do something on a certain occasion. Another is how it can be that this is not always so. A particular case of the problem is this: how can it be that an agreement on signals for a single occasion always constitutes the adoption of a convention?

Before considering Lewis's theory in the light of these issues, I should note that signaling is not the only activity of a linguistic sort that appears to be governable by one-shot conventions. In fact, probably any activity of a linguistic sort is in the same position. Here are two examples. Someone is asked to list her favorite colors. She says: "Let's see, before I begin, I can't recall the name of the color of your dress—I'm not sure if it's called 'purple' or 'mauve.' So for the purposes of my list, let's call that color 'mauple.' " She then lists her favorite colors (mauple comes second). It seems natural enough here to say that she and her interlocutor agreed on a certain linguistic convention, namely, that "mauple" refers to, or is to refer to, the color of the interlocutor's dress. Another example is a notational convention. A lecturer, deciding on the spur of the moment on a way to represent some notion on the blackboard: "I'll use '?*' for now. I don't like it much, and next time I'll think of something more attractive." So much, then, for the possibility of one-shot conventions.[17]

V. Lewis and One-Shot Conventions

Let us look, now, at what David Lewis says on the topic of "one-shot conventions." Lewis does consider the matter fairly explicitly in his discussion of signaling. It is clear there that he does *not* allow that a convention is automatically involved when people agree on signals for a single occasion. Lewis evidently wishes to say that, in a case where "the sexton and Paul Revere agreed upon signals for a single occasion" we do not yet have a case involving convention, or at least, convention in the sense of Lewis.

> In other cases, the same signaling system . . . may occur repeatedly, without need for fresh agreement every time. The regularity whereby communicators and audiences use such a pair of contingency plans is a convention [p. 125].[18]

With respect to our concerns, I take it that Lewis's gist is roughly this: after an agreement on and use of particular signals for a single occasion, the occasion, say, of my needing to communicate to you the results of a certain battle, a similar situation may occur later. We may need to get a similar message across, and may feel that the best way to do so, given that we have this time made no specific agreement; is to use the same signals for *battle lost* or *battle won*. The message may, as a result, get across. As relevantly similar situations recur again and again, then, we may continue to use the signals we originally agreed to use on a single occasion, even though the original agreement made no reference to later occasions. According to Lewis, only when there is a repeated use of signals is there a signaling convention in his sense: an original agreement on signals for a single occasion, though it may be the beginning of a process leading to the existence of a convention, does not in and of itself involve a convention.

It is possible that Lewis's pretheoretical intuitions included the judgment that those agreeing on signals for a single occasion have not adopted, and will not conform to, a (signaling) convention. But his claims about signaling conventions may rather be straightforwardly derived from his general theory of convention. Lewis's presentation of his ideas suggests that this is so. Signaling is discussed after the general theory of convention has been developed in its fullest detail, on the basis of a consideration of regularities arising within coordination problems and without explicit agreements. The theory, meanwhile, appears to overdetermine the judgment that conventions are not involved when signals for a single occasion are agreed upon. For, according to the theory, conventions are or involve regularities in behavior in recurrent situations, and I am assuming that a regularity of this kind exists only when the relevant situation has occurred more than once along with the relevant behavior. Now, if such an "actual regularity" view of conventions is correct, then first one could not allow that any *agreement* on signals for a future occasion or occasions could *ipso facto* involve a convention; second, one could not allow that a convention could be *conformed to just once;* third, insofar as a "recurrent situation" must be a *type* of situation, which can have recurrent instances, as opposed to a particular "individual" situation, Lewis could not allow that anyone can adopt a convention with respect to a single, *particular, individual occasion.*

Suppose, then, that one who finds Lewis's theory of convention otherwise attractive is faced with the fact that we do—according to common, established usage—speak of one-shot conventions. We do speak naturally of the adoption of a signaling convention, for instance, for use on one and only one occasion. Rather than deny this fact, in deference to the theory, they might seek to amend the theory, to cope with this fact.

Can an amendment to allow for one-shot conventions be made without changing Lewis's account in a radical way? In this connection, let us look at Lewis's discussion of the topic of convention contrasted with agreement (pp. 83–88). Like his remarks on signaling, his remarks on agreement come after he has developed his theory of convention in general. There are two main aspects of his discussion that should be mentioned. First, the actual regularity view of conventions is, as far as one can tell, maintained. Agreements cannot by themselves, as it were, immediately bring conventions into the picture. Conventions only come in when actual regularities in behavior do. Lewis does allow that conventions may be "begun by agreement." But he fills this in at one point as follows: If . . . we agreed . . . by exchanging noncommittal declarations of intent, *the resulting regularity* would be a perfectly good convention at once" (p. 84, my stress).

The second main aspect of Lewis's discussion of agreements in relation to convention is more congenial to the idea that conventions may come into the picture exactly when a particular type of agreement is made. In order to start a convention "at once" an agreement must not amount to an exchange of "self-binding promises," but rather to no more than "a noncommittal declaration of intent." Looking back to Lewis's definition of convention in general, we see that the governing idea here is that the conditions on preferences ([3] and [4] in my summary) must still hold. These conditions will not hold if each party to the agreement considers him or herself to be bound by a promise: each will now prefer to conform to the relevant regularity no matter what the others do. This aspect of Lewis's thought on agreements could be incorporated into an account of convention which was not an actual regularity account. To abandon the idea of conventions as actual regularities is to make a radical revision of Lewis's account of conventions. Nonetheless, an amendment of his conditions on convention like the following does retain the "coordination problem" aspect of his thought on convention:

a population P has a convention if and only if it is true and common knowledge in P that—by reason of precedent or by reason of an agreement—it is the case that if particular situation s or a situation of type S were to occur among members of P, (1) everyone would perform a certain type of action A in s or in that instance of S. . . . [and so on, as in Lewis's original definition].[19]

Let us now consider this amendment in relation to the data on one-shot conventions. On this account, if you and I agree to use a signal, Z, to signify that z on a particular occasion O, and we consequently, as a result, fulfill all the stated conditions, then we will have a convention, a convention arrived at by an agreement with respect to conformity on a single occasion. So far, so good, one might feel. However, part of the data on one-shot conventions was that it was clear that an agreement to do a certain action, A, on a certain occasion, O, does not always involve the adoption of a convention. If the amended Lewis account is to be considered satisfactory with respect to the data noted on one-shot conventions, it must make the right predictions with respect to cases in which a convention is not adopted by agreement. This, however, it does not seem to do.

Consider again the case of the members of Jane's seminar. Let us now more fully specify the situation of the members, when their agreement occurs. Let their preferences about what to do conform to Lewis's conditions on preferences. That is, let it be the case that each one prefers to go to the cafeteria if most others do, but prefers to go to the Pancake Shoppe if most others go there, or to go off alone if the others go their separate ways. Let this be common knowledge. Now let them agree to go to the cafeteria in today's break. Assume that everyone now expects everyone else to go, not because the agreement is regarded as a binding promise, but because of their expectations about the other members, and their preferences for doing what most others do. Have they adopted a convention, at this point? My own intuition on the case is still clear, and negative. They have agreed to go to the cafeteria in the seminar break today. They have not adopted a convention.

I conclude, then, that the amended Lewis account, whatever its other merits, fails to cope with the facts about one-shot conventions. For it makes at least one important false prediction about when there will be such a convention. Evidently it cannot distinguish cases in an adequate fashion. So much, then, for the amended Lewis account.

Let me now consider some ways the original Lewis account might be defended in the context of the usages about "convention" that I have noted. A reply that Lewis has given to a critic in another context might be suggested as a possible reply here. Lewis writes:

> I gladly concede that we may properly call something a convention, although it does not meet the defining conditions I gave, because we hope that it will come to meet them, or we wish that it did, or we contemplate

the possibility that it might have, or we believe that it used to, or we pay lip service to the fiction that it does.[20]

This remark is deserving of more comment than I can give it here. First, though, one should be clear about what Lewis is claiming. When he says "we may properly call something a convention" I presume that he does not mean "we can call something a convention, and what we say can be literally true." Surely, if what we said was literally true, and what we called a convention did not meet the defining conditions Lewis gave, that would simply mean that Lewis's analysis had been refuted by a counterexample. I take it that his idea must be something like this: it is permissible, sometimes, to call something a convention, though it is not really a convention. This will be the case if we hope that it will become a convention, etc. Perhaps one could put the idea more carefully in general terms this way: Suppose we have a proposed analysis of concept *C*, and claim that nothing which is thus-and-so instantiates *C*. Take any putative counterexample of the form: but we say that *X*, which is thus-and-so, instantiates *C*. It may be that we can indeed properly say that "*X* is *C*" (or "instantiates" *C*) but that the putative counterexample is not a real one because "*X* is *C*" is not to be taken literally, but rather as expressing a hope, or as elliptical for "*X* used to be *C*" or "*X* could eventually become *C*," or something of that sort.

Applying this idea to the facts about one-shot conventions noted, one might try to argue that when we say, of people who adopt a signal for use on a single occasion, that they have adopted a (signaling) convention, we are not to be taken literally. Rather, such remarks are to be construed as elliptical for, say, "their agreement on how they will signal that such-and-such on a certain occasion, and their subsequent use of that signal on that occasion, could lead to a regularity of using the relevant gesture (or whatever) as a signal that such-and-such and hence could lead to a convention." More particularly, one making this move on Lewis's behalf would assert that remarks about putatively one-shot conventions are properly construed as elliptical for, or analyzable in terms of, an agreement's relation to a regularity in behavior that fulfills Lewis's other defining conditions for convention.

Our present problem, however, is in part one of distinguishing cases, and what are we to do with the fact that an agreement to go to the cafeteria in today's seminar break seems not to be properly describable as the adoption of a convention? Such a description seems to be improper, period. Yet one might well believe that going to the cafeteria in the seminar break could become a convention: the members of the seminar could come to have a convention, perhaps as a result of the initial agreement, that they go to the cafeteria together in the break. It looks as if we ought to be able to use "convention" elliptically here, if we can use it elliptically in the other case.

In any case, making use of this move with respect to putative positive instances of one-shot conventions seems illegitimate. It seems that a convention really is adopted when two people agree on signals for a single occasion. It seems that it is strictly and literally true that—in some established sense of "convention"—they have adopted a convention. (Meanwhile, in the seminar break case, it is strictly and literally true that no convention has been adopted by the agreement to do something today.) In other words, the one-shot signaling convention case presents a counterexample to Lewis's theory, and cannot be correctly explained as involving ellipsis because it does not. I do not say that the move Lewis seems to be making in the last quotation is never quite apposite in the defense of a proposed analysis of a concept. Sometimes apparent counterexamples in terms of what we say do involve ellipses. But if pretheoretical intuition has no sense that an ellipsis is involved, the claim that there is one nonetheless is difficult to uphold. Clearly Lewis's move cannot be used sweepingly to dismiss any proposed counterexample to any analysis.[21]

At this point another strategy in defense of Lewis's account of convention suggests itself. Perhaps the "common, established" notion of a convention which is involved when we speak of a signaling or linguistic convention is *sui generis*. Perhaps it is, in other words, a quite distinct concept, quite unconnected with the concept of convention which Lewis has attempted to analyze.[22] In other words, we might just as well speak of linguistic "noitnevnocs," for instance. Then we could without any obvious problems speak of people adopting linguistic noitnevnocs and conforming to them on single occasions, yet failing to have a convention of any sort, retaining "convention" in one standard sense of the term, a sense distinct from *noitnevnoc*. Something like this could be right. If it is, however, it looks as if there will be serious consequences regarding the relevance of Lewis's analysis of "convention" to our intuitive understanding of the nature of language. It will be useful at this point to reconsider the "platitude" which evidently prompted Lewis's account of convention.

VI. On the Platitude "Language Is Ruled by Convention"

Recall that Lewis set out to elucidate the platitude that "language is ruled by convention." He proceeded to explicate this with remarks such as: "Words might be used to mean anything" (p. 1). Prior to acquaintance with anyone's theory of convention, it would be very natural to construe the root idea here as concerning the character of "language" in the sense of languages: of any language, used by any person. Lewis could be held to be referring, in particular, to a form of the idea that, roughly, the relation between words—as yet uninterpreted—and the concepts which they express in a given interpreted language, is entirely arbitrary: that is, any sound, mark, or possible linguistic vehicle could, in principle, express any expressible notion. This idea will surely command "the immediate assent of any thoughtful person" (p. 2). It is, in other words, a platitude. Since it is a platitude about what we might call the "sound-sense link," I shall refer to it as the "sound-sense platitude."[23]

At least one thing about "language" in the sense of language *use* follows trivially from the sound-sense platitude. Suppose we use the word "white" in the sense of *white*. Then it follows from the sound-sense platitude that we do not *have* to do so, at least insofar as any other word could in principle, at least, have been used in this sense; similarly, the word "white" could in principle have expressed any other (expressible) sense. The passage in which Lewis's platitude is introduced could quite naturally be read as describing a version of the sound-sense platitude in conjunction with a trivial consequence in terms of language use. It would be perfectly natural, evidently, to use the term "convention" in expressing a version of the sound-sense platitude. Here, then, is one possible use of convention which appears to need explanation in a general theory of convention. (I shall say more about what I take the explanation to be in the next section.)

In this essay I have focused on a particular set of uses of "convention": a class of cases in which it seemed that we could talk of one-shot conventions. As far as language is concerned, it was apparent that people could, by explicit agreement, adopt signaling conventions, or more clearly "linguistic" conventions, for use on a single occasion. Now, just as it is possible to construe the platitude that "language is ruled by convention" in terms of the relation of words to their senses, as that relation is fixed in a given language, so it seems possible to construe the idea of "adopting a linguistic convention" in general in terms of the adoption of a particular sound-sense link. I have noted that it might be suggested that, to save Lewis's theory of convention, he renounce an interest in our talk of "adopting a linguistic convention" as an immediate result of explicit agreement. It now looks as if the renunciation of interest in such talk will involve Lewis in renouncing an interest in the platitude which motivated his whole enquiry, or, at least, an interest in the most natural interpretation of what the "platitude" he set out with is about.

There are other possible interpretations of the claim that "language is ruled by convention" and perhaps Lewis has been influenced by them. It has in recent years become something of a platitude among philosophers that language is a matter of social convention, of "socially established rules,"[24] or, more vaguely, of something to do with the behavior of groups of people. I cannot possibly address the large amount of literature in this area here, but I should like to make two points.

First, there are indeed pedestrian interpretations of the claim that language is a matter of social convention and the like, which will "command the assent of any thoughtful person." For example: There are social conventions with respect to language use. We are all (except a few unlucky ones) born into social groups and webs of social convention, including conventions of language. A child inclined to call her father "Mom" will, in America, be gently pressured into calling him "Daddy" or whatever the family wants. The same goes for all words: parents and teachers exert pressures of various kinds to get children to use the language they themselves use. People are linguistically conservative: they prefer to stick with the language they have, and not to keep learning new languages. All this is certainly platitudinous. Important as such facts are, they do not appear to touch the topic of the character of languages as such or language use as such. As far as these facts go, there could in principle be languages and language use in the absence of any social conventions and, indeed, in the absence of any societies or social groups. Insofar as they *are* platitudinous, these and similar facts have no obvious conceptual or philosophical import.[25]

Second: the deeper question, about which philosophers seem to be increasingly agreed, is whether language use in general requires, as a condition of its possibility, a social context, a context of social conventions or, more vaguely, sets of people behaving in various ways. It has become something of a platitude among professional philosophers and their readers that the answer to *this* question is affirmative. Wittgenstein's later philosophy is a dominant influence here, though Wittgenstein's writings are notoriously difficult.[26] If we take one important interpretation of Wittgenstein, however, the nonplatitudinous nature of his claims, from the point of view of the nonphilosopher, is very clear.

In his interpretation of Wittgenstein, Saul Kripke has clearly delineated a striking argument at a very deep level. What is important for us here about this interpretation is that Wittgenstein can plausibly be construed as a *skeptic* in the Humean mold, arguing passionately and with great force against deeply engrained habits of thought, in particular against the thought that whether an individual uses a word in a certain sense or not—or more generally, uses a language or not—is solely a matter of facts about that individual considered in isolation from any social context. Insofar as Wittgenstein suggests as the truth of the matter something that may be alluded to in crude slogans like "language has a social nature" or "language involves social conventions," and the like, he is, then, to be construed—on this interpretation—as proposing something that runs strongly counter to the commonsense view of what it is to have and use a language, what it is to use a word in a certain sense, to "follow a rule for the use of a word," and so on.[27] It is not to be expected that most thoughtful people would give immediate assent to a deep interpretation of Lewis's "platitude" along such sceptical lines, provided that they have not already been convinced by philosophical argument on the subject.

Lewis's project, as set out at the beginning of his book, was to elucidate a common commonplace, not a philosopher's commonplace. If he has in fact elucidated the sense of "convention" involved in a current philosophical commonplace, or in some pedestrian platitudes about language, so be it. There still remains the sense of "convention" that is involved when we say "they adopted the following signaling convention" and the like, and when we interpret in terms of the nature of the sound-sense link such remarks as ". . . language is ruled by convention. Words might have been used to mean almost anything." (*Convention*, p. 1) and ". . . the syllable 'big' could have meant 'small' for all we care, and the red light could have meant 'go' . . ." (Quine [1969], p. xii).

However we are to interpret "convention" in these cases, the concept at issue can evidently be used to state an important idea about language, a platitude about language, something about its essential character as far as our pretheoretical intuitions go. If in defense of Lewis's account of convention one says that account has nothing to do with "conventions of language" or "linguistic conventions" as they are conceived of in *these* cases, it leaves the account as an explication of a notion that may or may not have any relevance to the character of language as such. Whether or not it has any such relevance appears to depend on the truth of a skeptical philosophical thesis of great depth, but which, like all deep philosophical skepticisms, is entirely repugnant to commonsense, and hence, in itself, automatically and eternally suspect.[28]

VII. Speculations

I have argued that Lewis's work on convention leaves unsolved the nature of the concept of convention involved in our talk of one-shot signaling conventions, and in one natural interpretation of the platitude that "language is ruled by convention." More generally, we have the question of how these and other uses of "convention" tie up. Is there after all a "concept of convention in its full generality" that is susceptible of precise analysis in terms of a set of conditions individually necessary and jointly sufficient? (If so, then this discussion has shown that Lewis's analysis does not capture it.) Or do we, rather, have a set of uses involving different, distinct concepts? (If so, there is one such concept, at least, which Lewis's analysis evidently does not capture. The question remains whether Lewis's analysis captures some other concept commonly expressed by the term "convention.") Again, perhaps there is a unique concept of convention, but one that is "an especially messy cluster concept," to use Lewis's description of a concept he contrasts with that of a convention, that of a rule.[29]

I shall not attempt to answer these questions in a definitive way here. What I shall do in this section is to compare and contrast our use of "convention" in remarks about one-shot signaling conventions and the like, and another important range of uses. My method here will be to look at each use in isolation, first, and to suggest an interpretation which might be given if that were the only use of the term in our language. I shall then compare the resulting interpretations. I shall compare the concept one might naturally take to be involved in our talk of one-shot signaling conventions and linguistic conventions in general with the concept one might naturally take to be involved when we say things like: "there's a convention in this community that after a dinner party one sends a 'thank-you' note to one's hosts" or "there's a convention in our town that if a telephone call is cut off, the original caller calls back." I shall—without idiosyncracy—call conventions of the latter type "social conventions." One mark of such conventions is that they are the conventions of a social group or, more generally, population. They will not, evidently, just concern our "social lives" in the narrow sense.

I shall not argue that a unique concept of convention is involved in the cases of both linguistic and social conventions, nor shall I deny this. I shall argue simply that these uses do appear to be closely related: the existence of convention appears to depend on related features in each case. Thus I shall argue, in effect, that the notion of convention involved when we speak of the adoption of a one-shot signaling convention, and the like, is not a completely isolated notion, unconnected with the concept expressed in other uses of "convention." This is a satisfying conclusion, but one that cannot be taken for granted.

Let us look first at signaling or more generally linguistic conventions. We have considered certain cases in which two or more people have agreed to adopt a certain linguistic convention for use on a single occasion. Evidently, they could equally well have adopted the convention for use on several particular occasions, or for the indefinite future. It is important to note that, prephilosophically at least, we also allow that one person may adopt a linguistic convention for private use. (I may say to myself such things as: "Let me use a large asterisk to mark this special day in my diary"; "I shall use a small 'q' in my diary to indicate quarrels with my spouse"; and so on.) Given that individual people can adopt linguistic conventions for themselves and on their own, it looks as if the prephilosophical or intuitive notion of a linguistic convention and the idea of adopting and conforming to such a convention are not to be understood in terms of facts about populations of more than one person.

In this connection, let me refer again to David Lewis's discussion of convention and its relation to language use. For Lewis, to have a language is to be party to a convention in his sense: to participate in a regularity in the behavior of members of a population of agents with certain preferences for coordination. As Lewis notes in "Languages and Language," this seems to imply—contrary to our natural assumptions—that it is not the case that "a man isolated all his life from others might begin—through genius or a miracle—to use language, say to keep a diary" (op. cit., p. 26). It also seems to imply the impossibility of something more mundane, of an individual who is part of a society but devises for himself and is the only one to use a new language (a potential rival to Esperanto, say). In discussing this issue Lewis admits that, with respect to his definition of "convention": "taking the definition literally, there would be no convention" (ibid.). He continues: "But there would be something very similar. The isolated man conforms to a certain regularity at many different times . . . he has an interest in uniformity over time. . . ." (ibid.). And Lewis finally suggests that "we might think of the situation as one in which a convention prevails in the population of different time-slices of the same man" (op. cit., p. 27).

Now, in the case of a diarist Lewis's suggestion has some attractions. Typically, I suppose, one writes a diary at least in part so as to make a lasting record of one's activities, a record which will be accessible to oneself, at least, on later occasions. One wants, then, to ensure that if one uses a word in a given sense in making a certain diary entry, one will interpret that word accordingly when one reads the diary later. One has, in other words, an interest in uniformity of interpretation over time. However, as noted earlier, it is possible, intuitively, to adopt a one-shot linguistic convention and to conform to such a convention on a single occasion, without thought for the future.

Though I have, in this essay, focused on cases where more than one person was involved, and where an interpersonal agreement was made concerning a one-shot convention, it seems equally possible that one person on his own could decide to adopt a one-shot linguistic convention, and could conform to it on a single occasion only, without any intentions regarding future uses or beliefs about past ones. (Such a procedure may seem likely to have little point, but it seems not inconceivable. Perhaps one is a poet and decides to make up a poem in one's head about a certain dog whose name one does not know. So one decides that for the purposes of one's fleeting creation (in which the dog will be named only once, of course) one will name him "Bonzo." One then begins: "Ah, Bonzo! . . .".) In the case of a single use of language by a single user uninterested in coordination with himself over time, it is hard to see how to view the matter as one in which a convention in Lewis's sense prevails, or how it can be said in this case to prevail in a "population" of more than one person, or, if you prefer, "item." To say that this is the "limiting case" of something involving many persons, or items, or indeed, of a speaker-hearer interaction would seem to be simply question-begging (perhaps the limiting case should make the law).[30]

The appropriate way of looking at things, then, still appears, to me, to be this: the notions of a linguistic convention and of the adoption of and conformity to a linguistic convention, are not to be understood in terms of facts about many-membered populations.

If we now ask what seems to be going on when we talk of a linguistic convention, a natural way of putting things, eschewing philosophical worries about the terms, would be that what we have in mind is something like a *rule* that "binds" or links a sound or sign of some kind with a sense or meaning. When we adopt a certain signaling convention, we agree to abide by a rule linking a sign—a black flag, say—with a certain signification or meaning—say *danger,* or *battle won.* What I am saying is that it is natural to put things this way, to rephrase or translate, in this way, talk about adopting signaling conventions or linguistic conventions in general. But when we say that we have adopted a linguistic convention, more seems to be included than simply reference to a rule of some sort. It seems natural to add that the rule is *arbitrary,* if what is adopted is a linguistic *convention.* As noted before, it is easy to construe the idea that "language is ruled by convention," particularly when illustrated by remarks like "red could have meant *green,*" and so on, as expressing the platitude that the sound-sense links involved in any language are arbitrary—from the point of view of what we might call "in principle expressibility"; that is, any sign might in principle express any sense; any sense might in principle be expressed by any sign. Trivial but true, and perhaps the clearest truth about the essential nature of languages.[31] So let us take it that, whatever problems lurk beneath the surface of this characterization, the common concept of a linguistic convention is, roughly speaking, that of an arbitrary rule that links sounds and senses. One cannot with certainty pull the "convention" part of the notion out to see it on its own, so to speak. It is going to be the notion of an arbitrary rule, apparently, at least.

Let me turn now to social conventions. A first and obvious question is whether David Lewis has in fact produced an analysis of the concept of a social convention, as expressed when we say things like, "there's a convention in our town that when a call is interrupted the original caller calls back," and so on. I do not believe that Lewis's conditions are logically sufficient for social conventions in the relevant sense. Moreover, I do not think that in order for there to be a social convention there must be a regularity in behavior, a general belief that people will in fact conform to the convention, or an underlying preference structure that would naturally be called a "coordination problem."[32] Instead of arguing these points here, I sketch an alternative view, which I call the view of conventions as norms.[33]

According to this view, social conventions involve, by definition as it were, beliefs about what ought to be done by members of the group in question. David Lewis himself argues that conventions according to his definition are norms, that is, "regularities to which we believe one ought to conform" (p. 97). If they are not regularities, however, they are not precisely that. Moreover, it is the underlying coordination problem structure of Lewisian conventions that, according to Lewis, will provide the "presumptive reasons, according to our common opinions, why that action ought to be done." If conventions do not require such a structure, then Lewis's argument for their normativeness will break down. Finally, and most important here, if—as it would seem Lewis allows—others might not share our "common opinions" about what ought to be, the normativeness of conventions, on Lewis's account, will be a purely contingent property of them: there could be conventions which were not perceived as norms in the groups whose conventions they are. On the contrary, according to the view of conventions as norms, their normativeness is to them as being unmarried is to bachelorhood.

It is worth pointing out that, in recent years, it has generally been thought that commonly known expectations of conformity to convention are crucial to convention, where an "expectation" is taken as a belief about what will in fact be done. (Such a view is endorsed by a number of critics of Lewis, who do not accept his coordination problem account.)[34] One reason that such a view may seem plausible is an accompanying view that conventions are or involve commonly known regularities of some sort—either "actual" regularities or vacuous ones. Even if one does not take a regularity view of any kind, however, there is an ambiguity in the use of "expectation" in English that could smooth the way for acceptance of this condition. For "I expect you to come" may have a partially normative sense; it may include the idea that I believe that you *ought* to come.

According to the view of conventions as norms, it is "ought" beliefs of a normative kind, rather than beliefs about what will be done, that are crucial to our concept of convention.

It is important, in further developing the view of social conventions as norms, to say more about the type of "ought" belief involved and its role in the constitution of social convention. Very brief remarks must suffice here, as to how this might be done.

Concerning the type of belief: when there is a social convention people will say that one ought to do such-and-such, where the "ought" does not constitute a claim about the intrinsic moral value of what one "ought" to do. There could be a convention in an office that interoffice memos were handwritten; it would be absurd to suggest that if there is ever such a convention then the parties to it must believe that there is some intrinsic moral value in handwritten interoffice memos. Further, the "ought" used here is not simply that of "practical rationality" in one narrow sense of that phrase: it is not seen as simply expressing the idea that the person to whom it applies should do such-and-such, his or her current personal preferences being what they are. There could be a convention in an office that interoffice memos are handwritten, even though most people would find it more congenial to type memos, and, in abstraction from the existence of the convention, would prefer that memos be typed.

With respect to the two features just noted, the "ought" of convention evidently parallels that of explicit, verbal agreement. It is clear, meanwhile, that the "ought" of social convention is not simply that of explicit agreement. Certainly a social convention can exist in the absence of any explicit agreement to conform to it, as David Lewis rightly stresses. Further, consideration of cases like that of the agreement to take tea in today's seminar break shows that an explicit agreement does not automatically give rise to or involve in any way a social convention.

It is natural at this point to suggest that a social convention involves something closely related to an explicit agreement, possibly an agreement of some special, tacit kind. I do not think that what is literally speaking a form of agreement is involved in social convention. In what follows, however, I speculate that a phenomenon bearing an important relation to actual agreements is involved; I shall dub this phenomenon a "quasi agreement" for reasons I make clear. The particular label does not really matter, though, and the working definition of "social convention" that I arrive at can be presented without any reference to agreements or use of the notion of an agreement.

Let us return for a moment to explicit agreements. One might judge that the crucial upshot of an actual explicit agreement is that it is common knowledge among the parties that they now believe that each one ought to do what they have agreed to do (an obligation or requirement on their conduct created, as it were, by the fact of agreement itself). Now suppose we have a situation in which it is common knowledge in a certain group that members of the group are going about prescribing (or proscribing, or permitting) doing action A to each of the members, using an "ought" (or "ought not," or "may") characterizable negatively in the way the "ought" of agreement has been characterized above, but where there has been no actual agreement. Assume, to start, that there is no alleged justification for these "oughts" (and so on). They say things like: "You ought to do A, that's all." It seems that it would be very fitting to say in such a case that it was *as* if these people had agreed, or that they had a quasi agreement to do A.

Let us for present purposes define the phrase "quasi agreement" in terms of such a case. Evidently, a quasi agreement as defined may generate a further set of "oughts," which implicitly refer to the quasi agreement: "I ought to, because not only do I believe that I ought to, but most other people believe that I ought to. . . ." In not acting in accordance with the quasi agreement, I would not only be going against my own prescription, but against my fellows' prescriptions also, and it would be known that I know I am doing this. Quasi agreements as defined above, then, may be used to support "ought" judgments.

Note, now, that where there is a social convention people will not only prescribe (etc.) certain actions for members of the group, but will often justify their prescriptions with such locutions as "that's what one is supposed to do, that's all." One might feel that in the absence of such locutions or the corresponding thoughts, we did not have a case of a society whose members fully accepted or endorsed a certain convention. This suggests that we might best think of a social convention not simply as a quasi agreement as defined above, but as something more. As a working hypothesis, then, let us say that a population *P* has a *social convention SC* that one is to do *A* in circumstances *C* if and only if: there is common knowledge in *P* that generally speaking members of *P* believe that they ought to do *A* in *C* because there is a quasi agreement in *P* that one do *A* in *C* ("quasi agreement" will be defined as above). We might dub this account, for short, as the view of social conventions as norms of quasi agreement. For the purposes of what follows, let us assume that the view of social conventions as norms of quasi agreement is correct.

We may now ask how social conventions, characterized as above, compare and contrast with linguistic conventions, viewed as abstract, arbitrary rules that are part of, or help define, a given language. At least one striking connection exists: insofar as a social convention is partly constituted by a generalized belief about what ought, normatively speaking, to be done in a certain situation, it may be seen as a type of norm or, in other words, as a type of rule. What, next, of arbitrariness?

Is there a link between the idea of a norm of quasi agreement and some kind of arbitrariness? I think that one can perceive a link here. Consider again for a moment the case of linguistic conventions and the idea that the rules determining a given sound-sense link are essentially arbitrary. One way of describing the way in which or sense in which the rule is arbitrary in this case is as follows: a different rule would have been equally valid, would have been just as much a rule, as any given rule, since neither is based on the nature of things; in this case, neither has to be based on the intrinsic nature of sounds or senses in order to be a valid linguistic rule. The rule's legitimacy, in other words, does not depend upon its content. This also seems to be true in the case of norms of quasi agreement.

Let us look at the case of norms of quasi agreement in a little more detail. First, when there is a quasi agreement as defined above, there is common knowledge in a group that most members prescribe a type of action with an "ought" that has certain important negative characteristics: it holds irrespective of the morality of the action, and it is not the "ought" of practical rationality. It appears that one could also put things more positively: the prescription or requirement in question is created or imposed by those formulating the prescription, the individual members of the group themselves. It is not independent of human *fiat,* but rather created by it. Second, those who accept certain norms as *based on* quasi agreements will perceive a certain requirement on their conduct as immediately founded, not in their desires or in morality, but on something like majority *fiat,* stipulation, or decree. This will be to see the requirement as of such a kind that, had people in their group thought otherwise, they might have been subject to—subjected themselves to—a different requirement. So one might put it this way: they will perceive that, given its nature as a norm of quasi agreement, it might have been different—something different might have replaced it, but still been a norm or rule. For, had the quasi agreement had a different content, there would have been something else they should have done, where the "should" had the same force as far as its basis in quasi agreement went.

Given the considerations of the previous paragraph, we may say, then, that social conventions, insofar as these are accepted norms of quasi agreement, exist only when there is a group of people who acknowledge certain requirements on or rules of conduct which, *qua* requirements, they perceive as arbitrary. More precisely, to the extent that this behavior is seen as required, it is also perceived that some alternative, incompatible behavior might equally well have been required, insofar as some other quasi agreement, quasi agreements being what they are, was equally possible.

It is important to note that all this would not mean that parties to a given social convention must believe that there is nothing to be said for their convention as opposed to other conventions they might have had in its stead. Nor does it follow that conventions are not criticizable from a variety of standpoints. These are desirable results, from the point of view of an analysis of our everyday concept of a social convention.[35] The analogy with linguistic convention is preserved here, for a given linguistic convention—arbitrary rule linking sound and sense—may nonetheless be especially good or bad from some particular point of view: it may be too unwieldy, say, or very onomatopoeic.[36]

In the case of both social convention and linguistic convention the idea of convention, then, can be argued to involve the notions of both rule and of arbitrariness. There is the following evident difference. In the case where we say that "language is ruled by convention" and mean to refer to the arbitrariness of any given sound-sense link, we are not obviously talking about arbitrariness perceived by any language users or intelligent creatures. A convention of this type might aptly be called the "convention of a language,"[37] in that the locus of the convention here is "in" the language as it were, that is, "in" an abstract object. Meanwhile, social conventions are "in" the social groups they characterize: such conventions only exist when there is common knowledge in a group that a certain norm is held to and is perceived to be a norm of a certain special kind. The arbitrariness of social conventions is a special kind of perceived arbitrariness— according to the view of conventions as norms of quasi agreement.

VIII. Conclusions

In *Convention* David Lewis set out to elucidate the platitude that "language is ruled by convention." I have argued that, insofar as this is a genuine platitude and has to do with the nature of languages and linguistic behavior as such, Lewis's account of convention does not help to elucidate it. In order to show this, I focused on the possibility of one-shot signaling conventions, conventions adopted for conformity on a single occasion. Lewis's theory seemed unable to cope with the sense of "convention" or type of convention involved here. I then argued that insofar as Lewis's platitude is a genuine one, the type or sense of "convention" involved appears to be the same as that involved in talk of one-shot signaling, or more broadly, linguistic conventions. Finally, I sketched a positive account of linguistic convention and a positive account of social convention. If these accounts are more or less right, then we see at least a family resemblance between these two types of entity, in particular the notions of rule and of arbitrariness seem properly to characterize each one. Nonetheless, these are entities of very different sorts, and, in the context of the foregoing discussion the following central point should be noted: linguistic conventions can be involved in a situation when no social conventions are involved. There can be social conventions relating to language, to which language to use, just as there can be explicit agreements of this kind (once some language is possessed already), but these are a kind of metaconvention; they are conventions about what type of linguistic convention to use. (We might call them "conventions of language" as opposed to the "conventions of a language."[38]) Social conventions regarding language are not involved in the case where an isolated individual adopts or conforms to a set of linguistic conventions; nor are they involved when people agree on a one-shot signaling or linguistic convention. That is, when we say that they have adopted such-and-such a convention, we are not in this use of "convention" speaking of social conventions.

I do not pretend to have solved all problems about our concept (or concepts) of convention here. I hope I have shown, however, that if it is a platitude that the nature and use of language as such can be characterized in terms of a type of convention, then Lewis's theory of convention does not capture the type, nor is our common, everyday notion of a social convention the relevant one.[39]

Notes

1. Lewis (1969, 1975). The influence of Lewis's work on conventions is evident in many places, including Schiffer (1972), Bennett (1976), and Ullman-Margalit (1977). Page references in the text refer to Lewis's *Convention* unless otherwise stated.

2. I shall not attempt any direct discussion here of the writings of Quine and White to which Lewis refers, nor question the accuracy of Lewis's characterization of the issues. In this section I mean simply to note the explicit motivation for Lewis's theory of convention.

3. Lewis's own definition, given at p. 24, is in fact ambiguous. See Chapter 5. I here adopt one of the possible interpretations: none of the arguments of this essay is materially affected by the choice.

4. Schelling (1960) suggested that situations like the telephone case ("coordination games" in his terminology) probably underlie the "stability of institutions and traditions" (p. 91). This is not a claim about how anything is to be defined. Lewis's definition of "coordination problem" and his idea of defining "convention" in terms of coordination problems, are his own. An earlier antecedent is Hume, who seems to say that in a situation with a certain

structure of preferences akin to that of a Lewisian coordination problem, a certain practice can only become established as a result of a certain type of convention. See Chapter 3, note 1, above.

5. See Chapter 5, which discusses Lewis's use of the mathematical theory of games in detail. See also Chapter 3, section IV, above.

6. Lewis (1969), p. 70. See Chapter 5 here.

7. See Chapter 5. Lewis gives his initial "coordination problem" condition what he sees as a "natural extension" in his final account of convention (p. 78). (He discusses the nature of the change at pp. 68–70.) The need to amend Lewis's account in the light of his own argument from arbitrariness still applies to the final version.

8. In the definition of "convention" in Lewis (1975), there is no explicit reference to a recurrent situation S. (The definiens is: a regularity *R*, in action or action and belief, is a convention in a population *P*.) One might think that Lewis has here abandoned any "actual regularity" requirement. However, in conversation (May 1977) Lewis has stated that he intended no change from the *Convention* definition in which conventions involved regularities in behavior in recurrent situations, and there is no reason to think that he has abandoned an actual regularity view assuming he originally had one. I shall, in any case, consider later in this essay a possible change in Lewis's *Convention* definition which would involve its ceasing to be an actual regularity view, as I have defined that here.

9. There are various ways one might define "common knowledge." That given here is taken from Lewis (1975). See also Lewis (1969), pp. 51–57. See Chapter 3, this volume, section III, for further references.

10. Lewis (1975), p. 7 ff. I briefly discuss Lewis's account of "actual languages" below, note 25.

11. On the survival of the "actual regularity" view, see note 8 above.

12. Lewis uses the phrase "signaling convention" in a special, technical sense; I should not be taken to be using it here.

13. Cf. Lewis (1969), p. 129, where Lewis refers to a "one-shot" signal. I discuss this passage below.

14. As Saul Kripke pointed out to me, the idea that there could not be a convention conformed to on a single occasion may recall to mind Wittgenstein's query about rules (which evidently invites a negative answer of some kind): "Is what we call 'obeying a rule' something that it would be possible for only *one* person to do, and only once in that person's life?" (*Philosophical Investigations*, 1, section 199; I have slightly ammended the translation). However, Wittgenstein does not seem to go so far as to imply here that in no context whatsoever could there be a particular rule that was obeyed only on one occasion (and by one person only). I shall say more about cases in which only one person is involved below, in section 7.

15. Sometimes our use of the term "convention" may suggest that it can simply mean explicit agreement or thing explicitly agreed upon; as when we

speak, for instance, of the Geneva Convention. According to Hume (see the *Enquiry*) the central use of the term in his day was to refer to an explicit promise or contract. Given that there is such a sense of "convention" or that one be stipulated, it is clear that convention in a different sense is (also) involved in the cases of signaling just discussed. If we "bracket" the former sense of "convention," we can still say, quite properly, that a convention is involved in these cases—a convention has been adopted by virtue of an agreement. This is certainly not true of all cases in which there is an agreement to perform an action *A* on a particular occasion, *O*, as the example in the following paragraph will show. In all of what follows, I intend that we assume that any sense of "convention" in which it means explicit agreement or thing explicitly agreed upon is not at issue. I might note that Lewis (1976) discusses the case of the so-called *Third Hague Convention* of 1907 (p. 114), citing several possible explanations for such a usage. Those he seems to prefer involve our not regarding "*Convention*" as a literal description here. He also notes that "this agreement" may be "called a convention because it is one in some technical sense that has grown up among international lawyers." Possibly such a technical sense could be an outgrowth of a once-common usage along the lines Hume noted. In any case we seem to be looking here at what is now rather a special usage: I waive further discussion of it here.

16. Except, of course, in the special usage mentioned in footnote 15, above.

17. It may be objected that these examples do not give true one-shot conventions for the following reason. Consider the lecturer: it is true that she may only write down her new symbol, '?*', on one occasion. But, insofar as she intends to refer back to what is written down, and intends her students to do so also, in the course of the ensuing discussion, is it not the case that she in fact intends this "notational convention" to be used or conformed to on several occasions? This objection is, I think, well taken, as long as we mark "insofar as" in the previous sentence. For it is surely possible, in practice, that one invents some notational convention such that one intends it to be conformed to on only one occasion, and, indeed, that one's intention is fulfilled. For instance, in the case of the lecturer, it could be the end of the lecture and the lecturer may want to represent the basic theorem arrived at so that everyone can see it set out before them momentarily before they leave.

The main question here is not whether one-shot signaling, notational, or linguistic conventions are typical or common, but whether, intuitively speaking, they are possible.

18. Lewis means something rather complex by his term "signaling system," and his "signaling convention" is defined in terms of the former notion. See his p. 135. For the purposes of this discussion I ignore a number of special details that do not affect my argument.

19. The "by reason of" clauses rule out a case where the other conditions hold because of the conspicuous virtue of one of the possible solutions to the coordination problem. Adding such clauses probably ensures less tampering with Lewis's ideas.

20. Lewis (1976), pp. 113–14.

21. Suppose someone "analyses" "*X* is rich" as "*X* has no more money than most other people." One certainly does not get the correct result if one dismisses the putative counterexample of David Rockefeller ("But don't we say that David Rockefeller is rich?") by replying: "We can of course properly say that D. R. is rich, but that is only because we are expressing the hope that he will be rich (since, for egalitarian reasons, we hope that he will come to have no more money than other people)." In fact of course, the reason that we can properly say (in 1982) that D. R. is rich, is that he is literally speaking rich, and any analysis having the consequence that this is not so has to be false.

22. Compare what Lewis himself says (1975), p. 24, "there are other so-called rules of language which are not conventions of language and are not in the least like conventions of language: for instance 'rules' of syntax and semantics. They are not even regularities."

23. I do not say that this "platitude" cannot usefully be discussed and its import clarified. For some further discussion, see below. A classic reference in this area is Plato's *Cratylus,* which I cannot approach directly here. I thank Malcolm Schofield for reminding me of the reference.

24. A phrase used by Winch (1958), p. 33. I discuss Winch's argumentation concerning the social nature of language in *On Social Facts.*

25. I do not take it as obvious that the idea that a particular language, *L,* the language of a population, *P,* is to be explicated in terms of a common, established notion of a social convention, even though there may in fact be such conventions regarding language use in all human language-using groups. Nor do I take it that this idea is to be explicated in terms of conventions in the sense of Lewis. Nor, finally, do I believe that a population *P* will use a language *L* if and only if there is a convention of truthfulness and trust in the population—Lewis's hypothesis in Lewis (1975). (I discuss this last point briefly in Gilbert [1974], p. 86.) My own guess is that something less complex than social convention or convention in the sense of Lewis will be required. Perhaps—in order for *L* to be the unique language of a population *P*—we just need common knowledge in *P* that individual members of *P* will "utter" sentences of *L,* if of any language, and will interpret those sentences in accordance with the semantics of *L.*

Note added here: In Chapter 10, I explore aspects of a *group's* language, construed as a language that has been agreed upon by group members. Given a group's language, in this sense, interpreting the sentences of *L* in accordance with the semantics of *L* will not just happen by chance, but by virtue of an underlying agreement. The last account envisaged in the previous paragraph is a summative one: according to it a population's language may be no more than a set of idiolects that (as is commonly known) happen to coincide. Obviously a population can have a language in this sense. Some problems inherent in such a situation are noted in Chapter 10.

26. Another influential philosopher who endorses a view of the kind under discussion is Quine, in various writings.

Those influenced by Wittgenstein include Peter Winch and Michael Dummett (see "The Social Character of Meaning" [1974] in Dummett [1978]). Outside the circle of professional philosophers, in the social studies, for instance, one often hears and reads that Wittgenstein has shown that language is "public" and the like. The precise nature of what Wittgenstein is alleged to have shown is often left obscure in such references.

27. See Kripke (1982). Wittgenstein's positive views, as Kripke sees them, are quite subtle, and of course crude slogans of the type cited hardly capture their detail.

28. Of course, if in fact Wittgenstein's positive views, as Kripke sees them, are correct, the question remains as to whether conventions in Lewis's sense come into the correct picture of language use as such. There is no space here to expand on the subtle nature of the views, or to discuss their connection with conventions in Lewis's sense or in any familiar sense. See *On Social Facts*, Chapter 3, for some exposition and discussion of Kripke on Wittgenstein.

29. Page 105. Lewis remarks that the concept of a rule seems to be one in which the "relative importance of different conditions varies with the subject matter, with the contrasts one wants to make, and with one's philosophical preconceptions." I take it that the idea of such a concept is something like this: an "analysis" of such a concept would not consist of a set of conditions individually necessary and jointly sufficient, logically, for application of the concept, but, rather, of a set of conditions such that the concept may apply when only some proper subset of the conditions is satisfied. The idea of a "cluster concept" is to be distinguished, evidently, from the idea of a concept such that, though there is a set of logically necessary and jointly sufficient conditions, we sometimes *speak as* if the concept applies in a case where it literally does not, because we speak elliptically.

30. Perhaps I should stress that this case does not have to be thought of in terms of a radically isolated person, one isolated from others "all his life." It is enough to imagine someone fully integrated into a society and with a shared language—like the reader—who decides on a one-shot linguistic convention for some purpose or other.

31. The "in principle expressibility" point of view must of course be distinguished from the point of view of a person or persons choosing what sign to adopt in order to express a certain thought. I suppose that there is a possible language or system of signs in which a person's flying to the center of the sun means *five*. This will be a language that is pretty hard to use. Every time I want to "say" that two plus two equals five, for instance, in this language, I shall have to bring it about that someone flies to the center of the sun. It is probably impossible to do this, in fact, so I could never utter a sentence in this language involving the word for *five*. Similarly, there is a possible sign system in which leaving a baseball bat on the kitchen table means or signifies that I have gone to the baseball game. This is relatively easy to use, and the sign is

perhaps a "natural" one to choose. But a squashed tomato or a glass of water could in principle be endowed with the same signification. Significations or meanings are not choosy about their mates; humans are more choosy about the words or signs they are willing to adopt. They care, among other things, for what is manageable, aesthetically congenial, and obvious within their frames of reference. (I make this point in response to questions from Barry Richards, Paul Ziff, and Paul Grice, in Tallahassee, 1980.)

32. See Chapter 3, above, and *On Social Facts*, Chapter 5, for further discussion of these issues.

33. See also Chapter 3, above. In *On Social Facts* I criticize this account of social convention, and develop another which though different in important ways has some important affinities with this one. Similar things can be said of social conventions as I would now characterize them, in relation to linguistic conventions (see below in the text). My current view of a social convention as a "jointly accepted *fiat*" is invoked in Chapter 2, section VIII, this volume. It is discussed further in *On Social Facts*, Chapter 5.

34. See, for instance, Schiffer (1972).

35. I should have liked to develop the points made in the previous three sentences in greater detail here, but space forbids it.

36. See also note 26, above, on this issue.

37. Lewis uses this phrase in *Convention*, p. 51. He construes it in terms of "regularities." I, of course, do not.

38. Lewis has used both phrases, without marking a distinction (I believe). In fact "linguistic convention" and "convention of language" seem to be phrases that are hard to keep free of ambiguity. I have tried to keep my own intended meaning as clear as possible throughout the discussion.

39. Most of the work on this essay was done while I was a Visiting Fellow at Princeton University. Versions have been read at the Philosophy of Language conference, Tallahassee, Florida, 1980, and elsewhere. I thank Saul Kripke, especially, for comments. Section III has been shortened substantially for this volume, as have some of the notes.

5

Game Theory and *Convention*

Introduction

Recently David Lewis has proposed an account of conventions that, he maintains, enables us to see precisely how it can be that "language is ruled by convention."[1] Lewis's work on convention has, rightly, received some enthusiastic responses.[2] While it represents a substantial and stimulating contribution to the philosophy of language, it is also essential reading for philosophers of social science and any others concerned with phenomena like social conventions. As well as Lewis's proposal concerning conventions, a number of his key notions—for instance "coordination problem," "common knowledge," "actual language of a population"—are of independent interest and have stimulated discussion.[3]

It is with the first mentioned notion—"coordination problem"—that I shall be most closely concerned in this essay. This notion lies at the center of Lewis's account of conventions: conventions are, according to Lewis, and roughly, practices established within coordination problem situations. Lewis's notion of a coordination problem is explained in game-theoretical terms.

Lewis's book has been admired for its "deft use" of the mathematical theory of games.[4] No doubt many readers have been impressed by the way game theory has been used to provide a technical underpinning for Lewis's philosophical project. At the same time, I think it probable that many readers, like myself in the first instance, have tended to take the details of this underpinning for granted, skimming these particulars lightly. It is the purpose of this essay to examine whether Lewis's technical underpinning gives his work as rigorous a basis as first appears.[5]

I. An Argument Linking "Coordination Problems" to Convention

Prior to his proposed analysis of the notion of a convention, Lewis presents us with descriptions of eleven situations that he calls "sample coordination problems" (p. 5). One of these is roughly as follows (see Lewis, p. 6, and also Schelling, 1960, p. 94, where there is a similar example): two people—call them "*A*" and "*B*"—are talking on the telephone, when they are unexpectedly cut off. Each wants the connection restored. What should they do? Lewis describes the problem thus: they must each "choose whether to call back . . . in order to call back if and only if the other waits" (p. 6).

One can quickly see a connection between conventions as ordinarily conceived, and the situation of *A* and *B* in the telephone case. *A* and *B* might, one supposes, already be parties to a convention that, say, when a telephone conversation is cut off the caller calls back. If this is so, we would expect *A* and *B* to have no real problem of choice when their conversation is interrupted. *Ceteris paribus,* we would expect the caller to call back and the person called to wait, each conforming to the convention. In other words, we can see that a typical convention may apply to, or "cover," a typical "coordination problem" situation, and in fact render that situation, when it occurs, unproblematic.

Now, Lewis does not merely claim (unexceptionably) that conventions may cover problem situations analogous to the telephone case and help to solve them. His view is that the very existence of a convention, *C*, is logically dependent on the existence of a coordination problem situation, *S*, which it covers. That is, as a matter of logic, there is a convention in a population *P* only if (almost) whenever a certain coordination problem *S* occurs among members of *P*, the members of *P* concerned do action *A*.[6]

Lewis cites a number of examples that seem to fit this contention about convention. One can also glean from Lewis's text the outlines of an argument for it.

First, there are some basic intuitions or premises about the notion of a social convention: (A) a convention in a population, *P*, is a "regularity" in the behavior of members of *P* when they are agents in a certain situation, *S*. (B) A convention is, in some sense, and to some degree, in the interests of all parties to it; or, to use Lewis's words, "coincidence of interests predominates" among the parties (in section III below I discuss Lewis's various uses of the quoted phrase). (C) Social conventions occur, at least in clear cases, among rational agents[7] who have "common knowledge"[8] of each other's rationality and each other's preferences relating to situation S. (D) Conventions are "arbitrary" in some intuitive sense.

I do not necessarily accept claims (A) through (D), but for the purposes of this essay I shall in general not dispute them. I shall be more critical of them elsewhere, when I present an alternative account of conventions.[9]

Second, there is an abstract argument linking conventions as characterized above to certain features found in "coordination problems." In particular the "arbitrariness" of conventions is linked tightly to the "nontriviality" of choice-situations and (hence) to "coordination problem" situations. We shall see in the detailed argument of this essay that Lewis does not really have a well-defined notion of "coordination problem," since he does not define his key notion of a "proper coordination equilibrium," which is central to his definition of the former notion, and no clear definition of "proper coordination equilibrium" can be deduced from his writings. In this preliminary section, however, I will write, for simplicity, as if Lewis has given clear accounts of "proper coordination equilibrium" and "coordination problem." For one can display the form of Lewis's abstract argument without attempting to define his key technical terms. The argument runs roughly as follows. (The argument refers at all times to choice-situations involving [ideally] rational agents with "predominant coincidence of interests" and common knowledge of the matrix of preferences and of each other's rationality.)

1. Unless a choice-situation has multiple "proper coordination equilibria" it will be trivial. (For example, if a situation possesses a unique "coordination equilibrium" [and hence has fewer than two proper coordination equilibria] the situation will be trivial; it will be common knowledge among the agents that each one should do his part in the unique coordination equilibrium.)

2. Let S be a trivial choice-situation. Let action "A" be what rational agents should do in S. In a population of such agents a regularity of doing A in S will not then be an *arbitrary* regularity, and hence it will not be conventional. (For example, a regularity of doing one's part in a unique coordination equilibrium will be a regularity of doing what one should do, and hence will not be arbitrary, and hence not a convention.) We ignore the case of conformity to some other action in this situation, since we are considering the case of (ideally) rational agents with common knowledge of each other's rationality.

3. Let S be a nontrivial situation, i.e., one having two or more proper coordination equilibria. A regularity R occurring among rational

agents in such a situation *will* be arbitrary. It will be a regularity of doing one's part in one of the proper coordination equilibria; but there will be at least one other regularity R' which might have been conformed to among these agents, that of doing one's part in another of the proper coordination equilibria.

4. It follows that the only situation in which arbitrary regularities (and, hence, conventions) obtain among agents who are (ideally) rational, etc., is a situation with two *or more proper coordination equilibria;* and any regularities arising in such a situation will be arbitrary.

5. Now, there is a class of intuitively similar "problem" situations arising among agents who are rational (etc.), which may be introduced by means of examples (like the telephone case) and which we may call "coordination problems." A consideration of examples makes it clear that a general, distinctive, and important feature of the members of this class is their lack of triviality. We may reasonably define "coordination problem" in terms of whatever is responsible for this nontriviality. By premise 1 above, this is the possession of more than one proper coordination equilibrium. Hence we may define a "coordination problem" as (roughly) a situation in which there are multiple proper coordination equilibria.

6. In conclusion, then, conventions—arbitrary regularities among rational agents—depend on the existence of coordination problems. More specifically, a regularity is a convention only if it is a regularity of doing one's part in a particular proper coordination equilibrium, in a coordination problem situation.

Some such argument is, as I have said, at least implicit in Lewis's text. Whether or not it, or something similar, informed Lewis's thought on convention, if it were acceptable it would be a powerful argument in favor of Lewis's account of conventions as they are ordinarily conceived.[10]

In the following sections of this essay I address myself explicitly to Lewis's use of game theory in his discussion of *coordination problems.* Certain of the claims he makes in the course of that discussion, however, bear crucially on the acceptability of the abstract argument just presented. My arguments against these claims will, in effect, also destroy the above abstract argument linking coordination problems to convention, along with some possible variants on it.

In particular, I shall argue, against Lewis, (in Section III below) that situations possessing a unique "coordination equilibrium" (and hence *not* possessing two [proper] coordination equilibria) are *not* necessarily "trivial" in any intuitive sense; in particular, it need not be obvious to each agent that he should do his part in the unique coordination equilibrium; in general it need not be obvious to him *what* he should do. More generally, two proper coordination equilibria are *not* a necessary condition of nontriviality. Once this point is made, premise 1 above is refuted, and the abstract argument making coordination problems necessary to conventions collapses.

Among other things, it will emerge, in addition, that it is not the case that rational agents should always do their parts in a unique *proper* coordination equilibrium, nor need they always do their parts in one particular proper coordination equilibrium when there are several. (In other words, the regularities arising in the latter type of situation need not always be as is supposed in premise 3.)

I shall agree with Lewis that, on the basis of his eleven examples, a "coordination problem" might reasonably be at least partially defined as having two or more "proper coordination equilibria."[11] However, contrary to the whole drift of Lewis's game-theoretical argumentation, this is not because all and only such structures are "nontrivial."

Generally speaking, the central idea of the "triviality" of a choice situation needs more attention than Lewis gives it, and I shall attempt to go some way toward providing this.

II. Coordination Problems: Preliminary Issues

Lewis's discussion of coordination problems proceeds as follows. After presenting his eleven examples of sample coordination problems (p. 5), among which is the telephone case mentioned above, he sets out to "see how to describe the common character of coordination problems" (p. 8). He then moves through a small thicket of game-theoretical definitions and argumentation to an eventual definition of "coordination problem" (p. 24) explicitly motivated by the argumentation. At no point in all this is the supposed relation of coordination problems to convention explicitly alluded to. We are, in effect, invited to consider the nature of a coordination problem independently of that of a convention.

Once "coordination problem" has been defined, Lewis moves on to his definition of "convention." He notes that if among the agents in some instance of some coordination problem there is a precedent of doing one's part in one particular "proper coordination equilibrium," then *ceteris paribus* precedent will determine what happens next; in brief, precedent will be followed, and we shall get a "metastable self-perpetuating system of preferences, expectations and actions, capable of persisting indefinitely" (p. 42). There follows Lewis's "first, rough definition of convention":

> A regularity R in the behavior of members of a population P when they are agents in a recurrent situation S is a convention if and only if, in any instance of S among members of P, (1) everyone conforms to R; (2) everyone expects everyone else to conform to R; (3) everyone prefers to conform to R on condition that the others do, since S is a coordination problem and uniform conformity to R *is* a coordination equilibrium in S.[12]

As noted above, Lewis has an implicit argument linking (nontrivial) coordination problems and (arbitrary) conventions which allows him to take it that this account really is an account of convention, and convention "in its full generality." This argument, however, is not alluded to in these pages.

Before examining the argumentation which leads to Lewis's definition of "coordination problem," I shall point out, in this section, some problems relating to its conclusion. These have to do with an ambiguity in Lewis's eventual definition of "coordination problem," with his subsequent (different) characterizations of the preference structure underlying conventions, and with his initial examples of coordination problems.

i. Lewis's account of "coordination problems": an ambiguity

Lewis's preferred account of coordination problems is as follows: they are "situations of interdependent decision by two or more agents in which coincidence of interests predominates and in which there are two or more proper coordination equilibria" (p. 24). In this section I note that the important notion of a "proper coordination equilibrium" is explained ambiguously.

Unfortunately, Lewis does not explicitly define "proper coordination equilibrium" in spite of its centrality to his account. However, he does define some related terms. First, an "equilibrium" *simpliciter is* a combination of agents' actions such that no one could have done better by acting differently himself, given the others' choices (see Lewis, p. 8. This notion of an "equilibrium" is standard in game theory. Compare Luce and Raiffa, p. 62). A "coordination equilibrium" is a combination in which no one would have been better off had *any one* agent alone acted otherwise, either himself or someone else. [p. 14]

Finally, a "proper equilibrium" is a combination of actions such that

each agent likes it *better than* any other combination he could have reached, given the others' choices. [p. 22]

Now, given these definitions, what are we to understand by "proper coordination equilibrium" (I henceforth abbreviate this to "p.c.e.")? It may seem that a p.c.e. will be a coordination equilibrium which is also a proper equilibrium. In other words, then, it will be a combination of the different agents' actions such that (a) no one would be better off had any one agent acted otherwise, and (b) each likes it better than any he could have reached, given the others' choicest. Richard Grandy interprets Lewis in this way in his review of *Convention* (Grandy [1977], pp. 130–31). Lewis "interpreted" himself this way, also, in conversation with the present author (spring 1977).

There is, however, another, not implausible, way of construing "proper coordination equilibrium" given the previous definitions. According to this construal, the restriction of "properness" applies to *coordination equilibria* as it does to equilibria *simpliciter*— strengthening in a global way the restrictions imposed by the other condition. In other words, a p.c.e. will be a combination each agent prefers to any other in which some one agent, *himself or another,* had acted otherwise. This was in fact the interpretation which first occurred to me. And Edna Ullman-Margalit seems inclined to make it.[13]

Now, if we understand "p.c.e." according to the first ("weak") interpretation above, it does not follow that in a p.c.e. each agent will prefer any lone nonconformist to conform. Each could, evidently, be *neutral* with regard to the other's conformity and some nonconforming state. Such neutrality is not possible in a p.c.e. in the second ("strong") sense. Nor is it possible in the structure posited in Lewis's final account of the preferences underlying conventions in *Convention* or in the later paper "Languages and Language." Lewis's fourth condition in the paper is (in part):

There is a general preference for general conformity to (regularity) *R* rather than slightly-less-than-general conformity—in particular, rather than conformity by all but one. [p. 5]

We might put the point this way: were we to cull account of "p.c.e." from these accounts of convention, we should define it using the *strong* sense of "p.c.e." noted earlier.

Recall at this point Lewis's condition in the definition of "coordination problem" that "coincidence of interests predominates." This does not occur in "Languages and Language." Someone might then conjecture that in "Languages and Language" two original conditions (the "coincidence clause" and a *weak* p.c.e. requirement) have been elided to produce a requirement of two or more p.c.e. in the strong sense.

It turns out that we have to reject this conjecture. In the *Convention* section on coordination problems, Lewis explicitly defines what he there means by a situation in which "coincidence of interests predominates"; that is: "the differences between different agents' payoffs in any one square (perhaps after suitable linear resealing) are small compared to some of the differences between payoffs in the different squares" (p. 14). Now, we can construct a "game matrix" showing a situation with two p.c.e. *in the weak sense only,* which fulfills the stated requirement of the coincidence clause.

	A	B	C
1	5 / 5	4 / 5	0 / 0
2	5 / 4	0 / 0	3 / 4
3	0 / 0	4 / 5	5 / 5

Fig. 5.1.   (See note 14 for key.)

Here, the 2 p.c.e. (weak sense) are $A1$ and $C3$ (see Figure 5.1).

It is clear, then, that the coincidence clause does not have the effect of bringing the two possible definitions of "p.c.e." together. It has no bearing on either p.c.e. requirement, nor they on it.[14]

ii. Shifts in Lewis's thinking

If Lewis started intending a weak interpretation of "p.c.e." in the definition of "coordination problem," by "Languages and Language" he has implicitly changed his definition to one using a notion of p.c.e. in the strong sense. If in fact he always intended a strong interpretation of "p.c.e." he has still changed his view of the structure of preferences underlying conventions, for he has now dropped the further require- ment that coincidence of interests predominates. Either way, then, he has changed his view, since the original account of coordination problems contained the very specific "coincidence clause" we have noted.

Lewis has also clearly adopted a requirement of what are, in effect, two p.c.e. in the strong sense by the time he reaches his final definition of "convention" in *Convention*. Thus "we require that all share the conditional preference of each for his conformity to R" (p. 69). If there has been a change here, it is neither noted nor argued for. Of the requirement just noted, Lewis writes: "if S is a self-contained problem of interdependent decision, this . . . requirement makes uniform conformity to R a proper coordination equilibrium" (p. 69). This may suggest that Lewis thinks that a p.c.e. in the strong sense is what was at issue all along, but of course the last remark is consistent with a weak interpretation of "p.c.e." Moreover, though in this section Lewis explicitly intends only to alter his conditions on *Convention* in ways irrelevant to our present discussion of the structure of coordina- tion problems (see p. 68), he makes what amounts to a fairly major change in the area of the overall coincidence of interests that is required in the situation at the base of conventions. For consider that at this point in *Convention* the original coincidence clause has gone, while a *new* clause has appeared: in the problem situation to which the convention applies, every agent must have "approximately the same preferences regarding all possible combinations of actions" (p. 78; see also p. 69). This is perhaps supposed to be a somewhat vaguer statement of the original coincidence requirement, but in fact it looks quite a bit stronger. In any case, Lewis himself regards it as entailing that every proper equilibrium in the situation must be a proper coordination equilibrium in the strong sense (see p. 69). Since the original coincidence clause does not entail this, it will certainly be stronger than that clause if it has this entailment.

Since defining "coordination problem," then, Lewis certainly changed things in *Convention* with a new clause about overall coincidence of interests that is different from the original coincidence clause and probably much stronger. Another change—depending on where he started—may be that from a weak to a strong p.c.e. requirement. That he ends with a strong requirement is clear. "Languages and Language" differs, finally, from the last *Convention* statement by a final dropping of any clause about overall coincidence of interests.

The strong interpretation of "p.c.e." requires, in effect, a specific area and type of "coincidence of interests" among agents. By "Languages and Language" Lewis conjectures that the requirement that a p.c.e. in this sense underlies a convention may be *all* that is needed in respect of the coincidence of interests involved in conventions (p. 16). Apparently abandoning his old technical definition of predominant coincidence of interests, and the requirement in terms of it, and abandoning the later approximate-agreement-in-preferences clause in *Convention,* he writes that the requirement of an underlying strong p.c.e. "serves to distinguish cases of convention, in which there is a predominant coincidence of interest, from cases of deadlocked conflict" (ibid.).

Now, as far as deadlocked conflict goes, a strong p.c.e. requirement does serve to rule out zero-sum situations; but so, in fact, would a *weak* p.c.e. requirement. Leaving aside the question of conventions in the everyday sense, some obvious questions arise with respect to coordination problems. Is the requirement of two p.c.e. in either sense necessary for the specification of the structure of coordination problems, and if so, which? Is the necessary p.c.e. requirement, if any, sufficient with respect to the "coincidence of interests" required? Or is some further "coincidence of interests" clause necessary, and if so, which? Let us see if the discussion preceding Lewis's definition of "coordination problem" can help us, as might be expected.

iii. Lewis's examples: two distinguishable structures

Lewis explains his procedure with regard to the definition of "coordination problem" as that of introducing a class by means of examples, and taking the "defining features" of the class to be "those distinctive features of the examples which seem important for an understanding of their character'' (p. 24, fn.). In this section I point out that in one of Lewis's examples there are two p.c.e. in the weak sense, but there are not two p.c.e. in the strong sense. This being so, one might think that Lewis must opt, if anything, for the requirement of two p.c.e. in the weak sense. However, there could be reasons for excluding this case from the class of coordination problems.

First, let us look at a case that appears to involve two proper coordination equilibria in the strong sense: the telephone case cited earlier. The matrix for the case could look like this:

Call Back   *Wait*

	10	0
10		0

Wait

	0	10
0		10

Call Back

Fig. 5.2.   Telephone Case: Diagram 1

Second, consider the stag-hunt case:

Suppose we are in a wilderness without food. Separately we can catch rabbits and eat badly. Together we can catch stags and eat well, but if even one of us deserts the stag hunt to catch a rabbit, the stag will get away; so the other stag hunters will not eat unless they desert too. Each must choose whether to stay with the stag hunt or desert according to his expectations about the others, staying if and only if no one else will desert. [p. 7][15]

Now, if starving is the option if we don't at least get a rabbit for ourselves, the matrix could presumably look something like Figure 5.3.[16]

If one were looking for formal differences between the cases cited so far, it might be noted that in the staghunt case, as diagrammed above, there is a choice for each agent which uniquely "maximizes his

	Staghunt	Separate
Staghunt	100 100	80 0
Separate	0 80	80 80

Fig. 5.3.   Stag Hunt: Diagram 1

security level'' or maximizes his minimum possible payoff. (This is the choice of separating from the others.)[17] It is true that in the telephone case, as diagrammed above, there is no unique ''maximin'' strategy available. This does not seem, however, to be essential to one's sense of the case. Consider that there would be a maximin strategy in this case if, say, one spent some money whenever one made a call, whether the party called was reached or not. The strategy of waiting would then maximize each agent's security level, even if the cost of calling, both in monetary and other terms, was relatively very low, as in the version of the telephone case in Figure 5.4. Consider also that Lewis himself makes it clear (see below) that he does not see coordination problems as having to involve a *perfect* coincidence of interests. In his own version of the telephone case he writes ''it matters little to either of us whether he is the one to call back or the one to wait'' (p. 6) and this is as true of the telephone case-with-a-maximin-choice as of the case without it.

In any case, there is at least one important difference between the original version of the telephone case and the stag-hunt case which *also* differentiates the latter from the ''amended'' telephone case, *both* being cases where each agent has two choices of action and one possible maximin strategy.

The amended telephone case has two proper coordination equilibria in the strong sense, while the stag-hunt case possesses only one equilibrium of *this* kind, plus one proper coordination equilibrium in the *weak* sense only. This means, in more concrete terms, that the

Fig. 5.4.   Telephone Case: Diagram 2

hunters are not so dependent on their fellows as the people in the telephone case. If a hunter chooses to hunt rabbits, as he may well do if he is unwilling to risk starvation, he will have no particular desire that the others hunt rabbits with him—in other words, when he himself does. He doesn't in fact care in this case *what* the others do. (This is made explicit in Rousseau's version of the case, incidentally.) He will therefore only care what the *others* do in *one* case—the case where he himself stays with the hunt. Compare this with the telephone case: whatever each chooses (maximin choice or not) he cares what the others involved with him will do. There is no way in which he can put himself out of the reach of the others so that he does not care whether or not their actions are appropriately coordinated.

Now, we could redescribe the stag case as one in which everyone prefers that *no one* starve. Then the matrix could be redrawn, as, for instance, in Figure 5.5 below. In such a case coordination over separation clearly is something each one desires in itself. Yet Lewis's description of the case gave no reason to suppose it was of this kind.

The point about there being an obvious maximin strategy for the hunters still stands, indeed stands firmer, with Figure 5.5, but, substituting Figure 5.5 for Figure 5.3, the case would then resemble cases like the telephone case in what is a salient, and maybe an important, respect. Figure 5.5 but not Figure 5.3, involves two proper coordination equilibria in the strong and not merely the weak sense.

These considerations might suggest the use of the strong definition of p.c.e. in a definition of coordination problem, but Lewis says

Staghunt   Separate

	Staghunt	Separate
Staghunt	100 100	80 0
Separate	0 80	90 90

Fig. 5.5.   Stag Hunt: Diagram 2

nothing about them. Besides, perhaps the salient feature in question could be argued to be unimportant, so that the stag case as diagrammed in Figure 5.3, Stag Hunt Diagram 1, and the telephone and other cases, in fact resemble each other in important respects which can motivate their coclassification, and the adoption of a requirement of two p.c.e. in the weak sense. A look at Lewis's examples, then, makes one eager to follow the arguments that provide the basis for his definition.

III. Lewis's Game-Theoretical Argumentation

At the outset of his discussion of "the common character of coordination problems" Lewis makes some purely descriptive comments. He writes that "the outcome of any action an agent might choose depends on the actions of the other agents" (p. 8). As already noted, this point does not cover a natural interpretation of the stag-hunt case, for on this interpretation *one* action of each of the agents reaches a certain payoff whatever the other agents do. If we wished to leave this case in, we could describe the cases as situations in which the payoff of *at least one* move of each agent depends on the actions of the other agents. Neither this latter description, nor the former, can be *distinguishing* marks of coordination problem situations. Nor is the next feature Lewis notes: that in all his examples there are equilibria. These, as Lewis says, can occur in cases of pure conflict, and, Lewis implies, coordination problems are *not* situations of pure conflict.

This still leaves us with a large range of situations. Lewis suggests that his coordination problems are "at or near the pure coordination end of Schelling's spectrum" (p. 14). He does not, however, "want to require perfect coincidence of interests" (p. 14). In all his examples he does, with intuitive reasonableness, leave room for the players' rankings of the possible outcomes to differ at least somewhat from the point of view of both rank order and relative value. Thus he introduces his requirement that coincidence of interest predominates. As we have already seen, this is a relatively weak requirement; in itself it leaves room for the prayers' rankings of the various outcomes to vary quite considerably, in both order and relative value.

Lewis next notes that all the sample coordination problems have two or more different coordination equilibria (p. 16). Here description of the cases ends and some *a priori* reasoning comes in. It is reasoning to the conclusions, first, that a coordination problem should be defined as having two or more coordination equilibria, and, second, that it should have, by definition, at least two p.c.e.

This reasoning might be expected to reveal the sense intended for "p.c.e." and, more generally, to explain the significance of Lewis's final account of coordination problems. However, the reasoning is often obscure and, I shall argue, mistaken.

The basic (unstated) intuition behind Lewis's reasoning appears to be that it is a distinctive and important feature of coordination problems that they are nontrivial choice-situations. Hence Lewis's purpose is, evidently, to isolate those features of coordination problems which are responsible for their nontriviality, and to define them by reference to those features. His attempt to do this is what appears to lead him eventually to his conclusion that there must be two or more p.c.e. in a coordination problem.

One central claim about which Lewis is mistaken is the basis of his argumentative defense of an initial minimal requirement on all coordination problems—that they have at least two *coordination* equilibria. The claim I have in mind is this:

If there is no considerable conflict of interest, the task of reaching a unique coordination equilibrium is more or less trivial. [p. 16]

The above claim is in fact not entirely perspicuous. It seems to break down into two related claims. First, a general claim seems to be implied, namely that if there is a unique coordination equilibrium (in a situation without considerable conflict of interest), then it will be the outcome most desired by each agent. This claim will be refuted shortly.[18] Second, Lewis implies that, while all are trivial, there are varying degrees of triviality in situations with unique coordination equilibria—and he proceeds to discuss, in sequence, the general case and then a special case involving "dominance." There are many obscurities in this discussion. Unravelling it will take longer than the original discussion.

To begin, consider Lewis's claim about *the general case*. He argues that situations with a unique coordination equilibrium (or "c.e." for short) are always such that the unique c.e. will be reached:

> if the nature of the situation is clear enough so that everyone makes the best choice given his expectations, everyone expects everyone else to make the best choice given his expectations, and so on. [p. 16]

This claim is not very clear. For one thing we could take Lewis to be talking only about what I shall call a "one-off" case (see below), or rather, about all possible cases with a unique coordination equilibrium.[19]

By a "one-off" situation, here, I mean something rather specific: a situation like one of Lewis's examples in which it is common knowledge that no one has or can come by any (justified) expectations about what the other agents involved will do in advance of his own decision about what to do—*except* what he can glean by considering that there is common knowledge among the agents concerned of their shared rationality and of the matrix. We might say that, in such a situation, no one has any *external basis* for expectations about what will be done. Typically this will be in cases where the situation has never occurred before among these agents, but a case's being of this kind is not sufficient for its being one-off in the sense I have in mind. For instance, though these agents may never have been in this situation, it may be common knowledge among them that certain other people have, and have successfully resolved the question of what to do in a particular way. This may justify expectations of each other's acting in the relevant way. It is clear that in a one-off case as defined, agents have to decide what to do without resorting to *communication*. (Lewis himself does not mention communication in these pages.)

Consider, then, that we are talking about a one-off case. Then Lewis's claim about "ordinary" unique coordination equilibria could be construed something like this:

(1) the best (most desired) combination for each agent individually will be that equilibrium (this is the general claim noted earlier); therefore (?)
(2) given only common knowledge of the matrix and of the agents' rationality, each one will expect everyone else to do his part in the coordination equilibrium, and hence, being rational,
(3) each will do his own part, and thus the unique coordination equilibrium will be reached.

That something like this was meant is indicated by some remarks Lewis makes later (p. 70), thus:

Recall the discussion . . . of the triviality of any situation with a unique coordination equilibrium and predominantly coincident interests. We are now in a better position to describe this triviality: common knowledge of rationality is all it takes for an agent to have reason to do his part of the one coordination equilibrium. He has no *need* to appeal to precedents or any other source of further mutual expectations. [my stress]

(Lewis's discussion of his concept of "common knowledge" and of types of sources of "mutual expectations" have come after the passages on matrix structure that we are considering.) I take "have reason" here as "have a sufficient (decisive) reason."

Now the interpretation of Lewis's claim in terms of one-off situations is not the only one possible. Lewis could be taken to be making a claim about all possible (relatively unconflicted) cases with a unique coordination equilibrium, and not merely one-off cases. To phrase this interpretation as similarly to the former as possible, it would run:

(1) the best combination for each agent individually will be the unique c.e. Therefore (?)
(2) *Whatever "external" bases for expectations each player has,* in advance of making his move, about what the others will do (precedents, agreements, and so on), these will always be *irrelevant* to his decision, whatever they are, since,
(3) common knowledge of rationality and of the matrix will *always* give each agent sufficient and indeed overriding reason to expect everyone else to do his part in the c.e. and hence,
(4) each will do his part, and thus the c.e. be reached.

In brief, the claim is that all cases can and should work exactly as if they were one-off cases: the crucial basis for expectation and action will be the same. Remarks of Lewis that seem to support *this* idea occur in another later passage. Referring to "a regularity whereby we achieve unique coordination equilibria" Lewis writes: "we would conform to it simply because that is the best thing to do. *No matter what we had been doing in the past,* a failure to conform . . . could only be a strategic error (or compensation for someone else's anticipated compensation, etc.)" (my stress: p. 70).

These two interpretations of Lewis are not equivalent. I now argue, in any case, against the claims made in each of them.

First I introduce some terms of my own. These will be useful now and later also. Let an *absolute best point* be an outcome such that every other outcome is *worse* for every agent. Let a *best point* be an outcome such that no other outcome is *preferred* by any agent. (Thus there may be more than one best point but not more than one absolute best point in a given situation.)

Now, suppose that in a one-off situation with an absolute best point there is group common knowledge of rationality and of the matrix. Then the *best combination* for each will (by definition) be the point in question and will be obvious to all. Will it be true that agents in such a situation will always expect the others to do their parts in the absolute best point combination, and that each will do his part? (Let us assume that each option an agent has is equally accessible, or that difficulties in reaching a given option are already incorporated in the matrix.)

I suggest that, in general, an absolute best point will not be the obvious thing to aim for or to expect others to aim for under the assumptions stated.[20] If there are grave possible losses involved in the relevant course of action compared with others, the agents surely will have reason to be apprehensive of it. Similarly the possible losses for others may make each one less secure in any expectation that the others will do their part in the absolute best point combination: less secure, that is, that common knowledge of rationality and of the matrix, plus their own preferences, will dictate that course of action. Thus consider a matrix such as that shown in Figure 5.6.

What should rational agents choose here in a one-off case with lack of communication? One can imagine "Row," the player whose payoffs are given in the bottom left corner of each cell, reasoning somewhat as follows.

(1) If I take option 1, and Col (the other player) takes his option *A*, I'll get my best possible outcome, namely 5. However, if Col does anything other than *A*, I'd be best off *not* doing 1, in fact

Col

	A	B	C	D
1	5 \ 5	−500 \ −500	−500 \ −500	4 \ 1
2	−500 \ −500	3 \ 3	3 \ 3	3 \ 3
3	−500 \ −500	3 \ 3	3 \ 3	3 \ 3
4	1 \ 4	3 \ 3	3 \ 3	4 \ 4

Row

Fig. 5.6

I'd be best off doing 4 in every such case. Indeed, even if Col does *A*, my doing 4 gets almost as good an outcome as my doing 1. And my doing 4 absolutely avoids my getting -500, *whatever* Col does. It looks as if I should do 4 unless I *know* that Col will do *A*, in which case I should do 1.

Well, *do* I know that Col will do *A?*

Row might continue as follows:

(2) Let me try to look at the situation from Col's point of view, since it is only by considering his reasoning that I might come to see that he will do *A*. He, then, may be expected to reason much as I have, *mutatis mutandis*. But then he will, first, be left wondering whether he knows that I will do 1, just as I was

left wondering about him at the conclusion of stage (1) of my reasoning.

Row might then continue:

(3) Now suppose Col tries to replicate *my* reasoning, as I tried, in phase (2) of my reasoning, to replicate his. He will then arrive at my question at the end of (1): do 1, Row, know that Col will do *A*? He may go on, further, to replicate phase (2) of my reasoning, and he will then see that I am having to replicate *his* reasoning—and that I will realize that he is wondering whether he knows that I will do 1.

The final phases of a rational Row's thinking might run thus:

(4) I could go further in this attempt to replicate Col's reasoning, but this seems fruitless. Clearly this attempt at reason replication gets us nowhere.

(5) It is true that, insofar as he is rational, Col will do *A* if he knows that I will do 1; but while I *do* know that Col is rational, I *don't* know that he knows that I will do 1. Indeed, he can't know that I will do 1, since I appear to have no good reason to, and I am therefore going to choose 4, for reasons already considered.

Here, then, it is at least *not obvious* that one should do one's part in 1, or *A*, in a one-off case of this situation; 4 and *D*, rather, seem to be the options, if any, that players should choose in a real one-off case with lack of communication. It is an option that minimizes each one's possible loss, and is guaranteed to get him relatively near to his personal absolute best outcome. There is an absolute best point in this situation: it is, not *D4*, but *A1*.[21]

What if there were, say, numerous precedents known to Row and Col in which the agents involved in their situation did their parts in some one combination of actions? Suppose there is a precedent for doing one's part in *D4*. Now, it is not clear what consequences, if any, common knowledge of such a precedent should have for rational agents in their deliberations. (See Chapter 2 for a skeptical argument on that score.) In the case supposed, however, if it does have any force it will presumably reinforce the idea of doing one's part in *D4*, not *A1*. In short, it seems that, given this matrix, it will only be rational to choose to do one's part in *A1*, the absolute best point combination, when the other's doing his part is pretty well guaranteed. The other's mere rationality, however, will never effect such a guarantee. It does not effect it in a one-off case; adding the (common) knowledge of a contrary precedent will, clearly, not effect it either.

Let us now turn to Lewis's coordination equilibria. Lewis might be thought to imply that (at least where there is predominant coincidence of interests) a unique coordination equilibrium will be an absolute best point, when he speaks of the (apparently obvious) "task" or reaching a unique coordination equilibrium in such circumstances. We may refer also to Lewis's argument, on page 17, for a claim about "any finite two-person game of pure coordination with a unique equilibrium." One of the premises is "(R1, C1) must be the unique equilibrium, and $P((R1, C1))$ must exceed every other payoff in the game." (Here P = payoff.) Now, while it is true that in a finite pure coordination game a unique (coordination) equilibrium must be an absolute best point, this is certainly not true for games of slightly-less-than-pure coordination, as I shall show. And Lewis clearly means his remarks on triviality apply to such games.

Lewis himself notes (p. 8) that it is not the case that an *equilibrium* combination, *simpliciter,* "must produce an outcome that is best for even one of the agents." This is also true of Lewis's *coordination* equilibria; it is true of them in general and of unique coordination equilibria in particular. Thus consider Figure 5.7.

Here $A1$ alone is a coordination equilibrium. The situation is one of "predominantly coincident" interests on Lewis's definition. Yet $A1$ is clearly neither an absolute best point nor a best point. Indeed there are none such in this whole situation. Nor is $A1$ an outcome that would be best for even one of the agents. So much for the claim that unique coordination equilibria must be absolute best points, or indeed best points, in relatively unconflicted situations.

Now it may be argued that Lewis never implies that unique c.e. had to be absolute best points, but rather that (for some reason) rational agents should in any case aim to reach (and thus do their part in) such equilibria. Perhaps this is so; however Figure 5.7 surely shows that the latter statement also is false. For surely if one thing is clear about this situation it is that A and I are not the obvious things for rational agents to do in a one-off case; and the same goes, *a fortiori,* in a situation where it is common knowledge among the agents that there is a precedent of doing one's part in, say, $C3$. Yet $A1$ is a unique coordination equilibrium.[22]

What we have above, then, is a situation in which we have a unique

	A	B	C	D
1	6 6	0 0	0 0	−1000 −1000
2	0 1	0 0	−1000 −1000	0 0
3	−1000 −1000	1 0	90 89	89 90
4	−11 −10	−10 −11	0 0	0 0

Fig. 5.7

c.e. which is (1) not an absolute best point, hence not the most desired combination for each agent individually; (2) not such that in a one-off case each player will, given common knowledge of rationality and the matrix, expect the others to do their parts in it, and (3) not such that in a one-off case each should do his part in it if rational. There is, hence, (4) no reason to suppose that rational players will end up doing their part in this c.e. in a one-off case, and (5) there is even less reason, if that is possible, to suppose that a case *with* an external basis for expectation should always be treated as it was alleged a one-off case should be treated. This case, therefore, provides a counterexample to all of the Lewisian claims concerning the "triviality in general" of situations with a unique c.e. that we have considered.[23]

I have noted that—perhaps contrary to Lewis's drift—unique coordination equilibria do not have to be absolute best points. Nevertheless they may be. If there is a unique coordination equilibrium in a situation and also an absolute best point, these must be the same point. For all absolute best points must be coordination equilibria. However, we found that, as with coordination equilibria in general, the absolute best point combination is *not* always the obvious thing for rational agents to do their parts in a situation with, or without, any external expectations. Our conclusions about absolute best points in general, and about unique coordination equilibria in general, also go for those absolute best points that are also unique coordination equilibria.[24]

My conclusion on situations with a unique coordination equilibrium, then, so far contradicts Lewis's claims. In sum, it is not apparent that where coincidence of interests predominates, in Lewis's sense, situations with a unique c.e. are generally "trivial."[25]

Lewis next draws our attention to a special class of situations with a unique c.e. that are "still more trivial (and more deserving of exclusion)" (pp. 16–17). He first singles out situations in which all the agents have a *strictly dominant* choice—"actions they prefer no matter what the others do."[26] Such situations, Lewis notes, "can have only one equilibrium (and *a fortiori* only one cordination equilibrium), namely the combination of dominant choices" (p. 17).

Lewis could be taken to imply that it is (at least in part) the fact that these situations must have a unique coordination equilibrium that makes them trivial. Now, it seems clear from my discussion so far that the existence of a unique coordination equilibrium in a situation does not make that situation intuitively trivial in any way. It is worth turning explicitly to the idea of a "trivial" situation at this point. (Except where noted, what follows should be understood as referring at all times to situations involving rational agents with common knowledge of rationality and of the matrix—the kind with which Lewis is concerned.)

An intuitive judgement that a certain choice-situation, involving agents with common knowledge of rationality and of the matrix, is trivial, may be based on a tacit assumption that the agents' choices are to be made under certain particular circumstances. Let me give an example.

There may seem to be something trivial about situations with an absolute best point, on an initial consideration of these. I suggest that one reason we might be tempted to view such situations as trivial *simpliciter* is that, *if* allowed to make binding agreements prior to making their moves, rational agents would have no trouble in coming to an agreement maximally satisfactory to all: clearly they would agree to do their parts in the absolute best point combination. They would then act in accordance with their binding agreement and each would reach his best payoff. Something similar seems to go for best points also, for one might suppose that rational agents making an agreement would agree to let a coin-toss decide between best points, since they are supposedly neutral about which best point they reach.[27] Absolute best point situations may, however, seem more clearly trivial than best point situations because, in the absence of preplay communication, *if* each follows the rule "do your part in a best point," this automatically leads to the point in question. Clearly, if there are several best points, then each one's following this rule guarantees nothing.

Let us now try to describe things more precisely. Let us say that a situation is *success-trivial in conditions C* if and only if, *in C,* rational agents (with common knowledge of rationality and the matrix) will reach a best point in that situation. A situation will be said to be *maximally success-trivial* if, in general, rational agents (with common knowledge, etc.) will reach a best point in that situation.

Now, in the absence of preplay communication, as we have seen, things may look problematic for a rational agent as he tries to decide what to do, even in a "pure" coordination game with an absolute best point. Though he might *like* a guarantee that all players will follow the rule "do your part in an (absolute) best point," no such guarantee appears to be forthcoming in such situations in general, even given common knowledge of rationality. A rational agent may, it appears, be justified in doing his part in something other than an absolute best point. Therefore, while it may be correct to say that absolute best point situations are success-trivial, *given* the agents' ability to make binding agreements, or *given* common knowledge that the rule "do your part in a best point" is being followed, it is wrong to say that, *in general,* situations with an absolute best point are success-trivial; these are not then, in general, *maximally success-trivial* situations.

If a situation's only claim to triviality is that it is success-trivial given some special condition (like the ability to make binding preplay agreements) it will surely only be misleading to call it "trivial" without qualification. A maximally success-trivial situation, however, would appear to be aptly called "trivial" without qualification. Such situations can certainly exist, as we shall see.

It appears that even in the absence of maximal success-triviality a situation may aptly be called "trivial" without qualification. This will be the case, it seems, when there is one particular choice that rational agents should always make in that situation, whatever the others do.

Let us say that a situation will be *maximally choice-trivial* if and only if there is some action *A* for each player such that he should always do *A* in this situation; this is to be so, in particular, whatever the other players are expected to choose. We can talk also, analogously, of the "choice-triviality" of a situation under certain conditions. Thus a situation will be *choice-trivial in a one-off case* when there is some action *A* for each player, such that he should always do *A in one-off cases* of the situation. (As will emerge, a situation can be choice-trivial in a one-off case even though it is not maximally choice-trivial.)

As with success-triviality, if a situation's only claim to triviality is that it is choice-trivial under some special condition, it will be misleading to call it "trivial" without qualification. A maximally choice-trivial situation does appear, however, to be aptly called "trivial" without qualification.

It is *clearly* apt to call a situation "trivial" without qualification when it combines maximal choice-triviality and maximal success-triviality: that is when it is maximally choice-trivial, and the intersection of the choices each agent should make is an absolute best point or best point. As well as being certain what to do, whatever the others do, a rational agent can, in such a situation, be certain of success (given common knowledge of rationality and the matrix).[28]

We may now apply the above distinctions and considerations to the case of situations with a unique coordination equilibrium, rephrasing our previous conclusions in terms of them.

We have already seen, in effect, that a unique coordination equilibrium (in a situation of predominant coincidence of interests) does not ensure that a situation is either maximally success-trivial or maximally choice-trivial. Hence an unqualified attribution of "triviality" to situations with a unique coordination equilibrium does not appear appropriate, even on the assumption of common knowledge of rationality. Moreover, it is not even true that in one-off cases at least unique coordination equilibria entail or produce success-triviality or choice-triviality. There is, more generally, no reason to suppose that situations with a unique coordination equilibrium are in general to be appropriately described as "trivial" in any sense relevant to Lewis's discussion.

Let us now turn to the case of situations where each agent has a *strictly dominant* choice. Let us call the intersection of each player's strictly dominant choice, where each has one, a point of "universal strict dominance" or "u.s.d." In what way is such dominance related to intuitive triviality?

Consider first a famous case Lewis himself cites, that of the so-called "Prisoner's Dilemma."[29] Here the combination of dominant choices is, as Lewis says, a noncoordination equilibrium. Perhaps more to the point, its apparent maximal choice-triviality through dominance conflicts with the goals of the agents in an extreme way: each player gets only his third best payoff (out of four), and, relatively speaking, this could be very bad.

In view of the conflict between dominant choices and goals, it may appear that it will *not* really be clear to a rational player what he should do in this situation.[30] Yet assuming that each player wishes to maximize his own payoff (the usual game-theoretic assumption), then it is surely trivially true that each player *should* opt for his strictly dominant strategy, whatever his expectations about what the other player will opt for. One can simply echo Luce and Raiffa's rueful observation that "two 'irrational' players will always fare better than two rational ones."[31]

Situations with universal strict dominance, then, *are* maximally choice-trivial. They thus appear to be quite aptly thought of as trivial choice-situations in general. As the typical Prisoner's Dilemma case indicates, however, they need not be success-trivial. (The dilemma, in other words, is not a matter of it not being clear what one should do; it is rather a matter of the correct decision on the part of all parties leading unfortunately to an unsatisfactory outcome.) In fact, situations with universal strict dominance may approach success-triviality in various ways without achieving it. Thus even Prisoner's Dilemma–type situations can approach success-triviality, depending on quantitative aspects of the situation.[32] Again, players might get their second best outcome at the intersection of dominant choices, and this may be relatively close to their best outcome.

What, now, of cases of u.s.d. with a unique coordination equilibrium? As Lewis points out, if a situation has both of these features, the unique coordination equilibrium and the u.s.d. point must be the same point.

Now it turns out that in order to have a unique coordination equilibrium in a situation of u.s.d. the coordination equilibrium must also be an absolute best point or a best point.[33] Then *a fortiori* we have a situation which is trivial intuitively. This triviality can evidently be perspicuously characterized without reference to the existence of a unique coordination equilibrium. For we have a situation in which (a) it is obvious what agents should do (choose their dominant strategies) and (b) the intersection of dominant strategies reaches at least a best point. In other words it is maximally choice-trivial and success-trivial at the same time.

I have argued, then, that if we wish to rule out cases that are trivial in general it appears that we must rule out cases of universal strict dominance as such. In particular, then, we must rule out the special case of universal strict dominance plus a unique coordination equilibrium. At this point in our discussion, it is clear that while the feature of universal strict dominance is sufficient for the appearance of intuitive triviality in a situation, the feature of a unique coordination equilibrium, *pace* Lewis, is not. At the point in Lewis's reasoning that we have reached so far, Lewis is concerned explicitly with unique coordination equilibria, and with ruling out cases with this feature, including (as a special case) those which have this feature plus that of universal strict dominance. Lewis effectively excludes both unique coordination equilibria and universal strict dominance by introducing a requirement of *at least two coordination equilibria* in a coordination problem.

As my discussion of unique coordination equilibria in general has shown, Lewis's two coordination equilibria requirement is too strong if it is intended to rule out only intuitively trivial situations. (*A fortiori* it is too strong if intended only to rule out situations trivial in a one-off case.) Having introduced this already overstrong requirement Lewis points out that trivial cases remain. In other words, he implies that while necessary to rule out trivial situations, the two coordination equilibrium requirement is not *sufficient*. He is, presumably, aiming at a condition that is both necessary and sufficient for nontriviality.

The trivial cases cited by Lewis as remaining, given fulfillment of the two coordination equilibrium requirement, are Figures 5.8 (matrix A) and 5.9 (matrix B), (Lewis's Fig. 14, p. 21).

Of these, Lewis writes, first:

> There is still no need for either agent to base his choice upon his expectation of the other's choice. There is no need for them to try for the same equilibrium—no need for coordination—since if they try for different equilibria, some equilibrium will nevertheless be reached. [p. 21]

Now, it is not immediately clear what bearing Lewis's remark about the equilibria in these situations has on their intuitive triviality. In fact, their intuitive triviality can be well enough accounted for without

(A)

Fig. 5.8

bringing in the equilibrium concept at all. Nor does there seem to be any need for either agent to reason in terms of equilibria in either example.

Note that in matrix A, one agent (Row) has a strictly dominant choice. Moreover, given only that Row makes this choice, a best point will be reached. It does not matter what Col does; if you like, he "should" do anything he pleases. Thus neither needs to "try for an equilibrium." Neither needs to know the equilibrium points in order to see what to do. Indeed, neither needs to know anything about the payoffs of the other. Col cannot affect Row's or his own payoff; everything depends on Row's doing what it is obvious he should do.

In matrix B, Row has a dominant strategy in the usual sense that there is one choice of action that in every case will get him as good an outcome as any other, and in one case (at least) will get him a better outcome. He would therefore, it would seem, be wrong, from the point of view of rationality, to aim for just "any old" equilibrium. He would presumably be better advised to "hedge his bets" even if he knows Col will act rationally, since he loses nothing by doing so. Col, meanwhile, can choose betweeen *C1* and *C2* arbitrarily and then always do at least as well as on any other choice, while sometimes he will do better. Thus we could see him as having, effectively, a dominant strategy in this case: choose arbitrarily between *C1* and *C2*. Hence, again, we can characterize what each should do in all circum-

(B)

	C1	C2	C3
R1	1 / 1	1 / 1	.2 / 0
R2	1 / 1	1 / 1	.5 / .2
R3	0 / .5	0 / 0	0 / 0

Fig. 5.9

stances without mentioning equilibria. Both situations are such that if each does what he obviously should do, irrespective of expectations about the other, a best point is reached. (One player in the first case can ensure by his own choice that he gets a best point, *whatever* the other does.)

Thus though I agree with Lewis as to the intuitively trivial nature of these cases, I find his diagnosis in terms of equilibria unhelpful. Further, for reasons that should now be obvious, I cannot accept his statement that "these cases exhibit another kind of triviality, akin to the triviality of a case with a unique coordination equilibrium" (p. 22). At this point Lewis introduces his requirement that there be at least *two proper coordination equilibria* in a coordination problem. He writes (of a particular matrix, but presumably intending a general claim): "the two proper coordination equilibria are sufficient to keep the problem non-trivial" (p. 22). (The matrix involves two p.c.e. in the strong sense.) Sufficient, but perhaps not necessary, Lewis notes: "we might prefer a weaker restriction that would not rule out matrices like those of Figure 16." One matrix is that in my Figure 5.10.

Lewis does not state why we might prefer not to rule out the matrices in his Figure 16. One assumes, obviously, that he regards them as nontrivial in some relevant sense. One thing is clear about the Figure 5.10 matrix, at least: neither player has a dominant strategy in either the strict or the ordinary sense.

Now, Lewis says, with respect to the Figure 5.10 matrix, that it "can be rescued even under the strong restriction we have adopted. Let $R2'$ be the disjunction of $R2$ and $R3$, and $C2'$ the disjunction of $C2$ and $C3$ in the left-hand matrix. Then the same situation can be represented by the new matrix in Figure 17, which does have two proper coordination equilibria. The other matrix in Figure 16 can be consolidated in a similar way" (p. 22).

This is supposed to mean, I take it, that the two p.c.e. requirement does not, after all, really rule out Figure 5.10, and hence is not, really, too strong after all.

It is true that, formally speaking, any situation which can be represented by Figure 5.10 can also be represented by Figure 5.11. The

	C1	C2	C3
R1	1 1	0 0	0 0
R2	0 0	1 1	1 1
R3	0 0	1 1	1 1

Fig. 5.10

Fig. 5.11   Lewis's Figure 17

following, however, might be noted. There could be situations for which Figure 5.10 seemed the more natural representation. For instance, in the case where we see ourselves as having three possible choices: go to Omaha; go to Boston; go to Davis. It may also seem that, when viewed in terms of Figure 5.10, this situation is choice-trivial in a one-off case, that a rational agent should avoid doing his part in (*R1, C1*) since he is most at risk from the other agent if he does this; if so, if both act rationally, they will reach a best point. Or suppose fifty cities are involved, and coordination is achieved when either both go to Omaha or each goes to any of the other forty-nine cities; it may seem rational for both players to avoid Omaha. This reasoning, meanwhile, does not seem to apply to Figure 5.11; when viewed in terms of that matrix, a situation does not seem trivial.

However, without any restriction on the type of actions the rows and columns in a matrix may represent, the matrices in Figures 5.10 and 5.11 represent the same situations, as noted, and the argument for the triviality of the situation represented by Figure 5.10 in a one-off case does not go through. On the other hand, an appropriate restriction on what the rows and columns represent is hard to define.

In any case, there are other situations, clearly lacking a matrix reducible to one with two p.c.e. (in either sense), which make it clear that Lewis's two p.c.e. requirement is too strong. In considering the case of the unique coordination equilibrium, we have already considered matrices neither trivial nor reducible in this way. Figure 5.12 represents a case which appears to be neither trivial in a one-off case nor maximally success-trivial nor maximally choice-trivial, nor trivial in general. Yet the two p.c.e. requirement would rule *this* out as it stands, and it is surely not representable by some matrix that does have two (or more) p.c.e.

In sum: Lewis's two coordination equilibrium requirement was too strong to rule out only nontrivial situations, and so, *a fortiori*, is the two p.c.e. requirement. It should now also be clear that, *pace* Lewis, the two p.c.e. requirement is not merely *apparently* too strong, that is, too strong only if we fail to take advantage of an inconsequential maneuver involving the reduction of one matrix to another.

Is Lewis's final requirement in fact *too weak,* or are two p.c.e. at least sufficient to keep the problem nontrivial as Lewis claims? It depends, as it often does, on what kind of triviality is at issue. We have, throughout, been considering situations in relation to various kinds of triviality, since Lewis's intentions on this point have not been clear; so let us continue to do so here. Consider the case represented in Figure 5.13.

Here there are two p.c.e. in the strong sense, *A1* and *B2*. *A1* is an absolute best point, far superior to *B2*. All in all, there does seem to be something that rational players should do here, at least in a one-off

3	1	0
3	1	1
0	3	4
0	4	2
3	1	2
3	1	1

Fig. 5.12

Fig. 5.13

case: namely, their respective parts in *A1*. Row, it seems, can reason as follows. Insofar as he neither has nor can come by any justified external expectations about Col, he might as well do his part in *A1*. He has little to lose if anything goes wrong (i.e., if Col does not do *his* part in *A1*), and no strategy of minimizing his possible loss, nor any other viable strategy, is left untouched. Thus it appears that, *ceteris paribus,* Row should do his part in *A1*, and that this is the rational thing to do. Now, *ex hypothesi,* Row and Col also have common knowledge of one another's rationality. It is hard to see how this can lead to the rejection of action *A* for Row. If doing one's part in *A1* is indeed rational for *both* players, given no external expectations about the other, and *ceteris paribus,* then Row's knowledge that Col is rational can only reinforce his reasons for doing his part in *A1*: Col will, if rational, do his part and Row's absolute best payoff will be reached if he follows suit. Similarly, for Row's knowledge of Col's knowledge of Row's rationality: Col's reasons for doing his part in *A1* will only be reinforced by his knowledge of Row's rationality; and so on.

This situation, then, is arguably trivial at least in a one-off case. It appears that rational agents should do their parts in *A1*, and if they do this—what they *should* do—they will reach an absolute best point. Each does depend on the other's acting rationally to get his own best payoff, but then success-triviality as we defined it is success-trivially for each member of a set of rational agents; some cases Lewis considered clearly trivial, like Figure 5.9 above, are of this kind. In a one-off case, then, this matrix is arguably choice-trivial and success-trivial.

For another kind of two p.c.e. case that might appear relatively trivial for similar reasons in a one-off case, see Figure 5.14. Here there are two p.c.e. (in the strong sense), at *A1* and *B2*. But one could argue that *C3*—*not,* incidentally, a p.c.e.—is what the agents should do their parts in, in a one-off case.

First, though there are no best points here, *C3* and *C4* are greatly preferred by both parties to any other outcome. It appears rational, when it is common knowledge between the parties that no one has any expectations about action external to the matrix, for Row to do C: there is no special risk involved and there is no countervailing strategy of, e.g., maximizing his security level. *Mutatis mutandis,* Col should

	1	2	3	4
A	6 6	5 5	5 5	5 5
B	5 5	7 7	6 6	6 6
C	5 5	6 6	90 89	89 90
D	5 5	6 6	7 6	7 6

Fig. 5.14

do 3 (3 dominates 4). Neither will be deflected from these courses of action by common knowledge of rationality. The situation is, then, arguably choice-trivial in a one-off case. While it is not success-trivial in such a case, it certainly approaches success-triviality, since one player reaches his absolute best payoff and another reaches a point only slightly worse than his absolute best payoff, at least in relation to the other possibilities.

Each of the two foregoing matrices is, then, arguably choice-trivial in a one-off case. Neither, however, is maximally choice-trivial as we defined this: there is, in these situations, no action *A* for each player such that he should always do *A* in an instance of the situation, whatever he expects the others to choose. Thus, if in the first of the two situations just noted, Row—for some reason—firmly expects Col to do his part in 2, he should himself do *B* rather than *A*, the thing he obviously should do in a one-off case.

Lewis's requirement of two p.c.e. then, taken either in its weak or in its strong sense, is neither necessary *nor sufficient* to rule out choice-triviality in a one-off case.

What of maximal choice-triviality? Even in its weak sense, the two p.c.e. requirement is sufficient to rule out *dominance* in both its strict and its usual sense. (Clearly, it is not *necessary* to adopt Lewis's requirement in order to rule this out.) Hence it appears that Lewis's two p.c.e. requirement does rule out maximal choice-triviality, as I have defined this.

What, next, of success-triviality? We have already seen that the first of the two matrices just considered is arguably success-trivial in a one-off case, in spite of having two p.c.e. So Lewis's requirement is neither necessary nor sufficient to rule out such success-triviality.

What, finally, of maximal success-triviality? Recall what that was: a situation will be maximally success-trivial if, in general, rational agents (with common knowledge of rationality and the matrix) will reach a best point in that situation. We previously noted one feature that guarantees maximal success-triviality: universal strict dominance, where the intersection of dominant strategies is a best point. *Prima facie,* it looks as if there could, in principle, be other such features. "*S* is maximally success-trivial" does not obviously *entail* "*S* involves universal strict dominance," etc.

Let me sketch a possible argument that, if acceptable, would show that the first of the two matrices considered above was not only success-trivial in a one-off case, but also maximally success-trivial.

Recall first a remark of Lewis's made in the context of his belief that situations with a unique coordination equilibrium are trivial:

> *No matter what we had been doing in the past,* a failure to do one's part in the unique coordination equilibrium, . . . could only be a strategic error, (or compensation for someone else's anticipated strategic error, or compensation for someone else's anticipated compensation, etc.). [p. 70; my stress]

One idea here seems to be that precedent, which may in certain situations serve rational agents as a basis for expectations about others, will not have a tendency to produce the correlative expectations in all situations.

Now, one case that could give rise to this idea is that of a situation with a unique coordination equilibrium *plus* universal strict dominance. Rational agents in any such situation will presumably choose their strictly dominant strategy and expect the others involved to do the same, insofar as they are rational, contrary precedents notwithstanding. If they (or others known to them) *had* somehow done something else when this situation occurred in the past, this would have had to be a matter of strategic error, but at this point, where there is, *ex hypothesi*, common knowledge of rationality, each one knows what he should now do, and what the others may be expected to do, given that they too are to act rationally. Another way of putting the situation here is this: it is rational to treat each case as a one-off case. (In fact, of course, given universal strict dominance, no agent needs to bother for a moment about *what* he expects the other to do in this instance, before choosing his own strategy.)

Is it possible to reason in this fashion about any cases *other* than those involving dominance? Lewis apparently thought so, since he (rightly) did not believe that unique coordination equilibria occurred only where there was dominance. However, we have seen that it is not always rational to do one's part in a unique coordination equilibrium, even in a one-off case; indeed, rationality may not determine any strategy in such a case. So one cannot reason in the above fashion concerning unique coordination equilibria in general, as Lewis may have thought one could. Can we, however, use similar reasoning against Lewis, with respect to some cases involving two proper coordination equilibria?

One would, I think, have to reason somewhat as follows. Rational agents with common knowledge of rationality should treat all cases of a situation S as if they were one-off cases if they are success-trivial in a one-off case. Only if the one-off case is not success-trivial will factors other than common knowledge of rationality and the matrix be considered. At this point agents would be looking for clues from outside the matrix as to how to proceed. Precedent, then, would only be considered at this stage.

Were this reasoning valid, then in situations like that of the matrix now under consideration, which are success-trivial in a one-off case, precedent would not tend to generate any expectations about action, nor would anything do so except common knowledge of rationality and the matrix. If this were a correct picture of truly rational proce-dure, then the case we are considering would be maximally success-trivial, and hence would reasonably be thought of as trivial without any qualification. Moreover, though by my definition it would not be maximally *choice-trivial,* it would possess a property similar to maxi-mal choice-triviality. For it would be the case that there is some action A which each one should do in all cases: *not* irrespective of what the others are *expected* to do, but, rather, irrespective of what the others may *justifiably* be expected to do, given common knowledge of ratio-nality. For the others, being rational agents, etc., could then only justifiably be expected to do something fully supporting one's decision to do action A.

Without trying to assess the correctness of this or some similar reasoning here, we can see that (a) it is reminiscent of and may represent some reasoning of Lewis's, and (b) if it were valid, it would show that his p.c.e. requirement has less power than might be thought, since it would be neither necessary nor sufficient to rule out maximal success-triviality.

So much, then, for the details of Lewis's game-theoretical argumen-tation in *Convention.*

Conclusions

The game-theoretical reasoning that underlies Lewis's eventual defini-tions of "coordination problem" and "convention" contains a number of serious flaws, many of which have been outlined above.[34] In brief, Lewis's program of ruling out all and only trivial situations among agents with predominant coincidence of interests is not carried out successfully. We noted that (1) Lewis's eventual two proper coordina-tion equilibrium restriction was ambiguous, and that (2) he did not make clear during his discussion whether he was concerned with triviality *simpliciter* or rather with triviality in a one-off case. (Nor did later passages force conclusions on either of these issues.) However, we have still reached definite conclusions. Lewis's two p.c.e. restriction, in *either* of the two possible interpretations, is too strong with respect to *both* kinds of triviality (and not in a merely innocuous way). In addition, though Lewis's restriction is sufficient to rule out the phenomenon of dominance, it is too weak to rule out all situations that are intuitively trivial in a one-off case, and it may be too weak to rule out all cases which are trivial *simpliciter*.

In this concluding section, I ask what follows from the foregoing discussion, first, for the definition of "coordination problem," and, second, for the definition of "convention."

i. Coordination problems

Let us consider to begin what might be the point of progressively ruling out trivial situations in the definition of "coordination problem," when this is viewed as a matter of perspicuously characterizing Lewis's examples. It might be suggested that trivial situations should be ruled out in the definition of "coordination problems" at least insofar as the triviality associated with absolute best points, such as it is, is lacking from such problems.[35] If this was one's idea, then it is clear that the two-or-more p.c.e. requirement (on either interpretation) would not *guarantee* this feature of the situation, nor is it *necessary* to produce this feature in a situation.

A related thought at base of a nontriviality requirement might be that in these situations, in one-off cases at least, *coordination is a problem:* these agents want to coordinate their actions in one of, say, two preferred ways (say by all driving on the left *or* all driving on the right) but this is not going to come about without some sort of special push from outside common knowledge of the matrix: common knowledge of rationality and of the matrix is not enough. We have seen, however, that the two-or-more p.c.e. condition (on either interpretation) is not *enough* to make situations nontrivial in this way: there could be an absolute best point *(and* no reason not to aim for it) or some other relevant feature. The two p.c.e. requirement is also (on either interpretation) too strong to rule out *only* situations that are trivial in this way. (It is therefore both too strong, and too weak, if this was Lewis's intention for it.)

In my view, whatever Lewis himself may have thought about them—

and that is not clear—this idea and the foregoing are at least not appropriate to Lewis's *examples*. As he describes his eleven examples in turn, Lewis usually writes that "it matters little" to the agents which of the combinations of actions that are proper coordination equilibria result. This in itself implies that it may matter somewhat to all or some agents. Moreover, from his own description of the stag case, for one, it is clear that in that case, one of these combinations is in fact strongly preferred to the other by all parties. The stag case, it may be argued, is anomalous. Finally, however, it is surely not appropriate to Lewis's examples in general, and to examples intuitively like them, to stipulate that all parties not prefer one possible p.c.e. outcome over the others, even considerably prefer one to the others. Consider the case illustrated below, which appears to be intuitively analogous to Lewis's cases:

	Wood	*Cafeteria*
Wood	10 10	0 0
Cafeteria	0 0	1 1

Fig. 5.15

Here you and I wish to meet. We would *much* rather meet in the quiet woods surrounding the campus than in the noisy cafeteria. However, we would definitely rather meet than fail to meet by unilaterally going to wood or cafeteria. We get nothing at all out of going to either place alone.

This latter case is choice-trivial and, indeed, success-trivial in a one-off case—it is not going to be a problem among rational agents in a one-off case. Yet it is, surely, intuitively analogous to, if not identical to, cases Lewis presents.[36] (The stag-hunt case is different and more problematic in that the absolute best point strategy conflicts with an attractive maximin one.) It looks, then, as if "coordination problem" situations as envisaged by Lewis may involve a lack of complete or even relative indifference between the proper coordination equilibrium outcomes, and *may* involve an absolute best point, and (also) *may* be trivial in a one-off case, or *unproblematic* in such cases. The lack of cutting edge of the p.c.e. requirement here, then, may not have to be considered a failure with respect to the characterization of Lewis's examples.

Finally, one's idea might be that coordination problems are nontrivial in that, whatever is true in strictly one-off cases, given a certain set of external expectations, rational agents will act one way, given another set, they will act in a different way. In our terms, they are at least not maximally choice-trivial. This idea, at least, seems to fit all the examples.

Clearly, however, though it is *sufficient,* the two p.c.e. structure is not *necessary* to rule out maximal choice-triviality. Thus if what one meant to capture of coordination problems was the lack of triviality in *this* sense, the two p.c.e. requirement would be too strong, and therefore unacceptable.

What of the clause "coincidence of interests predominates," which Lewis includes in his eventual definition of a coordination problem? We have noted that for Lewis it is important to be realistic enough not to require perfect coincidence of interests. This seems right, given the examples. Apart from this, Lewis does not attempt to justify his precisely defined coincidence clause in the course of his game-theoretic argumentation, nor is it clear that it picks out anything very clearly salient in the examples. Consider a case: Brezhnev and Carter want to meet. They can do so by both going to Vienna, or both going to Oslo, or both going to Moscow, or both going to Washington. Their matrix of preferences might look like Figure 5.16.

Here the differences between the agents' payoffs in squares *W, W* and *M, M* are surely not "small compared to some of the differences between payoffs in the different squares." Yet this is not intuitively unlike Lewis's examples, I would say. At the least, it is not clear that this case should be ruled out from the class of coordination problems, given Lewis's actual examples.

Now, rather than working from the abstract idea of nontriviality to a definition of "coordination problem," one might simply try to describe how it is with Lewis's examples and intuitively analogous cases (if we feel we *can* extrapolate); we might look simply for maximally specific common features. Let us briefly consider this approach here. Looking back at Lewis's examples of coordination problems, it does look as if

Carter

Brezhnev	V	O	W	M
V	5, 5	0, 0	0, 0	0, 0
O	0, 0	5, 5	0, 0	0, 0
W	0, 0	0, 0	1, 10	0, 0
M	0, 0	0, 0	0, 0	10, 1

Fig. 5.16

they all at least have two or more proper coordination equilibria in the weak sense. Most involve two or more proper coordination equilibria in the *strong* sense: everyone prefers that any one more do his part in this combination of actions if the rest do. Given that a situation has either of these features, it will then lack maximal choice-triviality; rational agents must then take into account who happens to expect what of whom, for whatever reason. (This is not, of course, to deny that there are situations with *other* structures in which rational agents will have to do this.)

Where there are two or more p.c.e. (in either sense), agents are susceptible to external expectations in precisely the following way: if *A* expects everyone else to do his part in a given p.c.e., then *A* has a sufficient reason to do his own part (at least given no thought to his action's possible repercussions in the future). This is true even if this p.c.e. gives *A* far from his best outcome in the total situation. Thus where there are two or more p.c.e. in a situation, the way is open for expectations about others, perhaps arising out of a knowledge of precedent or agreement, to determine a population's practices. Lewis's two p.c.e. requirement, then, appears to be motivated relatively well by a search for features common to the examples, and to examples that appear intuitively analogous.

We may relate to this observation the question whether each p.c.e. in a coordination problem situation must be better than any non-p.c.e. combination for each agent. (This feature is implicit in Ullman-Margalit's account of coordination problems, and is implicit in some remarks in Lewis.)[37] This is not part of Lewis's formal account of coordination problems, nor is it clear that it should be. As is shown in my Figure 5.14, all the p.c.e. in a situation may be inferior to *some* other point or points that are not p.c.e., though not, by their nature, to all. Even where this is so, the usual need to take account of existing expectations about action, and the possibility for precedent to generate continuity, obtain.

Consider the following case. Two friends, Natalie and Anna, are to meet at the theater. They have no means of prior communication. It is common knowledge between them that: each one could wear jeans, trousers, a black velvet dress, or a flowered print dress; each one prefers that if either one wears jeans or trousers, the other one wears the same thing. Natalie would most like, however, to wear her velvet dress, as long as Anna dresses up also, wearing either a velvet or a print dress. On the whole, Natalie would rather Anna avoided the less dressy print, and wore velvet also. Anna, meanwhile, also prefers that both dress up; she believes that Natalie looks best in black velvet, and should wear it as long as she, Anna, dresses up too. She herself, however, marginally prefers that they wear contrasting dresses than two black velvets. So both prefer velvet-velvet, or Natalie's velvet and Anna's print, to any other combination possible. The payoff matrix in Figure 5.17 seems roughly to represent the situation.

Here "coincidence of interests predominates" in Lewis's sense. The p.c.e. are marked with an asterisk. Neither p.c.e. is a best point, nor does every agent prefer one p.c.e. to any other point. However, there is the usual need to take account of expectations about action which are known to obtain; and it is at least not clear that this case should be ruled out. (For what this is worth, the label "coordination problem" seems quite apt for this case.)

Let me come finally to the question whether anything should have us define "p.c.e." in the strong rather than the weak sense, given Lewis's examples. Though after an initial ambiguity on this matter Lewis settles down with an implicit strong interpretation, the impor-

Anna

Natalie \ Anna	jeans	trousers	velvet	print
jeans	1 ★ / 1	0 / 0	0 / 0	0 / 0
trousers	0 / 0	1 ★ / 1	0 / 0	0 / 0
velvet	0 / 0	0 / 0	2 / 3	3 / 2
print	0 / 0	0 / 0	0 / 0	0 / 0

Fig. 5.17

tant features of p.c.e. so far noted in this section— their exclusion of dominance, the specific force of expectations of conformity—are shared by p.c.e. in both the weak and the strong sense. Nowhere does Lewis explain his position. It might, perhaps, be explained simply by the naturalness of an interpretation with two or more p.c.e. in the strong sense when we diagram most of Lewis's examples. The stag-hunt case could then be seen as an anomaly, on one interpretation of it.

Another justification for distinguishing cases here might be this. Suppose we all regularly conform to a certain p.c.e. (strong sense) in a certain recurrent situation. I would have all the more reason to conform on another occasion if I thought that one *ought so* to conform. Well, at one point Lewis argues that conventions are "norms: regularities to which we believe one ought to conform" (p. 97ff.). He explains this: not only do we desire to conform if others do, but the others desire our conformity also. Hence there are two good reasons for conforming—one relating to our own preferences, one to the preferences of others—such that clearly we ought, *ceteris paribus* to conform.

This justification for using a p.c.e. requirement in the strong sense is not that strong: according to Lewis's own statements, if we prefer to conform, and we know that the others are neutral between our conformity and our nonconformity, then we believe that we ought to conform. However, given a strong p.c.e. requirement, the "ought," it may be argued, is better supported. So there is perhaps some reason here to define "p.c.e." in the strong rather than the weak sense: coordination problems (or a subclass of them) have p.c.e. in the strong sense, and this is an important feature of those that have it; it is a feature, at least, which has consequences.

Lewis, meanwhile, never explicitly distinguishes the two senses, and so apparently does not see that his game-theoretical argumentation requires supplementation if he is to adopt the stronger interpretation, which he clearly does, as his account of the preference structure allegedly underlying conventions progresses.

Perhaps Lewis could simply say that he has the intuition that underlying *conventions* we have the structure of two or more p.c.e. in the strong sense. If so, this claim can be discussed on its own terms. We should then, of course, have moved beyond the issue of how to characterize coordination problems as exemplified in Lewis's examples.

ii. Conventions

Where do we now stand with respect to conventions as ordinarily conceived?

Recall the abstract argument making conventions depend upon coordination problems, which I adumbrated in section I of this essay. Central to the argument was the claim that coordination problems are nontrivial situations.

In sketching the argument I left open the nature of Lewis's use of the key term "trivial." I later distinguished two things Lewis might have had in mind: triviality *simpliciter,* and triviality in a one-off case. Triviality *simpliciter,* it appeared, might be a function of maximal choice-triviality, or dominance of some kind, or of maximal success-triviality, given which agents who are rational (etc.) would always reach their best payoff in a situation.

We have now seen that coordination problems as defined by Lewis *can* be trivial in a one-off case. However, they cannot be maximally choice-trivial. Perhaps, also, they cannot be maximally success-trivial, though we have noted an argument derived from remarks of Lewis's that, if valid, would show that coordination problems need *not* lack maximal success-triviality.

Now recall that Lewis's abstract argument also relied on the claim that coordination problems alone are nontrivial. However, it is now clear that situations other than those meeting Lewis's requirements on coordination problems can lack maximal choice-triviality and maximal success-triviality. In particular, situations with a unique coordination equilibrium, considered by Lewis to be paradigmatically trivial, may lack these kinds of triviality. They may in fact lack triviality in any possibly relevant intuitive sense.

It is clear, then, that flaws in Lewis's game-theoretical reasoning make his underlying argument for the dependence of conventions on coordination problems unacceptable.

Let me turn briefly to another term in Lewis's argument: "arbitrary." Conventions, according to Lewis (and others) are necessarily "arbitrary," and Lewis in effect argues that only coordination problems give rise to regularities which have the "arbitrariness" of conventions, at least among rational agents. This—according to Lewis—is because regularities occurring in trivial choice-situations cannot be arbitrary, and coordination problems—again according to Lewis—are the only nontrivial situations that occur among agents of the relevant sort. Given our discussion, there are two ways one might attempt to secure a connection between a kind of arbitrariness and nontriviality on Lewis's behalf.

We might define a "nonarbitrary*" regularity as a regularity in which rational agents regularly choose their dominant strategy, and define an "arbitrary*" regularity, as any regularity that is not nonarbitrary*. It is now clear that all regularities arising within Lewis's coordination problem situations will indeed be arbitrary*, but coordination problems will not, contrary to Lewis's suggestions, be *alone* in engendering arbitrary* regularities.

We have seen that Lewis himself may believe that situations that are success-trivial in a one-off case inevitably lead to intuitively nonarbitrary regularities, at least among rational agents with common knowledge of rationality who never act against reason's dictates. Let us assume for the sake of argument that this belief is correct. Let us now define a "nonarbitrary! regularity" as a regularity that is either nonarbitrary* or is a regularity (among rational agents with common knowledge of rationality) of doing, in a certain situation S, what one would do, if rational, in the success-trivial one-off case of *S*. An "arbitrary! regularity" will be one that is not nonarbitrary!. Here again it is now clear that coordination problems will not be *unique* in engendering arbitrary! regularities; in addition, some regularities arising in coordination problem situations could be nonarbitrary! regularities.

Now, suppose conventions were necessarily nonarbitrary* or necessarily nonarbitrary!. It follows from the argument of section III of this essay that Lewis could not argue that for this reason conventions necessarily *depend* upon the existence of coordination problems as he defines them. For regularities of these sorts can arise in situations that are not coordination problem situations. Nor, in the case of nonarbitrary! regularities, could Lewis argue that all regularities arising within coordination problem situations *were* conventions.

Let me now turn to an example. I hope that it will be clear that it is an example of the following things. First, a choice-situation *not* involving two p.c.e. Second, a situation out of which a *convention* might arise. If this is indeed a situation out of which a convention might arise, then it will of course be a situation out of which a regularity arbitrary in the way that conventions must be arbitrary might arise. I shall not try to say anything more positive here about what kind of arbitrariness this has to be, if any. It will certainly not, however, be a kind of arbitrariness dependent on Lewisian coordination problems, since the situation underlying it will not *be* a coordination problem in Lewis's sense. Consider, then, the following case. Natalie now only has jeans and a print dress as clothes in which she might go to the theater. Anna has trousers, a velvet dress, and a print dress. For a matrix representation of what their preferences with respect to the total situation might look like, see Figure 5.18.

One can surely imagine that, either after some discussion, or perhaps by force of precedent, Natalie and Anna arrive at a *convention* of wearing jeans and trousers, respectively, to the theater. Though in doing so they reach, in fact, what is a p.c.e., there are no others in this situation. This is not, of course, to say what a convention is. But surely one could arise as stated out of this matrix of preferences.

There is no space here for a more detailed discussion of the intuitive arbitrariness or indifference (if any) of conventions or of the nature of conventions themselves. However, in the light of the foregoing we surely cannot agree that our initial intuitions on the subject have been adequately explicated or properly refined in *Convention*.[38]

The details of Lewis's final account of conventions have been

Anna

	trousers	velvet	print
jeans	2 3	0 0	0 0
print	0 0	3 2	2 3

Natalie

Fig. 5.18

queried elsewhere for a variety of reasons.[39] To my knowledge, however, neither the clarity nor the force of Lewis's use of game theory in his discussion of coordination problems has been seriously questioned. Nor has the relation between game-theoretic considerations and Lewis's final account of *conventions* been made clear.

I hope that in this essay I have shown that Lewis does not simply assert that conventions depend on or arise within coordination problems as a matter of dogma, on the one hand, or the fitting of examples to hypothesis on the other. He has, rather, an abstract *a priori* argument to the effect that conventions, being what they necessarily are, must arise out of coordination problems, these being what *they* necessarily are. I hope that I have also shown that, and why, Lewis's implicit abstract argument is unacceptable in its own, game-theoretical, terms; in other words, I hope I have shown where the fallacies lie. Independently of questions about Lewis's implicit abstract argument, I believe I have shown that some of his game-theoretical concepts are not clearly defined, and many of the particular game-theoretical claims in his discussion are incorrect.

Lewis's *Convention* is a rich, rewarding, and stimulating work, with many facets. One of these facets, which has generally gone without criticism or challenge, is Lewis's use of game theory. It should now be clear that this particular facet is importantly flawed.[40]

Notes

1. Lewis (1969), p. 1. See also Lewis (1975). Lewis has replied to some criticisms in Lewis (1976). Unless otherwise stated page references to quotations from Lewis are from Lewis (1969), henceforth referred to in these notes as *Convention*.

2. See for instance Bennett (1973 and 1976); Schiffer (1972); Ullman-Margalit (1977). See also Gilbert (1974).

3. In addition to the works cited above, see, for instance, Peacocke (1976) and Heal (1978).

4. Quine (1969), p. xii.

5. For present purposes I follow Lewis and characterize game theory roughly thus: it concerns situations in which a number of players have a number of alternatives open to them. It is assumed that each player's preferences among the possible combinations of players' actions are linearly ordered, allowing indifference, and can be represented on a scale of arbitrarily chosen units, so as to show the rank order and relative value of the combinations to the player in question. For a note on the origins of mathematical game theory, and contributions of Schelling (1960) relevant to Lewis on convention see Chapter 3, note 3.

6. This condition is given what Lewis characterizes as a "natural extension" on pp. 68-73.

7. In general, in *Convention*, "rational agent" seems to mean something like "agent whose actions and beliefs are based on reasons which justify them (and with whom justifying reasons lead to actions and beliefs)." I shall construe "rational" and its cognates here accordingly. I take it that Lewis-rational agents will, also, strive to maximize their payoffs in a game.

8. I here take it that it is "common knowledge" in a population P that . . . , if and only if (1) everyone in P knows that . . . , (2) everyone in P knows that (1), and so on. This account of "common knowledge" occurs in Lewis (1975). I shall assume for the sake of argument here that the "infinitistic" condition so specified is realistic. (See Chapter 3, this volume.) In *Convention* Lewis gives a more subtle account in terms of a finite set of conditions: see pp. 51-57.

9. See Chapter 3, this volume, and *On Social Facts,* Chapter 5. In particular I argue that it is questionable that conventions should be identified as regularities of a certain sort, an assumption shared by Lewis and critics of Lewis such as Stephen Schiffer (op. cit.).

10. We get nearest to an explicit formulation of this argument in *Convention,* p. 70:

> This is why it is redundant to speak of an arbitrary convention. Any convention is arbitrary because there is an alternative regularity that could have been our convention instead. A convention that is *not* arbitrary, so to speak, is a regularity whereby we achieve unique coordination equilibria.

Because it is not arbitrary, it does not have to be conventional either. We would conform to it simply because that is the best thing to do. No matter what we had been doing in the past, a failure to conform to the "nonarbitrary convention" could only be a strategic error (or compensation for someone else's anticipated strategic error, or compensation for someone else's anticipated compensation, etc.).

11. Though I shall show that Lewis's key term "proper coordination equilibrium" is ambiguous, and shall note (in my concluding section) that there are arguments on both sides (of the ambiguity) with respect to the precise definition of "coordination problem."

12. (3) should in fact read " . . . uniform conformity to R is a *proper* coordination equilibrium in S." (There are some other places where it is surprising to find that Lewis does not qualify "coordination equilibrium" by "proper." It is clear that the "properness" qualification was omitted in error here, at least.)

13. In Ullman-Margalit (1977): "*A* proper coordination equilibrium . . . is a coordination equilibrium in the strong sense" (p. 81). (In fact her explicit account of a p.c.e. is surprising, and unjustifiably weak; it must surely involve an inadvertent slip. Thus she writes that a p.c.e. is "a coordination equilibrium such that at least one agent would have been worse off had any one alone acted differently" [ibid.]. Why "at least one"? No reason is given for not having "both" agents here.)

14. If we do have two p.c.e. (on either interpretation) we do not then necessarily have "coincidence of interests predominating" in Lewis's sense. See the matrix in Figure 5.19. (This represents a game with two players. Call them "Row" and "Col" Row's alternative actions are represented by labeled rows of the matrix, Col's by labeled columns. The squares or "cells" of the matrix thus represent combinations of the agents' actions. Row's payoff from a given combination of actions is represented by the number in the *lower left* corner of the relevant square, Col's in the upper right.)

Here A1, B2 are p.c.e. on the strong interpretation, but it is not the case that the differences between the players' payoffs in any one square are "small compared to some of the differences between payoffs in different squares." Finally, if we *posit* coincidence of interests in a situation, we do not automatically have one or more p.c.e. on either interpretation; see Figure 5.20.

15. That the stag-hunt case is peculiar has been noted by others. See, in particular, Ullman-Margalit (1977), pp. 121ff. Her discussion at p. 122 is somewhat confusing as to the significance of the existence in the stag case of a maximum security level choice as such. See my discussion below.

16. This represents, of course, some analogous *two-person* case.

17. Cf. Ullman-Margalit (1977), p. 122.

18. A slightly different claim might be implied here: that a rational agent should (for *some* reason) always do his part in a unique coordination equilibrium. This too will be refuted in what follows.

	A	B	C	D
1	3 3	0 0	0 0	0 0
2	0 0	3 3	0 0	0 0
3	0 0	0 0	-15 15	0 0
4	0 0	0 0	0 0	15 -15

Fig. 5.19

19. In all of what follows I shall be talking about agents who take no account of any possible repercussions their actions in this play of the game may have on *subsequent plays* of the game (or on subsequent occasions). David Lewis says nothing about such considerations, and in his examples the agents do not appear to have them in mind.

20. Cf. Luce and Raiffa (1957), p. 70, second matrix.

21. If we don't conform to Lewis's "coincidence of interests predominates" restriction, this point can be made more forcefully: make Row's *D1* payoff and Col's *A4*, be -1000. It can be made slightly less forcefully, if we restrict ourselves to situations of pure coordination. Here alter *A4*, and *D1*, to yield "4" for each player.

22. In the case we are considering here it may be noted that each player prefers *C3* or *D3* to anything else, and each knows this, etc. However, nothing seems to follow from this about what each should do. This case is similar to that in Figure 5.6, which has a risky absolute best point. Surely all that Row

Fig. 5.20

can be sure of is that *if* Col does *C*, he himself should do *3;* Col meanwhile can be sure that *if* Row does *3*, he should do *C*; and each can be sure that the other is sure of these things, and so on. But beyond this they cannot go, on the basis of common knowledge of rationality alone. In particular, Col cannot infer that Row will place himself in Col's hands by doing *3*, so Col can be sure *C* is the right thing to do himself. Meanwhile, there is a maximin choice available to each, which avoids the great possible losses of other possible choices. Without any guarantees about the other's future action, a rational agent who wishes to maximize his security level will do his part in *B4*.

23. We must also reject as invalid an implied inference in Lewis's drift as characterized in my account of it. It looks as if Lewis accepts the following conditional: if a rational player knows that the other players will be doing their parts in a particular coordination equilibrium, he should do his part. This, however, according to the definition of "coordination equilibrium" is just not so. Consider Figure 5.21.

Here *A1* is a unique coordination equilibrium. Yet it is not the case that if Row knows Col is to do his part in *A1*, he will or should do his in *A1*. He might just as well do his part in *B1* he will get the same payoff. The same goes *mutatis mutandis* for Col. Indeed, in this case both Row and Col have a dominant strategy (see below), such that they would be well advised to do their part in it whatever their expectations about the other. In this case Row should do *B* and Col *2*. Thus we can expect rational players in this situation to end up doing their parts in *B2*, even where they expect their opposite numbers to do their parts in *A1*! (See below, on Prisoner's Dilemma situations.)

24. See Figure 5.22. Considering the risks involved in choosing *A* and *B*, Row will presumably not find the choice of A obvious in a one-off situation; similarly for Col's *1*. All that each one can say is that if the other does his part in *A1*, then he should do his part. But there are no guarantees that the other

Fig. 5.21

Fig. 5.22

will do his part. Given an expectation that, say, Row will do *B*. Col will hardly do his part in the unique coordination equilibrium. (We might expect the players to end up at *C3*, in a one-off case.)

25. I discuss "triviality" in more detail below, shortly.

26. This is not entirely perspicuous. What Lewis seems to mean here (cf. his next paragraph) is that a choice of action *C* is (strictly) dominant for an agent *A* if, by making *C*, *A* will have a higher payoff than any he would have got through any other choice, whatever the others do. (A weaker notion of dominance is more standardly employed in the game-theoretic literature. Cf. Luce and Raiffa, p. 287.)

27. Consider in this connection Luce and Raiffa (1957), p. 59: "if both players have the same preference pattern over the outcome, then everything is trivial since both players prefer the same outcome above all others." This seems to assume an *absolute* best point in all games of pure coordination, which is, of course, not the case. However, all such situations must have one or more *best* points.

28. If the assumption of common *knowledge* of rationality is removed, we cannot say that each (rational) agent will *know* that success is certain. Even removing the assumption, there still remain situations in which a rational agent can be certain of success: it could be that no player is at risk from any other; in particular, he may be able to ensure that *he* gets his best payoff whatever the others do, that is, whether the others act rationally or not. At the limiting case, it may be that neither can fail to get a best point whatever *he* does, though we seem hardly to have anything worth calling a "choice-situation" here.

29. For the matrix Lewis gives (on p. 16) see Figure 5.23.

30. Cf. Watkins (1970), "I say that there is no optimal solution, that the idea of optimality breaks down here" (p. 205).

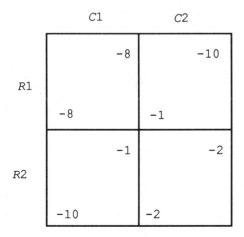

Fig. 5.23

31. Luce and Raiffa (1957) believe that it is clear that agents should pursue their dominant strategy. (See p. 112.) Recall that in my discussion I exclude from the agents' consideration anything about future plays of the game. Such considerations appear to alter the picture in the "iterated Prisoner's Dilemma" case. See Luce and Raiffa, pp. 97–102.

32. Quantitative aspects of game-theoretical situations may, clearly, effect their intuitive triviality. This is so even when the agents' dominant choices "meet" at an outcome only better than their worst; suppose each one likes every outcome but the worst pretty much, while considering the worst outcome to be a terrible disaster.

33. We can prove that if there is a unique c.e. that is also a point of u.s.d., then the c.e. must also at least be a best point. Let "Col" and "Row" be the players in a game represented in a matrix according to the conventions adopted in this essay. Let C be one of Col's strategies, represented by a certain column of the matrix, and let I be one of Row's strategies, represented by a certain row of the matrix.

Let CI be the u.s.d. point. Let CI also be a c.e. Then Col prefers CI to anything else in its row (because of the u.s.d. property) and also likes CI at least as well as anything in its column (by the c.e. property). Col also prefers anything in column C to anything else in the corresponding row (because of the u.s.d. property). Let $B2$ be any point distinct from CI. Then $B2$ is either as good as or worse than CI for Col. Hence CI is as good as or better than any other point for Col. The same goes for Row, *mutatis mutandis*. Hence CI is at least a best point.

Though this argument refers to a two-person case, it appears to be generalizable to cases involving any number of players.

34. Two further points, noted by Saul Kripke:

(1) A difficulty arises in Lewis's treatment of "dominated" choices in games of pure coordination. Lewis defines a choice to be (strictly) *dominated* if "no matter how the others choose, you could have made some other choice that would have been better" (p. 17). After proving that in a finite two-person game of pure coordination with a unique equilibrium at least one action of some agent is dominated (pp. 17–19), Lewis supposes that since it is common knowledge that "everybody ignores dominated actions" (p. 19), and since the deletion of a dominated action still leaves a game of the same type, the original game can be transformed, by a series of deletions, to one where both players have only one action (p. 19). So he thinks this proves the triviality of a finite two-person game of pure coordination with a unique equilibrium, though he acknowledges (pp. 1–21) that this method does not carry over even to all games of pure coordination.

However, the idea that "dominated" choices can be ignored is not well-founded, so that Lewis's proof of triviality fails. Consider Figure 5.24. There C is "dominated" but should Row ignore it? In fact, a theorist who recommends maximization of security level would recommend C. C is especially attractive

	1	2	3
A	11 / 11	0 / 0	11 / 11
B	0 / 0	11 / 11	0 / 0
C	10 / 10	10 / 10	10 / 10

Fig. 5.24.

here since it guarantees 10 while the others risk 0 for only a slight gain over 10 (cf. the "minimax regret" criterion). (Note that if Row chooses *C*, he excludes all the coordination equilibria!)

Probably it would be more usual to call a player's choice "dominated" if some other choice available to him is at least as good always and exceeds it sometimes. It is reasonable to suppose that a choice that is dominated in this sense can be ignored; but it is not true that, in this sense of "dominated," in a finite two-person game of pure coordination with a unique equilibrium, at least one player must have a dominated choice.

(2) There seems to be no special justification for ignoring infinite games; sometimes real situations are probably best treated (or idealized) as infinite games. If they are allowed, there are two-person games of pure coordination with a unique (coordination) equilibrium where the equilibrium is far from a best point and, moreover, it is by no means obvious that rational players will "do their part" in it. (See Figure 5.25.)

35. Cf. Ullman-Margalit (1977), p. 80 (lines 1–12).

36. It is virtually identical to one of the matrices in Lewis's text; see his Figure 20, center matrix, p. 26, described without qualification as a "coordination problem."

37. See Ullman-Margalit, p. 82: " . . . each of these co-ordination equilibria is still much preferred to any of the non-coordination equilibria," and Lewis, p. 73: ". . . suppose the coordination equilibrium we would reach by conforming to *R'* is [so] much worse than the one we reach by conforming to *R* . . . that it is only slightly preferred to some of the outcomes that are not coordination equilibria."

38. Cf. Quine, foreword to *Convention*, p. xii: "The key-note of convention-

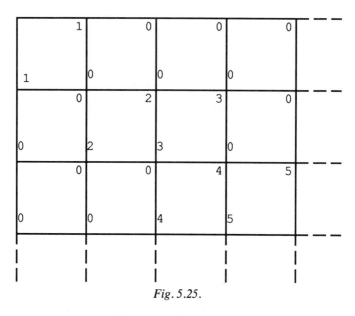

Fig. 5.25.

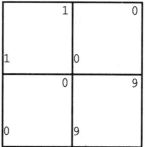

Fig. 5.26

ality is a certain indifference. . . . Such is the initial intuition; but the appropriate sense of indifference . . . needs a lot of refining. It gets it, thanks to Lewis's deft use . . . of the latter-day theory of games and decisions.''

39. See for instance Schiffer (1972), pp. 151 ff., and Burge (1975). See also *On Social Facts*.

40. I thank David Lewis, Tim Scanlon, Anne Jacobson, Mark Sainsbury, and, especially, Saul Kripke for discussions of my work in progress.

Part II

Sociality: Introducing Plural Subjects

The essays in this section address in a variety of ways the nature and range of social phenomena and introduce the author's *plural subject* theory—the theory that plural subjects as she characterizes these are fundamental parts of the human social realm.

Essays 6, 7, and 8 present and defend accounts of three important phenomena of everyday human social life: the omnipresent phenomenon of *doing things together* (exemplified in walking together), talk of what *we* believe, and the sense that a marriage or similar relationship involves a positive kind of *fusion* of the parties. In each case it is argued that the phenomena in question are plural subject phenomena—involving or arising from the existence of a plural subject.

Essays 9 and 10 approach the question of the social nature of language. The first cautions against too easily assuming that language as such is social, pointing out important pitfalls for arguments in this area. The second sketches an account of what it is for a group to have a language, connecting this with Wittgenstein's doctrine that an "inner process" stands in need of "outward criteria."

Essay 11 discusses the characterization of social phenomena in general, and touches on a variety of topics relating to plural subject theory, including the nature of crowds, and the possibility of group emotions.

6

Walking Together: A Paradigmatic Social Phenomenon

If one were asked to characterize the standard concerns of contemporary philosophy of social science, two different problem areas would most likely come to mind. The first has to do with methodology broadly speaking. Key questions include: Are the methods of natural science appropriate to the study of social phenomena? Can there be a properly so-called social "science" at all? The second problem area is a matter of ontology. Usually the question posed is a relational one. Roughly, what is the relationship between human social groups and the individual humans who are their members? Are groups simply aggregates of individuals, or what?

On the whole, those who have focused on the above questions have tended to work with a relatively inarticulate, intuitive understanding of the nature of social phenomena in general, and of social groups in particular. Though a more articulate understanding may not be required for certain purposes, one would think that it would benefit discussions of these questions. Thus it is plausible to suppose that an important task for the philosophy of social science is the detailed articulation of our central intuitive concepts of social phenomena.

In this essay I approach a concept crucial to this task, the concept of a social group or collectivity in general. I begin by focusing on something far less grand and general—the everyday concept of going for a walk together. The essay is intended to introduce some of the main ideas in my book *On Social Facts* through a relatively self-contained discussion.[1]

I. A Proposal about Social Groups

The sociologist Georg Simmel wrote:

Sociation [roughly, the process of forming a social group] ranges all the way from the momentary getting together for a walk to founding a family . . . from the temporary aggregation of hotel guests to the intimate bonds of a medieval guild.[2]

This suggests an idea that I endorse for my own reasons, as I shall explain.

The idea is that we can discover the nature of social groups in general by investigating such small-scale temporary phenomena as going for a walk together. This idea is attractive insofar as it should be relatively easy to understand what it is to go for a walk with another person. It may also seem somewhat far-fetched.

When sociologists and others give examples of social groups they tend to mention only such enduring, complex phenomena as families, guilds, armies, even nations. And, clearly, important distinctions can be drawn between such phenomena as going for a walk together and families, armies, and so on. Be that as it may, such small-scale phenomena as two people going for a walk together, having a conversation, and the like, do occasionally find their place among sociologists' examples, witness the quotation from Simmel above. As I shall argue, there is good reason for this.

I shall propose, more precisely, that analysis of our concepts of "shared action" discovers a structure that is constitutive of social groups as such. To this extent, then, going for a walk together may be considered a paradigm of social phenomena in general.

I start by arguing for a particular account of what it is to go for a walk together. This will be the major part of the discussion. I then argue that a plausible account of social groups in general can be given in similar terms. In an essay of this length, some sketchiness is inevitable.[3]

II. Going for a Walk Together: Preliminaries

What is it for two people to go for a walk together? Let us start with one person who is out on a walk alone and see what minimum addition allows us to say that this person and someone else are out on a walk together.

Imagine that Sue Jones is out for a walk along Horsebarn Road on her own. Suddenly she realizes that someone else—a man in a black cloak—has begun to walk alongside her, about a foot away. His physical proximity is clearly not enough to make it the case that they are going for a walk together. It may disturb Sue precisely because they are *not* going for a walk together.

It is possible, of course, that she is glad he is there. She has recognized him. He is Jack Smith, and she wants to get to know him. She waits for him to say something. He is in the same position. Thus they could be walking along next to each other, each wanting this to continue. Is each one's possession of the goal that they continue walking alongside each other logically sufficient for their going for a walk together? I would say not. Note that it is possible that each one's possession of the goal in question is not known by either one. Sue may look worried and Jack may suspect that she would rather be alone. Jack may be famous for his reclusiveness, leading Sue to conjecture that he is hoping she will stop and turn back. Once this possibility is made explicit it seems particularly clear that we must reject what I shall call the *weak shared personal goal analysis*. (Why I say "weak" here will be clear shortly.)

What precisely is the problem here? One general, informal hypothesis is that giving both participants the personal goal that they walk alongside each other puts them no closer together *as far as they are concerned*.

Let us now consider the *strong shared personal goal analysis*. On this account, it is logically necessary and sufficient for a case of going for a walk together that it is *common knowledge* between Jack and Sue that each one has the goal in question. By this I mean, roughly, that each one's goal is completely out in the open as far as the two of them are concerned.[4] Such common knowledge could arise in various ways. In some contexts it may be enough for both parties to continue walking alongside each other for several minutes without any sign of discomfort. In any case, I shall now argue that even assuming that the conditions in question are fulfilled, a crucial feature of going for a walk together will be lacking. Let me first say something about the feature in question.

Let us assume that, at some point in time, Jack and Sue are indeed going for a walk together. That is, we assume that at this juncture the relevant logical conditions are fulfilled, whatever these are precisely.

Now suppose that Jack starts drawing ahead. Failing some special circumstances, it would be odd if he were not to notice this. It would, moreover, be odd for him not to make any attempt to bring them closer together. So much is true, of course, if Jack genuinely desires that they walk side by side. For if this is what he wants, he will be acting against his interests if he fails to monitor the situation relatively carefully and to act accordingly. But there is more.

If Jack and Sue are indeed going for a walk together, and Jack has apparently drawn ahead without noticing what is happening, we can imagine Sue taking action in various ways. She might call out "Jack!" with a degree of impatience. She might catch up with him and then say, somewhat critically, "You are going to have to slow down! I can't keep up with you." In both of these cases she rebukes Jack, albeit mildly. She might not do this, of course, but it seems that, again failing special circumstances, her doing so would be *in order*. In other words, it seems that in the circumstances Sue is *entitled to rebuke* Jack. We would expect both Jack and Sue to understand that she has this entitlement.

The existence of this entitlement suggests that Jack has, in effect, an *obligation* to notice and to act (an obligation Sue has also). Particular acts Jack might perform in fulfilling his obligation to rectify matters include stopping and waiting for Sue to catch up, slowing his pace, smiling encouragement, asking if she is getting tired. These are the kinds of thing we expect to find if one party realizes he has drawn ahead of the other. Though he may not be obligated to do any one of these things, he is obligated to do something along these lines. The point can also be put in terms of *rights:* each has a right to the other's attention and corrective action. We would expect those out on a walk together to *realize* that they have the obligations, and the rights, just noted.

The foregoing suggests the following test for a putative analysis of the notion of going for a walk together. Are the proposed conditions such that the participants' failure to acknowledge the noted obligations and entitlements would necessarily throw doubt on the idea that the conditions are fulfilled?

I propose that the strong shared personal goal analysis fails the above test. In a word, those who are supposedly going for a walk in the sense defined by this analysis can deny that they have the obligations and entitlements at issue without necessarily bringing the supposition into doubt. Some clarification of this claim is in order.

Suppose Jack knows that he and Sue both have as a personal goal their continuing to walk alongside one another. (We can take this to follow from the common knowledge condition.) It is possible that Jack will judge that, all else being equal, both he and Sue have *moral duty* to see that the goal is achieved. For this way overall happiness will be maximized. It seems equally possible, however, that Jack will not see things this way. In other words, he may fail to judge that either of them has a moral duty to promote the shared personal goal. Given that this is possible, it cannot be argued that his failure to draw the moral conclusion would necessarily throw doubt on the original supposition about what Jack knew. In order for this to happen we need some premise about Jack's moral views.

The reference to moral duties raises a more general question: Must those who lack the concept of a moral duty altogether be incapable of going for a walk together? This is not particularly plausible on the face of it. Nonetheless, if I am right, people out on a walk can *for that reason* be expected to recognize certain responsibilities and rights. This suggests that the rights and obligations in question are not moral rights and obligations. I take this to mean that they will have a different basis from that of moral rights and obligations. This is something that a satisfactory analysis should illuminate further, for it should indicate what the grounds of obligation and entitlement are in the case of going for a walk together.[5]

Morality aside, if Jack's goal is to walk alongside Sue, *prudence* obviously requires him to monitor the situation carefully and to take what action he can to keep the two of them together. Common knowledge that Jack and Sue have the same personal goal seems to add to the prudential reasons available. Let us take it that, given common knowledge, Sue will know that Jack knows that both have the goal in question. She may well, in that case, deem Jack to be both irrational and inconsiderate of her if he fails to monitor the situation, and this could lead her to stop wanting to be with him. So it can be argued that the addition of common knowledge gives Jack an extra prudential reason to pay attention to and deal with the growing distance between them. In any case, one can say that, from a prudential point of view, that is what Jack is *obliged* to do. This does not help us save a shared personal goal analysis, however.

As is well known, H.L.A. Hart has stressed a conceptual distinction between "being obliged" and "having an obligation."[6] It is clear that there is a significant distinction here. The distinction at its broadest is between a feature generated by prudential considerations, whatever we call it, and a feature differently derived. In the first case, we argue for the feature simply by noting what a person wants, and how he must act in order to get that thing. In the second case, such premises are insufficient. It seems clear that in the case of going for a walk we are dealing with something of the latter kind. In this case, I have not only argued for the presence of an obligation—prior to that, I argued for an entitlement to rebuke. These features appear to be closely connected: *the obligation is such that Jack's failure to perform entitles Sue to rebuke him.* But in the case of the feature stemming from prudential considerations only, which Hart refers to as "being obliged," there is no such tight connection between the feature and an entitlement to rebuke.

Supposing only the fulfillment of the conditions of the strong shared goal analysis, is there any basis for inferring that Sue is now entitled, all else being equal, to rebuke Jack for carelessly drawing ahead? On the contrary, fulfillment of these conditions does not seem to entitle her to interact with him in any way at all. By this I mean, roughly, that it does not by itself—without special ancillary premises—generate a right of some kind to interact with him. If this is so, one can infer, of course, that the right kind of obligation has not been generated either, by whatever means.

Someone in Sue's position may well feel herself to be in the following fix. She would like to call out to attract Jack's attention. Indeed, she would like to put the kind of pressure on him an appropriate rebuke would produce. But she does not feel entitled to behave in these ways. Quite generally, she does not feel entitled to *interfere* with his actions in any way. More precisely, she does not feel that the existence of such an entitlement has been *established* between them.[7]

In various places Charles Taylor has suggested that when there is common knowledge of some fact between two persons this does not yet make it what he calls "*entre nous*" between them: according to Taylor it is not at this point "in public space." Meanwhile Taylor indicates that once the fact in question has been communicated, particularly by the use of language, it will be "*entre nous*," "in public space." This suggests that it is worth seeing if there could be a difference for our purposes between the general common knowledge case and a case involving linguistic communication. What if, rather than simply positing common knowledge of the shared personal goal, from whatever source, we suppose it to be common knowledge that each has *told* the other that he or she has the goal in question?[8]

Here things are a little delicate, since more may be conveyed than is actually said, and more or less may be accomplished depending on the circumstances. But let us suppose in this instance that each is taking the other purely at face value, and this is common knowledge. (Perhaps it is common knowledge that they are members of the Literalists, or of the G. E. Moore Society.) Suppose, then, that Jack says, somewhat quaintly, "My goal right now is to go on walking in your company." Sue replies, "And my goal is to go on walking in your company!" In spite of this change in the situation, the crucial element needed to establish that the parties are out on a walk together seems to be missing. As before, each is safe in the knowledge that the other party will (if prudent) do what he or she can to ensure that the shared personal goal is reached. But, as before, neither one seems to have to conclude that any one has any obligations to the other to perform satisfactorily, or that anyone is entitled to rebuke the other for not doing what they can to reach the goal.

This is true even if each has averred: "I intend to do all I can to achieve my goal. For instance, if you draw ahead without noticing, I plan to call out to catch your attention. Given your own goal, this should help you attain mine." This does not seem crucially to change things. In the case now envisaged Jack will, if you like, be "entitled to expect" that Sue will call after him if he unknowingly draws ahead, and Sue will be "entitled to expect" that he will not be surprised at her doing so. This might make her less timid about doing these things. But here, saying that they are "entitled to expect" these things is just another way of saying that their evidence is such that they can infer that performance will take place, all else being equal. No one yet seems to have the right type of *obligation to perform* or the corresponding *entitlements to rebuke* and so on. (Is a rebuke in order at all? This depends on whether one is entitled to complain about violations of *one's beliefs about what will be done.* Presumably Jack might in fact complain in such a way as this: "I believed you would alert me, so I was less concerned to monitor the situation." Here I suggest the implicit appeal would be to moral considerations. Jack might add: "You *should have realized* that I might rely on you." Given a case of genuine walking together, however, he could afford to be much more peremptory, appealing to an *established understanding:* "Why didn't you alert me!?")

So far, then, three accounts of going for a walk together appear insufficient. I focused on the strong shared personal goal analysis, requiring common knowledge that it is each party's personal goal that the two of them walk along side by side. In such a situation reasons of morality generally, prudence, or, indeed, of "care" could prompt each person to monitor the actions of the other and to do what they could to ensure that the goal each pursued was reached. I argued that, nonetheless, in this situation certain key obligations and entitlements fail to be generated. As long as people are out on a walk together, they will understand that each has an *obligation* to do what he or she can to achieve the relevant goal. Moreover, each one is *entitled* to rebuke the other for failure to fulfill this obligation. It is doubtful whether the core obligations and entitlements in question are moral obligations and entitlements. At the same time, they are not merely a matter of prudence or self-interest. Importantly, they seem to be a direct function of the fact of going for a walk together. Thus, though certain "external" factors or considerations may lead to their being ignored, they are "still there." How might these various judgments about going for a walk together plausibly be accounted for?

III. Going for a Walk Together: Outline of an Account

Suppose Jack Smith coughs to attract Sue's attention, and then asks if she is Sue Jones and would she mind if he joins her? "No," Sue says, "that would be nice. I should like some company." This is probably enough to produce a case of going for a walk together. Once the exchange has taken place, both parties will be entitled to assume that the attitudes and actions appropriate to their going for a walk together are in place.

What were the crucial elements in this transaction? I suggest, as an initial characterization, that each party has made it clear to the other that he is willing to *join forces* with the other in accepting the goal that they walk in one another's company. There are other ways of putting the point. I might have said that each has manifested his willingness to bring it about that the goal in question be accepted *by himself and the other, jointly*. For now, let me sum up by formulating my suggestion as follows: in order to go for a walk together each of the parties must express willingness to constitute with the other a *plural subject of the goal* that they walk along in one another's company. "Plural subject" is a technical term of my own, whose meaning will be more carefully specified shortly.

I conjecture, further, that once this willingness to form the plural subject of the goal in question has been expressed on both sides, in conditions of common knowledge, the foundation has been laid for each person to pursue the goal *in his or her capacity as the constituent of a plural subject* of that goal. Thus we can consider that each one's expression of willingness to walk with the other, in conditions of common knowledge, is logically sufficient for them to be plural subjects of the relevant goal, and hence to go for a walk together.

If that is right, then once all this has happened, the relevant obligations and entitlements will be in place, and we can expect the parties to know this. Let me now argue that this will be so, provided that we construe the notion of plural subjecthood in a particular way. As it turns out, the way I (independently) want to put things bears a striking resemblance to the language of some classic political theorists.

Let me first say what I want to say about plural subjecthood. When a goal has a plural subject, each of a number of persons (two or more) has, in effect, offered his will to be part of a pool of wills that is dedicated, as one, to that goal. It is common knowledge that, when each has done this in conditions of common knowledge, the pool will have been set up. Thus what is achieved is a binding together of a set of individual wills so as to constitute a single, "plural will" dedicated to a particular goal.

The precise mechanism by which this binding is understood to take place is rather special. The individual wills are bound *simultaneously and interdependently*. Thus we do not have, here, an "exchange of promises" such that each one unilaterally binds himself to the goal in question, leaving himself beholden for release to someone else upon whom, through this particular transaction, he has no claim. Nor is it that one person in effect says: "You may regard me as committed once you have made a commitment," leaving it up to the other person to make an initial unilateral commitment. Rather, each person expresses a special form of *conditional commitment* such that (as is understood) only when *everyone* has done similarly is *anyone* committed. Thus all wills are bound simultaneously and interdependently. The character of each one's commitment is then as follows: no one can release himself from the commitment; each is obligated to all the others for performance; each is (thus) entitled to performance from the rest. This, I believe, is what is achieved in interchanges such as the one in my example, where Jack asks if he may join Sue, and Sue says that he may. Once this transaction has occurred, then all else being equal, the commitments in question are in place.

How can we best describe the content of the commitment? I have said very generally that the pool of wills is dedicated, as one, to the relevant goal. This, though vague perhaps, is the guiding idea. Thus we might say that: each must act as would the parts of a single person or subject of action in pursuit of the goal. Or: they are to act as members of a single body, the body comprising them all. As we have already seen, in a concrete case one's sense of the range of responsibilities and rights becomes relatively precise.

Note that the obligations and entitlements can now be characterized further. Each is obligated to all *qua* member of the whole; each is entitled to certain actions *qua* member of the whole.[9]

The above account of what it is to become a participant in a plural subject can be used to throw light on, and is to that extent supported by, a semantic phenomenon involving the pronoun "we." [Since noticing this I have found that Wilfrid Sellars has remarked on it previously. See, for instance, Sellars (1963).]

It seems that premises of the form "We seek goal *G*" license certain inferences about action. Thus, Sue's premise "We seek to walk along side by side" in conjunction with the premises "Jack is drawing ahead" and "The best way I can help achieve our goal is to tell Jack to slow up" seems sufficient to determine that (all else being equal) Sue should tell Jack to slow up. In other words we would expect Sue, if rational and accepting the premises, to act accordingly. Intuitively, I suggest, the conclusion follows from the premises without any kind of decomposition of the "We" premise giving some premise about, say, Sue's personal goals.[10] Accepting this, how can we explain it? It turns out that the hypothesis that "we" refers to a plural subject in the sense just elaborated gives us a satisfying account.

If "we" refers to a plural subject of a goal, it refers to a pool of wills dedicated *as one* to that goal. In Sue's case, her use of "we" refers to a pool of wills of which her own is a member. She understands her will to be bound in the service of the pool's established inclination. Hence she understands herself to be bound to perform what will best serve the goal in question. This gives her a (quite strong) reason to act accordingly. No reference to her own goals is necessary to effect the inference to this conclusion. For a premise about "our goal" is as effective as one about "my goal" in establishing a reason for action for a participating individual. In sum, then, the account of a plural subject in terms of a pool of wills dedicated as one to a given end, in conjunction with the assumption that "we" refers to a plural subject of which the speaker is a part, plausibly explains the apparent inferences from an undecomposed "we" premise.

Now, those out on a walk would quite appropriately refer to one another as "we," at least in relation to their walk. They would quite appropriately say such things as "Shall we stop here?" "Shall we go through the woods?"[11] And inferences of the sort noted will seem appropriate at various junctures. This supports the idea that those out on a walk form a plural subject in the sense in question. For this assumption provides a satisfactory explanation of these uses of "we."

I have argued that going for a walk together with another person involves participating in an activity of a special kind, one whose goal is the goal of a plural subject, as opposed to the shared personal goal of the participants. Alternatively, going for a walk involves an "our goal" as opposed to two or more "my goals." I take it that there are many activities of this kind, which may be referred to as "shared," "joint," or "collective" action. Examples will include traveling together, eating together, dancing together, investigating the murder together, and so on.[12]

IV. Social Groups in General

What has all this to do with social groups? To say it quickly, in my view, human social groups are plural subjects. That is, in order to form a social group, it is both logically necessary and logically sufficient that a set of human beings constitute a plural subject. Clearly this is a thesis about a concept, namely, the open-ended lists of so-called social groups made by sociologists and others. These are not entirely unambiguous, but I believe the plural subject account gives them a plausible and compelling rationale.

Some immediate clarification of this thesis is in order. I have argued that those out on a walk together constitute the plural subject of a particular goal, roughly, the goal that they walk along side by side for a certain roughly specified period. Let us say that a given set of people have a "joint," "collective," or (in a strong sense) "shared" goal when they are the plural subject of a goal. Now, some situations which seem definitely to involve a social group, seem not to involve any joint goal in the appropriate sense. Witness, for instance, the committee imagined by John Updike (1981) in his story "Minutes of the Last Meeting" whose members are quite unclear about what general charge, if any, their committee has. Committees do generally have some sort of goal, it is true. But what about families? We are not talking here about the useful effects family life may have, such as the satisfaction of individual needs for psychological intimacy. I do not find it obvious that, in constituting a family, a set of persons must have a *joint goal* or goals.

Suppose that we assume for the sake of argument that it is *not* the case that all social groups must have a joint goal. This does not, in any case, refute the claim that social groups are plural subjects. For the general fundamental concept of a plural subject is not only embedded in our shared action concept, it can be found, for instance, in our concept of a shared or collective belief, and in the concept of a shared or collective principle.

There is no place here carefully to develop and defend detailed analyses of these particular concepts, but let us look at them briefly in action. Suppose that while they are out on their walk, Jack says: "What terrific weather!" and Sue concurs. If they subsequently run across Jill, a mutual friend, and she says "Whew! It's hot!" Sue could reply "Do you think so? *We* think it's great." It appears, in other words that the previous interchanges between Jack and Sue will count as having established a view that they may properly refer to as "ours." My contention is that, more precisely, they are now members of the plural subject of a view. This carries with it a set of obligations similar to those involved with a shared goal. Roughly, they must endeavor to appear to be "of one mind"—as we say—in relation to this view.

Similarly, Sue and Jack may constitute themselves the plural subject of a principle of action. Suppose that at each choice point, Jack tells Sue to choose where they will turn. After a while she chooses automatically, and Jack follows her lead. At a certain fork in the road, however, Jack seems to be "taking the reins." Sue says, with some amusement, "I thought I was supposed to make the decisions!" and Jack apologizes. Given some such scenario, we shall be able to say that Jack and Sue have come to constitute the plural subject of a principle of action. In this case the principle is a simple "fiat," which means, I would say, that there is now a *social convention* in this particular population. (Sue's utterance might have been tendentious, but as long as Jack goes along with it, the right attitudes will have been expressed, and thus by these acts themselves a plural subject will have been constituted.[13]

Plural subjecthood, then, extends not only to goals but also, at least, to beliefs and principles of action. On my account of social groups, in order to constitute a social group people must constitute a plural subject *of some kind*. And *any* plural subject is a social group. This makes the account less restrictive. Updike's committee probably has many collective beliefs and principles, as do most families, whether or not they lack any clear collective goal.

My claim in this essay has been that if we are looking for the key to social groups we can find what we want in the phenomenon of going for a walk together. This claim can now be articulated as follows: it turns out that in order to go for a walk together two persons must constitute a plural subject. The key to social groups is the concept of a plural subject. For social groups are plural subjects. In the space that remains let me briefly attempt to back up this view of social groups.

Evidently, those who form a plural subject of whatever kind may properly refer to themselves as "us" or "we," to "our goal" or "our belief," and so on. This supports the idea of a connection between plural subjecthood and social groups. "We" is often used to emphasize or create a sense of group membership. Political rhetoric abounds with such phrases as "We Americans" and "We trade unionists." And compare Tonto's reply to the Lone Ranger: *"We,* white man?"

Mention of politics may raise a doubt. Is the analysis too broad? In groups such as nations, clubs, and even families political questions are endemic. It may not be immediately clear that such issues can arise in such a small-scale enterprise as going for a walk. And so one might wonder if we can really have a social group here. Further thought resolves this doubt. Those out on a walk have many problems to solve. For instance, for how long should they walk and where will they go? Will they talk, and if so, what about? Both collective decisions and joint principles are likely to result. One may always question whether such decisions and principles have been arrived at in a fair way and whether their content is acceptable. Is Jack forcing conversation on Sue? Is Sue forcing her slow pace on Jack? Are Sue's interests likely to be ignored, the way things are currently arranged? Clearly, then, even going for a walk together has a political dimension.

It is, indeed, rather striking that the language I have felt it most appropriate to use in describing the constitution of plural subjects closely resembles some key passages in classic works of political theory.

Early in *The Social Contract,* discussing when we have an association as opposed to a mere aggregate of people, Rousseau writes:

> Since men cannot engender new forces, but merely unite and direct existing ones, they have no other means of maintaining themselves but to form by aggregation a sum of forces . . . so that their forces are directed by means of a single moving power and made to act in concert.[14]

This is relatively obscure, and I do not claim, or need to claim, that I am certain what Rousseau had in mind. However, it and several other passages in the book clearly bear some resemblance to what I want to say about plural subjects.

So also does this, from Hobbes, who argues that in order to generate a commonwealth human beings must

> conferre all their power and strength upon one Man, or upon one Assembly of men, that may reduce all their Wills, by plurality of voices, unto one Will . . . this is a reall Unitie of them all, in one and the same Person . . .[15]

Hobbes includes as a possibility that the "one Person" in whom all are unified is an "Assembly of Men." In principle, this could presumably be the assembly of all the people. This does not seem such a far cry from the idea of people conditionally committing their wills to common goals or views, the goals, it could be said, of a single person, that person they together constitute. Consider also what Hobbes says about the mechanism that generates the "reall Unitie": "A reall Unitie of them all, in one and the same Person, made by Covenant of every man with every man, in such manner, as if every man should say to every man, I *Authorise and give up my Right of Governing my selfe, to this Man, or to this Assembly of men, on this condition, that thou give up thy Right to him, and Authorise all his Actions in like manner.*"[16]

These analogies with past accounts of association and commonwealth, neither necessary nor conclusive for my argument, do lend a degree of support to the idea of linking social groups in general with plural subjects. Though Hobbes and Rousseau were concerned with whole nations, it can be argued that the essentials of the mechanism they envisaged are involved even in such phenomena as two people going for a walk together.

Georg Simmel himself regarded the two-person group or "dyad" as importantly different from larger groups. Something he stresses is that, in a dyad, each person knows that without him or her in particular the group will cease to exist. As long as there are at least three people, the group can survive the loss of any given person. People in a dyad, then, may feel less as if the group is something "over and above" the individual members. One can accept this and related observations without having to reject the idea that a dyad can be counted as a fully fledged social group. It can simply be regarded as a social group with a special character.[17]

So much for the worry that, in embracing temporary dyads the plural subject account of social groups is too broad. One might also wonder if the account is too narrow. Let me briefly address two worries on that score.

First, it might be questioned whether there really is some jointly accepted principle, belief, or goal, in every social group. Consider the United States of America. Does every American constitute a plural subject with every other American? Let me answer this with another question: Is the United States of America a paradigmatic social group? By this I mean, does the population of the United States clearly satisfy the conditions for being a social group in a more than rough and ready way? Unless it does, a negative answer to the original question will not throw doubt on the plural subject account of groups. It is true that people often put nations in a list of social groups. And the United States of America is generally deemed to be a nation. But it is not obvious that all of the populations we are comfortable to think of as nations must be paradigmatic social groups.

The second worry I address concerns a type of population that has been the focus of much theorizing. Someone might ask, what of economic classes, such as the so-called blue-collar workers in a certain society? These are surely not always plural subjects. This I think is true, but I would not count that against the plural subject account. Usually the informal lists of social groups given by sociologists and others do not include economic classes as such. And the importance of such classes does not imply that they ought to be thought of as social groups. In sum, I do not think there is a problem in an account of social groups that may, in the event, not bring all actual economic classes within its scope. Of course, if a given class does constitute a plural subject then it will be counted a group according to this account. And recall that a plural subject may do no more than accept a certain credo.

In the end, I do not want to argue about a label. I have argued that those out on a walk together form a plural subject, and that there is some reason to suppose that our concept of a social group—that concept by virtue of which we list families, guilds, tribes, "and so on" together—is the concept of a plural subject. In any case, I would argue that the concept of a plural subject is a key concept for the description of human social life. It informs and directs a great deal of that life, in nations, clubs, families, and even in the taking of walks.

Postscript

There is no space here to inquire as to the implications of my argument for those methodological and ontological concerns mentioned in the preamble to this essay.[18] It is clear, however, that once the centrality of plural subjects to the human social world is agreed upon, a range of new and quite specific questions of methodology and ontology come into view.[19]

Notes

1. Given this expository intention, I shall not attempt to survey the literature in this area or to compare or contrast my views with those of others. One who has for some while been discussing the nature of such phenomena as going for a walk together in a detailed way is Raimo Toumela, whose work first came to my attention after my own analysis had been developed. See Toumela (1984, 1985), and elsewhere. I take Toumela's conclusions to be significantly different from my own. In particular he does not ascribe to the phenomena the special type of intrinsic normativity I take to be central. There will not be space for any detailed comparison of our accounts here.

2. Simmel (1908 [1971]), p. 24. My attention was recently drawn to this particular passage by the quotation in Walter Wallace (1988), p. 33. "Sociation" is a translation of the German *Vergesellschaftung*. "The process of forming a social group" is a more cumbersome but familiar-sounding rendering. Simmel prefers to talk of "sociation," a continuous process or event, as opposed to "society" or "social group," which have less dynamic connotations. Thus: ". . . society, as its life is constantly being realized . . . is something individuals do and suffer. To be true to this fundamental character of it, one should properly speak, not of society, but of sociation" (Simmel, "Fundamental Problems of Sociology," in Wolff, ed. [1969], p. 10. See also Wolff's note on his translation, p. lxiii).

3. For further relevant discussion, see *On Social Facts,* especially Chapter 4, and many of the essays in this volume.

4. "Common knowledge" is a technical term from Lewis (1969). See Chapter 1, note 4, for further references on this important topic.

5. I am connecting these and related points to the problem of political obligation in a monograph in progress (*Social Ontology and Political Obligation*). In the original version of this essay I said that I took moral rights and obligations to have their basis in "facts about objective value." It is not strictly necessary to make any such specific pronouncement. It is major philosophical task to say what moral rights and obligations amount to, as opposed to operating in terms of one's informal understanding—a starting point that suffices for many purposes, including my purposes here. See Chapter 12,

below, for more on the distinction among obligations indicated in this paragraph.

6. See Hart (1961).

7. Even once an entitlement of the right kind has been established between parties, one may not feel able to make use of this. Sue may be loath to assert herself in certain ways even when she is, and recognizes that she is, entitled to do so. She might be reluctant to call Jack in a rebuking way if she knows that he has an aversion to criticism, of whatever kind, and is likely to flare up at her. Such circumstances may well provide enough motivation to inhibit action to which one knows one is entitled.

When it is understood that no entitlement of the relevant kind has been established, this will tend to act as a *break* on action. This does not, of course, rule out the possibility of impulsive action, or action one justifies in terms of beliefs about moral rights.

8. Possibly closest to Taylor's paradigm would be the case where Jack says "Obviously you and I have as a goal our walking along in one another's company!" and Sue endorses this. That is, the fact of the shared personal goal is communicated in a single statement. My conclusion on the case in the text seems to stand for this case also. I would agree with Taylor that in interactions of the sort at issue here an important type of change in the situation occurs. As I would put it, Jack and Sue can now be said *jointly to accept* the view that they both have as a goal their walking in one another's company. For what I take this to amount to, see below and Chapter 7; see also *On Social Facts*, Chapter 5.

9. The last two sentences have been added to the previously published text.

10. For further defense of this idea, see *On Social Facts*, Chapter 7. In particular, I argue against the fairly popular view that all reasoning rationally productive of action must include a reference to the agent's personal desires.

11. I have argued elsewhere that "Shall we do *A*" is not *always* correctly said of a given speaker and hearer. See *On Social Facts*, pp. 175 ff.

12. A caveat: the phrases used in this area can be somewhat ambiguous. "Together" can mean little more than "in close proximity" and such phrases as "traveling together" may occasionally be intended accordingly. The head of a spy ring might say to a colleague "Kim and Don will be traveling together on Friday" meaning only that they will be on the same train and so on. He might add "Kim doesn't know Don will be there. I want Don to keep an eye on him." Generally, though, the phrase "traveling together" is used about those who are engaged in the special kind of activity at issue in this section.

13. For more on social conventions in the sense at issue here, see *On Social Facts*, Chapter 6, especially pp. 373 ff. For discussion of David Lewis's influential (and quite different) account from a variety of angles, see *On Social Facts*, Chapter 6, and, in this volume, Chapters 3 and 5 in particular.

14. Rousseau (1792/1983), Bk. I, Chapter 6, p. 23.

15. Hobbes (1651/1982), Part II, Chapter 17, p. 227.

16. Ibid., original emphasis.

17. Cf. Simmel, ". . . the simplest sociological formation . . . that which operates between two elements . . . itself is a sociation," "Quantitative Aspects of the Group," in Wolff, ed. (1969), p. 122.

18. For a discussion of the debate between "individualism" and "holism," given that social groups are plural subjects, see *On Social Facts,* Chapter 7. See also the introduction, this volume, on the holism in the notion of a plural subject.

19. An early version of this essay, entitled "Some Footnotes to Rousseau," was presented to the Philosophy Department at the University of Connecticut, Storrs, in 1986. A later version, approximating the present essay, was presented to the Philosophy Department at the University of Michigan, Ann Arbor, in 1989, and to the Philosophical Society, Oxford University, in 1990. I thank Stephen Mulhall for his comments as official commentator on the Oxford version. I am grateful to all who have commented on the material, and thank in particular Alan Gibbard, Saul Kripke, Peter Railton, Thomas Scanlon, and Crispin Wright.

7

Modeling Collective Belief

What is it for a group to believe something? A *summative* account assumes that for a group to believe that *p* most members of the group must believe that *p*. Accounts of this type are commonly proposed in interpretation of everyday ascriptions of beliefs to groups. I argue that a *non*summative account corresponds better to our unexamined understanding of such ascriptions. In particular I propose what I refer to as the "joint acceptance" model of group belief. I argue that group beliefs according to the joint acceptance model are important phenomena whose etiology and development require investigation. There is an analogous phenomenon of social or group preference, which social choice theory tends to ignore.

Introduction: An Important Phenomenon

It is natural to distinguish between the beliefs of groups, or collective beliefs, and the beliefs of individuals. But what does this distinction come down to? In particular: what is a collective belief?

In this essay I focus on two importantly different types of account of collective belief. One type is rather commonly proposed in interpretation of everyday ascriptions of belief to groups. As I shall argue, the other corresponds better to our unexamined understanding of such ascriptions. It also picks out an important phenomenon. There is some danger that an incorrect interpretation of vernacular speech could lead one to overlook this phenomenon. It is important not to overlook it, for whatever reason.

The discussion is relevant to the interpretation of many phrases in the literature, including "consensus," "shared belief," "belief held in common," and "social belief," as well as "belief of a group" and "collective belief." It has consequences, too, for the interpretation of such phrases as "social preference" or "group preference." Given the possibility of defining such phrases in widely different ways, it is obviously important that those discussing topics such as the etiology of consensus clarify their understanding of the terms in question in advance.

My discussion takes the form of an attempt to arrive at an acceptable account of everyday ascriptions of beliefs to groups. My main aim is to articulate and distinguish two radically different types of account, and, hence, to distinguish two radically different types of phenomena.[1]

I. Collective Belief Statements

We often say things like "Our group takes the view that we should go on strike immediately" or "The Zuni tribe believes that the north is the region of force and destruction." Call such statements *collective belief statements*. They may appear problematic. One may be tempted to say that only the members of groups, not groups themselves, can believe anything. Nonetheless, collective belief statements are frequently made. What, then, provokes them? What phenomena are they intended to pick out? What account of *collective beliefs* can be derived from an investigation of the truth conditions of our everyday collective belief statements?[2]

One common view of collective belief statements is expressed by Anthony Quinton in a well-known paper ["Social Objects" (1975–76)]. Quinton writes:

> We do, of course, speak freely of the mental properties and acts of a group in the way we do of individual people. Groups are said to have beliefs, emotions, and attitudes and to take decisions and make promises. But these ways of speaking are plainly metaphorical. To ascribe mental predicates to a group is always an indirect way of ascribing such predicates to its members. With such mental states as beliefs and attitudes the ascriptions are of what I have called a summative kind. To say that the industrial working class is determined to resist anti-trade union laws is to say that all or most industrial workers are so minded.

I shall use the term "summative" in a broader sense than Quinton's.[3] By a *summative account* of collective beliefs I shall mean one according to which for a group *G* to believe that *p* it is *logically necessary* that all or most members of G believe that p. One simple type of summative account, which I assume Quinton would accept, holds that in order for a group G to believe that p it is both necessary and sufficient logically that all or most members of G believe that p. (I note that Quinton himself puts the point linguistically.) The question arises whether some form of summative account is correct.

One of the founders of sociology, Emile Durkheim, may be read as denying the acceptability of a summative account. Indeed, in *The Rules of Sociological Method* Durkheim expressed the view that anything properly called a collective belief will be "external to individual consciousnesses."[4]

There is one rather bland interpretation of this claim in which it would be compatible with a summative account of collective beliefs.[5] The claim could be that the existence of a collective belief that p does not require that each individual member of the group in question believe that p. This claim seems plausible enough. Just because one particular group member had no beliefs about a certain strike, it does not seem to follow that the claim that the group thought a strike would be a good thing must be false. Quinton's analysis in terms of "most members of a group" may be displaying a sensitivity to this point.

Meanwhile, examination of Durkheim's text as a whole suggests that he would say, more strongly, that the existence of a collective belief that p does not require that any individual member of the group believe that p. In other words, he can be read as rejecting any form of summative account.[6] Though I cannot spend more time here on questions about the exegesis of Durkheim, I shall in what follows present some considerations that I take to go against a summative account of collective beliefs and will propose an account which could be expressed in something like Durkheim's terms.

First, I note some problems connected with two types of summative account.

II. The Simple Summative Account

According to the simple summative account, a group C believes that p if and only if most of its members believe that p. Let me here draw attention to one particular problem with this account.

Suppose an anthropologist were to write "The Zuni tribe believes that the north is the region of force and destruction."[7] Now suppose that the writer went on to give his grounds for this statement as follows:

> Each member of the Zuni tribe believes that the north is the region of force and destruction, but each one is afraid to tell anyone else that he believes this; he is afraid that the others will mock him, believing that they certainly will not believe it.

Such an explanation might well, I think, be taken to throw doubt on the original statements.[8]

What conclusions can be drawn from this? It surely suggests at least that when we ascribe a belief to a group we are not *simply* saying that most members of the group have the belief in question. That is, it is surely not logically sufficient for a group belief that *p* that most members of the group believe that *p*.

It may now appear that the basic problem with the simple summative account is that a person's beliefs can, in principle, be kept private. It may seem obvious, on reflection, that a set of actual, but secret, beliefs will not be enough to constitute something we would refer to as the belief of a particular social group. Again, if everyone knows of everyone else's belief, but is under the impression that he alone has this knowledge, this may seem to fail to be enough. The same may appear to go for the *next* order of knowledge.[9]

III. A Complex Summative Model: The Common Knowledge Account

Given such considerations, one may be drawn to a more complex kind of summative account, using a technical notion of "common knowledge," defined along the lines of David Lewis (1969) and others.[10] It is not part of my brief here to present or assess the many different accounts of common knowledge that have been given. The general aim is to define a concept which is realistic and at the same time captures the idea that some fact is "out in the open" or "entirely public" with respect to certain individuals. Evidently common knowledge is an important phenomenon.[11] To fix ideas here, we can think in terms of the following popular definition of common knowledge: it is common knowledge in *G* that *p* if and only if (a) p; (b) everyone in *G* knows that *p*; (c) everyone in *G* knows that (b), and so on, ad infinitum.[12]

Let us now consider the following complex summative account.

> A group *G* believes that *p* if and only if (1) most of the members of *G* believe that *p*, and (2) it is common knowledge in *G* that (1).

A group belief, according to this definition, is, one might say, a "commonly known general belief."

There are a number of prima facie problems with an account of group belief of this general type. When the conditions are fulfilled, we have a group, and it is out in the open that "most of us believe that *p*." Nonetheless, the intuitive aptness of saying that the group believes that *p* may seem doubtful when one considers that what is known by all group members, and so on, is something about what *most individuals* who are members of the group *personally believe*. (The simple summative account involves a similar problem.)

Related to the above point is the following. Though we here define the belief of a group in terms of what the *members of a group* individually believe, and what *group members* individually know that *members of their group* individually believe, and so on, the fact that a *group* is involved does not play any obviously essential role in what is going on. An analogue of group belief exists in many populations that are not intuitively social groups. It is probably common knowledge in the population of adults who have red hair and are over six feet tall that most of them believe that fire burns, for instance. (I take it that this population is not intuitively a social group, and that the existence of a commonly known general belief does not make it one.)[13] In brief, common knowledge in a population that most members of the population believe that *p* is not an essentially group involving phenomenon. Meanwhile, one might expect that for statements of the form "Group *G* believes that *p*" to be really apt, they would refer to a phenomenon involving a group in a more than accidental way. (This consideration, too, applies to the simple summative account.)

There is a kind of case that shows rather neatly that neither of the summative accounts considered so far can be correct. This depends upon the evident possibility that there can be coextensive groups; that is, groups with the same members. Assume that there are two committees—say, the Library Committee and the Food Committee of a residential college—with the same members. It seems quite possible to say, without contradiction, that (a) most members of the Library Committee personally believe that college members have to consume too much starch, and this is common knowledge within the Library Committee; (b) the same goes, *mutatis mutandis,* for the members of the Food Committee; (c) the Food Committee believes that college members have to consume too much starch, whereas the Library Committee has no opinion on the matter. It seems that one can infer that according to our intuitive conceptions *it is not logically sufficient*

for a group belief that p either that most group members believe that
p, or that there be common knowledge within the group that most
members believe that p.

IV. Toward a Nonsummative Account of Collective Beliefs: The Case of the Poetry Discussion Group

I now discuss in some detail a case where I think it would be apt to say that a group belief becomes established. Consideration of this case suggests among other things that it is not logically necessary that most group members believe that *p*, in order for there to be a group belief that *p*.

Consider the following fairly humdrum, commonplace kind of situation: a group of people meet regularly at one member's house to discuss poetry. The format followed when they meet, which evolved informally over time, is as follows. A poem by a contemporary poet is read out. Each participant feels free to make suggestions about how to interpret and evaluate the poem. Others respond, as they see fit, to the suggestions that are made. An opposing view might be put forward, or data adduced to support or refute a suggestion that has been made.

When discussion in this vein has gone on for a while a point is usually reached where one preferred interpretation seems to be emerging. No one is voicing any objections to certain ideas about how to read the poem. Someone asks if anyone wants to say any more. No one speaks up. The poem is then read out once more, stressed and phrased according to the preferred interpretation. Now suppose that the poem this time is "Church Going" by Philip Larkin, and that, according to the preferred interpretation, the last line of that poem is quite moving in its context. After the poem has been read for the second time, the group moves on to discuss another Larkin poem. The following dialogue then takes place. First Person: "The ending here is far more persuasive than that bathetic last line in 'Church Going'!" Second Person: "But we thought that line was quite moving!"

Apparently, by the end of the discussion of "Church Going" it would be quite natural for a member of the group to make one of the following statements: "We are agreed that the last line is moving"; "We accept that . . ."; We think that . . ."; "In our opinion, . . ."; "We decided that . . ."; "Our view at this point is that . . ."; "In the opinion of our discussion group, . . ."; "The group thought that . . .".

In general, then, in a context such as the kind of discussion sketched it would be natural and appropriate for group members to *ascribe a certain belief to the group as a whole*. I take it that one way of arriving at an account of what it is for a group to have a belief or opinion, intuitively, is to try to isolate those features of the present context that seem to substantiate the statement that the group has a certain belief. The following two points are especially relevant to the question of the acceptability of some form of summative account.

First, the truth of the statement that the group has a certain belief seems to be established by facts that would be perfectly compatible with the fact that even by the end of the discussion of "Church Going" most members of the group, in their hearts, judged the last line of the poem to be far from moving. Most of them might personally be inclined to judge it jarring, or bathetic. (Why, then, would they not have spoken out? Perhaps they were afraid to do so because one personally aggressive or sensitive person suggested that it was moving. That is one possibility. In any case, for whatever reason, they *did* decide to hold their peace.) What seems to be crucial is that all or most members decided to let a certain interpretation "stand" in the context of their discussion.

Second, the facts that make the ascription of group belief true seem compatible with the possibility that the majority of members of the discussion group did not have *any personal opinion* on the last line of Larkin's poem, either during the discussion or after the poem had been read out for the second time, after everyone had "had their say." If one member suggested that the last line was quite moving, in a firm and vigorous manner, other more passive and tentative souls might have been happy to let this opinion "carry the day" in the domain of the discussion—without being personally convinced. Again, it is the fact that this opinion was left to carry the day that seems to be crucial.

Given that these points are accepted, it seems that no form of summative account of collective belief can be correct as a general account. That is, *it is not a necessary condition of a group's belief that p that most members of the group believe that p*. Indeed, given the above, it seems that *it is not necessary that any members of the group personally believe that p*.

If this last conclusion seems to need further backing, consider that once a certain point is reached in discussion, a given view is established as the group view. It remains the group view, *ceteris paribus,* even if everyone subsequently comes to have a different opinion personally. Hence a group can believe something at a certain time without any member of the group believing it. It is not necessary that any member of the group ever believed it. Suppose one forceful person's statement stands unopposed and thus establishes a group view. It seems not to be necessary in any way that the forceful person in question believed what she said. A variety of motivations could lie behind her saying something she disbelieved or about which she had no current opinion of her own.[14]

People who were not personally convinced of the truth of an established group view might later speak like the first person in my imaginary dialogue. But, more likely, they would speak in a different vein, saying something like: *"I personally do not* think that the last line of "Church Going" is moving." That is, "personally" would be added as a special qualifier, perhaps in implied contrast with "as a person representing this group," or "in my capacity as a member of this group." Similarly, someone might deny having an opinion "of my own."

Let us now go back to my imaginary dialogue. Contrary to what one might expect, the first speaker contradicted the group view flatly and without preamble. The second person greeted this utterance with: "But . . .". I take it that the natural way to construe this is as a *rebuke* to the speaker. That a certain type of rebuke is in place if one has acted as the first speaker did appears to be an implication of our intuitive concept of a collective belief.

The existence and the precise nature of what I shall call the *predicted* rebuke is an important clue to the nature of our intuitive concept of collective belief. It will be useful to begin an examination of the rebuke by considering the difficulty it presents for the summative accounts previously considered. Suppose that what a group thinks is a matter of what most members think, or what most members think, as is common knowledge in the group. Then the "But . . ." in the dialogue will have to be explained in that light. This explanation could go various ways. None of the explanations open to the summative theorist seems to be right, however.

One thing the summative theorist could suggest is that the second person is saying something like: "How surprising that you think so differently from most other group members!" But this is not obviously a rebuke at all.

The summative theorist could try construing the response as doing duty for: "How bad of you shamelessly to flaunt your difference from the rest of us!" On this construal the response is indeed a rebuke. But it is a rebuke whose predictability depends on the conformism of a given respondent. The predictability of the predicted rebuke appears not to be so dependent.

The summative theorist might attempt to explain the response as a rebuke to the first person for not having given everyone the benefit of her dissenting opinion during discussion. ("Then we might all have ended up thinking differently!") This explanation is unacceptable for at least two reasons. Suppose the first person had not kept anything hidden, but had changed her mind after the end of the discussion. She could defuse the rebuke, so explained, by telling of her situation. But the predicted rebuke cannot be successfully defused by reference to a change of mind. This rebuke is directed specifically at the statement just made, in its current context.

A second, related problem with this explanation is that the predicted rebuke would apparently be in place whatever the first person had said during the discussion. Thus suppose she had indeed indicated that she thought the last line of "Church Going" was bathetic. Something presumably happened subsequently so that some other view was the one allowed to stand as a view of the group. Perhaps after she had spoken, someone interjected "Oh, come on now! How can you say that!" And then someone else said "Surely this line works very well. It is really quite moving." No one gainsaid this. Given some such context, the first person will still be considered out of order, if she repeats her original statement without preamble.

A rebuke, in general, is a claim that one has done what one ought not to have done. One may think that someone ought not to have done something for a variety of reasons, prudential for instance ("But you're on a diet!"). How, then, is the predicted rebuke to be understood? It appears to be understood as grounded *directly* in the existence of a group view that contradicts what the speaker says. More precisely, the understanding seems to be roughly as follows: once a group believes that *p*, then, *ceteris paribus,* group members are personally obliged not to deny that *p* or to say things that presuppose the denial of *p* in their ensuing interactions with each other. If someone does say something that implies that *p* is not the case, this person should give some sort of explanation, or qualify the statement, saying something like: "In my own view, *p* is not the case." A violation of these obligations is understood to be grounds for rebuke.

It would be good to have an account of collective beliefs that respected the fact that the existence of a group's belief is held directly to generate the noted set of obligations for the group's members.

V. Sketch of a Nonsummative Account of Collective Beliefs: The Joint Acceptance Account

Suppose we take the poetry discussion case as a paradigm.[15] The following account of group belief suggests itself (First Statement):

> A group G believes that p if and only if it is common knowledge in G that the individual members of G have openly expressed their willingness to let p stand as the view of G.

This has a certain opacity, however. Can we do anything about the occurrence of "the view of G" in this statement? It is true that the phrase occurs in an intentional context. But the account still uses the notion of the view of a group, the very notion that it is supposed to explicate and thereby clarify.

Let us start by approaching a different question. Is there any helpful way of characterizing what it is, in this context, to express one's willingness to let p stand as the view of a particular group? I find a clue in the fact that the existence of a group view is held directly to generate a personal obligation for each member of the group. How might that be? I propose that the following complex conception is at issue here. It is understood that in order to bring a group view into being each group member must openly express a certain conditional commitment. It is understood that if *all* openly express such a commitment they are then *committed as a body* in a certain way. That is, it may now be said that they *jointly accept* a certain proposition. It is understood that when a set of persons jointly accepts that p, then each of the individuals involved is personally obliged to act appropriately. Such action consists, roughly, in not publicly denying that p or saying anything which presupposes its denial. More positively, one is publicly to affirm p and to say things that presuppose that p when it is appropriate to do so. There is the escape clause indicated, that if one feels bound to speak against the group view, though one is not ready to challenge its status as the group view, one must preface one's remarks making it clear that one is speaking *in propria persona*.

We can now give an alternative formulation of the nonsummative account of collective belief at issue here (Second Statement):

> (i) A group G believes that p if and only if the members of G jointly accept that p.

(ii) Members of a group *G jointly accept* that *p* if and only if it is common knowledge in *G* that the individual members of *G* have openly expressed a conditional commitment jointly to accept that *p* together with the other members of *G*.

In a more elaborate discussion of this account I would say more about how precisely I prefer to define common knowledge. Details may be waived here.[16] I would also argue for an important aspect of the concept of joint acceptance of a proposition: any set of persons who jointly accept some proposition thereby become a social group or collectivity, intuitively. I cannot attempt to argue for this here.[17] However, I hope that it already has some plausibility, without argument.

I remarked earlier that if ascriptions of beliefs to groups are to appear genuinely apt, they will surely refer to a phenomenon involving a group in more than an accidental way. In the case of the summative views considered, it was possible that a set of persons could fulfill the conditions proposed for group belief (other than the condition that they *already* formed a group) and yet not thereby *become* a group. If I am right, it is otherwise with the nonsummative account proposed. Any set of persons who jointly accept some proposition thereby become a group, if they were not one before.

VI. Comments on the Joint Acceptance Account

VI.i. Against Certain Reductions of the Notion of Joint Acceptance

That *A* and *B* jointly accept that *p* neither entails nor is entailed by their individually accepting that *p*. It is important to stress this.

It might be queried whether joint acceptance of the view that *p* does not come down to this: each of a set of persons has promised to *act as if he believed that p*, just in case the others will make a similar promise. This is not the process envisaged. It is perfectly possible that a set of people exchange promises, or agree, that each will act as if they personally believe that *p*, and carry out such an agreement. However, they do not thereby jointly accept the proposition that *p*. Quite simply, the understandings involved are different. People are understood *jointly* to accept propositions *as a single body*. This is understood to have certain *consequences,* in particular certain consequences about how each one should behave. By and large, these consequences involve acting in such a way that one might be taken personally to believe that *p*.

While jointly accepting a proposition with certain others, it appears to be possible to admit that *personally* one thinks differently. This seems to show that participation in joint acceptance does not even *carry with it* an obligation to act as if one personally accepts something. It seems to show, further, that in committing oneself to joint acceptance of a view, one is not taking upon oneself an obligation *personally to believe* that view.[18]

People who participate in joint acceptance of a proposition *p* by publicly saying that *p* will view their situation in a way indicated by certain common phrases. Perhaps at a deep level, they will view themselves as speaking "in their capacity as group members," "as a member of this body," and so on. "I'm afraid that you did not meet our needs" says the department chairman to one of the unlucky candidates. Conscious of his role as a representative of the department, he speaks as such. He may personally think that this candidate was the best. Or he may have no personal opinion on the matter.

These considerations indicate something of what is going to be needed for the meticulous investigation of what individuals in a particular population *personally* think. Simply asking people for an opinion on some issue may well not be enough to elicit a personal belief. Someone may think he is being questioned in his capacity as the member of some group (a scientific research team, for instance). For this reason, or some other, he may answer in that capacity. Hence the fact that a given individual has checked a certain box must be interpreted with caution.[19]

VI.ii. *Collective Beliefs and Truth*

Given the proposed joint acceptance account of group belief, we may predict that those who help to create and sustain group beliefs will be influenced by many considerations in so doing. The desire that the group belief be true may be one consideration. But one may be willing to countenance the joint acceptance of a view that one does not consider true, or even possibly true. Why might this be so?

Here are three possibilities. First, insofar as it is reasonable to see group views as *negotiated,* then all of the usual constraints of rational negotiation may come into play. For instance, two people may settle on a compromise view, neither believing it. They may be willing to settle on a given resolution, in order that some resolution be achieved.

Again, someone may have a "threat advantage," and so prevail. Second, there are characterological and emotional factors that may influence the role a given individual is willing to play in the process of group view formation. Apathy, passivity, self-deprecation, and so on, could allow some to hold their peace and let what they know is a silly view stand as the group view. The case of conformism deserves special note. One may be susceptible to the influence of a particular party ("I'll say whatever he says") without thinking that his views are especially likely to be correct. One may think that one's imitative behavior will please this person. One may also be influenced by the fact that most others are saying some particular thing, and one wants to go along with the majority, not to appear the odd person out, and so on. One may have little interest in or hope of the truth. (Of course many group views concern vital matters such as values that are at best hard to decide from the point of view of truth.) Third, people may want the view that *p* to become the group view for reasons other than their own understanding that *p* is true. For example, an army commander, who despairs of his platoon's ability to win a given battle, may realize that he will increase the chances of success (meager as they are) by increasing the confidence of his soldiers. He thus goes round making it clear that he wants the group to accept that "We can win!" He believes that, once the group accepts this, the individual soldiers may embolden each other by acting and talking appropriately, hiding their initial personal fear or despair.

Given the preponderance of motives other than truth seeking that may be involved in their genesis, I conclude that there is no obvious reason to think that group beliefs in general have a high probability of truth, or that they are likely to be superior in this respect to the beliefs of individuals.

VI.iii. *The Influence of Collective Beliefs*

There is no need for one who holds a joint acceptance account of group belief to deny a close connection between the collectivity of a belief and its generality at the individual level. If I want the group's belief to be true, then I am surely likely to push my own beliefs as those the group should accept. Even if I am not especially concerned with the truth of the group's view, if there are no special constraints it seems that my own contribution to discussions is likely to be what I personally think. Hence we can assume that there will be many cases where a group's view reflects the view of at least some individuals.

Meanwhile, once formed, any group belief is apt to have an influence on the beliefs of individuals. In the first place, one would expect the personal beliefs of many people eventually to mirror those of their group, whatever views they held prior to formation of the group views. Conscious hypocrisy is probably harder on the nerves than sincerity. If someone feels constrained to mouth and act some doctrine at all public points in her life, then she will have some motivation to come to believe it personally. We can imagine mechanisms by which this could come about: avoidance of evidence conflicting with the doctrine; repression of doubts when they come to consciousness. (This being so, it can obviously be quite a grave decision, from a personal point of view, jointly to accept a particular view with certain others. If one's personal view is distinct from that which is jointly accepted, one automatically faces an unpleasant choice: between an uncomfortable tension within oneself, and erasure of one's own original standpoint.)

A second form of influence is through parents and teachers. A child may tend to presume that his parents believe what they tell him, though they may only be acting as members of a group in so speaking. Knowing them to be more experienced than himself, he may assume that they are right, and so believe what they say.

In sum, getting others to join you in jointly accepting a certain view is a good means of making that view the personal view of those others, of those in a wider circle, and, indeed, of oneself.

VI.iv. *Generality of the Account*

Let me summarize my reasons for preferring something like the proposed joint acceptance account of the semantics of everyday collective belief statements. When we examine some of the fine-grained detail of talk in the context of an acknowledged group belief that p, we find that certain obligations are presumed to have been incurred by each party. One is apparently required to act in a way appropriate to the group's accepting that p as a body. Apparently one is not required to believe (or attempt to believe) p personally. But if one personally believes that p is false, one is required not to express that belief baldly, without preamble, but to make it clear that one is speaking for oneself alone, and not for the group.

The idea of something resembling an *agreement* to accept that p as a body is strongly suggested. Meanwhile, it is implausible to suppose that an explicit verbal agreement is required. The account proposed does not require that people explicitly agree jointly to accept a certain view. Evidently one can communicate one's conditional commitment to participate in joint acceptance in quite subtle, nonverbal ways. It will be understood in advance by all that once everyone has openly expressed such a conditional commitment with respect to some proposition p, then they do jointly accept that p as a body. (I take it that one cannot express the relevant conditional commitment without already understanding this. For unless one understands it, what is expressed cannot have the right content.) Thus joint acceptance can be brought about without explicit comment.

The question of the generality of the account may be raised. There are some contexts in which group belief statements are properly made which may seem to diverge radically from the joint acceptance account. Nonetheless a case can be made for the general relevance, and, indeed, the primacy of the account given. It can be argued to describe the central or basic case of group belief. When we consider other cases where group belief statements can properly be made, it seems that these can be assimilated, in one or another way, to the case I suggest is central. This is also the simplest or most primitive type of case. There is therefore reason to suppose that it provides us with the model by which we extend our talk of group belief to more complex cases.

I can only touch briefly on one complex case here. This is the case where a government believes something, and that belief is ascribed to the group or nation as a whole. Example: "The United States believes that the invasion of Afghanistan was an unconscionable act." Many U. S. citizens have no knowledge of the invasion of Afghanistan. Yet we may allow ourselves to ascribe a belief about this invasion to the nation. I find it plausible to argue that we allow ourselves to do so because we allow ourselves to presume that a certain complex setup exists. We presume that the citizens at large have endorsed the idea that what their government as such thinks may be regarded as what they as a nation think. This presumption can be further articulated in terms of the notion of the joint acceptance of a view. We presume that the citizens have endorsed the idea that they may be regarded as jointly accepting whatever propositions the government itself accepts. In cases where no such presumption is correct, it is not clear that we can properly ascribe the "government's" view to the people in question.[20]

VII. Conclusions on the Joint Acceptance Account

Leaving aside the question of conceptual analysis, I conjecture that the joint acceptance model of collective belief picks out an important, real phenomenon, worthy of investigation in its own right. What has already been said makes clear the importance of phenomena corresponding to this model. Evidently, to use a phrase of Durkheim's, a collective belief on this model has "coercive power." On the one hand, the individual parties to a collective belief necessarily understand that their behavior is subject to a certain constraint, the obligation to speak and act in certain ways. On the other hand, given this intrinsic feature of collective belief, we can expect collective beliefs to affect what individuals personally think. Whatever we as theorists choose to call it, then, collective belief as a jointly accepted view is a dynamic phenomenon, a phenomenon with consequences. A few further points may be mentioned.

On this model one's group's belief may presumably become one's own without one's endorsing any particular reasons for believing the proposition in question. At any rate, collective beliefs do not have to come packaged with collective reasons for believing. They may be so packaged, however. When they are, they will presumably be apt to produce "reasoned" beliefs in individuals, by the usual mechanisms. A special case here is the context of teaching; one often teaches "the reasons" for believing in certain things. Teacher and pupil may jointly accept that this is the evidence for such and such, and so on.

As noted, on this model a group can in principle believe that p even though everyone in it personally believes the opposite. This looks as if it will be an unstable situation in practice. (Recall the Hans Christian Andersen story "The Emperor's New Clothes.") But its possibility raises interesting questions. Which way will things go? Will the individuals' beliefs change? Or will the group's belief explode? On what will this depend?

It would surely be unfortunate if social theorists and others, accepting a summative account of group belief, ignored the existence of jointly accepted views. If I am right, we all have the concept of a jointly accepted view at our fingertips. Indeed, we express that concept when we talk of what groups think, in everyday discourse. And it is expressed when we participate in the thought of a group. Nonetheless, it is not easy to articulate. Perhaps for that reason, if no other, theorists have tended to adopt a summative account of collective belief.

Before concluding I should like to focus briefly on one obvious development of the joint acceptance model of collective belief I have adumbrated here. Social choice theorists often assume that no sense can be given to the notion of a social preference (or a group's preference) except in terms of (some function of) the personal preferences of the individuals concerned.[21] I would argue that this is not so. Given that preferring *A* to *B* is something like accepting that *A* is more desirable than *B*, it is clear that we can give a model of collective preference that is analogous to the joint acceptance model of collective belief.

Clearly the notion of collective preference I have in mind does not involve the notion of a group mind which is independent of the minds and wills of the people involved. It involves, rather, the notion of a meshing set of conditional commitments to accept a certain preference or ranking as a body. I take it to be a real issue whether and when such a preference could ever be regarded as not representing "what *the group* really prefers." Of course one may always question whether what a group has preferred (according to the joint acceptance model) is what it should have preferred, according to some standard of assessment that one deems important.

To conclude: an account of our intuitive concept of group belief as the concept of a jointly accepted view has much to recommend it. Jointly accepted views are important phenomena. A jointly accepted view is not necessarily, as a matter of logic, a view that most of the people in question personally accept. Given a tendency in the literature to assume that the belief of a group is to be defined as a belief that most members of the group personally accept (whether or not it is something else as well), discussions of "collective belief,""shared belief," "social belief," "consensus," "social preference," and so on should start with a careful specification of the intended subject matter. I hope that expression of these personal views of my own will help to produce consensus in all of the senses discussed here.[22]

Notes

1. Shorter versions of this essay, under the title "What is a Collective Belief? Some Considerations," have been presented at the American Philosophical Association meetings, Chicago, 1985; the New Jersey Regional Philosophical Association meetings, Rutgers University, 1985; and at the Universities of Connecticut, Storrs, and Illinois at Urbana-Champaign. *On Social*

Facts, Chapter 5, contains a fuller discussion of collective belief, including more discussion of summative accounts. Important aspects of my nonsummative account are further elaborated in Chapter 15, this volume. I am grateful to many people for discussion, and thank in particular Raymond Geuss, Anne Jacobson, John Tienson, and Steven Wagner for comments on written material.

2. I shall assume that we can talk of *truth* here. Possibly, if collective belief statements are best characterized as metaphorical, some other notion is more appropriate. This issue need not concern us here.

3. "In some cases, which may be called summative, statements about social objects are equivalent to statements otherwise the same that refer explicitly, if at some level of generality, to individual people. To say that the French middle class is thrifty is to say that most French middle class people are" (Quinton [1975], p. 9).

4. Fr. "*consciences*."

5. Cf. Lukes (1973), p. 11.

6. See Durkheim, especially page 56: "If it is general, it is because it is collective." For extended discussions of Durkheim, see *On Social Facts*, Chapter 5, and my later article (1994a).

7. Cf. Durkheim and Mauss (1963), p. 44.

8. In conversation one learned anthropologist, who had, off the cuff, put forward the simple summative account, withdrew it immediately, after I brought up this consideration.

9. Compare Lewis (1969), p. 59: "the cases become more and more unlikely, but no less deserving of exclusion."

10. For further references see Chapter 1, note 4.

11. Bach and Harnish (1979) define a related concept, "mutual belief that *p* in a collectivity *G*." They claim that if and only if something is mutually believed in a group *G*, is it "socially or intersubjectively real for *G*" (p. 270).

12. See Lewis (1975), Schiffer (1972), and Aumann (1976). The account I currently prefer is more complex to spell out but not open to certain familiar objections. See *On Social Facts*, pp. 186–97 and elsewhere. The differences do not affect the points made in this section.

13. There is no space in this essay to do more than state intuitions on this matter. I discuss the everyday concept of a human collectivity at length in *On Social Facts*, especially Chapter 4. See also this volume, Chapter 6 and elsewhere.

14. John Tienson gave a nice example illustrative of this possibility when he commented on my presentation at the New Jersey Regional meetings.

15. On the reasonableness of doing so, see *On Social Facts*. I there argue in particular that *conversations* in general are situations of the same general type. A more formal analogue is a committee in session. Thus the poetry discussion case has both more formal and less formal analogues.

16. For the role of my preferred definition of common knowledge in a "joint acceptance" view of collective belief, see *On Social Facts*. I argue there that

there is an important *family* of concepts akin to that of joint acceptance of a view as sketched here.

17. See *On Social Facts*.

18. If it did carry with it the last mentioned obligation, it would not follow, of course, that anyone had managed to live up to his or her obligation. That is, it would not follow that those who jointly accepted that p actually did believe that p personally. I take it to be harder to change one's views than one's actions, particularly if one is not aware of any new evidence against one's initial view.

19. Cf. Pollock (1955). This excellent discussion rightly casts doubt on the meaningfulness of questionnaire answers in relation to a summative conception of public opinion.

20. Cf. Plato's discussion of the virtue of "moderation" in a city in the *Republic, Book V.* Roughly, his view is that in order for a city to be deemed wise by virtue of the wisdom of a certain small group within the city, all of the citizens must accept that the members of that group are those who properly do the city's thinking.

21. See, for instance, Sen (1970).

22. This last remark, among other things, indicates the obvious possibility of a strong "mixed" model of collective belief in which we require that p be jointly accepted by certain persons, each of whom personally believes that p. My own sense of our everyday concept is that it is not this strong. Meanwhile, as noted, I take the following to be an important empirical question: when do collective beliefs according to the weaker, nonsummative, joint acceptance model give rise to collective beliefs according to the stronger model? If we only had the stronger model, we might not see this question.

8

Fusion: Sketch of a "Contractual" Model

"... love ... is neither you nor him. It is a third thing you must create." (D. H. Lawrence)[1]

"... [In] a good love relationship ... to some extent the two people have become for psychological purposes a single unit, a single person, a single ego." (A. H. Maslow)[2]

"... fusion ... central to all loving." (W. Gaylin)[3]

I. Introduction

The terms "fusion" and "merging," and related phrases, are often used to describe a common and desirable feature of long-term intimate relationships such as marriage. Such terms occur in theoretical contexts in sociology and psychology, as well as in poetry, fiction, and in private thoughts. Sometimes it is said that two "selves" or "egos" merge or fuse.[4] And people may be said to become "a single unit," even "a single person" or "a single ego." (All three phrases are used by Maslow, quoted above.) Often merging is associated with phenomena such as responsibility, care, and concern. The sociologist Pitirim Sorokin writes: "The successes and failures of one party are shared by the others and elicit their concurrence, aid, and sympathy."[5]

Reference to the merging of two selves may be fine as a "picture" of a real process, but how much theoretical illumination does it give us? What is a "self" or "ego" and how can two distinct egos fuse?

In *The Symposium* Plato envisions the fire-god Hephaestus asking two lovers: "Do you desire to be joined in the closest possible union? ... I am ready to fuse and weld you together in a single piece."[6] Lovers may indeed sometimes imagine a complete *bodily* merging of

215

one with the other. But we know *this* does not actually happen. Is there something that *does* happen that might aptly be referred to as the fusion of two people?

In the literature of clinical psychology and family therapy, terms such as "fusion" are often used to refer to an actual phenomenon. However, when the parties involved are an adult couple, this phenomenon is commonly deemed pathological, or at least a sign of immaturity. Thus according to M. Karpel, the term "fusion," when applied to adult couples, refers to the "transactional and experiential phenomenon that is created when two minimally individuated persons form a close, emotional relationship." Karpel contrasts fusion with "dialogue": "a mature relationship between individuated partners."[7] And M. Bowen writes, "In mature families, individual family members are contained emotional units who do not become involved in emotional fusion with others."[8]

The term "fusion" may be an apt label for certain problematic forms of marital relationship. At the same time, many people have obviously thought that something aptly referred to as "fusion" has the capacity strongly to enhance a marriage. Witness my opening quotations from Gaylin, Maslow, and Lawrence. It is this thought that provokes the present essay.

Can one describe an actual phenomenon for which the label "fusion" is apt, and which has the capacity strongly to enhance a marriage? To echo Wittgenstein on meaning, "Is there a model for this?" In this essay I propose one such model.[9]

Fusion in my sense is an actual state of affairs necessarily involving two persons in a symmetrical fashion. It is a state of affairs of which the parties may be expected to be aware: they may be expected to have a "sense of fusion." But fusion is not simply a matter of two persons having a certain sense of their relationship to one another.[10]

The model I shall propose can be characterized as a "contractual" model in a broad sense. Some may find this surprising. Sorokin, for instance, labels relationships involving a high degree of fusion "familistic" while the contrast case is labeled "contractual." Can fusion itself be a function of something resembling a contract or agreement? People may, of course, espouse different ideas as to what is essential to a contract or agreement. Suffice it to say that the model of fusion presented here has some clear affinities with models of human association in classical contractarian political philosophy.[11]

I take the phenomenon I shall refer to as "fusion" in this essay to be central to human social relationships in general. It can be long or short-lived, and admits of degrees: two or more people can be more or less fused together at a given time. Meanwhile, a lasting marriage may well involve an intensive, continuing fusion. Though all fusion has inevitable cost in terms of individual freedom, an intensive continuing fusion has the capacity strongly to enhance a marriage.

In the second section I argue for and sketch a model for the general idea of the fusion of two or more persons. In the third section I discuss why one might think of fusion in my sense particularly in connection with marriage and family relations, and indicate how fusion can enhance matters in these contexts. I stress that fusion can co-exist with a variety of background states of the self, and that this is relevant to the evaluation of the total situation in which it occurs.

II. Fusion

How might we interpret the phrase "fused egos" in the present context? Let us start with an account of a "self" or an "ego." For present purposes I shall make use of the first person singular pronoun "I." An individual person can represent herself as "I," and her qualities, including her goals, values, and beliefs, as "mine." (What we call an "ego"-centric person, by the way, appears to be one who *focuses* to some high degree on what is *hers:* her thoughts, needs, wants, achievements, and so on.) I shall stipulate that a person who makes explicit references to herself in terms of "I" and "mine" *has an ego,* or, equivalently, *is an ego.* Now consider two egos (as defined), Jill and Jack. How might they "merge" or "fuse"?

One idea might be that Jack must make Jill's ideas his own, while retaining his own ideas, and vice versa. An obvious problem arises, though, if, say, Jack is a Democrat and Jill is a Republican. Without difficulty Jack himself can hardly be both a Democrat and a Republican. If, to avoid generating a whole set of inconsistencies in belief, we insist that Jack take on Jill's ideas *while discarding his own,* and vice versa, there seems to be no more reason to call Jack and Jill "merged" than when they had their original ideas. They've just switched sides.

It may be suggested that "fused egos" are (by definition) those who care for each other's well-being: I care both for my own well-being, and for yours, equally, and vice versa. Here again there is the problem of seeing why we should talk of "fusion" here. It is perfectly consistent with the idea of an ego developed so far that egos care deeply about others. (This is also the case with the resembling notion of an agent in game theory with a personal utility function.) I may want you to be happy. I may intend to provide for your future, whatever else I do. If we want some appropriate general definition of "fused egos" or "merged egos," then, this seems the wrong way to go.

It is true that one fairly natural way of expressing the thought that I care for your welfare as I care for my own is to say that I "identify" with you, or, indeed, that I love you. In spite of this, "fusion" seems too strong a term in this connection. In addition, if we define fusion in terms of mutual concern and caring, we cannot explain instances of the latter in terms of fusion. Yet in many discussions fusion is seen as an explanatory concept, something that can help to explain at least some instances of concern and caring. Though its development was not influenced by this idea, the model of fusion that will be presented below will give it such an explanatory character.

I shall now stop focusing on the first person singular pronoun, and turn to the first person plural pronoun—"we." This is quite often invoked in connection with love and marriage, and Sorokin refers to "the egos of the interacting parties" as being "fused together *in one* "we.""[12] Use of "we" cannot of itself solve the problem of providing an articulated model of merging. However, as I shall argue, one can provide a perspicuous account of a phenomenon one might well name "fusion," if one focuses carefully on certain uses of "we" along with the pronominal adjective "our," and so on.[13]

Clearly, someone may represent herself as *part* of a "we" and may represent herself as *participating* in "our" opinions, goals, values, and so on. When is this justified?

Consider "our opinion." Is Jill's use of this phrase justified just in case she and Jack individually hold the same opinion? Perhaps sometimes "our opinion" is used in this way. But in many cases the appropriate interpretation for "our opinion" is not of this "summative" kind. Nor, indeed, is it a necessary condition for the proper use of this phrase that at least some of the parties hold the opinion in question.

As I have argued elsewhere, a paradigmatic situation for "our opinion" is roughly as follows: each of a set of people has openly expressed personal willingness to accept a certain view *jointly* with the others. Once this has happened, joint acceptance of the view is established. It is then appropriate to speak of "our opinion." The process that generates a jointly accepted view is *agreement-like*, though it does not have to involve any explicit agreement. Like those who explicitly agree on something, the participants are, by their own acts, *simultaneously* and *interdependently* "bound" to behave in certain ways. In particular, *it is now incumbent upon the parties to act as the members of a (single) being with the view in question,* at least in certain relevant circumstances. Rebukes of one participant by another are in place for failures to comply with this requirement.[14]

Those who jointly accept a certain view have, in effect, jointly constituted themselves the single subject of a view. They will understand this (since they have the concept of joint acceptance) and now see themselves as constituting in effect, the members of a single being, or, as we might put it, a single "body" or "person."

For an example of this complex phenomenon on the ground, consider a typical statement made in the context of a family. Mr. Jones says, "We think you should be home by midnight, Johnnie." Mr. Jones may himself see no reason why Johnnie should not come home any time he pleases. Ms. Jones, meanwhile, thinks Johnnie should be home by ten, and, if it was up to her, would still make this ruling. But the Joneses have discussed the matter and compromised. They have arrived at what they may properly characterize as "our view"—not his, nor hers, but "ours," and in this case, ours only. Each understands that it is now incumbent upon each one to express "their" view (that is, the compromise view) in front of Johnnie. For instance, if Johnnie says to Ms. Jones, "Must I *really* be home by midnight?", she must answer affirmatively if she does not qualify her answer in some way (see below). Thus the Joneses may be expected to express the compromise view, and behave appropriately. For all Johnnie knows, both hold it personally.

It is important to see that the change in each of the Joneses in generating a view that is, as they say, "ours," is not a superficial one. This is so even when, as above, each personally holds a conflicting view. In particular, neither one is *pretending personally to believe something*. Rather, they now conceive themselves as the members of a single body (or person) that does believe that thing, a status requiring specific behavior on each individual's part. This behavior, not surprisingly, coincides to some extent with that of one who personally believes the thing in question. Consider, however, that Mr. Jones could tell Johnnie, with *logical* propriety, "I personally still think we do not have to be so restrictive." (Most likely it would be imprudent of Mr. Jones to make his own view known.)

"We" may not only have opinions, but also *values, principles of action,* and *aims*. Bob and Sue could have the *joint aim* of cycling from Storrs to Willimantic together. A salient aspect of this case is that Sue and Bob will need constantly to monitor each other's behavior, making sure that they are keeping up with one another. If Bob has a fall, it will be incumbent upon Sue to do something about it. A plausible course of action will be to stop herself, help him up from the ground, and ask if he needs to stop and rest for a while. Here, then, at least the simulacra of caring and concern are likely to come into play.[15]

Those with a joint aim are only obligated thereby to behave in a caring manner insofar as this is necessary to promote their joint aim. Thus the primary joint aim of a given couple, Belle and Ben, could be "keeping Ben happy," and Ben may derive pleasure from hurting Belle. Insofar as Belle has to exist and be capable of suffering pain in order that Ben have his pleasure, Belle's continued survival and her continuing sensitivity to pain, at least, will be a matter of concern for both. This will tend to produce a minimal degree of caring behavior on Ben's part. Clearly, though, that may be all the caring behavior that Belle receives from Ben (or from herself).[16]

I have elsewhere referred to those who participate in a joint belief, or a joint goal, principle, or the like, as the members of a *plural subject*. I have also argued that there is a correlative central sense of the pronoun "we" such that "we" refers to a plural subject.[17] I now suggest that one possible model for *fusion* is that of *plural subject formation,* or *"we"-formation* in the correlative sense. I propose that two egos may be said to have fused just in case the people in question form a plural subject of some kind.

Note that, on this account, an alternative to the phrase "fused egos" is *persons with egos, who fuse* (that is, come to constitute a plural subject). As the example of the Joneses makes clear, the fusion of two egos, on this construal, *does not require the obliteration of the egos in question*. Mr. and Ms. Jones can still *be* egos, on my definition, while being fused in relation the belief that Johnnie should be home by midnight; that is, while jointly believing this. Indeed, each can maintain a personal belief antithetical to their group belief. Their fusion does entail corresponding constraints on their behavior, of course. Some previously possible plans become inadmissible. For instance, Mr. Jones cannot now appropriately plan to tell Johnnie that he is welcome to stay out as long as he likes.

According to this account, it is part of the structure of all fusion that the parties accept an obligation to attend to one another and to act in such a way as to promote their joint "cause." This is most obvious in the case of joint pursuit of an aim, but it is true of jointly accepted beliefs, values, and principles also. Mr. Jones will need not only to watch his own words, but to pay some attention to what Ms. Jones is doing. (It is, one might say, his business.) If he sees that she is about to say the wrong thing to Johnnie, he is both entitled and obliged to step in and do something, if he can, to prevent her from slipping up.

It appears that there is a sense in which the parties to any instance of fusion are obligated to come to one another's aid. By definition, each one is committed to promoting their "cause." When he intervenes with Ms. Jones, Mr. Jones is helping her to fulfill her commitments, along with his own. "Thanks," Ms. Jones might respond, "I nearly slipped up."

All fusion, then, will promote a particular species of aid to another, with a concomitant gratitude on behalf of the person helped. This is one inherent comfort of fusion in general. There can also be some comfort in being noticed. If another person is providing these comforts, one is likely to feel a degree of affection and kindness toward them.

There is, of course, another structural aspect of fusion that seems apt to generate positive emotion. Every instance of fusion provides a basis for a *sense of unity,* even a sense of *intimacy* or *closeness* within the single "we" that is involved. Human beings may tend to find this sense of things gratifying and those gratified in this way are likely to feel some affection and kindness toward those with whom they are fused.

In sum, on my account fusion in general is such that for structural reasons a degree of positive emotion stands to occur between the parties.

III. Fusion in Marriage

On the above construal, fusion is a matter of degree. That is, two (or more) people can be fused together to a greater or lesser extent.[18] Fusion can also be of long or short duration. Two strangers might start talking on a bus and converse until one has to leave. A conversation generally involves a joint aim (conversing with one another) and generates various views that are jointly accepted at least for the duration of the encounter.[19] These conversationalists will, then, be fused temporarily to a degree, in relation to a certain goal and a certain set of views.

If strangers can fuse, why think of fusion in relation to marriage in particular? The answer is clear. Marriage is liable to produce an intensive, long-term fusion.

There is no obvious reason to think that fusion of the kind common in marriage cannot exist without benefit of legal marriage. Marriage, though, is its usual locus in our culture as things stand. There are familiar aspects of marriage in our culture that will help both to encourage and to make salient the special kind of fusion it can involve. Marriage is often entered into in an emotionally charged public ceremony with a public exchange of vows, often under religious auspices, and has legal implications at least some of which are known to the parties.

Marriage, I suggested, is a fruitful field for fusion. Of course a given marriage may contain more or less fusion. But many will involve the following components. First, the parties have one or more major long-term joint projects, such as living together harmoniously for the rest of their lives ("'til death do us part"), creating and maintaining a comfortable home, raising a family, and so on. Such projects generate a plethora of smaller joint projects, both long- and short-term, such as maintaining a joint bank account, buying a car, visiting parents, and taking the kids to the zoo. Second, over time negotiations take place and agreements are reached on a multitude of issues, major and minor, such as whether we can afford to buy a house, who is the best babysitter, and how often we should eat fish. Such agreements arise in part in the course of carrying out joint projects. There are also many random conversations that result in joint acceptance of some proposition, value, or principle. A given issue may be debated many times, and the parties may agree to differ more or less often. (Joint acceptance of the view that you disagree on some issue is itself, of course, an agreement of sorts.) In any case, the parties come continuously jointly to accept numerous beliefs, values, and principles of action. In addition, there is a variety of beliefs and so on that are jointly accepted for a time.

In a situation like this, a host of major and minor projects, and a host of views, values and principles, characterize the same pair, the same "we" at a given time. The parties, then, are fused in many respects. I shall say that the fusion is *intensive*. They are also fused in this intensive way over time. This intensity and continuity of intensity can be expected sharply to stimulate the sense of unity and closeness fusion in general supports.

It is also significant that, in a situation like that described, there is a lot of stability in the way the parties are fused: they continuously sustain certain particular long-term projects, and certain particular views, values, and principles. What I shall call *stable* fusion has its own special import. Even when difficult compromises have been made over an opinion or a principle of action there is some likelihood that when a couple continuously cohabits and interacts, personal preferences will pale or get converted. The couple's practices may, as a psychological matter, so predominate that the individual has no countervailing tendencies any longer. Being committed to acting and speaking a certain view in Mr. Jones's presence, Ms. Jones may eventually lose hold of her own original view: it may cease to be her personal view. Indeed, there is some normative pressure upon her to let this happen. For each party will probably better sustain "our view" in being if they have no countervailing tendencies, and they are committed to sustaining that view as best they can. There is some likelihood, then, that stable fusion will also be *untrammelled*. There will be no countervailing tendencies within the individuals concerned.

Stable untrammelled fusion is likely to be reflected in a fully justified, strong sense of mutual trust. For over time each has trusted the other to do his or her part in promoting their jointly accepted "causes," and the trust has regularly been fulfilled. Moreover, by hypothesis, it has become easy for each one to fulfill that trust. That this is so will most likely be common knowledge between the parties.[20] This will increase their trust in the domains in question. Trusting the other will likely become second nature. This strong mutual trust will itself most likely be common knowledge.

Any situation involving a good deal of stable untrammelled fusion stands to provide both a sense of unity and common knowledge of mutual trust irrespective of what the fusion relates to. Essentially structural or formal features of the situation ensure that this is so. Insofar as a sense of unity and mutual trust themselves provide a degree of comfort or subjective satisfaction, then all such situations stand to engender some positive emotion in the participants, including a degree of positive feeling one for the other.

Meanwhile, it should be recognized that there are a number of importantly different possibilities in a situation where there is much stable untrammelled fusion.

It may be that in a given marriage practically everything is "ours" and the parties have no views, goals, interests, and so on, of their own, or little to speak of. This is a case where the people concerned barely have egos in the sense defined here. Plato sometimes seems to have something close to this as an *ideal* for the members of his "guardian class" in *The Republic*. The opposite pole will be the totally "unfused" ego, the "unjoined person," to use a phrase from Carson McCullers.[21] These types seem possible at least in the abstract. The case of "ego-less" fusion may deserve to be seen as pathological, or simply bad, something that is dangerous at least from the point of view of individual survival. That is something worth pondering. However, it should be stressed that it is not necessary in principle that a large amount of stable untrammelled fusion involve the virtue demise of the ego.

First, in principle each party may personally endorse all the joint values and so on. As already indicated, there exists some normative pressure to organize one's mental life so as to satisfy the commitments of joint acceptance with ease. But this need not involve leaving oneself with no personal views at all. One will satisfy this demand simply by bringing one's own views into line with the jointly accepted views. And, of course, in many cases one will do this easily or not need to change at all. Let us call the case where a joint value or whatever is personally endorsed by each of the parties *positively correlated fusion*. It might be labeled *deep* fusion. One would expect this particular form of fusion to be particularly comfortable for the parties.

Note that each person may or may not have views of their own outside the areas of fusion. This brings us to the other possibility. Even if there is much stable fusion that is completely uncorrelated with any personal views on the topic in question, there may be areas of thought and value that simply do not overlap the areas of fusion. Hence there may not be a total loss of ego. One's spouse may know little about one's work, for instance. One may love going to the ballet and one's spouse may hate it. One hundred years of living together may be incapable of changing these preferences. There is much space for the ego, then, even given the comforts of much stable untrammelled fusion.

Conclusion

Whether a relationship in which much fusion occurs is good overall depends on a number of facts extraneous to the presence of fusion itself. While this is undoubtedly so, fusion as such clearly has the capacity emotionally to enhance a marriage or similar relationship. Particularly when it is stable, it provides a ground for important positive experiences, and, through these, a basis for cherishing and caring for the other person or people. A marriage (or any relationship) in which little fusion develops may have many charms. But, by hypothesis, it will mostly lack ideas, values, principles, and goals shared in the strong sense of joint acceptance. There may be a coincidental complementarity of ideas and values. But there will not be the interlocking commitments of plural subjecthood, with its capacity to generate a sense of partnership (as opposed to mere similarity) and mutual trust. The parties may well feel "loose and separate" from each other, lacking the sense of unity that fusion engenders.

It is clear that fusion does not guarantee that the parties will be subjectively comfortable overall (however others evaluate their union). There could be a marriage involving much fusion in my sense, but where there is also much conflict between the fused and unfused (ego) portions of the individuals concerned. In the extreme case, each of the parties personally strains against each of the jointly held opinions, values, and so on. Here we have much *negatively correlated fusion*. For obvious reasons, this is likely to be uncomfortable for the parties. Perhaps most importantly, each party is likely to be conscious at some level of inner conflict. They may feel "stifled" or "suppressed" all the time. Clearly there can be degrees of conflict here. Even in a situation of negatively correlated fusion, if there is real fusion there, particularly stable fusion, this may help to explain how the situation could still have some attractions in terms of a sense of partnering and "knowing where one is" with the other person.

Fusion as an ideal must, clearly, be viewed with caution. The main point of this essay is to indicate how something aptly named "fusion" is possible, something that has the capacity strongly to enhance a marriage from a subjective point of view.

The word "love" was used in all of my opening quotations. George Eliot has aptly referred to it as that "jack of all words." One hesitates to say "what love is." Meanwhile, it seems quite plausible to suppose that at least the most comfortable cases of stable fusion will involve something worthy of the name "love."[22] Even in cases repugnant to outsiders the sense of unity and mutual trust may be valued, and the parties may see themselves as loving each other—not entirely bizarrely. Love is often associated with a sense of unity, with "being one." And wherever there is much genuine fusion, particularly that which endures, one can see why someone might feel moved to say: "We have created a third thing, and each of us is one of the parts."[23]

Notes

1. Lawrence, *The Rainbow*, p. 176; quoted in Gaylin (1987).
2. Maslow (1953), pp. 75–76.
3. Gaylin (1987), p. 116.
4. See Sorokin (1947), p. 100: "a complete merging of their selves," and (of a contrasting case) "the egos of the parties remain unmerged" (p. 103). I learned of Sorokin's discussion from Lindgren (1988).
5. Sorokin (1947), p. 99; cf. Maslow (1953), p. 76.
6. Plato, *Symposium*, p. 192.
7. Karpel (1976), pp.70–71. Karpel aims to summarize the trend in a body of literature on "fusion" in clinical psychology.
8. Bowen (1965), p. 219.
9. This is based on work that was not itself focused on this particular theme. See in particular *On Social Facts*. The topics of love and marriage are briefly touched upon at pp. 223–25 and 471.
10. Cf. Gaylin (1987), p. 103: "The concept of fusion as I will use it literally means the loss of one's identity in that of another; a confusion of ego boundaries; the sense of unsureness as to where I end and you, the person I love, begin; the identification of your pain with my pain and your success with my success; the inconceivability of a self that does not include you; and the inevitability that your loss will create a painful fracture of my self-image that will necessitate a long and painful rebuilding of my ego during a period of grief and despair."

In this account each party's sense of the relationship appears to be central to fusion. In fact it looks as if fusion can be wholly one-sided (unilateral). It also looks as if our being fused one with another is a matter of each of us having the relevant sense of how things are, while this sense is not answerable to the world in any way. (It could not be mistaken.)

A realistic definition of fusion does not have to make it a function of subjective states in this way. On the account I develop below, *the fusion of two persons is not purely a matter of each party's sense of things.* Fusion in my sense may lead to the type of sense of things Gaylin alludes to, as will emerge.

11. That connection will not be pursued here. But see *On Social Facts,* especially pp. 197–98 and 415–16. See also Chapter 6, this volume.
12. Sorokin (1947), p. 142, my emphasis; see also pp. 100 and 103.
13. There is a detailed discussion of the semantics, broadly construed, of "we" and cognate terms, in *On Social Facts.* See in particular Chapter 4, pp. 167–203, and Chapter 7, pp. 417–27. What follows in the text draws upon that discussion.
14. For further elaboration of these ideas see Chapters 7 and 14, and the introduction, this volume. See also *On Social Facts,* especially Chapter 5.
15. For further discussion of joint aims or goals see Chapter 6. See also *On*

Social Facts, Chapter 4, especially pp. 157–202. On jointly accepted (or group) principles, see Chapter 2 here, and *On Social Facts*, Chapter 6, pp. 373 ff.

16. These last remarks suggest that there is nothing in the concept of a joint aim or jointly accepted view that prevents these from amounting on occasion to a *folie à deux*.

17. "We" may sometimes be used more broadly, but this narrower sense is often at issue. See *On Social Facts*, Chapter 4.

18. The idea that there are *degrees* of fusion is assumed by Sorokin (1947). Though he writes (of such relationships as that of a landlord and tenant) that the egos of the parties "remain unmerged in any real 'we' " (p. 103), he does accept that in such relationships there is a degree of fusion or merging. Cf. Max Weber on "communal" versus "associative" relationships in *Economy and Society*.

19. In *On Social Facts* I argue for a model of conversation in general as the negotiation of jointly accepted views, pp. 294–98.

20. Roughly, something is common knowledge between two persons if it is entirely out in the open between them. For references to the literature, see Chapter 1, note 4. For discussion of the role of common knowledge in plural subjecthood, see *On Social Facts,* Chapter 4, especially pp. 186–97 and 202–3.

21. McCullers (1985).

22. Cf. Lurie (1985).

23. The original version of this essay was drafted as a comment on Lindgren, "Models of Marriage," 1988ms. A version was presented to my colleagues at the University of Connecticut, Storrs, December 1988. I thank everyone present for their comments. Particular thanks to Susan Anderson, Len Krimerman, and Carol Masheter for written comments. I alone am responsible for the views expressed here. In addition, I thank Bob Moffat for his recent reference to Lon Fuller (1969), Chapter 1, in connection with my discussion of the not-necessarily-explicit agreement-like process by which jointly accepted views and such, and their associated obligations, are formed. I have not yet had a chance carefully to study Fuller's discussion at this point, but there does seem to be at least some congruence in our thoughts. See for instance Fuller's reference to "the patterns of a social fabric that unites strands of individual action." He goes on: "A sufficient rupture in this fabric must—if we are to judge the matter with any rationality at all—release men from those duties that had as their only reason for being, maintaining a pattern of social interaction that has now been destroyed" (p. 22; see also the following paragraph). Tempting though it is, there is neither space nor time, at present, to compare and contrast my views and Fuller's.

9

On the Question Whether Language Has a Social Nature: Some Aspects of Winch and Others on Wittgenstein

I. Introduction

That *language is social* has become something of a commonplace among philosophers and others. Doubtless there are many possible ways of explicating the claim that language is social. Some of these will make it obviously true, or probably true as an empirical matter: clearly an important function that a shared language can fulfill is interpersonal communication; probably individual members of the biological species *homo sapiens* will not come to use language unless they grow up among language speakers and so on. Meanwhile, it has been held that there are philosophical arguments that lead to the more general conclusion that language as such has a social nature. Such arguments are presumed to hold for any language used by whomsoever, for whatever purpose. Many believe that Wittgenstein has put forward effective arguments of this sort in the *Philosophical Investigations.*[1] Clearly, what precisely is at issue when it is claimed that language as such has a social nature remains in need of further explication.

In this essay I focus on two claims that occur in much expository writing on Wittgenstein. They do not occur without reason, but are clearly based on remarks of Wittgenstein's. However, both of these claims must be handled with care. If they are not, the route to a thesis about the social nature of language may seem easier than it is, and almost certainly easier than Wittgenstein thought that it was. I should note at the outset that my sense of Wittgenstein's own position has been influenced by Saul Kripke's interpretation of the central line of thought about language in the *Investigations*.[2]

My most general aim in this essay is not so much to discuss the details of Wittgenstein's difficult text, or those of particular commentators, but rather to make clear the problematic nature of the two central claims found in much existing argumentation regarding the social nature of language.

The first claim I discuss is what I shall call the "intelligibility claim." This may itself be regarded as a possible explication of the claim that language as such is social, and has been regarded by many as the central thesis about language to be found in Wittgenstein. Here are various versions of the intelligibility claim. (Each one of (1)–(5) starts with "There cannot be a language that" and continues slightly differently.)

There cannot be a language that:

(1) "another person cannot understand" (Wittgenstein, sec. 253);
(2) "could not possibly be understood by anyone other than the speaker" (Linsky, p. 172);
(3) "not merely is not but cannot be understood by anyone other than the speaker" (Malcolm, p. 182);
(4) "it is logically impossible that anyone but the speaker should understand" (Thomson, p. 183);
(5) "is private" (Wittgenstein, sec. 269).

and

(6) "What is ruled out in the . . . private language argument is not the imaginary soliloquist (solitary or in groups) but one whose concepts, rules, and opinions are essentially unshareable rather than contingently unshared. Wittgenstein's argument would not lose its point even if we possessed innate concepts" (Hacker, p. 222).[3]

I shall argue that in spite of the sense Wittgenstein's expositors evidently have that their formulations make precise what Wittgenstein wishes to claim, all these locutions subsume at least two importantly distinct theses. One of these, I shall argue, appears intuitively to be relatively trivial and easy to accept, while the other is prima facie false and in clear need of very strong support, as is any strongly counterintuitive doctrine. Meanwhile, the existence of the kind of ambiguity involved could obviously have the effect of lending unwarranted support to an otherwise counterintuitive claim, as well as more generally obscuring important issues.

The second claim that I shall address here—the claim that a standard of correctness is necessary or, for short, "the standard of correctness claim"—is derived by many commentators from what are among the most quoted passages in the *Investigations,* in part from section 258:

> Let us imagine the following case. I want to keep a diary about the recurrence d a certain sensation. To this end I associate it with the sign "S" . . . I impress on myself the connection between the sign and the sensation.—But "I impress it upon myself" can only mean: this process brings it about that I remember the connexion right in the future. But in the present case I have no criterion of correctness. One would like to say: whatever is going to seem right to me is right. And that only means that here we can't talk about "right."

and related remarks such as "justification consists in appealing to something independent" (sec. 265).

From these and other passages commentators have constructed an argument that has been supposed to support the thesis that language is social, in some form of that thesis. I believe that in the form in which many have conceived of and presented this argument, it contains a crucial lacuna, which arises, in effect, from insufficient attention being paid to one possible application of the idea of a standard of correctness. This is not to say that Wittgenstein's own argumentation contains this lacuna. Rather, his remarks can be seen as having been torn from their larger context, with the effect of leaving out an essential part of his own argumentation.

II. Winch on Wittgenstein

The intelligibility claim and the standard of correctness claim are both salient features of one quite influential exposition of Wittgenstein, that of Peter Winch in a well-known work in the philosophy of social science, *The Idea of a Social Science.* Winch argues here for the social nature of concepts, language, and action, in ways explicitly inspired by Wittgenstein. His arguments are based on what he takes to be Wittgenstein's views on language and rules; the main exposition is given in a section entitled "Rules: Wittgenstein's Analysis" in the second chapter of his book. Many whose primary interest has been the philosophy of social science have first encountered Wittgenstein's thought through these pages, and much time has been devoted to critical discussion of Winch's "Wittgensteinian" position, by both professional philosophers and social scientists.[4]

To focus my discussion, I shall concentrate to a large extent on Winch's formulations of the claims in which I am interested. I should stress at the outset that I shall not be attempting a complete survey of the section from which these formulations are drawn.[5] The section is highly compressed and often rather obscure. The formulations I shall focus on are clearly regarded by Winch as expressions of crucial points, however, and what I set out to argue here is, in part, that taken in themselves these formulations are importantly problematic. Among other things, I shall argue that certain natural, if "naive," and perhaps ultimately untenable ideas about the use of language are likely to affect an uninitiated reader's response to Winch's formulations. In one case, intuitive assumptions may muddy understanding of what is being said. In the other, a clear understanding that certain intuitive ideas are regarded as inadmissible is required if an argument that is presented is to make much sense. Since these ideas are the natural ones, their supposed untenability must be made clear. I am of course aware that many Wittgenstein aficionados will take it that Wittgenstein has demonstrated the untenability of these ideas. But any purported *exposition* of Wittgenstein's argumentation needs to make as clear as possible both why and that these understandings are untenable. Otherwise, at certain crucial points, what is being said will be more obscure—and much less persuasive—than is necessary.

In what follows, though Winch purports to expound Wittgenstein, I shall generally refer to "Winch's" assumptions, conclusions, and so on. Since Winch evidently endorses the claims in question, and it is more questionable whether Wittgenstein would do so, this is clearly the least question-begging thing to do.

Let me sketch a couple of preliminary points about the relation of language to rules as Winch sees them. Winch says things that suggest that he sees us starting with the following theses as acceptable to all.

(1) If someone uses a word in a certain sense on a certain occasion, then he grasps a rule that he takes to "govern the use of the word." To give an example: when I say "that's a blue mountain," if I use the words "blue" and "mountain" in different senses, then I associate different rules with these two words.

(2) In the case of a term like "mountain," I will call certain things "mountains." A given rule for the use of the word "mountain" will

determine what things I may correctly call "mountains." It will, in other words, and roughly, determine for every thing in the world whether or not it is correctly called a "mountain."

(3) To follow such a rule correctly is to "go on" in one's linguistic practice in accordance with that particular rule. Winch evidently sees Wittgenstein as proposing an "analysis" of "the concept of following a rule" that is involved in the above theses or premises. I shall consider some of Winch's statements about rule following in terms of these starting points and ask: how plausible, intuitively, is what Winch tells us about language, rules, and rule following?

Winch's summary of Wittgenstein's conclusions runs as follows:

> What Wittgenstein insists on . . . is, first, that it must be in principle possible for other people to grasp [any rule a person is following] and judge whether it is being correctly followed; secondly, that it makes no sense to suppose anyone capable of establishing a purely personal standard of behaviour if he had never had any experience of human society with its socially established rules. [op. cit., p. 33]

III. Meaning-Shareability versus Meaning-Identifiability

Let us first consider the point that it must be "in principle possible for others to grasp a person's rule and judge when it is being correctly followed." This evidently involves a version of what I have called the intelligibility claim: someone's language or the meaning of someone's words must be intelligible to or graspable by others. As I have already indicated, such a view about what Wittgenstein stresses, even about his whole doctrine of language, is not peculiar to Winch.

Now one thing I want to point out is that this sort of claim is ambiguous. On one reading it expresses something that is immediately plausible from an intuitive point of view. On another, it expresses something much stronger, which is at least not so immediately plausible. In this part of my discussion I shall not use the term "rule," but will speak rather, and more colloquially, of using a word in a certain sense or grasping a concept, and what is intuitively involved in these activities.

First, let me say what I think is probably is a truth about language as intuitively conceived. (This statement will be rough, but it should indicate the logical structure of the point.)

(1) If a person, *P1,* uses a word in a certain sense (with certain semantic properties) then there could be another person, *P2,* who uses that word in that sense (with those properties).

To put this succinctly: senses or meanings are in principle shareable. The analogous point for concepts runs:

(2) If *P1,* has grasped concept *C,* then there could be another person, *P2,* who grasps that concept.

In other words, concepts are shareable.

I do not want to argue for the truth of these claims given our intuitive understanding of what concept grasp or language use is, though I believe that they do reflect this understanding. Let me just deal, briefly, with one possible objection. This concerns those of someone's concepts that relate to the felt or phenomenological qualities of their experiences. Could another person have *those very concepts?* It seems that, from an intuitive point of view, this may be answered affirmatively: surely one person, *P2,* could in principle have experiences with the same felt qualities as those of another person, *P2.* (Clearly this is *not* to say that *P1* could experience *P2's* experiences.) But if so, then, surely, *P1* could in principle have the concept of any phenomenological quality that *P2* experiences. This could be so, whether or not the people in question know, or have any way of telling, that they share the concept in question.[6]

It may seem a little strong to think of claims (1) and (2) above as claims about the *social* nature of language or thought. For one thing, though more than one person or individual is mentioned in this formulation, I do not think that just any state of affairs in which two people are involved (even when both are actual) is properly described as a social state. Nor does it seem, prima facie, that the (potential) relationship between *P1* and *P2* here—viz., their sharing a given concept—is enough to give us one.[7]

The nub of claims (1) and (2) may, in fact, seem to be expressible in terms that do not mention "concrete" individuals at all, as follows:

(3) concepts (or meanings) are objective particulars.

Given that something is an objective particular, it would seem that it must be, in as sense, "open to all," provided that they have the requisite capacities and experiences, if any. Someone might object to

(3) as begging the question in favor of Platonism, perhaps as beginning to move away from "prephilosophical" intuition. However, I suspect that whether any form of Platonism about concepts is right or wrong, a form of Platonism is a very natural view. I am not, of course, claiming that any nonphilosopher you ask will say "of course concepts are objective" but that a view so expressible is naturally inferred from ordinary modes of thought and talk. (Perhaps one might allude to such garden-variety dialogues as: "Do you get the idea?"; "Yes, I think so"; etc.)

Let us in any case return now to (1) and (2), the theses about the shareability of concepts and meanings: these surely have some plausibility from a prephilosophical point of view. Let us say that these claims express a condition of *meaning-shareability* or *concept-shareability*.

A condition of meaning-shareability such as that noted must be distinguished from what I shall call a condition of *meaning-identifiability*, which would be of the following general form:

(4) If one individual, *P1*, uses a word in a certain sense, then some other individual, *P2*, should in principle be able to discover that *P1* is doing so.

In other words, someone else should be able to discover something about *P1*, in particular, to discover what he means by the word in question.

Now, Winch seems to hold to a rather strong form of meaning-identifiability condition. His various formulations of what must be in principle possible, in their context, suggest that he holds to something like this:

(5) If *P1* follows a rule *R* it must be possible for someone else to tell that this is so *by monitoring P1's behavior* (including the external circumstances in which *P1* utters sentences containing the term in question).

Sometimes the idea is expressed more behaviorally, as follows for instance:

it must be possible "for someone else to grasp what [he] *is doing,* by being brought to the pitch of himself *going on that way* as a matter of course." [p. 31, my stress]

These claims regarding the potential role of a rule-follower's overt behavior are surely not immediately acceptable. I cannot mention all the difficulties here, but will just refer to one natural objection.

Note that the claims made seem to be somewhat complex: a person's following a given rule in his use of a word is supposed to carry with it sufficient behavioral accompaniment to ensure that another person would:

(a) be able to grasp the rule involved on the basis of the behavior;

and

(b) be able to tell that the person in question has grasped it.

(Cf. Winch, p. 30: "it is only in a situation in which it makes sense to suppose that somebody else could in principle discover the rule that I am following that I can intelligibly be said to follow a rule at all.")

The natural objection in question involves a familiar type of example. Suppose someone has two distinctive types of ache in her shoulder which she, in soliloquy, calls "*x*-type" and "*y*-type" aches. There are no clear behavioral differences or environmental features associated with the phenomenologically distinct types of ache. Perhaps she is paralyzed. She frequently exclaims: "Oh, I have an *x*-type ache . . . ," "Now I have a *y*-type ache." She has, in other words, grasped, and continues to follow, rules for the use of the words "*x*-type" and "*y*-type." Intuitively this seems easy to imagine and the description has nothing obviously self-contradictory about it. Yet it is pretty clear that all else being equal no one could, on the basis of the behavioral evidence, grasp the rules for use of "*x*-type" and "*y*-type" that she is following, and so know that she has grasped those particular rules.

An apparent contrast case, I suppose, is that where someone who is judged to be "of sound mind" uses a term like "tree" while pointing to various items in the "public" world. From such a series of ostensive uses one may (as we would say) get to grasp a concept, and have reason to suppose it is the concept the speaker grasps (though not conclusive reason).

Now, why might someone be inclined to deny that, after all, the sensation case is a possible scenario? I note that though Winch ultimately allows that

It is . . . possible, within a human society as we know it, with its established rules of language and institutions, for an individual to adhere to a *private* rule of conduct [p. 33]

he insists that it must always be possible for others to "grasp that rule and judge when it is being correctly followed." This seems to rule out the sensation case, insofar as the "grasping" and the judgments in question are to be based on a putative rule-follower's behavior.

In answer to the question, why might someone be inclined to accept an insistence on "graspability" on the basis of behavior, let me first refer back to the plausible condition of meaning-shareability that I noted earlier. I find it interesting to note that, given a certain form of ambiguous formulation, whose ambiguity may easily not be noticed, it is easy to slip from this to a strong meaning-identifiability condition.

Consider the following formulation:

(6) If *P1* follows a rule, it must be possible for someone else, *P2*, to come to grasp *P1*'s rule.

This could be interpreted as stating the requirement *either* that *P2 come to grasp a certain rule,* or that *P2* come to learn something *about P1* (as well as grasping a certain rule).

Many of Winch's formulations, and those of others, seem to be ambiguous in this way. One also finds what may be unconscious shifts in the literature. Once one has become attuned to the ambiguity I have in mind, passages in various authors become unclear, and seem to call for more perspicuous formulation.

Consider, for instance, the quotation that I gave earlier, from Hacker's *Insight and Illusion.* This is an account of the point of Wittgenstein's "private language argument," in terms of the essential "shareability" of concepts. It hardly seems ambiguous, apparently expressing a point that is immediately plausible intuitively; that is, what I chose to call the concept-shareability point. To propound this point hardly seems like a possible philosophical breakthrough, however; certainly not an anti-Platonic one. Does Hacker not mean something stronger? Just previously to the passage I quoted, he in fact wrote:

> The necessary conditions involved in the existence of language (and hence of thought) imply . . . possible sociality, . . . the possibility of interpersonal discourse. [p. 222]

Now mere concept-shareability does not in itself seem to imply the possibility of interpersonal discourse, if "to imply" is read as "to be sufficient for." In a case like that of the *x*-type and *y*-type sensations mentioned earlier, two people might, intuitively speaking, both have such sensations without any behavioral correlate: they might even use the same terms to refer to them, but it is hard to think that they could have something we would call genuine communication over their use of "*x*-type" and "*y*-type," insofar as they would presumably have no adequate way of telling whether they did indeed use their terms in the same way. (We can assume that the occurrences of the different sensations seem to conform to no regular pattern in either case.) Concept shareability is, intuitively, only a *necessary* condition of true "interpersonal discourse." While it is fairly evident that Hacker in fact wants to make the stronger point, i.e., to refer to the meaning-identifiability thesis, his summary of his point in terms of *shareability* can only tend to confuse the issue.

Again, writing of Frege's views on language, Michael Dummett has said that

> Frege insisted on the objective character of sense: sense is something which can be communicated from one individual to another (in a way in which he thought mental images and the like cannot).[8]

Now if what I have said so far is right, this statement of Frege's view should seem puzzling. In general the intuitive connection between objectivity and communicability is by no means clear. Apart from questions about the proper exegesis of Frege in particular, it seems that in emphasizing the objectivity of senses or meanings one might be expected to have in mind the intuitive shareability of meanings or concepts. Two speakers can use a word in one and the same sense, intuitively speaking, while —to allude to Dummett's statement—they cannot associate one and the same mental image with it. Though the shareability or objectivity of senses may be a necessary condition for communication to take place, it does not, once again speaking intu-itively, *imply* communicability. Communication might fail because of a lack of meaning-identifiability, as I have stressed above. Sensitivity to the distinction stressed in this section makes Dummett's remark on Frege puzzling; it appears to stand in need of further explication or perhaps revision.

If someone *has* slipped to a meaning-identifiability condition via the ambiguity I have pointed out, he may feel that some behavioral or environmental correlate of language has to be essential, since how else could other people be expected to have any confidence they have learned the rule one is following? Thus we have a fairly simple route, via an ambiguity, to Winch's claim that:

the language in which we speak about our sensations must be governed by criteria which are publicly accessible. [p. 33]

(Winch does not elaborate on what it is to be "governed by criteria.")

I believe that once one has accepted a strong meaning-identifiability condition it may be possible to find chains of relatively simple reasoning from a priori principles even to Winch's strong conclusion about the logical necessity for a language user actually to have been a member of a society at some time (though I do not have room to go into this here). Meanwhile, a meaning-identifiability thesis in terms of the "availability to others" of one's language through correlated nonlinguistic behavior and circumstances might in itself, I suppose, be termed a thesis about the "social nature" of language. It implies, at any rate, that one individual cannot use a language unless others could, by observing him or her, get to share his or her language and know that they share that language. To have a language, then, would involve being at least potentially part of a linguistic community. It is perhaps more natural or perspicuous, however, to put the immediate implication of meaning identifiability in terms of the "public" rather than the "social" nature of language. The notion of "publicity" itself, however, is a somewhat slippery one.

One thing that strong meaning-identifiability clearly implies here is that one's language must be "public" in the sense of not residing, as it were, "in the sphere of the mind." (Recall section 358 of the *Investigations*, where Wittgenstein's interlocutor exclaims that surely "meaning" something by a word is what gives language sense, and is "something in the sphere of the mind.") This explication of "publicity" still leaves things open, evidently. As the foregoing discussion of Dummett on Frege suggests, we might think of something as not residing in the sphere of the mind, for the reason that it is an abstract, objective particular. In the case of strong meaning-identifiability, however, the publicity of language is not its necessary relation to an abstract objective particular, but rather its openness to everyone's view in the way in which tables and chairs are open to view: its residing in the physical world of objects open to sensory perception. Strong meaning-identifiability seems to imply that to have a language is to have a body or at least to be able to affect the rest of the world in some way, so it would be logically impossible for a disembodied spirit, detached from the rest of the world, to talk or think "in language."[9]

I do not want to claim that a strong meaning-identifiability thesis of some perhaps rather subtle kind may not be supportable by argument.

Winch himself, having repeated a claim of this sort a number of times, does present what looks like a supporting argument in favor of it, which is what I want to look at next.

My main point in this section has been that whereas it may be that intuition (perhaps I should say "naive" intuition) does assume that *meanings are shareable,* there is no quick and easy route from this idea to *strong meaning-identifiability*, in terms of accompanying non-linguistic behavior and external circumstances. In particular, one must guard against simply confusing the latter with the former claim.

IV. The Appeal to the Need for "External Checks"

In a passage toward the end of his exposition of Wittgenstein on rules, Winch presents what seems intended as a self-contained argument for strong meaning-identifiability, for the idea that, roughly, it is a necessary condition of one person *P1*'s use of language that there be behavior correlated with his utterances of words that is sufficient to enable others to discover what rules *P1* is following.

As this argument is presented, it appears that Winch believes that strong meaning-identifiability will follow directly from some simple and obvious facts that everyone will accept. Before presenting the argument Winch makes a variety of other points. Obviously, a full account of his work must take account of these, but nonetheless it is important to consider whether the argument in question has the complete and obvious character suggested by the passage I consider. Other expositors have presented more or less the same argument as relatively self-contained and based on obvious assumptions about the nature of rules as "standards of correctness."[10] Probably in some cases later expositors have been influenced by Winch's own exposition.[11] Meanwhile, in viewing the argument as complete in this way expositors seem ultimately to be relying largely on *Investigations,* section 258, quoted earlier. Whether or not Wittgenstein himself saw this passage as a self-contained argument from obvious premises is, however, open to question. Let me now look at the details of Winch's presentation.

I shall first quote or paraphrase three salient remarks of Winch's that might be taken as truistic and then turn to a fourth that can be argued to involve a crucial gap from the point of view of "naive intuition." Here, then, are some of Winch's claims in what looks like an argument in support of strong meaning-identifiability.

(1) The notion of following a rule is logically inseparable from the notion of *making a mistake:* if it is possible to say of someone that he is following a rule, that means that one can ask whether he is doing what he does correctly or not. (p. 32, Winch's stress)

(2) A mistake is a contravention of what is *established* as correct. (ibid., Winch's stress)

(3) Whether or not I make a mistake in following a rule for the use of a word cannot just be a matter of my decision or say-so.

So far, one might say, so good. Intuitively speaking, that is, without special argumentation, these points might well be held to be immediately acceptable.

Then we get to:

(4) If I make a mistake in say, my use of a word, *other people must be able to point it out to me.* If this is not so, I can do what I like, and there is no external check on what I do; that is, nothing is established. (ibid., my stress)

One might think here that Winch is claiming something like this: that all rules must be socially established, that, if you like, genuine rule-following is to be seen as a collective activity requiring a multiplicity of participants. Winch, in fact, quickly forestalls any such idea. He notes that

it is, of course, possible within a human society as we know it, with its established language and institutions, for an individual to adhere to a *private* rule of conduct. [pp. 32–33]

So his final conclusion is roughly speaking this:

(5) One who follows any rules must initially be part of a community and party to "socially established rules" (p. 33)—one's first rule-following must be the following of socially established rules.

Regarding the relation of (4) and (5) to strong meaning-identifiability, (4) must be held to imply it for all rules I follow, (5) at least for those that come first in time. (Nonetheless, Winch seems in fact to hold a strong meaning-identifiability thesis for all meanings.)

Now, how could Winch or anyone else think that (4) or (5) follow from the truisms about following rules and mistakes noted above? Let me review what his drift seems to be, once again.

We start by accepting the apparently innocuous or agreed-upon idea that a rule governing the use of a word ("mountain," say) will determine what things I may correctly call "mountains." It will place constraints on such behavior. We then imagine someone "going on" in a certain way, calling each of a certain set of things "mountains." We ask: what can the standard or criterion of correctness be for such "calling"? There has to be one if he is indeed following a rule. (So far, so good.) We are told: the "reactions of others can and indeed must be available so as to serve." For, to repeat Winch:

> it is contact with other individuals alone which makes possible the external check on one's actions which is inseparable from an established standard.

Consider, however, some apparent logical possibilities. Most generally, "surely it is not self-contradictory to suppose that someone, uninstructed in the use of any existing language, makes up a language for himself."[12] Let me now, like Ayer, Strawson, and others, develop a version of a standard type of thought-experiment, a kind of "Crusoe" case.[13]

It does not seem self-contradictory to suppose that someone, call her "Maude," comes into being on a desert island and, by hypothesis, uses and "goes on" using the word "mountain" in the sense of mountain (perhaps as part of sentences using other words also in certain senses). But if this is so, it seems that, by hypothesis, Maude grasps a concept or rule for the use of the term "mountain." (This was one of the points that I noted seemed implicit starting points in Winch's discussion.) This, then, has to be something Maude does for and by herself (by hypothesis).

Now, why can't we accept all of Winch's truisms as true for her? If she *has* grasped a *rule*, this rule *will* by its nature determine when "mountain" is used correctly and when not, i.e., if she wishes to accord with this rule then it is determined what is correctly called a "mountain" and what isn't. So, of course, we can "ask whether she is doing what she does correctly or not"; and *the rule she grasps will establish what is correct.* Whether or not she makes a mistake with respect to this rule is not up to her; it is a function of the nature of the rule in question. It seems, then, that Maude can have a language and this is a function of facts about her considered in isolation from any society. In particular, it is a function of her grasping "in her head" as it were, a certain determinate concept or rule, which provides the standard for her rule-following linguistic behavior.

This suggests that whether or not we must accept some form of "society"- or "community"-based account of what it is to misapply a term or use it incorrectly is a matter of finding some flaw in the story about Maude (and similar stories). Winch, however, does not speak directly to this issue in presenting his argument from the possibility of mistakes.

In response to claims by Strawson and Ayer about possible language using isolates, Winch writes, roughly, that they have begged the question in saying that Crusoe "has a language." By what right do they speak of his having a language here, Winch asks. What I want to stress is that if we start from the standpoint of what seems obvious intuitively, it must be shown that those who write of language-using isolates have no right to do so. In other words, this question may indeed be begged, until it is shown that it is incoherent or otherwise inadmissible. Some flaw must be clearly shown in the picture of Maude's situation that I have sketched.[14] Clearly, appeal to the necessity of an (established) standard of correct use is not enough.

V. The Pull of the "Private Model" of Rules

I have already indicated the nature of the crucial omission in the above argument from the necessity of an (established) standard. Let me now say some more about it. Following Saul Kripke, one can see Wittgenstein's main thrust in the *Investigations* as an attack on a certain natural idea; the idea, roughly, that we "grasp" determinate concepts or rules "in our heads" or "in our minds" at some moment, and that these concepts or rules are such that they justify our use of words and provide standards of correctness for our continuing use of the words we associate with them.[15]

What precisely is Wittgenstein attacking? Not that we can properly say things like "He's grasped this concept," but rather a certain model of rule-following or concept-grasp which—with Kripke—we may call the "private model" of rule-following.[16]

Why is this model worth attacking? Because it is a very natural one. According to Wittgenstein, however, a private model of rule-following or concept grasp is ultimately impossible to articulate intelligibly.

Part of the attack is directed at the suggestion that to grasp a concept or use a word in a certain sense is to contemplate something like an explicit verbal formulation of a rule—say, " 'red' means *red*"—or a particular mental image or picture—of a fuzzy red patch, say. The problem with this suggestion, as is well-known by now, is that such a formulation or picture can be applied or interpreted in infinitely many ways. Evidently, association with such a "rule" cannot determine the correctness of future uses of a word; if a similar type of "rule" is invoked to provide an "interpretation" of the original, the problem of *its* application or interpretation will arise in the same way. Such "rules," then, seem not after all to provide any way of determining whether a word is used in accordance with them, or whether things are sorted in accordance with them. It is ultimately unclear, given this version of the "private model," what "in accordance with them" could *mean*.

There is another version of the "private model" of rules that seems better to characterize our intuitive understanding of the matter. This idea too is attacked by Wittgenstein, in part, it seems, because it is too inarticulate, too mysterious. In the case of a mathematical function, say addition, someone might suggest that in grasping the concept of addition, or grasping the meaning of "plus" where it means *plus,* there somehow comes into our mind the whole of the infinite table that specifies the addition function. This table will then determine how "plus" is to be used, or what it is to *add*. Evidently, in this conception, the table is not something which needs interpreting; it is, if you like, an interpretation itself. No question about its "application" is left open. In nonmathematical cases the suggestion may be even less precise. It may be said that what comes into our minds when we grasp the concept of redness, say, and associate it with the word "red," is just *something* that determines how the word "red" is to be used, or determines a way in which things are to be sorted. *It* determines the set of correct and incorrect uses of "red."

Now this conception may be strange and difficult; it may ultimately be incoherent or be rejected on other grounds. Nonetheless, it is surely this, if anything, which comes closest to our basic "naive" intuitive conception of concept grasp and of meaning something by a word. It is, I believe, ultimately this version of the private model which most needs attack, if one is to argue for the social nature of language as such. (One way of attacking it, which Wittgenstein at one point takes up—see below—is to say that it hardly constitutes a *model* at all.)

Wittgenstein himself does address this picture in many places. To cite just two:

It may now be said: "The way the formula is meant determines which steps are to be taken." What is the criterion for the way the formula is meant? . . . [*Investigations*, sec. 190]

"It is as if we could grasp the whole use of the word in a flash." . . . have you a model for this? No. It is just that this expression suggests itself to us. [Sec. 191]

I do not aim to discuss here whether Wittgenstein's attack on the private model succeeds, nor to discuss his alternative picture of language.

At any rate, unless we have shown that there are deep, indeed insuperable, problems connected with the private model or conception of rules, it seems that it will always remain an option, so that no argument appealing simply to "what, then, could provide the standard of correctness" can lead immediately to "only the standard of others' agreement" or whatever. Anyone who gives the impression that there is an easy quick argument from the need for standards of correctness to the need for rules to be located in some way in communities surely both misrepresents Wittgenstein (if he is their acknowledged source) and misrepresents the crucial issues.[17]

Notes

1. See, for instance, Dummett (1978): "Frege's account gives insufficient recognition to the social character of language. Of course, it was the later Wittgenstein who insisted most strongly on this" (p. 424). See also Winch (1958), especially Chapter 2, to which I shall shortly refer again. Outside the circle of professional philosophers, particularly among social scientists, many would echo the statement of anthropologist Clifford Geertz in a famous article: "Culture is public because meaning is. You can't wink . . . without knowing what counts as winking. . . . The generalized attack on privacy theories of meaning is, since early Husserl and Wittgenstein, so much a part of modern thought that it need not be developed once more here." (Geertz [1975], Chapter 1, p. 12.) That "meaning is public," then, appears to be part of current intellectual apparatus, and Wittgenstein is one of its acknowledged discoverers.

2. Kripke (1982).

3. See Wittgenstein (1958) (I generally refer to this work as the *Investigations* here); Linsky (1957); Malcolm (1957); Thomson (1971); Hacker (1971).

4. Some references here are: MacIntyre (1967), pp. 95–114; Ryan (1970); Hollis (1977).

5. I discuss Winch's text more fully in *On Social Facts*, Chapter 3, sec. 3.

6. Saul Kripke points out to me that, according to Bertrand Russell, thesis (1) above would be false for Russell's "logically proper names," which refer to momentary, nonrecurring mental particulars. We do not think of our everyday language of sensation types as being of this sort. Russell's is, evidently, a very special kind of language.

Wittgenstein himself may have thought that the meanings of the words of his hypothetical "private" language would be intrinsically unshareable, not just incommunicable. But this view surely contradicts what we would think at first blush, and certainly cannot be assumed as intuitively evident: rather, I have suggested, the contrary will be the natural assumption.

7. The fact that Jones in Galaxy *J* had concept *C*, and that Xenon in Galaxy *X* also had concept *C*, would not, prima facie, be an example of an intuitively social fact, though it may be a necessary condition of various intuitively social facts, such as Jones's buying a car from Xenon.

The question of what it is for something to have a social nature is the most general theme of *On Social Facts*.

8. Dummett (1978), p. 424.

9. This, it seems to me, would be quite a powerful conclusion to reach. Though many others may find it quite congenial, I myself find it hard to accept the idea that a disembodied mind is a conceptual or metaphysical impossibility. . . . But I should proceed to more mundane matters.

10. See, for instance, Linsky, op. cit., pp. 171–74; Pitcher (1964), pp. 294–97. I say that the argument is seen as "relatively" self-contained because some expositors address certain objections about the possible utility of memory, citing *Investigations*, sec. 265. These objections and replies about memory, however, are not obviously relevant, at least as usually presented, to the gap in the argument that I mean to discuss here. I shall therefore not address them in this essay.

11. See, for instance, Fann (1969), pp. 76–77. In these pages Fann closely echoes those parts of Winch's exposition that I shall focus on here.

12. Ayer (1968), p. 259.

13. Ibid.; Strawson (1954), pp. 70–99.

14. Winch may, of course, feel that he has already explained what the flaw in the picture is, at the point at which he responds to Ayer and Strawson. Though I have not attempted in this essay thoroughly to examine Winch's discussion as a whole, I do not feel that he has in fact done so: he has not examined what from an intuitive point of view seems to be the nub of the issue, but rather skirts it (particularly within his second paragraph, p. 26). In any case, my main point here is that the argument that has been sketched in this section from the necessity of a standard of correctness to a "social setting" for language is *in itself* inadequate to refute the picture of a language using Crusoe.

15. I should stress that what follows contains only a very rough sketch of

what (in part) Wittgenstein may be up to. No attempt is made to argue this particular characterization of Wittgenstein or to capture the subtleties of Kripke's lucid exposition.

16. See Kripke, p. 109. See *On Social Facts*, Chapter 3, sec. 4, for an extended discussion of the ''private model'' in relation to the attack envisioned by Kripke.

17. This is a lightly edited version of a paper presented at the Wittgenstein conference in Tallahassee, Florida, 1982. I thank Rogers Albritton and Saul Kripke for lengthy conversations about Wittgenstein's views.

10

Group Languages and "Criteria"

This essay draws attention to a notable aspect of a group's language (or "group language"). It does so in the context of a famous claim from Wittgenstein: an "inner process stands in need of outward criteria."[1] The literature on Wittgenstein suggests a specific understanding of what a criterion is. I argue that group languages need outward criteria precisely in the sense suggested there.

My argument does not concern language in general or as such. It appears to be consistent with the theses that someone living entirely outside a community could in principle have a language, that no behavioral or environmental criteria are necessary for the sensation-terms of languages other than group languages, and that a Fregean or Platonist account of linguistic meaning is correct. In other words, it is an argument for an "outward criteria" doctrine that is not (otherwise) particularly Wittgensteinian.

I. "Outward Criteria"

Wittgenstein's famous claim that an "inner process" stands in need of "outward criteria" has provoked much discussion.[2] A main question has been: what precisely are *criteria*?

Apparently the presence of a criterion for something is never logically sufficient for the presence of that thing. Yet a criterion is not merely empirical evidence for its presence either. It is empirical evidence, but it is something else as well. Pain behavior—the kind of behavior that people typically manifest when they are in considerable pain, such as crying and screaming—is generally assumed to be a criterion for pain. One would not be contradicting oneself if, without special reason, one denied that a man was "in pain" when he was manifesting pain behavior. Doubt would nonetheless be cast on one's knowing what the word "pain" means, rather than merely on one's inferential powers. I shall summarize the drift of the claims I have just sketched as follows: a criterion is *meaning-determining—but not quite.*

An "outward" criterion is a criterion that is part of the outer world observable to many, as opposed to the inner world of the mind. Pain behavior, if a criterion for pain, is an outward criterion.

Wittgenstein's outward criteria doctrine has often been construed as follows: no one could have a sensation term in his or her language unless that term had its own outward criterion. This is a *general* outward criteria doctrine: it concerns *any language that might be used by anyone.* It is a *strong* general outward criteria doctrine. For it concerns *all* of the sensation terms of a given language.

This doctrine appears to be highly counterintuitive. It seems easy enough to describe counterexamples to it without contradiction.[3] Even a *weak* general criteria doctrine that requires only that *some* of one's sensation or inner process terms have outward criteria may seem suspect on first inspection. Perhaps for this reason, many of Wittgenstein's commentators have focused on his outward criteria doctrine, seeing it as the exciting core of his work, and looking for a correlative "anti-private language argument."

II. An Outward Criteria Doctrine

In what follows I shall outline an outward criteria doctrine that is relatively easy to accept. This is not a doctrine about language in general. It is a doctrine about group languages as I shall characterize these shortly. There is nothing particularly *deep* about it. Nor is there anything particularly Wittgensteinian—except that it is a doctrine about the necessity of outward "criteria" *in the sense sketched above.*

It is necessary clearly to distinguish this more or less commonsensical outward criteria doctrine from the general, more controversial doctrines that have been ascribed to Wittgenstein. It would be unfortunate if an inarticulate acceptance of the commonsensical doctrine were to lead people too easily to accept either of the other views. It would also be unfortunate if the concept of a group language—as characterized here—were overlooked.[4]

In my discussion I shall talk freely, in an everyday manner, of speakers using a word in a certain sense, and so on, without asking how this phraseology is to be explicated philosophically. I do not assume the truth of any particular approach to such talk here, except insofar as everyday talk of speakers using words in particular senses, and so on, may contain within it the presupposition of some such truth.[5] I should stress that I do not assume the falsity of a broadly Platonist or Fregean approach to language and meaning in general, something that, I take it, Wittgenstein does reject.[6]

I first argue briefly that one line of reasoning which may seem attractive fails to get us to outward *criteria*. I then turn to group languages.

III. Outward Criteria Are Not a Requirement of Seriously Intended Attempts at Communication

It may be thought that a thesis regarding the necessity of outward criteria can be derived from a consideration of the conditions for linguistic communication. In a sense this may be so, but the sense in which it is so needs to be made out carefully. Let me note two senses in which it is not so. The concept of "communication" needs sharpening. First there is what we might call communication in the *thin* sense. This occurs just in case one person, *S,* utters term *"T"* using it in a certain sense; another person observes *S*'s utterance and understands *"T"* in the same sense. Communication in the thin sense could surely occur by sheer coincidence. In particular, it could occur without *S* intending it to occur, and without either participant knowing or having any evidence that it has occurred. No outward criteria doctrine flows in any obvious way from a consideration of the logically necessary or sufficient conditions on thin communication.

What, however, of seriously intended communication? Let us say that Jack *seriously intends* to communicate with Jill if and only if he has some bona fide positive reason to think Jill will construe his words as he does himself. Seriously intended communication, unlike thin communication, obviously requires more than the "sharing of a language" in the thin sense of "using the same language."[7]

The question is: how much more? Jack could have some bona fide reason to think Jill will interpret his words as he does under a variety of circumstances. He could have such a reason merely if he has reason to suppose that Jill has reason to suppose that he means such-and-such. In short, it is hardly obvious that seriously intended communication requires *criteria* as those have been characterized here.

IV. "Linguistically Free" Agents

It is now time to introduce the concept of a group language. This is to introduce a concept in terms of which, I take it, most of us operate most of the time. I believe that this concept has not been focused on or articulated previously. Focusing on it and attempting to articulate it with care is an important philosophical task. Only a rough and ready beginning can be made here.[8]

One way of introducing this framework is by an argument for the utility of group languages as they will be characterized here. The argument I have in mind refers to communication in the thin sense. But focusing on what is *required* for such communication will not get us to group languages.

Suppose we are a set of agents who are *linguistically free* in the following sense. Each of us is capable of associating any of an infinite variety of sounds and marks with a given sense. Suppose that for our personal purposes we are already reasonably well enough equipped conceptually and linguistically. If you like, we have all come from different places, having learned different languages in the places we came from.

Naturally enough, there has arisen among us a certain joint project: we seek to bring it about that, roughly, whenever one of us utters a given sound in the presence of another, both utterer and hearer will assign the same interpretation to it. In other words, we seek to maximize the occurrence among us of communication in the thin sense.[9]

Communication in the thin sense can, of course, occur by chance. But what is the best we can do to maximize its occurrence among us? The obvious thing to do, I suggest, is to agree upon a particular language as our language. To be specific, we should agree that "red" (say) means *red*, and so on, in the context of our communications with each other. As we might put it: "red" means *red* "for us."

It is worth considering briefly what things would be like given the understanding that there are to be no agreements on terms: people are free to choose and use words of their own at all times. Call this a situation of *linguistic anarchy*.

In a situation of linguistic anarchy if I wish to ask you if you have an apple, I could try to find out if you have a word for *apple*. Or I could try to teach you mine. Even if there is an apple in the vicinity, this may take a while. I could point to an apple, and you may think that the word I utter is my word for *fruit*. In other words, a single *ostension* is quite ambiguous. If there is no apple nearby, teaching you my word for apple may take much longer.

Moreover, in principle things appear to be very widely open. Suppose I manage to discover your current word for *apple*. This will not necessarily help me tomorrow. Such considerations show that linguistically free agents in a situation of linguistic anarchy are likely to encounter serious problems.

Possibly such problems can be solved or mitigated in more than one way. It is clear, though, that agreeing upon the assignment of meanings to terms is a good way of solving them, and there are reasons for thinking it to be the best way.[10] In short, agreeing on a language may well be the best way for linguistically free agents to maximize the thin communication that occurs among them.

V. Group Languages: Terms in General

Let me now give a preliminary characterization of a "group language" as a language in which the assignment of meanings to terms is established by interpersonal agreement.[11] We can see that there is an important point to group languages. How, though, are they to be formed? How are the people I have imagined to agree on a meaning for a given term?

This is no trivial matter. Intuitively the case differs radically from that of an individual deciding to stipulate a new sound-sense link, for purposes of a private diary, for instance. One may allow that the individual in question can simply decide that a certain word is to express a given concept or sense. Assuming that at the outset people have no common verbal language, a joint decision about such a thing cannot be so simple.

I cannot point to the concept or sense I wish our word to express, and thus obtain your agreement. I need to find some indirect way of indicating the concept in question. I suggest that after we have gone through the procedure outlined below we may reasonably take it that we have sufficiently well indicated the sense in question to each other, and hence take it that a given language has been agreed upon.

Given that we do not yet have any agreed-upon language in which to make explicit agreements, pointing, or ostension, will be a crucial component in the formation of an agreed-upon language. Agreeing on an ostension can be read as, in effect, a joint stipulation regarding what concept the word in question expresses in our language. We stipulate that the concept it expresses applies (at least) to a certain object to which we point. Agreeing on an ostension can thus be thought of as agreeing on a judgment with a special, definitional status.[12] I shall not try carefully to specify the special status here. Clearly, though, there is a sense in which a given agreed-upon ostension partially *fixes* or *lays down* the meaning of a term for the group. In other words, there is a sense in which it is (partially) *meaning-determining*.

A *series* of agreed-upon ostensions will obviously help adequately to pin down the meaning. How far, it may be asked, need we go? It is well known that from a philosophical or "in principle" point of view we could agree on the correctness of a million applications of the term "game," say, yet there still be infinitely many potential candidate concepts at issue. Nonetheless, in a given group of human beings with initially similar backgrounds, it is arguably reasonable to assume that something like the following is so as a matter of fact: if we have made sufficient agreements on particular cases for our subsequent noncollusive uses of a word to be congruent, then we have indeed individually latched on to the same concept.

Given that our project is to home in on a given meaning as well as we can, then, the definitional or meaning-determining agreements should go on until disparities in the noncollusive application of a term no longer occur (or turn out to be explicable in terms of factors such as poor eyesight, etc.). Each can then individually feel confident that, say, the concept of a game is the one at issue. When this is common knowledge it seems fair to say that our group language now involves the element: "game" means *game*.

Given the above considerations, it can be argued that the foundation of a group language will be precisely the sets of agreed-upon ostensions by virtue of which the meanings of the various terms in the group language get settled. Once the meaning of a given term is settled, members of the group in question are in a position to teach its meaning to newcomers by reference to new paradigms; that is, clear cases by reference to which the term with its established meaning could have been introduced into the language, but which were not actually involved in establishing its meaning.

VI. Sensation Terms in a Group Language

So far I have not mentioned sensations or "criteria." But now consider the case of the group faced with a decision on sensation terms.

Let us assume the correctness of the idea that sensations are in some sense "inner" processes. Let us take it that, accordingly, though I can focus on my own pain, I cannot point it out to you, expecting you to see or otherwise perceive what I am pointing at. Given that we have sensations that are important to us, we will desire to find some way of referring to them in our group language. So we need some way to agree that it will be pain that is referred to by, say, the term "pain."

In the case of pain and others of our important sensations, it so happens that they have natural behavioral manifestations. We spontaneously utter howls of pain, sighs of pleasure, and so on. Specific taste sensations are correlated with the ingestion of particular substances. And so on. Nothing is more obvious and natural, then, than to make use of such behavioral manifestations and environmental correlates, perhaps including some pointed reference to context. For the closest we can come to fixing meanings by interpersonal agreement in such cases is by reference to these manifestations and correlates.

What will be the result of using behavioral manifestations to fix meaning? Ostensions of behavior in attempts to fix the meaning of sensation terms clearly cannot be construed in exactly the same way as ostensions of public phenomena intended to fix the meaning of terms with public referents. If for terms of the latter kind we understand as our definitional judgment form, roughly, "The concept that term '*T*' expresses applies to *this*," we need something weaker for sensation terms. (Something like "The concept that term '*S*' expresses *standardly applies* to someone who behaves thus" or "A person who behaves thus will *generally be experiencing* the sensation to which '*S*' refers.")

One can see how, if the term "pain" is introduced into our language in some such way, then the behavioral manifestations used to pin down its meaning may be judged to provide more than mere evidence that the term "pain" applies. One can see why if Jill were to deny that Jack was in pain given the right sort of behavior and context we might feel justified in saying "If she denies that he is in pain now, she can't know what pain is (or, what 'pain' means)."

At the same time, however, given that it is the concept of pain that the term "pain" expresses, the presence of the behavior does not entail that there is pain: it is not logically sufficient for pain. In this way the term "pain" contrasts with terms introduced into the language with truly meaning-determining ostensions.

Inner process terms, then, may successfully be introduced into a group's language by appeal to outward *criteria*. That is, by reference to public phenomena that are meaning-determining—but not quite.[13]

Must *all* of the sensation terms in a group's language have public criteria? In the central cases of a group's term, members have together agreed on certain ostensions as fixing or—perhaps better—"quasi-fixing" the meanings of the terms. Within this framework it seems that there could be some terms for sensations that are not directly corre-lated with public phenomena. Such sensations could be regularly correlated with other sensations which had natural public expressions.

But what of terms for "radically uncorrelated" types of sensation—for types of sensation, if there are any, which are not usefully corre-lated with external phenomena even indirectly? Suppose a given indi-vidual, Jack, wishes to introduce such a term (*"S"*) into the group language. By hypothesis there is no way that, by observing the external world, other members of the group could come to figure out Jack's intended meaning for *"S."* More to the present point, there is no possibility of an agreement that *"S"* commonly applies to one who behaves thus (or to one in this specific context, and so on). In this special type of case, then, it may most forcefully be argued that it is only in a (far) less than full sense that a term can be part of a group's language. Thus even a strong outward criteria doctrine finds a fairly comfortable home in the domain of a group's language: an "inner process" stands in need of "outward criteria"—direct or at least indirect.

VII. A Caveat

The limited character of this conclusion must be stressed. It only concerns group languages: languages in which terms are associated with meanings by interpersonal agreement. For all that has been said here, an individual can have a language of his own, and in such a language there can be terms referring to "radically uncorrelated" types of sensation. There is no obvious reason not to think of such terms as terms of his language in the fullest sense.

The formation of group languages seems itself to depend on commu-nication at a more primitive, individual level. As Wittgenstein pointed out, a finger stretched away from the body could be interpreted very variously; luckily, we all tend to look along and past such a pointing finger, away from the body. We all, individually and naturally, interpret such a finger in such a way. Our meshing, individual languages, one might say, enable us to perform the ostensions that are the foundation of group languages.

VIII. Response to a Query

It may be suggested that the languages we use in real life are not group languages as I have characterized these—languages founded on joint stipulations and agreed-upon ostensions. In support of this contention, it may be argued that young language learners do not have much say in the language they learn.[14] This may well be so, but it does not entail that language learners are precluded from participation in something importantly like an agreement.

Consider the following case. A child, Sammy, points to a cat and says "dog." His mother says "No, Sammy, 'cat.'" In such a context, Sammy may well understand that, as far as Mother is concerned, he had better call things of this sort "cats," not "dogs." If he calls them "dogs" he will be reprimanded. I suggest that he is likely to understand something more subtle also.

One way of characterizing his understanding is something like this. Mother wants him to enter into a joint stipulation with her to the effect that things of this sort are called "cats." This will involve each one in accepting certain commitments. For instance, Sammy will accept a commitment not to deny that *this* (picked out by his or her ostension) is properly called a "cat."

Sammy may be willing to go along with his mother, and indicate his willingness to enter into such a joint stipulation. I suggest that it will then be perfectly plausible to say that, in learning English from her, he enters into an agreement of sorts, even though he is under pressure to do so.[15] Ultimately, he may come to see himself as the member of a wider circle committed to the same labeling practices.

Before leaving this issue, let me conjure a different scenario. Sammy is obstinate, refusing to use the word "cat" and insisting on using "dog" to refer to cats. Mother is exasperated, but finally capitulates in her talk with him. One day a friend hears her say "Sammy, where's the dog?" The friend queries "But you have a cat, not a dog!" Mother somewhat wearily explains: "Sammy refuses to use the word 'cat,' so *we call cats 'dogs.'*" Here, Sammy has forced his labeling preference on Mother. The language of their two-person group has been set up this way. (We do not expect Sammy to have such luck in the wider world.)

IX. Summary and Conclusion

The argument that led up to my outward criteria doctrine began with group languages characterized in a particular way. A group language is—on this account—a language the meaning of whose terms has been established by interpersonal agreement.

Given this account, the question of how group languages are possible arises: how do people agree on the meanings of terms? It appears that in general, and perforce, they do this by picking out public situations in which the terms are jointly stipulated to apply. Typically this involves focusing on a particular object and arriving at an understanding that the term in question applies to that object—because we now jointly stipulate that it does. Our intention is precisely to determine—or partially determine—the meaning of the term not in the sense of discovering or figuring out what the meaning is but rather in the sense of bringing it about that the word has the meaning it has.

A criterion plays a role in connection with our terms for "inner processes" that is closely analogous to that played by objects in the outer world in connection with the terms relating directly to that world. In the case of sensation terms we are thwarted by the nature of the phenomena: they are not open to public view. So our canonical meaning-determining procedure cannot be used here. In particular, we do not generate a set of cases for which the applicability of the term is not intelligibly open to question, failing special circumstances. Nonetheless, in the case of sensation terms what we do (using agreed-upon ostensions) and how we proceed (questioning whether someone knows the meaning of a term in related contexts) is closely analogous to what we do in the other cases. In short, it seems appropriate to bring the notion of meaning-determination into the description of what goes on here. One short way of doing this is to say that the phenomena in question are meaning-determining (in the relevant sense)—but not quite.

In conclusion, the following should be stressed. A "group language" as I use the term here is not identical *by definition* either (a) with a language that all members of a group individually use, or a "shared" language in that thin sense; or (b) with a language in which the meanings of terms are established by reference to publicly accessible phenomena. Given what a group language is, it is a "theorem" that group languages need to utilize such clues.[16]

The notion of a group language is worth investigation in its own right. A rough and ready start has been made here, by noting how well and uncontroversially a well-known, controversial Wittgensteinian claim which has been supposed to hold for languages as such sits with group languages in particular.[17]

Notes

1. Wittgenstein, *Philosophical Investigations*, section 580.

2. See Albritton's regularly cited review (1959), noting the afterthought added when this was reprinted in Pitcher (1968); see also Strawson's review of the *Investigations*, also reprinted in Pitcher.

3. For an example that conflicts with this strong general outward criteria doctrine, see Chapter 9, this volume (the example involving two distinctive types of ache). On the question whether Wittgenstein claims or needs to claim that every one of one's sensation terms needs its own criterion, see Kripke (1982), p. 102, note 83.

4. A number of philosophers have made suggestions as to what it is for a language to be the language of a particular population or group. See for instance Lewis (1969 and 1975), and Schiffer (1972). Lewis suggests that a particular language (abstractly defined) is the language of a particular population if there is a (social) convention of a certain kind in the relevant population, relating to the language in question. He understands what a social convention is in accordance with his own account (see Chapter 4, this volume). I understand social convention differently (see Chapter 1 [final section], this volume, and *On Social Facts*, Chapter 6). I do not think that precisely the notion of a social convention is required to explicate the concept of a group language, though I see both the concept of a group's language and that of a social convention as what I call "plural subject" concepts. The issue between the various options at this level is relatively fine-grained. See *On Social Facts*, pp. 389–90.

5. In *On Social Facts*, Chapter 3, I argue that it may. See section 3.9 in particular, and also section 4.4.

6. For a brief and clear summary of the Fregean point of view on meaning see Kripke (1982), p. 57. I discuss ways in which the Platonist-Fregean might attempt to counter the skepticism Kripke articulates on behalf of Wittgenstein in *On Social Facts*, Chapter 3. I take it that the philosophical debate on these matters is still open.

7. Cf. McGinn's explanation of what it is to "share a language": "to mean the same by their words" (1984, p. 89). This would not be enough for seriously intended communication. I note that though McGinn suggests that a shared language involves "agreement in judgements," sharing a language in his sense only seems to require agreement in judgments in the trivial sense that those with the same language are indeed equipped to make the same judgments, ceteris paribus. (They must, as he puts it, "agree in their use" of a given word.

But one cannot take it as obvious that they must have reason to think that they do.)

8. Those emphasizing the role of community in Wittgenstein's account of language may, of course, be influenced by a background sense of this framework (as may Wittgenstein himself). That our languages are group languages, however, and that group languages have certain features, is not in itself reason to conclude that all possible languages of all possible language users have those features.

9. I construe the notion of a joint project as the project of a *plural subject*; see Chapter 6. See also the introduction. For elaboration of the view that participation in a plural subject immediately involves obligations, see in particular Chapter 12 below.

10. I argue in Chapter 2, above, that, in a class of situations into which the many-person problem of assigning the same meaning to a given term on a given occasion fits, appeal to what happened last time—to precedent—is not an appropriate course for a certain type of rational agent. Insofar as we approximate such agents, even its being common knowledge that we have all been using a term in a given sense for some time is not a very solid basis for assuming that any one of us will so use it next time. Nor, as I argue in Chapter 1, is the salience of a given use a very solid basis either.

11. I shall not go beyond this characterization here. This could be seen as a characterization of a "primitive" or "simple" group language. Issues such as that of the possibility of a "division of linguistic labor" need to be raised in relation to languages which may reasonably be called "group languages." See *On Social Facts,* Chapter 3, section 6.4, for some discussion of the division of linguistic labor in relation to group languages.

12. Cf. Wittgenstein on agreement in judgments, as opposed to definitions, *Investigations*, section 242. (I only said "Cf.")

13. The sense of "criterion" could of course be characterized so as to be broad enough to allow that genuinely meaning-determining phenomena are criteria; in the case of sensations, however, what is called a "criterion" has a weaker relation to meaning; it is not quite meaning-determining. I shall not attempt to characterize a general sense for "criterion" that encompasses what is called a criterion here and what is more strictly meaning-determining.

14. The suggestion and argument are from Kent Bach's comment on my 1989 paper "Group Languages and 'Criteria' " presented at the American Philosophical Association meetings, Pacific Division, 19 March 1989. The material in this section documents my response.

15. The possibility of pressured or coerced agreements comes up in other contexts too, in particular the discussion of whether or not we have political obligations founded in something like an agreement. For an extended discussion of agreements entered into under pressure (more specifically, under coercion), and their ramifications, see Chapter 12 below.

16. In using the word "theorem" here I echo Kripke in his discussion of

Wittgenstein on criteria. Kripke expounds what he takes to be Wittgenstein's overall approach to language first, and explains how a kind of outward criteria doctrine falls out from it. (Precisely how "criteria" are best characterized within this interpretation is not something I shall pursue here.) There is no need either to affirm or dispute this account of Wittgenstein for present purposes.

17. Versions of this essay have been presented to colleagues at the University of Connecticut, Storrs, fall 1986, and at the meetings of the American Philosophical Association, Pacific Division, 1989. I thank Saul Kripke for comments on a late draft. Responsibility for the views expressed here is mine alone. Some further discussion of group languages can be found in *On Social Facts*, Chapter 3, section 6.

11

More on Social Facts

Response to John Greenwood's review of *On Social Facts*
in *Social Epistemology*

In his empathic and positive review, John Greenwood does not question my central conclusions (Greenwood, 1990). Indeed, he argues most supportively for their importance. He does have some queries, however. Invited to respond, I hope to clarify a number of points about my approach to social phenomena and the foundations of social science.

I. Concerning the Range of Social Phenomena

There is one general question that runs through a number of Greenwood's queries. He rightly sees me as primarily arguing for a particular analysis of our vernacular collectivity concepts. As he says, I argue that these concepts are what I call "plural subject" concepts, and this is a long and detailed argument. His question concerns the relation of this argument to the characterization of social phenomena in general and to the characterization of the subject matter of social science. These are issues with which I was, indeed, concerned. The progress of that concern is another matter, as I shall explain in response to Greenwood's question.

Greenwood writes: "The author . . . is not content to claim that social collectives form a proper and important part of the subject matter of social science. She claims that such phenomena constitute *the* subject matter of social science, and that the principles that . . . license our characterization of some populations as social collectives license our characterization of *any* phenomenon as social in nature."

Greenwood questions these claims about the range of social phenomena and social science. He suggests, in particular, that they are unnecessarily restrictive. Now, the proposals on the character of social phenomena in my book are in fact more nuanced than Greenwood's summary suggests. It is also significant that these proposals are mooted rather roughly and briefly toward the end of the book (pp. 441–42). Nonetheless, this was the broadest issue that concerned me, and it is raised in the book's opening pages. It seems worth sketching the progress of my concern with the nature of social phenomena in general, not so much in terms of the book as in terms of the work and thoughts that led to the book as it now stands.

As I shall explain later, I have some sympathy with what I think may be Greenwood's underlying worry about my proposals concerning the range of social phenomena. But first I should discuss the genesis and the precise nature of my position. The story in question is at least implicit in the text of the book, but it may not be entirely easy to discern through the detail of the whole.

II. Social Kinds

I start with some historical remarks. Max Weber and Emile Durkheim were perhaps the two major forces establishing sociology as a separate discipline. As is well known, their official pronouncements about what sociology involved were quite disparate. In particular, Weber stressed the interpretation of human actions (*Verstehen*); Durkheim did not. Nonetheless, both were moved to characterize sociology in terms of a single, special kind of subject matter. For Durkheim, "social facts" (*faits sociaux*) were at issue. For Weber, the fundamental subject matter was what he called "social action" (*soziales Handeln*). Now each of these classic writers attempted quite carefully to *characterize* the crucial phenomena. In the *Rules of Sociological Method* (1895/ 1982), Durkheim characterizes social facts as, among other things, phenomena that arise when and only when a number of people are associated in a particular way.[1] Weber carefully defines his technical concept of "social action" both positively, and by contrast with cases he deems to involve nonsocial action: social actions are, roughly, actions oriented toward persons other than the agent (see *The Theory of Social and Economic Organization* [1922/1978], p. 88).

In both these writers, then, we find a clear sense that one can give a *nontrivial, unitary* account of the subject matter (or "fundamental" subject matter) of sociology. By a "unitary" account I mean an account in terms of a *single kind of thing*. By a "nontrivial" unitary account I mean one that does not simply (and trivially) say that sociology is about social phenomena. The *single kind* in question is not just *socialness, sociality,* or whatever.

Is there just one *social kind* of thing—social action in Weber's sense, perhaps, or social facts according to Durkheim's account? On being presented with a nontrivial unitary account of the subject matter of sociology, one might wonder if this was so. If it were so, this would have clear implications for an analysis of our concept of a social phenomenon—for a characterization, if you like, of the kind *social*. For an acceptable analysis would then have to determine that no other kind of thing was a *social* kind.

My own initial interest—the project that ultimately led to my writing *On Social Facts*—was the analysis of our vernacular concept of a social phenomenon in general. When and why do we pick out some phenomena as "social" and deny others this description?

This question had been largely ignored in philosophy, in spite of the many salient references to sociality in different areas of the subject. These included not only the philosophy of social science but also the philosophy of language, the philosophy of law, and moral philosophy. It was often said that this or that "had a social nature" or "was a social phenomenon" but what was or might be meant was not examined or even seen as an issue. (At one point in *The Idea of a Social Science* [1958] Peter Winch claims that it is important to investigate the concept of a social phenomenon in general, but he does not go on to approach this question directly himself.)

In the light of my interest in the kind *social*, I considered Weber's characterization of the subject matter of sociology in terms of his concept of social action. My guiding question was, in effect, is social action in Weber's sense the only *social kind* of thing?

Now, I took it that a human collectivity was at least a social kind of thing. Indeed, collectivities were surely social things par excellence (p. 2). Thus it was hard to see how it could be argued that social action in Weber's sense was the *only* social kind of thing, unless perhaps the kind "human collectivity" could very simply be characterized in terms of Weberian social actions. Compare Weber: "When reference is made in a sociological context to a 'state,' a 'nation,' a 'corporation,' a 'family' . . . or to similar collectivities, what is meant is . . . only a certain kind of sequence of actual or possible social actions of individual persons'' (1922/1978), p. 102. (I have slightly amended the translation.)

I argued that it was impossible to give a simple, acceptable account of a human collectivity in terms of Weber's concept (pp. 34–42). Social action in Weber's sense, then, was not the only social kind. What precisely follows from this?

III. The Kind Social

Greenwood remarks that "The fact that our concepts of social *collectivity* cannot be explicated in terms of Weberian social actions does not entail that our concepts of *social* phenomena cannot be explicated in terms of them." I take his point, and take it to be as follows.

Suppose that I was right to argue that the essence of collectivities— that which makes them *collectivities* as opposed to mere aggregates—is not simply a matter of Weberian social actions. It could still be true, at the same time, that collectivities were deemed *social* entities by virtue precisely of their involving Weberian social actions in some way (perhaps as a necessary condition of collectivity-hood).

Now, at the point where I stopped focusing directly on Weber's social action concept, two issues highly pertinent to this possibility were discussed. First, I suggested that it was at least not obvious that Weberian social actions were even logically necessary constituents of a collectivity. Until we knew better what a collectivity was, this question could not be answered satisfactorily. Second, I noted that it could be questioned whether social actions in Weber's sense could properly be characterized as social phenomena in their own right. I had so far argued that Weberian social action was not the *only* social kind. I had yet to consider the question: is it a social kind at all? If it is not, then presumably collectivities would not be judged social by virtue of a presumed connection with Weberian social actions.

A doubt about the sociality of Weberian social actions could seem unnecessarily provocative. After all, why would we go on speaking of such actions as "social" actions if they were not, intuitively, part of the social domain? I had some conjectures about this (see pp. 53–55).

I noted that "it would be possible to find the label 'social' appropriate because one thinks of acts of the type in question as the building blocks of collectivities and their states. In other words, the label may be used solely because of a presumed relation to what one conceives of as a social phenomenon proper. . . . It is not clear how Weber saw the reason for his labelling, but this is quite possibly it" (pp. 53–54). I pointed out that Weber's original term for his concept of social action is *Gemeinschaftshandeln,* which makes a more overt connection with collectivity than does *soziales Handeln;* compare "societal" and "social."

I also suggested some ways of defusing an immediate inclination to think of Weberian social actions as social phenomena in a nonderivative sense. Further, I explained how it could be that while such actions were not, as such, social phenomena intuitively, it was nonetheless not *bizarre* to claim that they were. In brief, it could be that salient elements of any Weberian social action—its "having to do" with a plurality of persons, and the presence of a mental connection between one person and another—were necessary (but not sufficient) for a social phenomenon proper (pp. 54–55).

At this point it was clear that a necessary task in the quest for a deeper understanding of the everyday concept of a social phenomenon was the provision of a plausible analysis for our vernacular collectivity concepts.

IV. Social Groups as Plural Subjects

What are our data on the vernacular concept of a collectivity or social group? (In the book I use the term "social group" as equivalent to the more formidable "collectivity" and "collective." I take this usage to be quite standard, and should be understood accordingly in what follows. Greenwood is inclined to use the term "social group" more broadly. (I say something about one of Greenwood's examples of an "aggregate social group" in section 7, below.)

When sociologists and others introduce the notion of a social group (or sometimes the more technical sounding "social system" or "social unit") they frequently give lists of kinds of groups. Thus Weber lists: a state, a nation, a corporation, a family, an army corps. Durkheim lists, among the "smaller social groups" that are part of larger societies: religious organizations, literary societies. Often the writer will add "and so on" at the end of the list, indicating that the reader will know how to go on. A plausible analysis of our concept of a social group will make some sense of these lists, providing a plausible rationale for them, together with any other appropriate information (including negative data).

Of course, populations that are not social groups can be important and interesting, and people whose primary concern is social groups and their functioning will undoubtedly need to take account of such populations in fulfilling their aims. Nonetheless we have this question: what makes a population a social group?

I eventually came to feel that our everyday collectivity concepts could only properly be analyzed as *plural subject* concepts. I shall not attempt fully to explain the concept of a plural subject here. As Greenwood has indicated, plural subjects are formed when each of a set of individual agents expresses willingness to constitute, with the others, the (plural) subject of a goal, belief, principle of action, or other such thing, in conditions of common knowledge. "Common knowledge" is intended in roughly the sense introduced in Lewis (1969). Roughly and informally, that which is common knowledge among certain people is entirely out in the open between them. I present an account of my own in *On Social Facts,* Chapter 4, in the course of discussing plural subject formation.

A plural subject is, it seems, a special kind of thing, a "synthesis *sui generis,"* to quote Durkheim. Once it is formed, there are major consequences for the members of the association. In particular, they all now recognize an obligation to act in the light of the plural subject's goals, beliefs, and principles of action, even when their personal goals and so on are at odds with these. A striking corollary of this is that a member's action may often be explained without any reference to his or her own personal goals, values, or principles of action. I may be moving this way just because *we* are shifting the piano, and my moving this way is the best way I can contribute.

One characterization Greenwood gives underestimates the distinctiveness of the plural subject form of action-explanation. He says that "it makes reference to beliefs, reasons, etc., *other than one's own."* It certainly does do this. But that is not the whole story. Not surprisingly, Greenwood finds that the form of explanation he has described is not special to the members of social collectives. There may be many cases where someone "feels obliged publicly to endorse and act upon the attitudes shared by other members of an aggregate social group." Such cases, however, will surely be importantly different from cases where people act as members of a collectivity.

To allude to Greenwood's example, *why* might a particular woman feel obliged publicly to endorse beliefs most feminists hold, though these are not her own beliefs, and, by hypothesis, the population of feminists does not constitute a collectivity? Perhaps she is afraid of seeming to be antiwomen. This fear itself may stem from a desire to be liked, or at least not to be ostracized, by certain feminists. In that case a *personal want* is a crucial part of the motivational structure that moves the agent to mouth certain sentiments in this case. It is true that the explanation of her act makes reference to beliefs *other than her own*. But even so one can argue that this case does not involve the "most social" type of motivation, insofar as the agent's *own goals* still play a crucial role. What analysis of our collectivity concepts shows is that this is not necessary. (See especially pp. 417–27. See also my [later] discussion, "Folk Psychology Takes Sociality Seriously" [1989].)

It took some while to argue for the plural subject view of our collectivity concepts: the bulk of *On Social Facts* is devoted to this task. The argument includes critical discussions of a number of proposed analyses that do not incorporate the plural subject concept.

One of these is David Lewis's influential game-theoretical account of a social convention (see Chapter 6 and elsewhere, this volume). According to Lewis, the existence of a social convention is, roughly, a regularity in the behavior of the members of a set of rational agents when these are in a particular type of "coordination problem." The elements out of which a convention is built, on this analysis, are personal preferences and expectations, albeit expectations and preferences involving other persons. No one needs to see himself or herself as a member of anything, as "tied" to anyone or to any set of people in any particular way. I argue that our everyday concept of a social convention seems not to be captured by Lewis's conditions. An adequate analysis has to appeal to the notion of a plural subject, in this case the subject of a certain *fiat*. Again, it is common to propose that a group believes something if each (or most) of the group members believe that thing. Addition of a common knowledge condition may make this seem more plausible. Yet, I argue, when we talk of the belief of a group we often seem to have something else in mind—something that essentially involves a plural subject.[2]

The conclusion that our vernacular collectivity concepts are plural subject concepts is a striking conclusion in itself. What, though, of the very broad issue that had originally prompted my inquiries: the nature of social phenomena in general?

V. A Mark for the Social

Once I had stumbled across plural subjects, my basic thoughts with regard to my original question were these: if we use the one term "social" to cover both collective (plural subject) and noncollective phenomena, this is as likely to confuse as to illuminate. Meanwhile, if one has to plump for a nontrivial unitary account of social phenomena, an account in terms of collectivities or plural subjects would seem best.

Prompted by Greenwood's comment to look at it again, I have to allow that my discussion of the concept of a social phenomenon in the book is not just short, but somewhat cursory. That is partly because of exhaustion, partly because I had long ago run out of space, partly because I had written at some length on this topic in earlier work, and partly because the question no longer seemed as interesting as it once had. It was simply overshadowed by the intricate, important structure revealed by close inquiry into our collectivity concepts. Clearly, plural subject phenomena were *paradigmatic* social phenomena. If the concept of a social phenomenon was not the concept of a plural subject (and its derivatives) it seemed unlikely to be of great significance.

In discussing "Which are the social phenomena?" I noted, first, that "if we consider the variety of accounts social scientists and others have given of their subject matter, we may conclude that the phenomena aptly thought of as 'social' are a motley crew, including, for instance, social actions in Weber's sense and Durkheim's social facts" (p. 441). I then argue as follows for the primacy of plural subject phenomena in any such scheme.

Suppose that for the sake of argument we accept that social actions in Weber's sense are social phenomena, intuitively, or perhaps that all situations of common knowledge are. "It is still incumbent upon us to note that there is another order of phenomena, phenomena of plural subjecthood, which are arguably involved in all of the clearest cases of: . . . telling people things, giving orders, meetings, greetings, and so on, not to speak of established relationships and groups such as . . . families."

I contended that the plural subject phenomena are clearly the *most* apt for the label "social." So, if one had to choose among the kinds of things there are, and nominate one of these kinds the "social" kind, this would surely be it. (I intentionally echoed Durkheim here. In discussing the ways of acting that he thinks of as *faits sociaux* in the *Rules,* he writes: "to them must be exclusively assigned the term *social*. It is appropriate. . . . Moreover it is for such as these alone that the term is fitting. . . ." [1895/1982, p. 52]. What I say is less strong: not that the label "social" is appropriate *only* to plural subject phenomena, but rather that it is surely *most* appropriate to them, and hence, if its use is to be constrained at all, it should be reserved for them.)

I noted that the idea that plural subject phenomena are *the,* or at least the *paradigmatic,* social phenomena gains some support from etymology, in that the Latin *socius* means "ally." However antagonistic the parties to plural subjecthood, still participation in plural subjecthood of any kind is a type of alliance, a partnership of sorts. In contrast, when an action social in Weber's sense is performed, there need be nothing intuitively akin to an alliance between the parties. (Consider the case where someone out for a walk in the woods turns off the main path in order to avoid coming into contact with a stranger he has just spotted, before the stranger has spotted him. This person's act of turning off the main path counts as a "social action" in Weber's technical sense.)

I concluded that we have some reason to suppose that our concept of a social phenomenon is equivalent to that of a plural subject phenomenon. I did not review all of the considerations that might support this idea. In particular I did not mention the fact (alluded to above) that some uses of the qualifier "social" that seem to go against it may best be construed as derived uses, where the speaker has in mind the putative fact that, say, some phenomenon is *produced by* a collectivity, or that collectivities are *constituted by* such phenomena. In such cases the phenomena in question are deemed to be social by virtue of their presumed connection with collectivities in general.

Insofar as a use of "social" is of this derived, elliptical kind, it does not present a real challenge to a plural subject analysis of our concept of sociality. That would be challenged by an unshakable sense that, for instance, a social action in Weber's technical sense is a clear case of a social phenomenon not because such actions have some connection or other to collectivities, but simply by virtue of its involving an orientation to another person.

I granted that our concept of a social phenomenon may be or have become more capacious than the concept of a collective or plural subject phenomenon (and its derivatives). I suggested that there is still an argument for restricting the label "social" to plural subject phenomena, henceforth: we would then have a relatively precise concept that picked out a consequential range of phenomena. We would have, in short, a concept that might be *fruitful theoretically.* But I showed where my own concern was now focused by commenting, finally, that "it cannot be very profitable to worry about how or whether to limit the use of the label 'social.' What is of central importance is to bring plural subject phenomena into view . . ." (p. 442).

VI. On Science and the Social Realm

Where might we end up if we allow that social phenomena include all those that have ever been associated with the label "social," for whatever reason? Casting our net this wide, we would undoubtedly include phenomena whose description did not seem logically to involve plural subjects, such as social action in Weber's sense.

In a monograph completed before I had become aware of the structure of the plural subject concepts, I sketched a theory of social-ness based on such data.[3] I hazarded that from an intuitive point of view there were *degrees* of socialness. For if a single Weberian social action qualified as a social phenomenon, it must surely involve *less* socialness than any instance of common knowledge construed as in Lewis (1975) and Schiffer (1972): *A* knows that *p*, *B* knows that *p*, *A* knows that *B* knows that *p*, *B* knows that *A* knows that *p*, and so on. Meanwhile, other kinds of case seemed to involve less socialness than a minimal Weberian social action. What of someone who starts a bonfire and then disappears, inadvertently allowing a freezing beggar to warm himself? This action, I suggested, involved less socialness, intuitively, than did a minimal Weberian social action. Whether it involved something social at all was perhaps moot; but the term "social act" *has* on occasion been used as if to connote acts that quite simply *affect* others, without anyone intending to do so or foreseeing any such effects.

Considering that and how it seemed natural to *order* these cases, it seemed that an important factor in socialness would be *mental connectedness* between persons, something that itself admitted of degrees. So I arrived at the following tentative general hypotheses: First, "a phenomenon is a social phenomenon if and only if it involves one person's being connected either mentally or in some causal way with another person or persons."[4] As for degrees of socialness: "The degree of 'socialness' of a phenomenon is in general directly correlated with the amount and degree of mental connectedness between persons which it involves, and with the [amount and] degree of causal connect-edness between persons, where some mental connection always takes priority over any causal connection."[5]

In a concluding section, I noted that the notion of socialness characterized in these statements is not, intuitively, the concept of a "natural" kind of thing. It has some appeal, though, "in its openness and lack of prejudgment of issues. . . . Social scientists, or rather enquirers about the world, had better ask what questions they will and answer them if they can. Then, if they like, they can attempt to formulate concepts which bring out . . . the precise way in which the subject matter they deal with is . . . social."[6]

I have taken the liberty of reporting this earlier work here because it bears on suggestions and concerns that Greenwood expresses in his review. (In *On Social Facts* I refer to it only briefly in a footnote [note 20, p. 495], though shades of it surface here and there.)

It was clear to me then that if we cast the net of sociality as wide as we sometimes seemed inclined, it would cover so much as to be virtually useless theoretically. On the other hand, whether we cast that particular net widely or more narrowly, that would not in itself imply anything about what "enquirers about the world" should study. Obviously we do best to pursue whatever questions interest us, and yield clarifying answers, without worrying too much about how we label our enquiries (or ourselves).

Given that one is explicitly aware of plural subject phenomena, what is one to say about the subject matter of *social science*? First, plural subject phenomena are social phenomena *par excellence*. They are also without doubt an important family of phenomena. They seem to merit a good deal of focus. It does not seem odd to suppose that a whole branch of enquiry might be devoted to a discussion of their nature, genesis, functioning, and influence. If social science is the science of plural subjects, then, it can be seen to have an obvious set of tasks, an important focus. On the other hand, if we define sociality, and consequently social science, in a very broad way, such as that proposed in my earlier work, it is not at all clear that some particular branch of enquiry should focus on social phenomena as such. (See also Wallace [1983], who gives an account of a social phenomenon as an "interorganism behavior regularity.")

Can it do any harm to think of the social sciences simply as disciplines that are concerned with human aggregates and human interconnections in some way or other? Perhaps we would do better to forget about "sociality" and simply think, as Greenwood suggests, in terms of human science or the science of persons. It would certainly be a great loss if this or any other broad characterization of social science were to allow us to lose sight of the delicate, consequential, highly social structures of plural subjecthood. I think it highly likely that the assumption that the social *included* aggregate phenomena and, indeed, Weberian social actions as such, has had the effect of obscuring our understanding and even our conscious perception of plural subject phenomena.

VII. On Crowds

Greenwood refers to crowds as *aggregate social groups,* suggesting both that they are properly referred to as social groups and that they fall outside my plural subject analysis.

Now crowds do not normally figure in sociologists' lists of canonical "social groups," "social units," and the like, alongside such entities as families, literary societies, tribes, and so on. Is there some reason why one might incline to think of crowds as social groups nonetheless? I think that there is, but I also think that it is consonant with my account of social groups as plural subjects.

I suggest that many actual crowds are in fact plural subjects, albeit of a transient and spatially restricted sort. This fact may fuel a wish to characterize crowds in general as a kind of social group. At the same time, our concept of a crowd may not itself be the concept of a type of plural subject. This would explain why crowds are not generally listed in sociologists' lists of canonical social groups, though sociologists (Durkheim, for instance) may sometimes refer to a crowd as an example of a social group.

Let me briefly support the idea that crowds (along with other transient groups) may be plural subjects. Consider the 100 or so people crowded around a speaker at Speaker's Corner in London's Hyde Park. They may jointly accept that the speaker should not be heckled so strongly that he cannot utter an uninterrupted sentence. This could come about as follows; one persistent heckler is cried down by the others in a mutually supportive manner, and he finally makes it clear that he sees the point. Again, the members of the crowd may make it clear that as a body they endorse what the speaker says. Or there could be a welling up of anger which, by the way it is expressed, encouraged, and amplified, is aptly described as the anger of the group itself. (Though I do not give collective emotional states special attention in the book, I am inclined to think that there is a type of group emotion that should be analyzed along the lines of the other plural subject concepts. Durkheim implies a similar opinion when he writes of collective ways of acting, thinking, *and feeling*. This is of course much easier to accept once one has the general form of the plural subject concepts in view.)

As I said earlier, populations that are not social groups/collectivities may be of great importance. Even when it is very broadly defined (perhaps in terms of physical proximity and boundaries) the category "crowd" may well be a useful one. Precisely when and how crowds (broadly defined) become plural subjects is itself an interesting question. So is the question when and how crowds and mobs engaged in collective action are likely to lose their plural subject status. These questions would be important whether or not all crowds were *social* groups. They would, indeed, be questions for *social science* even if this is narrowly defined as the investigation of collective phenomena.

VIII. Social Phenomena and Social Explanation

In a few places Greenwood has not represented my views accurately. I do not think that the fact that sociologists study something is sufficient to treat that thing as a social phenomenon. Nor do I suppose that one should "characterize the subject matter of social science in terms of those phenomena that require a social explanation." Nor do I "criticize any characterization of social phenomena because it does not entail that it will have social explanations."

I do suggest that, for Durkheim, suicide rates counted as social phenomena just because they did in fact receive their proper explanation in terms of collectivity states. Had they rather been properly explained by referring to the weather, they would not have been social phenomena. The idea that having a social explanans is *sufficient* for being a social phenomenon (at least in a derived sense) seems reasonable enough, given the parenthetical qualification. That is of course not to say that it is *necessary* to have a social *explanans,* and I do not say this. As Greenwood notes, it cannot be presumed that the various aspects of plural subject phenomena all have plural subject (or social) explanations.

It is true that *Durkheim* was attracted by the idea that social facts require other social facts to explain them (at one point he straightforwardly asserts this). His core idea, though, was surely that the different elements of a group's culture will tend to be strongly interconnected, given a predictable pressure towards internal coherence. This is not so much a historical point as a thesis about synchronic functioning. It is a very important point, and is obviously relevant to an understanding of the properties of any given plural subject.

IX. Weber's Social Action Concept Revisited

In the chapter that focused on Weber's concept of social action I criticized the utility of this concept on several fronts. Not only was it not the key to the concept of a collectivity. It seemed unlikely to "carve nature at the joints," and so to figure in interesting lawlike generalizations. Nor was it clear that it picked out an intuitively "social" phenomenon. It is possible that in my desire to find a theoretically fruitful category, I have overlooked or downplayed a degree of felicity in Weber's social action concept. Prompted to reflect on this again, I ask myself why one might think that the concept of Weberian social action was in any way a pointful descriptive or classificatory concept. (Greenwood seems to, but does not explain why.)

As Wittgenstein once wrote, our concepts both direct and reflect our interests. Does Weber's concept pick out a phenomenon of significance to us as human beings? Obviously it is of the utmost importance to human beings in general that most other humans are endowed with the fundamental capacity to take others of their kind "into account" when they act.

I wrote in my book that certain acts of communication, which are social actions in Weber's sense, seem essential for the coming into being of plural subjects. Such acts could be termed "the foundation of all sociality" (p. 216). Insofar as we could not form groups without the general capacity to take others in account, Weberian social action itself is, of course, crucial to our social being as I have characterized it. (Once again, that a concept is worth keeping in play for some reason does not itself clinch the argument as to the social status of what falls under it.)

X. On Feelings of Unity

At one point Greenwood refers to my association of plural subjects with shared feelings of harmony or communion. He suggests that this may be a somewhat misleading way of indicating their importance and significance. I agree with this, insofar as no further "sense of unity" is needed to motivate individual action once there is the perceived unity of actual plural subjecthood with its associated commitments.

To say this is not, however, to concede that the subjective feelings that are predictable to some degree as a concomitant of plural subjecthood themselves lack explanatory importance. A sense of communion, unity, partnering, solidarity, and the like tends to enhance human life, and the desire for them surely motivates humans to form plural subjects in the first place, and to stay in them. There is some more than armchair evidence of the subjective importance of being a member of a plural subject in studies such as those of Michael Argyle and his collaborators on what makes people happy, and in studies of the individual costs of social breakdown, such as those of Kai Erickson. (See also Chapter 8, this volume.)

XI. Applications

Greenwood notes that only small portions of my book discuss the "potential explanatory significance of social collectives." This was in part a matter of space (and time), in part a sense that it was necessary to focus and convince on the matter of analysis rather than move too quickly to suggest or develop applications.

Clearly, the plural subject analysis gives us the option of a new kind of explanation of behavior. Behavior that might otherwise have automatically been explained in terms of the subject's personal aims or desires may rather be behavior as part of a real or supposed plural subject. Since at least some such behavior would not occur in the absence of an actual plural subject, a new type of explanatory variable has also been revealed.

Greenwood shares my faith in the theoretical importance for many areas of research of plural subjects as I describe them, and discusses this supportively. He refers to social psychology and social epistemology as examples. There are a number of classic social psychological topics to which the structure of plural subjects looks relevant. Greenwood mentions "risky shift" phenomena. In the book I noted some other such topics, including so-called social loafing (pp. 439–40).

As Greenwood indicates, the concept of a plural subject suggests significant questions about the growth of knowledge and, indeed, about what this amounts to. If groups can have their own beliefs, and, indeed, their reasons for believing (see p. 314), when and how can they be said to know things? Is the so-called "scientific community," or are individual scientific communities plural subjects? If so, how does this influence the growth of knowledge in scientific communities, and in general? How are individual members affected by the fact that certain beliefs, attitudes, and procedures have been jointly accepted by the members as a body? How are gestalt-shifts possible in this context? Who gets the genuinely new ideas and why? How can we tell when we are confronted with a concordance among individuals as opposed to a set of expressions of the group view?

I thank Greenwood for a perceptive and supportive review. I plan to work on various applications of my analyses, particularly in the areas of political philosophy and the philosophy of mind and action. I suspect that there are many more ramifications than I can hope to follow up. In the light of Greenwood's enthusiastic and forward-looking comments, perhaps I may hope that there will be others who join me in this endeavor.

Notes

1. See *On Social Facts*, pp. 243–54 for a discussion of Durkheim's conception of social facts as this is expressed in the *Rules*.

2. See *On Social Facts*, Chapter 5, and Chapters 7 and 14, this volume. See also the introduction.

3. Gilbert (1978ms). This manuscript, which carries the same title as my 1989 book *On Social Facts*, is substantially different in content. There is some further discussion of its conclusions in Gilbert (forthcoming a).

4. Gilbert (1978ms), p. 315.

5. Gilbert (1978ms), p. 315.

6. Gilbert (1978ms), p. 316.

Part III

Joint Commitment and Obligation

Essays 12 and 13 focus on a central phenomenon of ordinary life: everyday agreements. Agreements are taken to generate performance obligations for the parties to them. A particular understanding of the obligations of agreement is argued for here. These obligations are inherent in an underlying joint commitment, a fundamental aspect of any plural subject. The way in which joint commitments generate obligations is clarified, as is the normative nature of (a certain type of) group membership. It is argued that joint commitments and their attendant obligations can arise even in the context of coercion. Essay 14 approaches anew the topic of collective belief in the light of this understanding of joint commitment and its attendant obligations.

Essay 15 argues for a new approach to a classical philosophical problem of political obligation in the light of plural subject theory. Here the author proposes what is in effect a "nonvoluntarist" form of contract theory. Essay 16 argues that feelings of guilt over what one's group has done may be understandable in terms of plural subject theory. Several common assumptions about the nature of guilt feelings are thrown into question.

12

Agreements, Coercion, and Obligation

I. Introduction

Agreements and kindred phenomena are ubiquitous in human life.[1] They are a central source of obligation. Obligation is a forceful species of reason for action. It is therefore important to be clear about the nature of agreements and the obligations of agreement.

These matters have not as yet been well understood. Or so a number of common pronouncements suggest. Among these are some prevalent claims about the impact of coercion on agreements. Philosophers standardly claim that coerced agreements do not impose obligations to fulfill the agreement: they are not binding.[2] Many assert that coerced "agreements" are not agreements at all.[3] In my view both of these claims are false.

This essay offers an account of agreements and the obligations that flow from them. It brings this account to bear on the question of the possibility and bindingness of coerced agreements.

Section II is a largely critical section that addresses two common arguments for the impossibility of coerced agreements, questioning them from a pretheoretical standpoint. In section III, I present my positive thesis on the nature of agreements and their obligations. Although I believe that the impact of coercion on a promise is essentially the same as its impact on an agreement, I reject the standard view of an agreement as an exchange of promises. After explaining why I reject that view, I propose that typical everyday agreements are "joint decisions." I articulate the joint decision model of agreements in detail, arguing that obligations of a distinctive sort flow from every joint decision. This section of the essay is essentially self-contained with respect to the preceding and following sections. Working with the

281

joint decision model of agreements, I argue in section IV that coerced agreements are possible and that they all carry with them obligations of conformity. A number of implications of this claim are explored.

My conclusions bear on the interpretation and assessment of "actual contract" theories of political obligation, that is, theories supposing there to be widespread "political obligations" that derive from actual (as opposed to hypothetical) agreements. I touch briefly on the topic of political obligation in sections II and IV.

I should stress that I am here concerned with the notion of agreement expressed in informal everyday transactions, as opposed to any concept of contract in law.[4] Accordingly, the type of obligation at issue in this essay is something other than legal obligation.

II. Two No-Agreement Arguments

The Obligation Argument

The claim that coerced agreements are impossible is often defended with something like the following "obligation argument":

1. Any genuine agreement generates a moral obligation to abide by it: this is a conceptual matter.
2. If an apparent agreement is made in the face of coercion, there is then no moral obligation to abide by it.

Therefore:

3. A genuine agreement cannot be made in the face of coercion.[5]

In well-known writings on political obligation A. J. Simmons has suggested that the conclusion of the obligation argument can be extended. Consider those who appear to agree to remain in a state and accept burdensome duties of citizenship (such as military service) when their only option is emigration. Perhaps such people cannot be said to be *coerced* into agreeing. However, any so-called agreements exacted in this context are *unconscionable,* and so not morally binding. They are, indeed, not agreements at all.[6]

This is a strong conclusion in relation to actual contract theories of political obligation. According to Simmons, it would make no difference if agreements of the relevant kind appeared to be widespread. No such agreements are possible in standard political circumstances.

I shall not consider here whether Simmons has properly extended the conclusion of the obligation argument. Suffice it to say that the argument may extend beyond the context of coercion strictly speaking.

Interpreting the Obligation Argument

The argument is not entirely perspicuous as presented above. Let us say that one performs an "act of agreement" when what one does is sufficient from a behavioral point of view to constitute entry into an agreement, provided that any other relevant conditions are satisfied. Thus one might nod one's head emphatically, say "Sure" or "Fine" or "I will indeed," and so on, in response to some proposal by one or more others. Let us say that an "apparent agreement" occurs when two or more people perform matching acts of agreement, and this is common knowledge. (When something is common knowledge between persons *A* and *B*, then, roughly, it is "out in the open" between them.)[7] I take it that all genuine agreements are at the same time apparent agreements in the sense just defined.

Let us now construe the argument's first premise as follows:

1A. An apparent agreement is a genuine agreement only if, when it is taken together with its background circumstances, there is a moral obligation to abide by it: this is a conceptual matter.

The rest of the argument proceeds as before:

2. If an apparent agreement is made in the face of coercion there is then no moral obligation to abide by it.

Therefore:

3. An apparent agreement cannot be a genuine agreement if it is made in the face of coercion.

Or, in short:

A genuine agreement cannot be made in the face of coercion.

Given the above construal of the first premise, the obligation argument appears to be valid. It is nonetheless quite problematic, as I shall now argue. A number of other construals fare no better (see the section on revisiting the obligation argument in section III below).

The Knowledge of Agreements Assumption

In advance of theorizing about agreements, something like the following "knowledge of agreements" assumption seems plausible: if someone enters into an agreement, then she knows that she does. I should stress that this assumption concerns informal agreements as these are conceived of in everyday life, as opposed to contract in some particular legal system.[8] Without considering it further for now, let us consider its consequences for the obligation argument.

According to the first premise of that argument, whether or not one has entered into an agreement is a matter of the moral impact of one's circumstances. The argument assumes that coercion is *one* circumstance that prevents an apparent agreement from having the appropriate moral impact.

If we endorse the premises of the obligation argument, then, we apparently have to accept that in order to know that one is entering into an agreement, one must make what may in its context be quite a delicate judgment about the moral impact of one's circumstances. Thus one must know whether one is faced with the moral equivalent of coercion or, rather, with a form of strong pressure with different moral consequences. Given the knowledge of agreements assumption, we must accept that in order merely to enter into an agreement one must always accurately judge the moral impact of one's circumstances, however delicate a judgment that is in its context.

I find this implausible. Entering into an agreement and knowing that one does would seem to be a relatively simple business, possible even for creatures unable to make delicate judgments about the overall moral impact of their circumstances.

Agreements: A Rough Sketch

How firm is the knowledge of agreements assumption? Can we give it an articulate basis?

Consider the formation of a typical informal agreement. Mike says to Jane: "What do you say to my taking Fido for a walk at three and your feeding him at five?" Jane replies: "That's fine."

On the face of it, something like this seems to have happened.

CONDITION 1. Mike intentionally expressed to Jane his willingness to accept that he is to walk Fido at three and she is to feed him at five.

CONDITION 2. Jane did likewise.

These may be thought of as the "core" conditions. We may also add:

CONDITION 3. The fulfillment of the above conditions was common knowledge between Jane and Mike.

I shall introduce some important refinements in this rough account later.

If these or similar conditions capture the essence of this case, that would help to explain any initial plausibility of the knowledge of agreements assumption. It is already part of the full set of conditions that the fulfillment of the core conditions is common knowledge between Jane and Mike: it is out in the open between them. If something is out in the open between two people, then we can expect that each of them will know this is so.

The conditions roughly sketched also support the idea that agreement makers need have no understanding of the moral impact of various circumstances such as coercion. As to what it is intentionally to express one's *willingness* to accept something, I use this term to indicate only that a state of the agent's will is at issue or, more specifically, a positive inclination of the agent's will. The terms "readiness" or "preparedness" might have been used instead. Most to the present point, I take the state in question to be something of which the agent can be fully aware at the time he expresses it without reference to the circumstances leading up to it (such as coercion) or their moral consequences.

In sum: the premises of the obligation argument coupled with the knowledge of agreements assumption imply that some agreement makers must be able to make moral judgments of considerable sophistication. A rough sketch of the conditions that appear to produce a typical informal agreement both supports the knowledge of agreements assumption and confirms the independently plausible idea that agreement makers never require the capacity at issue. These considerations suggest that something is wrong with the premises of the obligation argument.

The Implications of Practice

The conclusion of the obligation argument would hardly matter if attempts to force another person to agree were never made. However, the existence of any such attempts makes that conclusion suspect. Further, we seem able to allow that such attempts succeed: certainly someone could say "He forced me to agree" without linguistic oddity.

Proponents of the obligation argument might contend that the sentence cited must always mean something like "He forced me to go through the motions of agreement," with the implication that "I did not agree in fact."

It is not clear how they could back this up. Consider the following dialogue. "Why on earth did you agree to do such a thing?" "He forced me to—I had no choice." It seems most natural to read *both* parts of this dialogue as presupposing that a genuine agreement took place.

Of course the second speaker could be misguided. It may be that her interlocutor could truthfully reply, "Then you didn't agree at all! (Thank goodness!)" But that the second speaker would be misguided cannot be assumed here: it is what is at issue.

Our usage is prima facie evidence against the obligation argument. In our pretheoretical judgments we do seem to allow the conceptual possibility of coerced agreements. Some argument must be found to show that, if we do this, we are somehow confused or misguided. And the argument must be a powerful one.

The Voluntariness Argument

What of the quite common voluntariness argument? This runs as follows:

1. Agreements are by definition voluntary: they cannot come about against the will of either party.
2. Coercion does not allow an agreement to be voluntary.
3. Therefore, coercion rules out the very possibility of agreement.

This argument may gain a spurious plausibility from an important ambiguity in the notion of voluntariness or of acting in conformity with one's will. Suppose that Betty has decided not to buy a certain house. However, a crafty trickster gets her to sign her name at the bottom of an agreement to purchase it without realizing what she is doing.

Perhaps he covers the agreement in such a way that she thinks she is simply giving him her autograph. We might say that she signed the agreement against her will in what I shall call the "decision-for" sense: she never made any decision in favor of signing the agreement in question.[9]

In contrast, if someone has a gun at Betty's head she may well decide in favor of signing the agreement. She may not only go through the motions of signing it but also have the intention of signing it. Then, though her signing it may be against her will in an important sense, or not be voluntary in an important sense, it will not be against her will in the decision-for sense. It seems, however, that only if Betty goes through the motions of signing against her will in the decision-for sense could she be said not to have signed the agreement.

Let us return to the voluntariness argument. The first premise appears to be uncontentious if and only if "against the will of either party" is interpreted in the decision-for sense. The rough conditions on agreement proposed earlier suggest that one who agrees must indeed decide in favor of something, in the foregoing technical sense. Let us ascribe that interpretation to the first premise, then.

The second premise appears to be false when it is interpreted accordingly. It seems to be false both if construed as a logical claim (as is presumably intended) and if construed as a claim of fact. As the above example indicates, one's rational choice in the face of coercion may well be to decide in favor of a course of action, or to agree to something.[10] Nor is it plausible to suppose that everyone becomes so unnerved in the face of coercion that they are incapable of making up their minds at all, that they are, so to speak, rendered witless. Some people may be so affected, but it is too bold to presume that all will be. There is surely no conceptual warrant for such a presumption. Compare Lord Scarman: "The classic case of duress is . . . not the lack of will to submit but the victim's intentional submission arising from the realization that there is no other practical choice open to him."[11]

Interpreted as I have suggested, then, the voluntariness argument must be rejected. The first premise uses the decision-for sense of voluntary. If this is the sense used by the second premise, that premise is false. Otherwise, the argument trades unacceptably on an ambiguity.

In the paper cited earlier, Simmons in effect proposes the following argument: agreements must be voluntary in order to be morally binding; agreements are necessarily morally binding; so agreements must be voluntary.[12] He believes that coercion rules out the type of voluntariness at issue. If he is right, then this type of voluntariness is not voluntariness in the decision-for sense.

If, in fact, agreements cannot be morally binding unless they are voluntary in some sense other than the decision-for sense, then it seems that—pace Simmons and many others—agreements do not have to be morally binding. For on the face of it there is nothing about agreements that entails that they must be voluntary in any sense other than the decision-for sense. Some argument must be given for the claim that they must be voluntary in some other sense. I know of no such argument.

III. Agreement and Obligation

Obligation in General

Now the common assumption that there is a conceptual connection between agreements and obligation of some kind seems to me correct: there is an important sense in which agreements generate obligations of conformity. As I shall argue, the obligations in question can be incurred in the face of coercion. I must first say more about agreements and their obligations.

Following certain pointers from common usage, let me start with some firm points about obligation in general.

It is clear that if someone, S, has an obligation to do A, then (at the least) S has a reason to do A. More precisely, an obligation is a *reason for acting* in the following sense: once you have such a reason, rationality requires that you act in accordance with it, all else being equal.

Now normally we do not count someone as having an obligation whenever they have a reason for action. Here are two cases in point.

First case: Alice is trying to win a race, and the only way she can do this is by running faster. She would now appear to have a reason to run faster. She may well say to herself, "I've *got* to run faster!" At the same time, it does not seem right to say that she now has an obligation to run faster. Second case: Molly decides to eat lunch in the factory cafeteria and has not at this point reconsidered and changed her mind. She would now appear to have a reason to eat lunch in the cafeteria. At the same time, it does not seem right to say that she now has an obligation to eat there.[13]

If an obligation is more than a reason for action, what more might it be? The foregoing discussion suggests a relatively precise negative characterization.

There is something special about a person's aims and decisions. All that is needed for their creation is the relevant act of that person's mind or will: the adopting of an aim or the making of a decision. This, too, is all that is needed to destroy them. The formation of an aim or decision may be preceded by deliberation, but it may not. It may have reasons behind it, or it may not. Nonetheless, once someone has taken up an aim or made a decision, she has a reason for acting. That reason disappears if she gives up the aim or rescinds the decision.

Let us say that *S* has a reason for acting that is *the creature of her own will* if the reason has this property: all that was needed for its creation and all that is needed for its destruction is an arbitrary act of will on *S*'s part. It seems that we do not call a reason an obligation if it is the creature of a person's will in this sense.

This thought is sustained when we look at a typical example of the use of the term "obligation." Suppose that Sally is out for a walk when a child trips in front of her and breaks its arm. There is no one else in sight. It may well be said that in these circumstances Sally has an obligation immediately to help the child.[14] Precisely what the implied ground of obligation is in this case is a moot question among theorists. But it seems clear enough that the obligation is not perceived as the creature of Sally's will in the sense defined above.

We have arrived at an apparent necessary condition on obligation that is relatively stringent: *S has an obligation to do A* only if *S* has a reason to do *A* that is not the creature of her own will (where this is understood in accordance with the above discussion). This gives us a partial characterization of obligation in general that accords with the plausible thought that the obligations that I have are not had solely "at my pleasure."

Now, decisions do not generate obligations, but they do generate reasons. It will be useful at this point briefly to consider how this can be so.

Decisions appear to generate reasons in a way which is independent of their content, their context, and their consequences. It doesn't matter what my decision is, or why it was made. As long as it is my decision it generates a reason for me.

How precisely it does this depends on what precisely a decision is and, indeed, on what a reason is. These are delicate and important matters which must to a large extent be waived here. However, there is at least one thing that can always be said in favor of the act in question, once the decision is made, and this may be crucial to the understanding that decisions generate reasons.

We understand that whatever else is true of it the act decided upon at least conforms to the agent's decision. It can then be argued that simply by deciding, I set up a situation in which a particular act is rendered the act it is appropriate for me to perform, all else being equal. It will also be inappropriate for me to accept new aims that conflict with my decisions, insofar as I have not yet changed my mind and rescinded my decision. The "appropriateness" in question is the appropriateness of simply being consistent: if my acts match my decisions I am at least being consistent. Such consistency has something "good" about it intuitively. This type of goodness is, equally evidently, only one aspect of goodness in general.

In my view agreements are importantly analogous to decisions: they too provide reasons that are independent of their content, context, and consequences. Unlike decisions, however, they generate obligations. To argue this I must say more about what I take an agreement to be.

Approaching Agreement

The standard proposal about agreements is that an agreement is, in effect, an exchange of promises.[15] In my view this is not so. I discuss this in detail elsewhere.[16] It will be useful to look at it briefly here before presenting an alternative account of agreement.

Let us focus on Mike and Jane's agreement that he will walk Fido at three and she will feed him at five. Mike says, "What do you say to my taking Fido for a walk at three and your feeding him at five?" and Jane replies, "That's fine." I shall consider for the sake of argument the simple suggestion that an agreement will have taken place if and only if the words of Mike and Jane were implicitly understood as a promise exchange as follows: Mike: "I promise to walk Fido at three." Jane (in reply): "I promise to feed him at five." Here each person promises the other to perform some act. I shall be taking these promises quite literally; in particular, each will be construed as making an unconditional or absolute promise. This is simply to fix the nature of the proposal I am focusing on.

There are two aspects of this exchange that make it inadequate as a representation of the agreement. First, as soon as Mike has promised to walk Fido at three, he has an obligation to do so. Jane has not yet incurred an obligation to feed Fido. This seems wrong: the parties' obligations surely arise simultaneously from their agreement.

More crucially, once both promises are made, Mike's obligation is logically independent of Jane's obligation, and vice versa. Even if Mike breaks his promise, Jane's promise—and hence her obligation to feed Fido at five—remains intact.[17] This too seems wrong: the obligations of the agreement appear to be (as I shall put it) *interdependent*. Among other things this means that if the agreement is broken by either party, neither obligation remains. Putting it with maximum generality: interdependent obligations cannot exist one without the other. Their independent existence is logically impossible.

We must therefore reject the suggestion that when we say a person "breaks" an agreement we are supposing that an agreement is a pair of promises, such that if one of the pair is broken the agreement as a whole is said to be broken. To clarify the problem, let us first define a new term, "shmagreement," as follows: when promises are exchanged there is a shmagreement. Let us say, further, that if one of the promises is broken the shmagreement is "broken." Let us now suppose that Mike and Jane have exchanged their promises and, hence, have entered a shmagreement. Mike breaks his promise, and hence the shmagreement is broken (in our stipulative sense). Both Mike's promise, and the shmagreement between Mike and Jane, are at an end. Yet Jane's *promise* is still unbroken. So she still has an obligation to act as she promised. I take it that if we are to capture the structure of our illustrative agreement, we cannot be left with such a dangling obligation. It seems, then, when we speak of the breaking of this agreement we mean something other than the breaking of one of an "exchanged" pair of promises.

Might one say that the agreement is a pair of promises such that we understand that if one of the promises is broken then (a) the agreement is broken, and (b) the other promise is broken too? What kind of pair of promises, though, is this? A promise which is broken given that another promise is broken is not so much a promise as . . . something else. (See the next section.)

In sum, I take it that the obligations arising from Mike and Jane's agreement are simultaneous and interdependent. It can be argued that no possible exchange of promises by one person to another, including exchanges involving conditional promises, can meet both criteria.[18]

In the next section I present a new model of agreements, which does meet these criteria. I shall here waive the question whether some forms of interaction that do not meet the criteria can still appropriately be referred to as "agreements." In particular I shall waive this question with respect to exchanges that are strictly and literally exchanges of promises. I shall go on to argue that agreements according to the model I present are possible in the face of coercion and that any such coerced agreements will be binding. I believe that analogous arguments can be made for single promises and thus for promises that are part of an "exchange." I shall not attempt to argue that here. I should stress, however, that the discussion in this section was in no way intended to imply that if the exchange of promise model of agreements were accepted, the conclusion that coerced agreements are impossible or nonbinding would be justified. It was intended only to show that the standard model of agreements is not adequate to capture the structure of obligations that characterizes typical everyday agreements and, thus, to prepare the way for the introduction of an alternative model.

Agreement as Joint Decisions

I shall now sketch a different model of agreements, developing the idea adumbrated in *On Social Facts* that an agreement is, in effect, a joint decision.[19] That is, the achievement of those who enter into an agreement is analogous to that of a single person who makes a personal decision; in this case, however, the achievement is a joint one. Precisely how this joint achievement is constituted needs some explanation.

If someone comes to a personal decision on a course of action, then, roughly, she comes personally to accept that she is to do such and such. As I understand it, the parties to a joint decision "jointly accept" that such and such is to be done by one or more of them. Joint acceptance, in the relevant sense, requires what I call a "joint commitment."[20] There must be a joint commitment jointly to accept that such and such or, alternatively, to accept that such and such as a body. When there is a joint commitment between two or more parties, there is what I call a "plural subject" or a (collective) "we."[21]

Before saying more about joint commitment, I address a query about describing an agreement as (in effect) a joint decision. Evidently our language allows us to speak both of "our agreement" and of "our decision." Given my analysis, the phenomenon referred to by these different phrases is essentially the same. Why, then, would we allow ourselves the two ways of talking when one might have sufficed?

There could well be a core phenomenon, a particular achievement, that is identical in each case. Meanwhile, we may speak of our decision when we mean to suggest the existence of one particular type of background circumstance, and we may speak of our agreement when we mean to suggest another. (Whether or not this has to do with the semantics of the terms, or something else, need not concern us here.)

I conjecture, more specifically, that we speak of a decision when we wish to suggest that before entering the decision-making process the parties already formed a we or plural subject. Perhaps they were committee members, or the members of a walking party. This usage may indeed suggest that in arriving at their decision, the parties were engaged not so much as separate individuals but, rather, as members of some relevant group or collective, with a single, jointly accepted agenda. We decide collectively. We speak of an agreement, meanwhile, when we wish to make no such suggestion. The parties to an agreement are viewed as separate individuals with (possibly distinct) personal agendas. We individually agree. Nonetheless it is true that, whatever our previous relationship, by entering an agreement we thereby constitute ourselves the members of a (collective) we.[22] In other words, we achieve the same immediate result as those who collectively decide: we come jointly to accept that such and such is to be done by particular people.[23]

I now return to the concept of joint commitment. In *On Social Facts* I argued that this concept lies at the core of a family of everyday concepts, our "collectivity" concepts. These include the concepts of a collective goal, a collective belief, and a social convention. I shall summarize those aspects of my discussion that are relevant here.[24]

The general idea of a joint commitment is the idea of a commitment that is *the commitment of two or more individuals*. In what follows I spell out this idea in relation to a case involving two people.

In order for Mike and Jane to form a joint commitment one with the other, each must express to the other his or her willingness to do so, in conditions of common knowledge. Both must therefore understand what a joint commitment is.

Of course the parties will not generally have the (technical) phrase "joint commitment" at their disposal. Nor need they be able to give an articulated analysis of the concept of joint commitment. They must possess that concept, however, in order to be parties to a joint commitment.

As Mike and Jane understand, their joint commitment is in place when and only when each of the necessary expressions of willingness has been made.[25]

With the joint commitment in place, Mike and Jane will understand that they are individually committed in the sense that each has a commitment. Nonetheless, these "individual commitments" are understood to flow from the joint commitment. In this respect the joint commitment of two people may be likened to a string that they hold taut between them. Neither can hold a taut string by this method unless the other does: neither is or can be individually committed through the joint commitment unless the other is.

Mike's "individual commitment" and Jane's "individual commitment" are in the following sense *interdependent*: they cannot come into existence or persist apart. This interdependence is a function of the joint commitment on which each of the "individual commitments" depends.

Mutual consent is required to rescind a joint commitment. The commitment produces, in effect, a single subject with its own commitment: we are committed unless we (together) change our mind. It may be true that one party can break a joint commitment with the result that it is henceforth no longer there to impose its former constraints on anyone. But those constraints exist in full force right up to the break. (A break requires something to be broken.)

Suppose, then, that Mike is party to a joint commitment. As he understands, the source of his own ensuing commitment is not an act of his own mind alone and he is not in a position to rescind that commitment unilaterally.

Mike's participation in the joint commitment immediately gives him reasons for acting. *Any* commitment on someone's part sets up a situation in which certain acts are appropriate for him and others are not. For some acts conform to his commitment and others do not.

Mike's participation in the joint commitment immediately gives him reasons for acting of a special kind, a kind that I previously had occasion to characterize in discussing the nature of obligation. These reasons are not the "creatures of Mike's own will" like the reasons that flow from his personal decisions or aims. In other words, unlike the reasons flowing from his personal decisions, these fulfill the necessary condition on obligation arrived at above.

As we have seen, even Mike's own "part" of the joint commitment required the act of another's will to bring it into being. As he understands, he is committed through it, unless and until the other parties concur in its dissolution.

Thus the reasons for action that a joint commitment produces for each participant cannot be created or destroyed by an act of that participant's will alone, as is the case with the reasons flowing from personal aims and decisions. The wills of one or more others are an essential part of the picture.

Insofar as a personal decision locks you into a course of action, you yourself have the sole key needed to turn the lock. In order to unlock yourself all you need to do is to change your mind: to rescind your decision. In contrast, insofar as a joint commitment locks you into a course of action, at least two keys are required to turn the lock. You have only one of these keys. Each of the other parties has another. Changing your own mind is not enough; all must concur.[26]

Changing the metaphor, one can say that the parties to a joint commitment are tied to one another or bound together. One who violates the commitment by acting inappropriately breaks that bond. Personal decisions as such involve no such interpersonal bond. One can act against one's own unrescinded decision without ignoring another's legitimate interest in the matter. What is at issue in the case of conformity to a *joint* commitment is not simply self-consistency. It is the maintenance of an acknowledged interpersonal tie or bond.

I propose that it is appropriate to speak of joint commitments as producing not just reasons for action but obligations. The word "obligation" comes, after all, from the Latin *ligare*, to bind.

More precisely, I suggest that a central use of the term "obligation" is to refer to a reason for acting such that he who has it (whom we may call the "obligor") is beholden to another or others (the "obligees") for eradication of that reason by virtue of the participation of both obligor and obligees in a joint commitment. If this is right, then any attempt to give a generic account of the everyday concept of obligation must take account of what I shall henceforth refer to as the *obligations of joint commitment*. I say more about an apparently distinct class of obligations shortly. But first I must come back to our everyday concept of an agreement.

I conjecture that the intuitive judgment that agreements generate obligations or are binding is responsive to the ineradicable presence, given the agreement, of obligations of joint commitment. A joint decision made by Mike and Jane involves a joint commitment: a commitment to accept as a body that such and such is to be done by one or both of them. They are thus obligated to uphold the decision: in particular, they must act as it dictates. In addition, they must not act to impede either one's conformity, for instance. These obligations have a single source: the joint commitment. They are arrived at simultaneously when and only when the joint commitment is in place. They are interdependent in the sense that they stand and fall together.

They both stand as long as the joint commitment stands; they cease if it is dissolved or broken. Their joint decision, then, involves both simultaneous and interdependent obligations, key features of their agreement.

I can now revise my original sketch of the conditions that produced Mike and Jane's agreement as follows:

> CONDITION 1. Mike intentionally expressed to Jane his willingness jointly to accept with Jane that Mike is to walk Fido at three and Jane is to feed him at five.
> CONDITION 2. Jane did likewise.
> CONDITION 3. The fulfillment of the first two conditions was common knowledge between Mike and Jane.

Given these conditions, Mike and Jane are jointly committed to accepting as a body that Mike is to walk Fido at three and Jane is to feed him at five. As a result, Mike's obligation to walk Fido and Jane's obligation to feed Fido will be simultaneous and interdependent.[27]

These conditions do not refer to a background social institution or practice of agreeing.[28] Nor are the obligations of agreement a function of such "external" phenomena as expectations of conformity or reliance.[29] On this account, obligation is intrinsic to the given particular agreement—something I take to confirm the account from a pretheoretical point of view.[30] That it is plausible to see the obligations of agreement as having such a "thin" source as that proposed here is supported by the fact that even the most trivial of agreements will appear to bind the participants in a way outside their personal control.[31]

For present purposes there is no need to investigate the nature of agreements in more detail. It is time to explore some ramifications of the joint decision model.

The Obligations of Agreement

Given the joint decision model of agreements, the obligations of agreement are of the type that derives from joint commitment in general.[32] As I have emphasized, obligation of this sort involves a relationship between persons of a precisely specifiable type. To the person with the obligation (the obligor) there corresponds an obligee or obligees who are instrumental in his having a certain reason for acting and whose concurrence is both necessary and sufficient (given his own concurrence) for the eradication of that reason. The obligees have their status by virtue in their participation with the obligor in an appropriate joint commitment.

The obligation here appears, then, to be of a type different from that in the injured child case. Though Sally's obligation has to do with the child, they do not stand in the precise obligor-obligee relationship referred to above.

That there is an apparently different kind of obligation involved here would perhaps be shown most clearly if we could find a case where we felt someone had an obligation of the relevant kind that had nothing to do with any other person. Possibly we are all obligated to do what we can to preserve endangered species of tree. There are no clear candidate "obligees" of the relevant kind here. Even if there is a supreme being, one might argue that He or She could not release us from *this* requirement in the relevant way.

If the obligations of agreement are the obligations of joint commitment, does this mean that they are not moral obligations? That depends, of course, on what one means by "moral obligation." More grandly, it depends on the nature of morality.

It is generally assumed that the obligation of agreement is moral obligation. Usually, however, this is just an unargued assumption. In this connection it is worth pointing out that a claim may have moral significance, in the sense of helping to decide what you ought to do morally speaking, without itself being a claim of "moral fact."

Thus consider the claim, "Your guests will all go blind if they eat that cheese." Taken at face value, this is a plain assertion of nonmoral fact, a fact about the predictable effects of certain behavior on the body. Yet it clearly has moral significance. Given its truth, you are presumably morally obliged not to serve the cheese to your guests. You could not be counted a virtuous person if you had a tendency to ignore such facts.

This could be the structure of the situation regarding agreements and their obligations. To say that the obligations of agreement are not moral obligations would not be to deny them moral relevance. The above argument presumes, of course, that it is not the case that any fact that is morally significant is therefore itself a moral fact.

R. M. Hare has suggested that to presume a form of obligation not to be moral obligation may be to grant it a status that could lead to uncritical compliance.[33] What seems to be the case with the obligations of agreement? Are they "absolute" in any sense?

Let us first consider how things seem pretheoretically. On the one hand, we normally allow that it is permissible to break an agreement in certain circumstances, all things considered. For instance, I may break an agreement to attend a party in order to save a life.[34] In describing how the permissible contexts of violation are determined we sometimes refer to our exercise of "judgment." On the other hand, what our judgment tells us is precisely when we may *violate* or *break* an agreement.

This suggests that the obligation of agreement is viewed as absolute in the following sense. Once it is in place through the existence of an agreement, it remains in full force whatever the further circumstances—only provided that the agreement remains in place.

Thus, if Mike and Jane agree that she is to feed Fido at five, etc., she then has an obligation to feed Fido, as long as the proviso is satisfied. We assume that even when the proviso is satisfied it may still be permissible for Jane not to feed Fido at five, all things considered. We understand, however, that her agreement will then still be "binding" in a central sense: she will have to break the bond. Even where it is true that she has an obligation to break it, all things considered, what she has is an obligation to break an agreement, thereby violating one obligation in the service of another.

Compare this with the following version of the case of the injured child. Sally is out on her walk. At 4:30 P.M., the child falls down close to where she is walking and breaks its arm. Let us assume that (as many would suppose) Sally now has an obligation of some kind immediately to help the child. Now imagine that before she can do this, at 4:31 P.M., an elderly person collapses with a heart attack in a nearby driveway. I take it that at this point Sally has an obligation of some similar kind immediately to go to the aid of the elderly person, who may otherwise soon die. Does she still have the original obligation immediately to help the child? Surely not. She certainly does not have an obligation immediately to help the child, all things considered. If we artificially limit the considerations available (in particular omitting any reference to the heart attack) we can say that she has an obligation to help the child given these considerations only. But if we expand those considerations (bringing in the heart attack), surely any obligation immediately to help the child simply disappears.

Someone may doubt this. Why not say that the obligation remains but is discounted or overridden by a more compelling obligation? One reason is this. We surely do not want to say that Sally violated an obligation to help the child if she rushes to the heart attack victim.

This can be disputed if one insists that an obligation immediately to help the child "remains." But I see no reason for such insistence. Though the *basis* for such an obligation remains, in the actual surrounding circumstances no obligation gets *generated*.[35] In order for the obligation to be generated, the right surrounding circumstances must obtain.

Pretheoretically, then, it appears that there are two quite different types of obligation: a type that is context sensitive in a certain way, and a type that is not. The first type is such that even when an obligation of this type is present in one context, it may in principle disappear if the context is enlarged and an obligation of the same type but with a different content stands in its stead. The second type is such that if an obligation of this type is present in one context (e.g., an agreement stands), then it does not disappear if the context is enlarged (e.g., the agreement still stands, but one can save someone's life by violating it). It may be discounted in the light of the additional considerations, but it does not disappear.

The joint decision model of agreements provides an explanation of how the obligations of agreement can persist in the way that they are taken to. The obligations of agreement stand as long as the corresponding joint commitment does. Whether or not the commitment stands is a matter for the participants to decide. They are in a position to keep it in existence through whatever changes in the circumstances.

The obligations of agreement are, then, absolute in a sense: they do not go away unless the agreement is rescinded. At the same time, they do not necessarily determine what must be done, all things considered. Once we understand this we see that the type of absoluteness in question here need not lead to uncritical compliance.

The obligation in the case of the injured child would normally be referred to as "moral" obligation. Though it may not matter for some purposes whether we call both of the types of obligation discussed here "moral"—though that may even have something to recommend it—it is important to note that our obligations differ widely in logical character. The obligation of agreement is of one type, which is in a sense absolute, or lacking in overall context sensitivity. It has its source (I propose) in an existing joint commitment that stands unless and until those who participate in it concur in its dissolution. Obligation of the sort in the injured child case is of the other, context-sensitive type. The nature of its presumed source is a controversial matter that I am waiving here.[36]

Whether we call them "moral obligations" or not, agreements

generate obligations, obligations that only disappear when the agreement is at an end. One who manifests a simple "take it or leave it" attitude to agreements has failed to understand what an agreement is.[37] Precisely when an agreement may reasonably be violated appears to be a matter of judgment that goes beyond our understanding of the logic of agreement itself.[38]

Revisiting the Obligation Argument

Let us now briefly look back at the original version of the obligation argument (in the first part of section I). Let us refer to the obligation of agreement as I have so far characterized it as "obligation(ABS)." The most clearly correct version of the first premise is this:

> 1B. Any genuine agreement generates an obligation(ABS) to abide by it: this is a conceptual matter.

Taking "obligation(CON)" to be a (completely) context-sensitive obligation, and hence an obligation of a distinct type from obligation (ABS), let us interpret the second premise of the obligation argument as follows:

> 2B. If an apparent agreement is made in the face of coercion there is then no obligation(CON) to abide by it.

Even if 2B is true, when coupled with 1B it does not give us the desired conclusion:

> 3B. A genuine agreement cannot be made in the face of coercion.

To think so would be to treat obligation(ABS) and obligation(CON) as the same. In other words, it would be to commit a fallacy equivocation.

I conjecture that the truth of 1B illegitimately gives rise to the common assumption that a similar premise about moral obligation is definitionally true, moral obligation being viewed as a form of obligation(CON). If I am right about agreements and their obligation, however, no putative facts about the disappearance of any obligation (CON) in the face of coercion could show anything about the impact of coercion on the genuineness of an agreement or the persistence of its obligation. They are simply beside the point.[39]

Suppose that we start with 1B: we assume that the "obligation" referred to in the first premise of the obligation argument is "absolute" given the agreement from which it derives. Then the second premise, to be relevant, must claim that if an apparent agreement is made under coercive conditions, there can be no agreement and, hence, no (ensuing) obligation. Why not? The argument seems to collapse into the bald assertion that coercion prevents an agreement from taking place.

IV. Agreements, Coercion, and Obligation

Coerced Agreements

In direct discussion of the relation between coercion and agreement I shall assume that agreements are joint decisions, though many of the following points should be independently plausible pretheoretically.

Nothing that has been said so far entails that coerced agreements are impossible. It is true that if two people have agreed, each is to that extent obligated to act in conformity with their agreement. Once we properly understand the nature of the obligations in this case, we should be less inclined to see this apparently logical consequence of agreeing as a ground for denying the possibility of a coerced agreement. The parties know they have these obligations. They have intentionally assumed them.

What could be the point of coercing agreement? Clearly there is a possible point. Namely, to introduce an extra motivational force into the situation: the force precisely of perceived obligation. Those who agree know that they are under an obligation. They may or may not understand that this leaves open the question whether they must fulfill it, all things considered. Simply knowing what an agreement is would not seem to give one this understanding. Nor is the outcome of a particular person's deliberations on the merits of keeping a particular agreement always obvious in advance. So getting someone to agree may, at the end of the day, amount to getting them to act, even when good judgment would not allow that the act was mandatory, all things considered.

Let us consider a gunman case: "Yes, I agree to marry Emily," says Ben, staring down the barrel of Emily's father's shotgun. Having agreed, he may or may not marry Emily in the end. If he does, it could be because he has agreed to do so.

"I don't owe him anything," Ben might say of Emily's father, "after all, he forced me to agree." We can construe this in ways conformable to my analysis so far. "Owe" here could allude to a context-sensitive type of obligation, distinct from the obligation of agreement. According to at least some conceptions, it could allude, that is, to moral obligation or an "owing" based on all morally relevant considerations.

It may well be that (in some appropriate sense) Ben's coercer is not morally entitled to his performance, does not morally deserve his performance, and will have no basis for complaint against Ben's moral character if he breaks the agreement, given what he himself did to bring the agreement about. It may be that Ben has no moral obligation to perform, that Ben owes his coercer nothing, morally speaking. However, all this can be true without it being clear what Ben should do all things considered. One thing to consider, or so it seems, is the fact that he agreed and has the corresponding obligation to conform.

Does the fact that Ben was coerced into agreeing in itself show that there was something to be said against marrying Emily from Ben's point of view? I have made no attempt here to define coercion or duress, preferring to operate on the basis of tacit understandings and cases assumed to be clear-cut. Nonetheless, our understanding of these terms is relevant here, and so must be (all too briefly) considered.

A standard way to define duress in the law is exemplified in the following statement: "Duress may consist of actual or threatened violence or imprisonment . . . [which threat] contributed to the decision of the person threatened to enter into the contract . . . even though he might well have entered into it all the same if no threats had been made."[40]

It is explicitly not made part of this account of duress that the person was pressured into entering an agreement he would not have entered except under such pressure. It is only that the pressure must in fact have motivated him in the situation under consideration. If we define a coerced agreement in terms of a threat of violence that in fact motivated a person to agree, the definition does not tell us that there are independent reasons against keeping the agreement once it is made.

Whether the agreement should in fact be kept will be a matter of judgment, in the light of all the relevant facts. Constrained by Emily's father's gun to agree to marry Emily, Ben might decide, after a thoroughly enjoyable evening with her, that he would very much like to marry her. There will then be no conflict between the agreement and his evaluation of the courses of action open to him. The agreement may well be instrumental in motivating his performance. He may be an indecisive person. His obligation under the agreement may be what moves him.

In contrast, constrained by an intruder's knife to agree to sit still while he rampages through the house, Emily may perceive that she has a moral duty to escape as soon as he leaves the room. In other words, she has a moral duty not to conform to the agreement. In such cases the cards are stacked against the coerced agreement, or so most people would hold.

It is evident that in some cases the coerced person agrees to do something she finds wholly repugnant, though she deems death to be worse. It may seem dangerous to argue that in such cases, as in others, there is an obligation to perform. This is surely not so, however, if it can also be argued that the other party has no moral right to performance, the coerced person is morally entitled to renege, and it only remains to consider whether she has adequate reasons for failing to conform. If to conform would be to bring about a great evil, perhaps her own terrible pain and anguish, then these reasons are presumably more than adequate. All things considered, she should violate the agreement if she can.[41]

Coercion and the Extent of Political Obligation

If I am right about agreements, there is no need to accept Simmons's claim that few people are in a position to agree to fulfill the duties of citizenship. Simmons argues that even in modern democracies the circumstances of the proposed agreement are generally analogous to coercion. If my argument here succeeds, it robs this argument of all force, for I have argued that agreements are possible in the face of outright coercion. I have also argued that whenever there is an agreement, there are corresponding obligations to conform to it. Thus the potential scope of an "actual contract" theory of political obligation is wider than Simmons's claim suggests.

It is standard to formulate the philosophical problem of political obligation as a problem about moral obligation. Whether or not the obligation of agreement is best characterized as a form of moral obligation, the obligations of agreement are surely highly relevant to the traditional questions concerning political obligation.

First, as far as the literature goes it appears that what is understood to make an obligation "political" is not so much the type as the context of the obligation. Political obligations are obligations *to obey particular laws, support particular political institutions*, and so on.

Second, the political obligations of interest have been contrasted with the "positional" or "institutional" obligations that some group or individual associates with a particular social position (such as the position of citizen). People may come by "positional obligations" in this sense without themselves having a new reason for acting.[42] One's participation in an agreement generates obligations that are reasons for acting. They are not merely positional obligations.

Third, contracts or agreements have always been considered important sources of political obligation in political philosophy. It appears that the situation has generally been this: the obligations intrinsic to agreement have not so much been ignored as misperceived, as in the obligation argument that takes coercion to rule these obligations out.

I argue elsewhere that we can give a plausible account of a central class of perceived political bonds in terms of obligations of the type agreement produces—in terms, more specifically, of the obligations of joint commitment. This surely has to count as a theory of at least one central kind of political obligation.[43]

There are a number of importantly different ways of modeling the psychological reality that underlies the persistence of political regimes of all kinds, including oppressive dictatorships. Sometimes obedience may be wholly motivated by fear. At other times conformity may be at least partly motivated by the sense of participation in an agreement or something like it. If people perceive themselves to be parties to an agreement to conform, this will provide an additional pull in the direction of conformity, a pull that works at the level of reason.[44]

I cannot explore the actual extent of agreements and agreement-like phenomena here. As I have explained elsewhere, I believe it to be quite wide.[45]

In sum, unless political theorists are clear about the nature of agreements, they are likely to misunderstand the scope of actual contract theory, to underestimate the potential extent of the obligations that derive from agreements and the like, to miss a crucial basis of perceived "political bonds," and to overlook a central type of political motivation.

V. Conclusion

In the course of this essay I have appealed to several judgments I suspect people would make pretheoretically: not thoughtlessly, but in advance of accepting any particular articulated theory of agreements.

These include the assumptions that those who enter into agreements know that they do, that there is a conceptual connection between agreement and obligation, that the obligations of agreement makers are interdependent, and that it is possible to force someone to agree.

There has not been space to argue for the independent plausibility of each of these judgments from a pretheoretical point of view, though such arguments can be given. In any case, the proposal about agreements and their obligations presented here provides indirect support for each of these judgments individually: the mere fact that it provides a single articulated basis for them all encourages the idea that each one is indeed an acceptable "ground-level" judgment. At the same time this systemizing role helps to confirm the acceptability of the account of agreements itself, given that there is at least some plausibility in the allegedly ground-level judgments. I take it that the account also has some independent plausibility of its own. Thus theory and ground-level judgments are (to a degree at least) in "reflective equilibrium," to borrow Rawls's phrase.

Given a certain picture of agreements, and a particular understanding of obligation, coerced agreements are possible and they all generate obligations of conformity. There is much that is speculative in this picture. At the same time, I am not aware of any more intuitively satisfactory picture of the way things are in our everyday conceptual scheme of agreements, coercion, and obligation.[46]

Notes

1. I argue that paradigmatic social phenomena such as social conventions have an underlying structure analogous to that of agreements in *On Social Facts*. See also Chapter 7, this volume, and elsewhere.

2. See, for example, Becker (1981), p. 100; Beran (1977), p. 267; Kavka (1986), p. 396 (not "morally binding"); Simmons (1979), p. 82 (with specific reference to "consent"), and (1984), pp. 812, 816; Walzer (1970), pp. xii–xiv; Woozley (1979), p. 104.

3. See, for example, Kavka (1986); Raz (1981), p. 126 (with specific reference to "consent"); Simmons (1979), p. 82 ("consent"), and (1984), p. 816.

4. That is not to say that legal judgments have no bearing on the discussion, or vice versa. Some legal judgments are referred to below, but I attempt no systematic consideration of legal discussions of contract in this essay.

5. There is a similar common argument about promises. I shall not explore this directly here.

6. Simmons (1984), especially pp. 809–17; and also (1979), pp. 99–100.

7. There is no need to fix on a precise definition for "common knowledge" here. See Chapter 1, note 4, this volume, for references to the literature, beginning with Lewis (1969).

8. Thus claims such as the following would not contradict the assumption: "By getting on a bus one concludes, whether or not one knows it, a legally binding contract" (Finnis [1980], p. 299).

9. The phrases "decision-for" and "decision in favor" may strike a more deliberative note than is apposite to make my point. I am assuming that if one acts with the intention of doing X, then this incorporates a "decision-for" X in the relevant technical sense: it incorporates a positive inclination of the will toward X. With this caveat, I shall stick with the phrase "decision-for," which I feel emphasizes the involvement of the person's will in the process, whereas "intention" seems rather to emphasize the understanding or cognitive component.

10. It is sometimes rational to do more then feign agreement, given that such feigning is possible. For example, the other party may have a nose for deceptions. See also note 27 below.

11. Quoted in Guest, ed. (1984), p. 242. Some earlier judgments, condemned by Guest (Anson) as "fallacious" argued that in "a successful plea of duress . . . the party affected must show that the compulsion was such as to vitiate his consent, to deprive him of any *animus contrahendi*" (ibid.). In these legal discussions, then, we seem to find an oscillation between a sense that a successful plea of duress is actually a plea of "nonagreement" and a sense that even if there is an agreement under duress, it should be "revocable" in law (Scarman). The main issue there, of course, is the determination of proper legal judgments. It may well be that what is an agreement intuitively speaking should sometimes be considered void, or at least voidable or revocable in law. The law has its own reasons, which have to do, among other things, with fairness and right (as well as history and tradition).

12. See Simmons (1984), p. 810.

13. That a decision provides a reason at all may appear to need arguing. It is implicit, however, in the way we think about decisions. Suppose that, having decided to eat in the factory cafeteria, and without first changing her mind, Molly starts in the direction of a local restaurant. We would surely judge that (all else being equal) something is amiss. More precisely, we would judge that Molly had a reason not to act in this way, a reason her decision provided. It may well be that there are importantly different types of reason, such that decisions and the like generate reasons of a special type. Bratman (1987) appears to argue along these lines, decisions and the like being what he calls "framework reasons." For present purposes, such distinctions need not concern us. The main point here is that from an intuitive point of view we regard decisions as reasons for acting in the broad sense at issue here. (I say more about some aspects of decisions below.)

14. Some philosophers have asserted that use of the term "obligation" in this type of case is improperly loose. However, the term is often so used in both everyday and philosophical talk. See Brandt (1965), p. 387.

15. A similar view is found in accounts of contract (or certain types of contract) in common law. That does not of course clinch anything with respect to the proper analysis of vernacular notions.

16. In Chapter 13, this volume. These discussions expand on some comments in *On Social Facts* (see p. 380).

17. In general terms, if a person X promises to do a certain act A on a certain occasion, no one else can break X's promise. X alone can break it, by not doing A when the occasion arises. The same goes for conditional promises. Suppose X promises that he will do A on a certain occasion, provided only that a second person Y performs act B on some prior occasion. Y still cannot break X's promise. If Y fails to do B when it is called for, X no longer has any option of performing his promise. But it has not been broken. Indeed, it never can be broken, now, since X will never have the opportunity not to perform when his performance is called for.

18. I argue this in Chapter 13, this volume.

19. *On Social Facts*, pp. 380–81.

20. See *On Social Facts* and elsewhere.

21. For more on plural subjects, see *On Social Facts* and elsewhere. I introduced the relevant notion of joint acceptance in "Modeling Collective Belief," Chapter 7, this volume.

22. Is it possible in principle for people to make an agreement without previously forming a plural subject? Insofar as "mutual recognition" on meeting in person itself creates a plural subject (see *On Social Facts*, pp. 217–18), this may be difficult. Perhaps this is an example, however: using electronic mail, I send out my part of an agreement to someone I know only by name. "Would you answer all my e-mail messages if I answered all of yours?" Were she to reply "Yes," we could have an agreement, it seems, without any prior "we" formation between us. Our only communication would be the communication of each one's individual willingness to form the agreement.

23. The "individualistic" nature of our focus in talking of agreement may be what has led many to assume that nothing of a contractual nature could lie at the basis of society. What those who agree *de novo* need, however, is only the power jointly to commit themselves in the area in question. They need in no other way be "asocial" or "atomistically conceived" either by themselves or anyone else. Those sympathetic to a contractual account of social groups are presumably sensitive to the "holistic" nature of what is achieved by agreements (i.e., of a joint commitment), whether or not they have clearly grasped what this achievement amounts to. See *On Social Facts*, Chapter 7, and Chapter 6, this volume, for some references to contract theory, Rousseau, and Hobbes in this connection. I hope to treat this matter at greater length elsewhere.

24. The original exposition here has been slightly changed. For some further observations see the introduction, this volume.

25. What precisely needs to be expressed is a somewhat delicate matter. Each party must evidently be "ready for joint commitment" as far as his will is concerned; yet (as he understands) only once a certain condition is fulfilled can he be committed as a function of the intended joint commitment. Thus one who says "Shall we dance?" indicates that, in effect, he will be committed to dancing if (and only if) his question is answered appropriately. This commitment to dance will be a function of the joint commitment then (and only then) created. One relatively crude way of describing what needs to be expressed is (as I have sometimes put it) a "conditional commitment." This description needs to be understood as indicated here.

26. John Deigh suggested the metaphor of lock and key(s) (personal communication, December 1992).

27. What of people who feign willingness to enter the relevant joint commitment? Can they avoid incurring the obligations of agreement by such a pretense? (Compare the idea of "mental reservation" to avoid lying.) Two brief comments must suffice here. First, there is some question whether the very idea of setting out not to incur the relevant commitment is intelligible, at least in the context of standard conventions. One cannot appropriately form just any intention one pleases, regardless of one's own other beliefs and commitments. (I thank Catherine Elgin for relevant discussion [January 1993].) Second, suppose that somehow Adam contrives to have Eve reasonably presume that they have made an agreement. Eve then relies on the presumed agreement between them, to her own detriment. Whether or not he has obligations under an agreement, Adam is morally responsible for whatever damage his manipulations produced, all else being equal. See below, in the text, for some discussion of the relevant contrast.

28. I am not alone in thinking that the obligatoriness of agreement can be understood without reference to social practices. For a recent discussion along these lines (though along different lines from this article), see Scanlon (1990), p. 199–226, and further references therein.

29. By an "external" phenomenon here I mean one that is not part of or logically derivable from the "conceptual essence" of agreement. It may be unusual, but as long as it is logically possible for there to be an agreement unaccompanied by the phenomenon in question, then it is "external" in the sense at issue.

30. In this article I appeal to several judgments I suspect people would make before accepting any particular articulated theory. There is no space here to argue at any length for the independent plausibility of each of these judgments from a pretheoretical point of view. I hope to do so in another place. For further comments on these appeals, see section V ("Conclusion"), below.

31. Even a silly agreement fabricated to make this point will have that quality. Try agreeing with a friend that after she leaves the room she will say

"Bip" and you will say "Bop." Presumably neither of you particularly cares to have this happen, and neither will base any future action on the other's performance. It is an entirely capricious and whimsical agreement. Nonetheless it seems to have the binding qualities any agreement has.

32. Given that an agreement is as described here, and that it therefore has an ensuing obligation of the kind described, is there something about conforming to any agreement that grounds another obligation to conform, an obligation of the kind, perhaps, that is at issue in the injured child case (see below)? This seems doubtful on the face of it. I shall not attempt to consider it further here. Any such obligation is likely to be a function of the existence of the first kind of obligation—the kind intrinsic to agreements as such.

33. See Hare (1989), pp. 8–9.

34. The case is similar to that of lying. Some may be inclined to think that a lie is never permissible morally. Some may feel the same about breaking an agreement or a promise. But the majority view goes the other way. Thus the view that one should not break an agreement even to avoid a great evil tends to be seen as absurd. (Possibly it stems from the perception that there is something "absolute" about the obligations of agreement. See below on the "absoluteness" of the obligation of agreement.)

35. As Sam Wheeler has pointed out to me, there is some concordant discussion in Davidson (1969), pp. 108–109.

36. If this sort of obligation is based on "where the most value lies," as some theorists would have it, one can see why it has the context sensitivity it does: enlarging the context at least potentially changes the value of any act. Perhaps some contexts are such that the context-sensitive obligation that arises within them will stand through however many possible enlargements of the context. The persistence of the obligation is then still a function of the character of the enlarged context.

37. Compare Robins (1984), p. 109, who—in contrast to Hare—suggests that unless we think of promissory obligations as moral obligations we will not take them seriously.

38. In *On Social Facts* and elsewhere I have suggested that the obligations of joint commitment are not moral obligations. I am inclined to think that this is a useful way of looking at things. Throughout the present article I attempt to be as agnostic as possible with respect to the definition of moral obligation. Everything of substance that I have to say about coerced agreements can be said without deciding that issue. The considerations raised in this section, meanwhile, are clearly relevant to that decision.

39. As I have already indicated, changing 1B by replacing "an obligation (ABS)" with "an obligation(CON)" does not give us a good argument. (i) If the new version of 1B refers to an alleged obligation(CON) that flows from an apparent agreement considered in isolation from its circumstances (of which coercion could be one), then the presumed fact that coercion left one with no moral obligation to conform to one's apparent agreement would not show that

there was no agreement at all. For it would have no bearing on the question of the implications of an apparent agreement considered in isolation. That is why in section II of this article I began by construing the first premise in terms of an obligation that stood in the light of all background circumstances. (ii) Suppose we now explicitly interpret the new version of 1B in terms of an alleged obligation(CON) that stands in the light of all background circumstances. As we have seen, though the desired conclusion 3B follows when the first premise is so construed, the premise is then implausible, at least given the limited understandings that seem to be necessary to enter an agreement.

40. Guest, ed. (1984), p. 240.

41. It is of some practical importance to stress that the fact that one agreed does not show that one was not *coerced into agreeing*. Judges have been known to rule against a verdict of rape on the grounds of the victim's consent to sexual intercourse. Surely the judgment of rape should focus on the presence and influence of coercion, not on whether there was acquiescence or some type of agreement. There is no space here to attempt a careful discussion of this important issue.

42. See Simmons on "positional" obligations (1979), pp. 16ff.

43. In ibid., Simmons takes as the primary datum for the theorist of political obligation an inclination to see ourselves as tied to our government and our country's institutions by "political bonds." I argue in Chapter 15 that the datum he focuses on can plausibly be accounted for in terms of the obligations of joint commitment.

44. Thus David Schmidtz (1990) is overly general when he writes: "The idea of a conqueror becoming justified by forcing his captives to pledge allegiance as the price of escaping with their lives is hardly plausible. I think it is more charitable to Hobbes to read his discussion as a purely descriptive account of the possible ways in which sovereigns can actually emerge, with no normative implications intended" (p. 98). My dispute is with "no normative implications." No *moral* implications of a certain sort, perhaps. But if captives enter an agreement or make a similar commitment, then this does have normative implications of an important kind. That is, it bears on what the captives have reason to do. Any genuine pledge or agreement has its own normative weight—as the conquering sovereign may well discern.

45. See *On Social Facts,* and elsewhere. See also M. Walzer (1970), Introduction, pp. ix–xvi.

46. The first draft of this essay was written when I was a Visiting Fellow of Wolfson College, Oxford University (1989–1990). That work was supported by an American Council of Learned Societies Fellowship for Research and a University of Connecticut sabbatical grant (1989–1990). Versions have been presented at the Political Theory Conference held at the New College, Oxford, January 1990, and at York University; the University of Connecticut, Storrs; Queens College, CUNY; M.I.T.; and Princeton University. I am grateful for

all comments. Special thanks to John Horton, Chris Megone, John Troyer, and Frank Stewart for lengthy comments on written material, and to John Deigh, Christine Korsgaard, and Saul Kripke for extended discussions. Responsibility for the ideas expressed here is mine alone.

13

Is an Agreement an Exchange of Promises?

(1) Hal: "So we'll both go to the bus stop at four?"
Mavis: "Yep."
(2) Rita: "Someone must walk Fido this afternoon, and Tibbles
has to be groomed."
Peter "Why don't you walk Fido, and I'll groom Tibbles?"
Rita: "Fine!"

The interactions depicted in (1) and (2) exemplify the process by virtue
of which an agreement is formed, an informal agreement of the sort
that permeates everyday life. Understanding what agreements amount
to is of the first importance. Their pervasiveness implies that no
descriptive theory of human interaction can be complete without an
account of them. Nor can we fully understand their role in our lives
without a clear comprehension of their nature. Then there is the
perennial claim that an agreement lies at the foundation of human
societies. I believe that although it is not strictly accurate, this claim
contains an important insight. Informal agreements such as those made
by Hal and Mavis and Rita and Peter represent in an especially clear-
cut way the normative structure of a phenomenon that lies at the core
of social union, a phenomenon I have referred to elsewhere as *joint
commitment*.[1] As I shall argue here, the standard account of agreements obscures this connection.

The standard assumption in the literature is that an agreement is an
exchange of promises. Thus, Michael Robins assumes without argument that an agreement is a "mutual exchange of conditional promises."[2] David Lewis refers to "an exchange of formal or tacit promises."[3] Annette Baier writes of "mutual promises."[4] Patrick Atiyah
refers to the general "equation of the concept of 'an agreement' with

313

mutual promises."[5] There is a similar legal theory regarding contract. In *An Introduction to the Law of Contract,* Atiyah accepts as the "most accurate" definition of contract the following (from the *American Restatement of the Law of Contracts*): "A contract is a promise or set of promises for the breach of which the law gives a remedy, or the performance of which the law in some way recognizes as a duty."[6] This view of contract may or may not have influenced those writers who see everyday agreements as promise-exchanges. Quite possibly, it was itself influenced by the corresponding view of everyday agreements (see the next section).

Although the idea that an agreement is an exchange of promises has some initial plausibility, I argue in this essay that it must be rejected.[7] More precisely, I argue that typical informal agreements of the sort made by Hal and Mavis or Peter and Rita cannot be construed as promise-exchanges. A set of criteria that any adequate account of such agreements must meet is formulated. I argue that no promise-exchange meets all of these criteria. The formulation of the criteria itself helps to reveal the nature of the type of agreement in question, and to explain the perennial tendency to see agreements in general as the foundation of a human society.

I. Note on the Everyday Concept of Agreement and Contract Law

I shall here pursue the everyday concept of an agreement, without essential reference to the law of contract. This is not to say that there is no connection between this concept and contract law. There clearly will be a connection insofar as the law of contract is seen by those who determine its content as the law-as-it-relates-to-agreements-as-intuitively-conceived. We shall then expect contract law to incorporate intuitive understandings about the nature of agreements. To what extent it does is a matter for the student of particular legal systems.

Could the everyday notion of agreement itself be an offshoot of developments in contract law? It is hard to believe that laws about contracts are historically prior to informal agreements. For present purposes, there is no need to pursue such historical matters. We have an everyday notion of agreement, one that people with little or no knowledge of law employ all the time. One way or another, in order to understand the relationship between this notion and legal notions of contract we need to ask the question: When ordinary people understand that they have agreed, what is it that they understand?

II. Three Criteria

Suppose that Hal and Mavis have agreed, by virtue of some such interaction as that depicted in example (1) above, that each of them will go to the bus stop at four. Their agreement explicitly assigns a particular future act to each participant. In what follows, I shall be concerned at all times with agreements of this sort, unless I make some disclaimer.[8]

We understand that the agreement generates for each participant an obligation to perform the specified act. I shall call this obligation the participant's *performance obligation*. In the case of Hal and Mavis, each gains a performance obligation to come to the bus stop at four. In the case of Rita and Peter (example [2] above), Peter gains a performance obligation to groom Tibbles, and Rita gains a performance obligation to walk Fido. Performance obligations may be unconditional, as in these cases, or conditional. My obligation may be to come to the bus stop at four if the sun is shining, for instance, or if I finish my work in time. When I write of "the obligations" of agreement in what follows, I should be understood to refer to performance obligations as those have just been characterized.[9]

I take our understanding to be that each party gains a performance obligation from the agreement given only that the agreement stands. A model of the sample agreements will be adequate, then, only if it meets the *obligation criterion:* the agreement directly generates the relevant performance obligation for each of the parties.

Let us consider promises for a moment. I take our understanding to be that a given promise directly generates a performance obligation for the promisor.[10] This simple correspondence may encourage the assumption that an agreement is just a pair of promises. As I shall argue, that assumption cannot be sustained.

To return to our sample agreements. The obligations that derive from them are surely simultaneous. That is, neither party has one until the other does. Consider the dialogue between Hal and Mavis. It is true that Hal speaks first. Yet he surely has no obligation to go to the bus stop at four until Mavis accepts his proposal. Only at this time are both obligations in place. The same seems true for Rita and Peter, *mutatis mutandis*. We can thus distinguish another criterion of adequacy for a model of these agreements, which I shall call the *simultaneity criterion*.

Speaking generally, the ability to produce simultaneous obligations is clearly a useful one. In many cases, a given party will have no desire to take on some particular obligation before the other party has taken on a corresponding obligation. Something about the sample agreements ensures that obligations are undertaken simultaneously by the parties, even though one may speak or relevantly gesture before the other. No one is *obligated first*.

A further criterion must be noted. Suppose that at noon Mavis sees Hal get on a plane headed for Los Angeles. Mavis knows that there is now no way that Hal can honor their agreement. To all intents and purposes, he has already defaulted on his own obligation. I take it that according to our common understanding, Mavis can now regard herself as free of obligation through the agreement.[11]

I waive here a question about the reason for Hal's default. Could it be that Mavis is only relieved of her obligation if Hal's act of default lacked proper justification? Suppose, for example, that he entered the plane in order to avoid being shot by a terrorist?[12] Rather than consider this, I shall suppose for the sake of argument that we are talking at all times about unjustified default. I take it that, according to our common understanding, if Hal deliberately defaulted for no good reason, Mavis no longer has any obligation through their agreement.

I also waive the question of how things stand with similar agreements according to which one or more of the parties is obligated to do many things, such as going to the bank, the supermarket, and the drugstore. Suppose these are Jenny's obligations, and she fails to go to the bank. Has she now violated her agreement in such a way as to absolve her opposite number from any or all of his obligations under the agreement? This may not be entirely clear. In the examples we are considering, in any case, each party's obligation is to do one particular thing. I take it that according to our common understanding regarding such cases, if one party defaults, the other's obligation will lapse.

One way of describing the aspect of agreements now under discussion is this: if Hal violates the agreement, he nullifies both his own and Mavis's obligation under it: *both* obligations are now "as nothing."

The agreement between Rita and Peter has a special feature that could possibly lead to confusion on this point. Suppose Rita calls Peter to say she has left town and cannot be back until the next day. She has, in effect, defaulted on her obligation through the agreement. Is Peter still obligated to groom Tibbles? It may appear that he is, since Tibbles is in need of attention. Indeed, Peter is probably obligated to walk Fido as well, since Rita will not be taking him out. Perhaps Peter is obligated to do both things. But this appears to have nothing to do with the agreement. The relevant question for present purposes is whether Peter still has an obligation *through the agreement to* groom Tibbles. The answer to this question is surely: no. No one has any remaining obligations through the agreement itself.

This implies, of course, that the agreement itself is at an end, given that a standing agreement generates its performance obligations. This observation suggests the following rough characterization of the conditions under which an agreement is held to stand or be in effect: an unrescinded agreement generates its obligations for the parties until either these obligations have been fulfilled or one party has defaulted. The concurrence of the parties is required in order to rescind the agreement. In what follows, I shall assume this understanding of what it is for an agreement to be in effect.[13]

In sum, it appears that the obligations of both sample agreements are interdependent at least in the following way: if one party defaults on his performance obligation, the other ceases to have his original performance obligation. This gives us another criterion of adequacy for a model of these agreements: the *interdependence criterion.*

The sample agreements are typical of informal everyday agreements in which performance obligations accrue to both parties. Is there any form of promise-exchange that will meet all the criteria noted and at least to that extent provide an adequate model of the agreements in question?

III. Different Kinds of Promise

Before looking at candidate promise-exchanges, it will be useful to distinguish a number of different kinds of promise. The discussion that follows is intended to be quite informal and to appeal to what are sustainable distinctions at least at first sight. These matters could be discussed much more fully, but I cannot attempt a more detailed discussion here.

One can distinguish, first, between unconditional and conditional promises. The following is an *unconditional promise:*

(i) "I promise to mow the lawn."

Conditional promises in general are expressible as (unconditional) promises coupled with an "if" clause (this can be read in all that follows as "provided that" as opposed to "provided that and only provided that"). Thus, the following is some kind of conditional promise:

> (ii) "I promise to mow the lawn tomorrow, if you do the laundry today."

Note that a promise is deemed conditional here because it can be expressed in a certain way. One can then distinguish two kinds of conditional promise. For want of some labels, I shall refer to these as externally conditional promises and internally conditional promises.[14] An *internally conditional promise* is a promise that one will do a certain thing, provided that a particular condition holds. The condition is a matter of the circumstances under which a certain act will (according to the promise) be performed. The condition is thus "internal" to the promise. To indicate clearly that a promise is internally conditional, I shall formulate it thus:

> (iia) "I promise this: if you do the laundry today, I will mow the lawn tomorrow."

The condition of an *externally conditional promise* is a condition of the existence of the promise as such. In what follows, I shall indicate that a promise is externally conditional by formulating it thus:

> (iib) "On condition that you do the laundry today, I promise to mow the lawn tomorrow."

Questions arise about both kinds of conditional promise. What I am calling an externally conditional "promise" to do A does not in fact become a promise to do A unless its condition is met. The question arises: At what time does it become a promise to do A, generating the appropriate promissory obligation? Suppose that on Sunday I make the externally conditional promise (iib). Later that day you do the laundry. Do I come by my own promissory obligation at the time you do the laundry? Or, given that you in fact do the laundry on Sunday, do I already have such an obligation when I give my externally conditional promise (an obligation that, to be sure, I may not be certain that I have)?

It is not easy to know precisely how to answer this question about externally conditional promises. On the face of it, these are not commonly made in everyday life. It would be most natural to interpret any linguistically undifferentiated promise as internally conditional. Thus, it seems one has to ask "What could be meant?" rather than "What is ordinarily meant?" by such an utterance.

If externally conditional promises are construed in a particular way, appeal to them can aid the attempt to construct an agreement out of a promise-exchange. For present purposes, I shall adopt this construal: an externally conditional promise to do *A* becomes a promise to do *A* and generates its promissory obligation *when and only when* its condition is fulfilled. If this construal is ultimately untenable, or indeed if the whole notion of an externally conditional promise is ultimately untenable, there will be less of a case for the analysis of agreements as promise-exchanges than I shall allow here. Indeed, it is not altogether clear that one should allow the *promise* exchange theorist the use of externally conditional promises, but I shall do so here for the purposes of argument.[15]

What of internally conditional promises? I take it that these generate their obligations at the time they are made. Perhaps this could be doubted. Evidently, the obligation generated is conditional. For the promise in (iia) it is an obligation for the promisor to mow the lawn tomorrow if "you" do the laundry today. Now the notion of a conditional obligation is not unproblematic. Is the condition "internal" to the obligation, does the obligation only come into being if its condition is met, or what? In the context of discussing internally conditional promises, it is surely plausible to construe the condition as internal to the obligation, for presumably one who makes such a promise intends a categorical promise, even if what is promised involves a condition. He intends, in other words, to *obligate himself* at once. His obligation, then, is an obligation *to mow the lawn tomorrow provided that you do the laundry today*. Given that we adopt this interpretation, it is natural to take it that the obligation does not cease if the condition fails to obtain. It simply becomes a conditional obligation that will never motivate: it will never generate an unconditional obligation to mow the lawn tomorrow. The discussion that follows will proceed in terms of these judgments about internally conditional promises.[16]

IV. A Simple Promise-Exchange

For present purposes, I shall construe the notion of an exchange of promises broadly: an exchange of promises takes place between *X* and

Y if and only if *X* makes a promise to *Y,* and *Y* responds with a promise to *X*.[17] As is clear already, an exchange of promises can take many different forms, and different forms will have importantly different properties. I shall now review a variety of forms of promise-exchange that might be thought to represent the gist of the agreement between Rita and Peter. I shall argue for each form that it does not satisfy all of the stated criteria for a model of this agreement.

It is important to stipulate that one of the rules of procedure here is to take the exchange in question at face value. In particular, each person makes a promise, and no more than a promise. The question is: If precisely these promises had (in effect) been exchanged, would the stated criteria have been met? Subsidiary to this question another question will be answered: What does the exchange of promises in question in fact provide by way of a structure of obligations? I shall thus in effect be comparing and contrasting the implications of different forms of promise-exchange and those of our sample agreement.

I start with the simplest form of promise-exchange: an initial unconditional promise and an unconditional "counterpromise." Suppose that Peter and Rita had explicitly exchanged promises as follows.

Promise-exchange 1

> Peter: "I promise to groom Tibbles this afternoon."
> Rita: "I promise to walk Fido this afternoon."

Does this promise-exchange fulfill the criteria? We may assume that the obligation criterion is fulfilled. If Peter's promise occurs before Rita's, however, Peter incurs a performance obligation through his promise before Rita incurs one through hers. Thus, the simultaneity criterion is not met.

It may be pointed out that this exchange only fails to meet the simultaneity criterion because the promises are made in a temporal sequence. If Peter and Rita were to "belt out" their promises in unison, then the simultaneity criterion might be met. This suggests that the criterion is relatively superficial. Various devices could surmount the obvious problem of "noise." If people communicated by pressing buttons that created "utterances" on a screen, they could simultaneously commit themselves by means of these promises.

Still, mutual promises uttered in unison are at present not generally practical. Effective communication of simultaneously *spoken* promises is unlikely. Meanwhile, in the common or garden communication processes that are taken to engender agreements, one person speaks before the other does, and we do not take that person to be committed before the other is. Evidently a simple exchange of sequential unconditional promises is not what is then at issue.[18]

There is a further problem. The interdependence criterion is not satisfied even by unconditional promises given simultaneously. Once Peter has made his promise, his ensuing obligation is independent of Rita's, and vice versa. Even if Rita breaks her promise, and fails to walk Fido, Peter's promise, and hence his obligation to groom Tibbles, remains intact.

Under what conditions is a promise held to stand or be in effect? I take it that the common understanding is close to that regarding agreements: a given promise stands until its performance obligation has either been fulfilled or violated, unless it is rescinded. Such rescission requires the concurrence of the promisee. In other words, the promisor requires to be "released" from his promise by the promisee. In that case, your breaking your promise cannot automatically affect the standing of my promise. For your breaking your promise cannot of itself release me from my promise.[19] Nor can it of itself fulfill or violate the obligation of my promise.[20]

In a related context, Charles Fried asks, "Does your breaking your promise cancel my reciprocal obligation to you or just give me a remedy for my disappointment? There is no obvious a priori reason for one or the other response. It does seem fairer to release someone from an obligation of trust to another who has shown himself unwilling to accept the same obligation" (Fried, 1981, p. 46 n.). Perhaps it is true that once you break your promise to me, I am not morally obliged to keep my (reciprocal) promise to you. There appears to be a clear a priori answer to the question, however: "Does your breaking your promise automatically cancel the obligation I would otherwise have through my standing promise?" The answer is: no. Your breaking your promise does not automatically affect the standing of my promise. Given that my promise stands, its obligation remains. There may of course be reasons that mandate or permit my not fulfilling these obligations, but that is another matter.[21] I conclude that an exchange of unconditional promises does not meet the stated criteria. Even if in special circumstances such promises can meet the simultaneity criterion, they do not meet the interdependence criterion.

It appears that enough has already been said to show that *no* exchange of promises can model our example agreement, for surely *none* can meet the interdependence criterion. Once I have a performance obligation through a promise, no one else can eliminate it by breaking some other promise. So no pair of promises can meet the interdependence criterion. What happens if conditional promises are introduced? This does not change things as far as the interdependence criterion is concerned. Conditional promises are alluded to by many of those who see agreements as promise-exchanges, however, and it is worth focusing on them directly. If one appeals to them one can indeed do more than can be done with a sequential exchange of unconditional promises. (I later consider proposals involving unconditional promises plus special understandings.)

V. Conditional Promises: Some Symmetrical Exchanges

Whatever the exchange of promises just considered failed to do, it succeeded in generating performance obligations for both parties. If we include externally conditional promises, not all exchanges of promises do even this. Thus, consider the following:

Promise-exchange 2

Peter: "On condition that you (unconditionally) promise to walk Fido, I promise to groom Tibbles."
Rita: "On condition that you (unconditionally) promise to groom Tibbles, I promise to walk Fido."

This interchange results in no obligations; it generates nothing. For no one makes an unconditional promise, so neither (externally) conditional promise has its condition met. Clearly, an agreement is not an exchange of externally conditional promises whose condition is an externally unconditional promise.[22]

What, then, of an exchange of externally conditional promises whose condition is an externally conditional promise? Someone might propose:

Promise-exchange 3

Peter: "On condition that you make an externally conditional promise to walk Fido, I promise to groom Tibbles."
Rita: "On condition that you make an externally conditional promise to groom Tibbles, I promise to walk Fido."

The fact that this rather elaborate promise-exchange is unlikely ever to be voiced need not disturb us here. The main question is whether—for all its stiltedness—it delivers the goods we are after.

There is a special awkwardness about what Rita says here, for the condition of her promise has patently been met. In normal, informal interactions one would probably only say, "On condition that such-and-such occurs, I promise to do so-and-so," when one does not know that such-and-such has already occurred. For present purposes, we may ignore this awkwardness. There is nothing logically problematic about the exchange. At the same time, there is some plausibility to the idea that what is implicitly—and crucially—expressed when people enter an agreement is in some sense the same for all.[23]

There is a major problem with promise-exchange 3, which may be dealt with at once. Suppose that Peter makes his conditional promise first. The stated condition of this promise is "an externally conditional promise to walk Fido." This condition would be met if Rita were to reply: "On condition that you climb Mount Everest first, I promise to walk Fido." She would then have given an externally conditional promise to walk Fido, which is all that Peter demands. Peter would at this point have a promissory obligation to groom Tibbles. Assuming that Peter is incapable of climbing Mount Everest, Rita will never have a promissory obligation to walk Fido as a result of the externally conditional promise she has given. It does not seem that the party who speaks first in the process of agreement making is open to such a frustrating response.

Peter would avoid this difficulty (and would accord with what was really intended here) if he proffered the following self-referential externally conditional promise, which can then only properly be met by Rita's identical response:

Promise-exchange 4

    Peter: "On condition that you make the very same externally conditional promise that I now make, I promise to do my part in the following pair of actions: Peter grooms Tibbles and Rita walks Fido."

    Rita: "On condition that you make the very same externally conditional promise that I now make, I promise to do my part in the following pair of actions: Peter grooms Tibbles and Rita walks Fido."[24]

This may look suspiciously "clever": Can these really be the thoughts expressed when people enter everyday agreements? We may waive such an objection for present purposes, for this exchange does not meet all the relevant criteria.[25]

It does meet the obligation criterion. It also neatly meets the simultaneity criterion. It fails, however, to meet the interdependence criterion: once the conditions of their promises have been met, Peter and Rita are in exactly the same position as they would be after a simple exchange of unconditional promises.

The practical felicity of this particular form of promise-exchange is clear. Unlike a simple exchange of unconditional promises, it satisfies a first promisor's desire not to be obligated before his opposite number is obligated. Its practical infelicity is also clear. Just like a simple exchange of unconditional promises, it does not satisfy a desire to be free of obligation if one's opposite number breaks faith. Thus, once they have exchanged promises in this way, Peter is obligated to groom Tibbles, whether or not Rita takes Fido for a walk.[26]

Let us now look at an exchange of *internally* conditional promises, where each party's obligation is to perform a given act provided that the other person performs a given act.

Promise-exchange 5

> Peter: "I promise this: to groom Tibbles, if you walk Fido."
> Rita: "I promise this: to walk Fido, if you groom Tibbles."

This exchange has the following evident practical virtue: if Rita makes it impossible that she walk Fido, Peter will not be left with an *unconditional* promissory obligation to groom Tibbles.[27]

As a modeling of the example agreement, however, the exchange has serious problems. In the first place, given that the promises are made one after the other, Peter has an obligation through the promise before Rita does. It is true that his obligation is only to perform a certain act if a certain condition holds. He has, nonetheless, a genuine obligation, from which Rita alone can release him. After he has spoken, she could refuse to make any promise and hence avoid becoming obligated to Peter in any way. She will in any case have the satisfaction of knowing that if she takes Fido for a walk Peter will then be obligated to groom Tibbles.

One can overcome this particular problem with a pair of promises both externally and internally conditional. This again involves a self-referential externally conditional promise.

Promise-exchange 6

> Peter: "On condition that you make the very same externally conditional promise, I promise to do my part in the following pair of actions if you do your part: Peter grooms Tibbles and Rita walks Fido."
>
> Rita: "On condition that you make the very same externally conditional promise, I promise to do my part in the following pair of actions if you do your part: Peter grooms Tibbles and Rita walks Fido."

This exchange meets the simultaneity criterion: Peter only incurs an obligation through his promise when Rita makes her promise, satisfying the external condition of his promise, which in turn satisfies the external condition of her promise. In addition, this exchange avoids the problem of an exchange of unconditional promises or of promise-exchange 4 above: neither party will be left with an obligation to perform a certain act whatever the other does. Each one's promissory obligation is to perform a specified act provided that the other performs a specified act.

Perhaps one could allow that agreement makers implicitly made the above avowals, though what they actually said looks snappier. But does this new exchange effectively represent the agreement between Peter and Rita? Apparently not. It has two problems surviving from exchange 5. First, it does not provide the parties with interdependent obligations. If one defaults, the other is left with the obligation consequent on any internally conditional promise, the obligation to perform a certain act if a certain condition is met. This may or may not be of much practical significance. Second, the *obligation* criterion is not met in the way appropriate to the agreement. There the parties would understand that each has immediately incurred an *unconditional* obligation—Peter has the obligation to groom Tibbles, Rita the obligation to walk Fido. Here, in contrast, the parties understand that the obligation each has is an obligation to perform a given act if the other person acts in a certain way. The practical difference between these cases is considerable.

Note that, if Rita understands that she does not yet have an unconditional obligation to walk Fido, and that she will only have one given that Peter grooms Tibbles, she as yet has no reason (through the promise-exchange) to walk Fido at all. She will quite reasonably pay attention to the question whether she can expect Peter to groom Tibbles. The existence of Peter's internally conditional promise is unlikely to give her much satisfaction on that score. For it provides Peter with no stronger a motivation than her promise provides Rita. So we seem to have a structure of obligations with, at the end of the day, little if any motivational force. This seems very different from the case of our sample agreements.

What of the interdependence of the obligations of agreement? Does this perhaps bring their motivational force close to that of conditional obligations? Not when the obligations that are interdependent are unconditional obligations, as in our sample agreements. Compare case 1, where it is common knowledge that (a) each of us has an unconditional obligation to perform action A, and (b) each will cease to have that obligation if the other person defaults (the obligations being interdependent), and case 2, where it is common knowledge that (a) each has an obligation to do A *if* the other does A, and (b) each one's obligation will remain even if the other defaults.[28] These situations have an important similarity: if one party defaults the other will have no *unconditional* obligation to act. They differ crucially in motivational force, however. This can be shown clearly in terms of the sort of situation dealt with in game theory.

Suppose that it is common knowledge between the parties that there are no facts bearing on their situation other than those just described. Suppose, further, that the parties are rational in the sense that they are motivated solely by reasons for acting. Then in case 1, we can expect both parties to do A; in case 2, we can expect neither party to do anything (since there is nothing in the situation to motivate them).[29] This argument should be enough to show the value of devices, like our sample agreements, that generate a structure of obligations of the case-1 type as opposed to the case-2 type. In both cases, the parties have an important degree of security: no one can be left with an unconditional obligation after the other defaults. Only in case 1, however, is the structure of obligations sufficient rationally to motivate the parties.

VI. Conditional Promises: Some Asymmetrical Exchanges

Joseph Raz has judged the following form of exchange sufficient to constitute an agreement.[30]

Promise-exchange 7

> Peter: "I promise to groom Tibbles, if you walk Fido."

Rita walks Fido. Peter's promise here could be construed as either internally or externally conditional. He could be saying either "I promise this: if you walk Fido, I will groom Tibbles," or "On condition that you walk Fido, I promise to groom Tibbles." In the first case, he makes an outright promise and hence immediately undertakes an obligation, an obligation to groom Tibbles if Rita takes Fido for a walk. In the second case, he avoids incurring any obligation to act until Rita has actually done something.

This is not really an exchange of promises, though performance of an act might perhaps be regarded as the "limiting case" of a promise to do that act: any such promise is thereby made redundant. Nor does it capture the structure of an agreement in which the parties simultaneously take on *obligations* to perform certain acts in the future. It is, clearly, a possible state of affairs, but it is equally clearly not the state of affairs that is the focus of this essay. It is in any case worth mentioning that Rita's position here has a serious disadvantage: she must herself *act* before Peter has an unconditional obligation to act through his promise, on either construal. Her position thus involves a special type of insecurity.[31]

Raz has characterized the following as "a special case" of the previous form of exchange and claims that here too "there is an agreement between the promisor and the promisee."[32]

Promise-exchange 8

> Peter: "I promise to groom Tibbles, if you promise to walk Fido."
> Rita: "I promise to walk Fido."

This has two possible construals. Peter may be saying, "On condition that you promise to walk Fido, I promise to groom Tibbles," or "I promise this: on condition that you promise to walk Fido, I will groom Tibbles." If we take the first construal, then Peter incurs no promissory obligations before Rita does. The simultaneity condition is fulfilled. If we take the second, then Peter incurs a promissory obligation at once. In either case, once Rita has made her promise, each has an independent unconditional obligation. Peter has an independent obligation to groom Tibbles, Rita an independent obligation to walk Fido. The interdependence condition is not met. The parties are in the situation they would have been in had they issued simple unconditional promises in the first place.

H. A. Prichard envisages two more complex asymmetrical forms of promise-exchange.[33] In each case, an initial internally conditional promise is coupled with an externally conditional one whose condition is the initial promise. Here is the first form of exchange, with emphases to aid comprehension:

Promise-exchange 9

> Peter: "*I promise* this: I will groom Tibbles, if you promise this: to walk Fido if I groom Tibbles."
> Rita: "On condition that[34] you promise this: you will groom Tibbles if I promise this: I will walk Fido if you groom Tibbles, *I promise* this: to walk Fido if you groom Tibbles."

Given this exchange, Peter is obligated to groom Tibbles, and Rita is obligated to walk Fido if he does so. These obligations arise simultaneously. They are independent, however. If Rita renders herself incapable of walking Fido, Peter is still obligated to groom Tibbles.

Prichard's second exchange runs as follows:

Promise-exchange 10

> Peter: "*I promise* this: I will groom Tibbles, if you promise to walk Fido."
> Rita: "On condition that you promise this: you will groom Tibbles, if I promise to walk Fido, *I promise* to walk Fido."

The ensuing obligations, which arise simultaneously, are independent of each other. Each is unconditionally and independently bound to perform the act their promise specifies.

I shall not discuss any further forms of promise-exchange, symmetrical or asymmetrical. It is clear that none will simultaneously generate a set of unconditional, interdependent performance obligations, as our sample agreement does. This is not just a matter of technical interest. In not fulfilling all three criteria, each of the promise-exchanges considered has had some serious disadvantage, in terms of riskiness for one or both parties or lack of motivational force. It is safe to say that every form of promise-exchange will involve some such disadvantage.

VII. Exchanges of Unconditional Promises Plus Special Understandings

At this point, someone may suggest that, in order properly to represent our sample agreements, what we need is two unconditional promises plus something else. More specifically, it might be suggested that we want an exchange of unconditional promises plus some special understandings about these promises or this exchange.

Here is one possible hypothesis: the agreement is an exchange of unconditional promises. The first promise is here understood not to take effect until the second promise has been given, however. This hypothesis takes seriously the criterion of (unconditional) obligation and the simultaneity criterion. It involves two obvious problems, however. One is that once both promises are set up, the interdependence criterion is not satisfied. The other is a problem of a different kind. If the first promise is indeed an unconditional promise, and understood to be such, then it *will* take effect before the second promise is given. That is what unconditional promises are like: they commit the speaker once they have been made, and immediately obligate him. One would, therefore, be better not using the term "promise" in the context of this hypothesis.

A more complex hypothesis could respect both the interdependence and the simultaneity criteria. According to this hypothesis, the agreement is a pair of unconditional promises such that it is understood at the outset by both parties that (a) the first promise does not come into effect until the second has been given, and (b) if (once both promises are in effect) one promise is broken, both promises are nullified, and no further obligations arise out of them for either party.

This more complex hypothesis, however, fails to respect the nature of promising in two ways. First, it fails to respect the immediate commitment and obligation of an unconditional promise. Second, it fails to respect the fact that, if you have made an unconditional promise that still stands, you are obligated by that promise irrespective of whatever other promises are kept or broken. In short, its apparent appeal to *promises,* like that of the previous hypothesis, is misleading. It is not a straightforward application of the notion of a promise to a special situation. Rather, it is an attempt to capture a different notion that has certain things in common with that of a promise-exchange.

VIII. A Conclusion and a Conjecture

I conclude that our sample agreements are not exchanges of promises, contrary to what the standard assumption in the literature would suggest. My discussion in this essay has, of course, used a specific understanding of what a promise is, an understanding I take to be the usual one. It might be suggested that agreements can accurately be characterized as promise-exchanges, given a broader notion of promise.[35] That is surely correct. Let us adopt (in this paragraph only) the following definition: someone makes a *promise* if and only if he deliberately incurs an obligation to perform an explicitly specified act from which he cannot be released without the concurrence of a specific person (the *promisee*). We could then claim that our sample agreements are promise-exchanges after all. To say this, however, obscures the significant way in which our sample agreements differ from all exchanges of promises in the standard sense.

As we have seen, some promise-exchanges produce unconditional performance obligations, some produce simultaneous obligations, and some do both of these things at once. There are promise exchanges that—by creating conditional obligations—ensure that neither promisor will ever be left standing with an unconditional obligation while the other promisor defaults on his promise. Some generate the appropriate conditional obligations simultaneously. But the promise-exchanges that maximize security in this way do so at great cost: a lack of motivational force.

If I have characterized them correctly, the sample agreements combine security and motivational force in a way that no exchange of promises is capable of doing. Their simultaneously generated unconditional obligations are interdependent. Among other things, this means that they all cease to exist if one of the parties violates his own obligation.[36] In contrast, promise-exchanges never generate interdependent performance obligations for the several promisors.

Now, agreements proper are not the only means of creating interdependent obligations. As I have argued at length in *On Social Facts* and elsewhere, interdependent obligations are a common feature of a range of paradigmatically social phenomena, including shared action and collective belief. Underlying these phenomena is what I have referred to as a *joint commitment*. In my view, the concept of a joint commitment is a central social concept, implicit in large tracts of human interaction. It may reasonably be regarded as the core of social union.[37]

For present purposes a brief review of some salient features of a joint commitment between two persons, X and Y, might mention the following. The way for X and Y to create a joint commitment is through mutual expressions of willingness to be jointly committed in some particular way. The joint commitment is understood to be in place when and only when *both* of the appropriate expressions of willingness have been made in conditions of common knowledge.

Once the joint commitment is in place both X and Y will be committed, but these "individual" commitments are understood not to exist independently of the joint commitment. The "individual" commitments of X and Y are thus interdependent in a thoroughgoing way: neither "individual" commitment can exist without the other. It is the joint commitment that generates interdependent "individual" commitments for the parties.

X and Y can aptly think of the joint commitment as "our" commitment in a distinctive sense. It is understood that a joint commitment can only be abrogated by mutual consent: only X and Y together can abrogate *our* commitment. Thus, my relation to a joint commitment in which I participate is different from my relation to a commitment "*of my own*" such as a personal decision, which is mine to abandon or revise unilaterally. A joint commitment therefore generates *obligations* for X and Y in the sense that it "ties" each to the other with respect to certain reasons for acting.[38]

The obligations X and Y accrue from their joint commitment arise simultaneously, when the joint commitment comes into being, and they are interdependent, both being a function of the joint commitment. If the commitment is broken for one it is broken for both, and ceases to impose the obligations in question.

I have argued elsewhere that our everyday concept of shared action involves the concept of a joint commitment *to accept a certain goal as a body,* that collective belief involves a joint commitment to *accept a certain proposition as a body,* and so on.[39] I have also proposed that an everyday agreement may best be understood as a "joint decision," where a joint decision involves a joint commitment to uphold a certain decision as a body.[40] A form of joint commitment may underlie promises also (see below). If X and Y are jointly committed to uphold as a body the decision that X is to do A and Y is to do B, then X will be obligated to do A, and Y will be obligated to do B, and these obligations will be interdependent by virtue of the nature of joint commitment.

If our sample cases of agreements are cases of joint decision, then the obligations of these agreements will be of the same type as those of joint commitment in general, and their interdependence will be a special case of the interdependence of the obligations of joint commitment. The joint decision model, therefore, not only provides an articulate basis for the intuited interdependence of the obligations of agreement, but clarifies the nature of the obligations that accrue to agreements—if these are indeed joint decisions. I say more about what promises and promissory obligation might be in the next section.

If I am right about the nature and importance of joint commitment, and if the typical agreements I have focused on are joint decisions in my sense, it is clear that such agreements have a good title to represent—even if they do not constitute—the basis of human social union. For agreements of the sort in question create a salient set of interdependent obligations (the set of obligations specified in the agreement), and interdependence of commitment and obligation is the basis of social union.

IX. Further Questions

I have argued that our sample agreements, typical of their kind, are not promise-exchanges. The claim that agreements are promise-exchanges is therefore not true as a general claim. Someone may query: Given that not all agreements are promise-exchanges, are promise-exchanges, if and when they occur, agreements?

It is worth noting that exchanges that are strictly and literally promise-exchanges do not appear to be common. Even when two or more people could appear to be exchanging promises, they may not actually be doing so. There will often be an understanding that the parties are arriving at what amounts to a joint decision though they could use the same words to be making promises. Often observation of the wider context will show this. Thus, Chloe may begin, "Let's see . . . how shall we organize things?" Phyllis replies, "I'll do the laundry." Chloe responds, "Okay, I'll do the dishes." This looks less like an exchange of promises once one notices Chloe's initial statement.

My sense of the matter is that when in the course of their everyday lives people think of themselves as entering an "agreement" they see themselves as, in effect, creating a joint decision with the appropriate structure of obligations. But what if two people do exchange promises? If we allow ourselves to say they have made an agreement, we are liable to become confused. Each form of promise-exchange is importantly different from a joint decision. Using the term "agreement" of both joint decisions and any given form of promise exchange will confuse in the relevant way.

To take one example, suppose that Rita and Peter initially understand that they are making the simple unconditional promises in promise-exchange 1, above. Rita then makes plans that will not allow her to fulfill her promise, and leaves Peter a note to that effect. Peter writes back: "We agreed that you would walk Fido and I would groom Tibbles. You've broken the agreement, so I am free not to groom Tibbles!" He characterizes what happened as an agreement and goes on to treat the ensuing structure of obligations as that appropriate to a joint decision. He regards himself as free not to groom Tibbles, irrespective of any appeal to considerations of justice or right. But, by hypothesis, he is not. What happened was an exchange of promises and Peter is still bound by his own promise.

Typical agreements that assign an act to each participant have the structure of joint decisions as I characterized these earlier. That seems reason enough to decide not to call pure promise-exchanges "agreements," if that is an option. If it is not, if pure promise-exchanges are standardly called "agreements" if and when they occur, then we need to be aware of the differences between agreements which behave like joint decisions and those which do not.

One reason that the exchange of promises model has so much currency may be that people feel clearer about what promises are than about what agreements are. In any case, they have assumed that the logical priority goes to promises. I disagree. That is not because I want to argue that agreeing is logically prior to promising exactly. I do not claim to understand precisely what a promise is, but I suspect that typical promises, like agreements, involve an underlying joint commitment. I cannot develop this point at any length here. But consider that in typical cases there is a promisee who in some sense "accepts" the promise. Moreover, there is some plausibility to the view that having accepted someone's promise one behaves inappropriately if one attempts to thwart their performance of it, all else being equal.

The promisor and the promisee apparently become partners, to a degree. If I promise to call you on Tuesday, only I have a performance obligation in the sense that I am the only person to whom a specific act has been explicitly assigned in our transaction, and I have an obligation to perform that act. There would be something untoward in your refusing to take my call on Tuesday, however, all else being equal. This suggests that you take on some obligations in the matter also. Insofar as we speak of "obligations" here, we may be sensitive to an underlying joint commitment.

Note that the concept of a joint *decision* does not require that some action must explicitly be assigned to all parties to the decision. We may decide that you will do the dishes, not specifying any action for me. We may decide that Jack will represent us at the meeting, and so on. Thus, there can be joint decisions that explicitly assign an act to one of the parties only. The ensuing obligations of the other parties are then somewhat vague, but at a minimum it would seem that they are obligated not to impede performance of the act in question.

Given all this, there is some temptation to see a typical promise as a joint decision to the effect that the so-called promisor will act in a certain way. Promises would then not be logically prior to agreements (assuming that agreements are joint decisions), they would *be* agreements of a kind. Would exchanges of promises then be agreements? No. They would rather be exchanges of agreements, agreements each of which assigned a particular act to one person only. It may seem that there will then be little reason for people to exchange promises rather than make the appropriate joint decision. They could have their reasons, however. Perhaps they want to incur independent performance obligations, for instance.

This could be what is desired in situations where people exchange promises. If X and Y exchange unconditional promises to love and to cherish one another, then each party will be committed to love and cherish the other irrespective of the other's failure in this respect. If that is the desired result, then a suitable exchange of promises will be in order.

To sum up: whatever we call things, our options are more varied than the standard promise-exchange account of agreements would have us believe. We have the ability simultaneously to generate unconditional, interdependent performance obligations for a number of different people, and this capacity is a valuable one. We avail ourselves of it when we enter into typical agreements, such as those between Hal and Mavis and Rita and Peter. We do not avail ourselves of it if and when we exchange promises.[41]

Notes

1. See *On Social Facts*. See also below.

2. Robins (1984), p. 105. Robins in the discussion from which I quote appears to use "agreement" and "contract" interchangeably. He does not focus on contracts in law, but rather on informal agreements.

3. Lewis (1969), p. 34, also pp. 45, 84. (On p. 84 Lewis refers to an exchange of "conditional promises binding us to conform to R only if the others do.") Lewis also contemplates two other models of agreement: "an exchange of [noncommittal] declarations of intent" (p. 34; also p. 84), and "a set of solemn and public oaths to conform . . . come what may" (p. 84). These will not be discussed directly here. It will be clear, however, that neither model meets the criteria of adequacy set out below. In informal discussion (p. 45) Lewis writes of an agreement in terms of a set of promises.

4. Baier (1985), p. 199: ". . . the social practice of promising, and of mutual promises. . . ." Baier reserves the term "agreement" for a phenomenon she takes to underlie the possibility of making a promise (and, presumably, a "mutual promise").

5. Atiyah (1981), pp. 204–5. See also Raz (1984), pp. 202–3, discussed in the text below.

6. Atiyah (1971), p. 23.

7. I argued briefly along these lines in *On Social Facts*, especially p. 380 and p. 489, n. 87.

8. Some contrasting kinds of case: (1) X says, "My charge for house cleaning is ten dollars an hour" and Y replies, "I'm perfectly happy with that." It seems that this may be no more than an "agreement on terms." Y may continue, "I'll let you know if I want you to work for me." (Cf. Atiyah [1981], p. 201.) The agreement between Hal and Mavis is rather an "agreement on acts." (2) Jill says to Jack, "So we agree that you will approach the chairman tomorrow?" Here it is not the case that *each* of the parties is explicitly assigned a specified act. My discussion will suggest a specific understanding of such cases. (3) More than one act is specified for each party. See the text below.

9. In my view obligations to perform the specified acts are not the only ones parties to an agreement take it to generate, but that need not concern us here.

10. We may ignore the special case of self-described "promises" to the effect that another person will do something.

11. In saying this, I do not assume that the point of the agreement in question here was to effect a meeting between Hal and Mavis. More generally, I do not assume that Mavis can regard herself as free of obligation because fulfilling her obligation would now in some sense be "pointless." Rather, Hal's default on their agreement seems in itself to suffice. In saying that Mavis "can

regard herself as free of obligation'' I do not mean that she is free to *disregard* her obligation. For present purposes I shall not distinguish between being able to regard oneself as free of obligation (in the sense in question) and simply being free of obligation. (The last four sentences have been added to the original for this volume.)

12. Conversation with Justin Gosling (summer 1990) prompted this query.

13. In some cases, it may be morally permissible, all things considered, not to conform to a given agreement. As I understand it, the agreement would still generate its usual obligations. At the same time, each party would be morally permitted not to fulfill the relevant obligation of agreement. See Chapter 12 for further discussion. I argue that we speak of agreements as immediately generating *obligations* because a particular type of *tie* or *bond* between persons is involved. There is a sense in which these are not *moral* obligations. See also section VIII below.

14. As Saul Kripke pointed out to me, Michael Dummett notes a similar distinction in relation to conditional questions, commands, and bets in Dummett (1973), pp. 388 ff.

15. Should an externally conditional promise be construed as a promise to promise? It is not so explicitly, nor does it obviously need to be so regarded. It seems that it will not properly be so regarded if it can be withdrawn without leave from any promisee before its condition is met. We may assume that this is so. Cf. Fried (1981): "A 'conditional promisor . . . is free to retract his offer at any time . . . before his condition is met,' " p. 47. Fried does not to my knowledge explicitly make the distinction between externally and internally conditional promises. Much of his discussion suggests that he is operating with the external notion.

16. I do not believe that the adoption of alternatives would allow us to save the promise theory.

17. Narrower notions are possible, but their adoption would not affect the substance of my argument.

18. See section VIII below for discussion of the suggestion that an agreement is an exchange of unconditional promises plus a special understanding.

19. This applies equally to a case where by breaking one's promise one ensures another's promise will never mandate action, as would happen with another's internally conditional promise whose condition will now not be met. The other's promise stands and its (conditional) obligation remains. Even in such an obviously special case as that where the promise *B* breaks is a promise not to release *A* from a promise to *B*, *B* breaks his promise *by releasing A*, rather than the other way round.

20. With respect to the special case of "promises" to the effect that someone other than the promisor will do something, it is not clear that the other person can exactly fulfill, or violate, the obligation of the promise, insofar as these count as genuine promises at all.

21. Fried's appeal to the "fairness" of "releasing someone from" his

promissory obligation "to another" suggests as much. We seem to have moved from reflection on the concept of a promise to reflection on the desirability of certain legal judgments given what seems to be fair. It is important to note that the argument that, morally speaking, if one person breaks his promise the other can ignore his obligation through the promise does not show an interdependence of obligation in the sense of the interdependence criterion. This concerns the disappearance, not the ignorability from some point of view, of the obligations of agreement, and, indeed, the collapse of the agreement itself.

22. Cf. C. Radford (1984).

23. This paragraph responds to comments from Frank Stewart (personal communication, 1992). See also note 34 (on "Since . . .).

24. In a lively discussion of my position at the Philosophical Society of Oxford University, May 1990, several people were inclined to think that roughly this promise-exchange would solve the problem (Michael Martin proposed that it might be adequate).

25. In discussion of this exchange, Saul Kripke, who had also envisaged it as a possibility, said that he was worried about this objection, and also about the possible pitfalls of introducing self-reference into the discussion. The argument in the text below shows that we need not be concerned with this further worry either, since the exchange does not fulfill the criteria of adequacy for a model of agreement in any case.

26. Even our sample agreements, as I have characterized them, have a degree of related infelicity. Once one has *already fulfilled* one's own obligation, one's opposite number may in the end not fulfill hers. She will have an obligation, but she may not fulfill it. What the structure of these agreements guarantees, however, is that one is no longer obligated under the agreement to act oneself, *given* the default of one's opposite number.

27. Once the condition of Peter's internally conditional promise is met, he has an unconditional obligation to groom Tibbles. If the condition fails to be met, he is left with a conditional obligation only.

28. To say that something is "common knowledge" between certain parties is to say, roughly, that it is "out in the open" between them. See Lewis (1969).

29. I discuss some cases similar to case 2 in Chapter 2.

30. Raz (1984), p. 203. Cited in de Moor (1987), pp. 112–13. De Moor's thoughtful article is a critique of the idea that a single promise might be the model for contracts in law. I shall make no attempt directly to discuss it here.

31. De Moor notes this problem, de Moor (1987), p. 116.

32. Raz (1984), p. 203. See also Radford, 1984, p. 582, who seems to endorse something like this as the proper account of what goes on when two people enter an agreement.

33. Prichard (1949), pp. 180–81. His own concern was to give an account of what it is for two people to exchange things in general, and he suggests that this is a matter of an exchange of promises in the broad sense of "exchange of promises" I have adopted here.

34. Prichard writes "Since," which is more natural given promises that follow each other in time, implying as it does that the necessary promise has already been given.

35. This discussion was added in response to queries from the editors of *The Journal of Philosophy*.

36. They also cease to exist, of course, if the agreement is dissolved (by mutual accord). There is a further contrast with exchanged promises here, for though one promisor's performance obligation ceases if he is released from his promise, this release of itself does not affect the status of the other promisor's promise.

37. The two paragraphs that follow in the 1993 version have been replaced by four new paragraphs. I now focus on a case involving two persons, corresponding to the promise-exchanges discussed in this essay. A joint commitment in general can be characterized roughly as an "our" commitment, which is not equivalent to "my" personal commitment plus "your" personal commitment, and so on. See the introduction, this volume.

38. I say more about this form of obligation and contrasting forms in Chapter 12. See also the introduction, which notes some issues not touched on here.

39. On shared action, see Chapter 6, this volume; on collective belief, see Chapters 7 and 14. See also *On Social Facts*.

40. See *On Social Facts,* and Chapter 12, this volume.

41. The first full draft of this essay was written while I was a Visiting Fellow at Wolfson College, Oxford University (1989-1990). I thank the American Council of Learned Societies for a Fellowship for Research for the same period, and the University of Connecticut Research Foundation for a sabbatical grant. The paper was completed while I was a Visiting Fellow at Princeton University, spring 1993. I thank D. Edgington, J. C. B. Gosling, C. Korsgaard, S. Kripke, A. de Moor, A. Orenstein, T. Scanlon, F. H. Stewart, and J. J. Thomson for discussion.

14

More on Collective Belief

Listen, Alexey Fyodorovitch. Isn't there in all our analysis—I mean your analysis . . . no, better call it ours—aren't we showing contempt for him, for that poor man—in analysing his soul like this, as it were, from above, eh? In deciding so certainly that he will take the money? [Doestoevsky, *The Brothers Karamazov*, 1943, p. 257]

Introduction

In daily life, people often say things like, "We decided that he would take the money," "In our view Jones would make a poor chairman," "We believe she is wrong." What is it for us to believe that such-and-such, according to our everyday understanding?

It is common to answer this question with some form of "summative" account. For *us* to believe that *p* is for all or most of us to believe that *p*.[1] Or perhaps a "common knowledge" condition may be added: for *us* to believe that *p* is for all or most of us to believe that *p*, while this is common knowledge among us.[2] Whatever the precise account given, the core of it is a number of individuals who personally believe that *p*.[3] Our belief is thus said to be constituted in large part by a "sum" of individual beliefs with the content in question. As I have argued elsewhere, there is another interpretation of such belief ascription—one I take to be quite standard—which connects them with a quite different phenomenon, a phenomenon of great practical importance.[4] I shall attempt to clarify further the nature of the phenomenon in question. I shall refer to it as *collective belief*.

I begin—in the next section—with an observation about the way in which some expressions of opinion are greeted with a certain special kind of shocked surprise. Those who know when to expect this type of shocked surprise are likely to be strongly affected by that knowledge. In particular, they are likely to censor their expressions of opinion. In the long run, the growth of human knowledge at both the collective and the individual level is likely to be affected. How does this shocked surprise response come about? Can it be avoided, or is it an inevitable part of human life? I go on to articulate my conception of collective belief and argue that the shocked surprise response is predictable given its presence.

I. Observation: The "Shocked Surprise" Response

Sometimes one will express an opinion and it will be met with a special kind of shocked surprise. This is not directed at epistemic qualities of the opinion itself such as its obvious falsity, its absurdity, its lack of known substantiation. It is, rather, directed at the speaker who expressed this opinion. It is directed at the speaker in the light of certain apparently nonepistemic facts about him or her. That is, the relevant facts do not relate to the speaker's perceived capacity to discern truths or reach justified beliefs in the relevant domain. The shocked surprise is not a matter of the observer's finding the speaker oddly obtuse, for instance, or, confused. Before I attempt a more positive characterization of the relevant shocked surprise response, some examples will be helpful.

(1) A group of acquaintances have been discussing a man they know, Jake Robins, and they have reached the conclusion that Jake is an unpleasant character. Greg, one of their number, subsequently remarks without special preamble, "Jake Robins is so *nice*." Now, there could of course be a kind of shocked surprise here at Greg's apparent and unexpected lack of judgment or simple ignorance. But there is in any case likely to be a significantly different kind of shocked surprise, the kind I am concerned with here. This is in some way a matter of Greg's participation in the conversational group that reached the conclusion that Jake Robins was an unpleasant character. One of the others might think, "How could Greg say that now, after what we've been saying?"

This example comes from an informal everyday context, and may seem relatively trivial. Apparently similar things happen in more formal contexts, however, such as the conduct of education, science, and politics. Here are two examples that relate to education and science, respectively.

(2) A class of students has been told by their teacher that modern science has a "masculine" bias. The existence of such a bias has subsequently been taken for granted in class discussions and tests. Toward the end of the semester Jessie raises her hand in class discussion and says, "You know, there's really no good evidence that modern science has a masculine bias." There could be shocked surprise here stemming from wonderment on the part of the students and the teacher that Jessie could be so ignorant, as she may indeed seem to be in their eyes. But a kind of shocked surprise with a different edge is in any case predictable: this stems in some way from the fact that Jessie has participated in the life of the class up to this point.

(3) A group of physicists are working together on some problems in string theory. One day in the course of a working lunch, Alphonse—one of their number—says, "String theory just isn't going anywhere!" Here again, there could be shocked surprise coming from the conviction that Alphonse is wrong, or from what is perceived as Alphonse's unexpectedly misguided thought. But a different target of such a response is also predictable: one of the group might perhaps think to himself, "How can he say that—he's one of us!"

Let us pause for a moment and consider what precisely this attitude of shocked surprise may amount to. I take it that, at a minimum, people who are shocked are "put out" in some way. They are "taken aback." They believe that something has gone wrong. This may or may not be true of all forms of surprise (see below). In any case, the type of surprise at issue here is indeed "shocked" at least in the minimal sense that the surprised person believes that something has—to some extent or in some respect—gone wrong.

Now there is more than this to the particular kind of shocked surprise I am concerned with, but it is worth considering this aspect of it in isolation for a moment.

The anticipation that one's utterance is likely to provoke the reaction "Something has gone wrong!" could be enough to prevent certain utterances from being made. In any case, more than the simple provocation of this particular negative *attitude* is likely to be at issue, given that it is provoked. It is clear enough that shocked surprise of this type is not something people tend to enjoy experiencing. They can therefore be expected not to deal entirely kindly with those who provoke it. They may frown at them, ridicule them, or shun them. In extreme cases those who provoke this response could lose their jobs or social positions. Fear of such losses would clearly be enough to explain the desire not to provoke shocked surprise in the first place.

Thus someone may be moved not to express an honest well-thought-out opinion—even something he or she takes to be certain knowledge, and something it is important to know.

So far I have characterized shocked surprise as (at the least) a negative attitude to the effect that "Something has gone wrong!", which could lead to behavior unpleasant or even disastrous to the person who provokes it. The particular type of shocked surprise at issue here can give rise to a special type of reaction, which will help us to characterize it more precisely.

Some typical expressions associated with this shocked surprise are "How can you say that?" and "*What* did you say?" or just plain "*What?*" With these expressions (uttered in the appropriate tone), one clearly expressed one's sense that the original speaker has behaved wrongly. One does more than this, however. One is not simply saying, "As I see it, it was wrong of you to say that!" Nor simply (in a less subjective vein), "It was wrong of you to say that!"

Observe that in the first of these cases, the original speaker could appropriately reply, "I regret that you think it was wrong of me to say that!" In the second case, the original speaker could appropriately reply, "Perhaps you are right!" or "That is unfortunate." As I shall explain, all of these replies would be inadequate in the context of the shocked surprise response at issue here.

The special reaction to which the shocked surprise response can give rise may in the first place be referred to as a *rebuke*. A rebuke—as I understand it—is, in the first instance, more than the simple communication to a person of a negative evaluation of that person's behavior. When one says, "It was wrong of you to do that," one is not necessarily rebuking the other person. Consider that statements like the following seem to be in order: "It was wrong of you to do that. I can't reproach you for it, of course. I've done the same thing many times myself. God knows the temptation is great!"; or "You did something wrong! I'm so glad! You were beginning to seem too perfect!"

What is it, then, to rebuke someone or to communicate a criticism in a rebuking way? What distinguishes remarking on a person's error to that person (or saying that there seems to have been an error) from *telling a person off*?

Let me return to the particular phenomenon of shocked surprise with which I am here concerned. What is involved when someone expresses this shocked surprise by saying "*What?*" in the relevant way?

One aspect of this reaction is that it would be appropriately answered with some sort of explanation. More particularly, it would be appropriately answered with an explanation intended to defuse the reaction, that is, with an excuse. Thus the original speaker might suggest that he was not fully responsible for what he did: "Honestly, I don't know what came over me." Or he might, as we say, explain it away: "I just wanted to see what happened if I said that! Of course I wasn't *serious*." He is quite likely to speak apologetically or to make an explicit apology, perhaps at the same time taking back the offending remark: "I'm sorry, I don't know why I said that! Of course string theory is going somewhere!" Such responses are clearly appropriate answers to "*What?*" and the like.

Other types of response are possible also. The original speaker might, for instance, defiantly repeat what was said before. For now, I want to focus on the appropriateness of apologetic excuses. Even a defiant repetition may well be preceded by such an excuse, as in "I'm sorry, but that's the *truth*. String theory just isn't going anywhere!"

Those who say "*What?*" suggest, it seems, that some kind of *offense* has been committed against *them*. Their shock, then, is by no means simply a matter of sensing an error or flaw somewhere. It involves a sense of offense: of being offended against. Their cry has in part the following ring: "Why are you doing this to me?" Or rather "to *us?*" For, importantly, any member of the relevant group might say "*What?*"—and, indeed, they might even say it in unison. They all lean forward: "*What???*" There is, indeed, something apparently impersonal about the offense. I, this person, am offended, but I am offended in my capacity as a member of this group.

A suggestion of offense suggests also that excuse and apology are in place. In contrast, if people simply point out to you that you have made some kind of error, they do not imply that it is appropriate for you to provide any kind of explanation, let alone an apology. (That is not to deny that many individuals would apologize in such circumstances, or that some cultural practices encourage this.)

Those who have been offended against by a person's action were, we may say, entitled at least to the absence of the action in question—a right that has been violated by the offender. This puts them in a special position in relation to the offender. They now have a basis for approaching the offender in a variety of related ways. They may engage in some kind of punitive behavior. They may demand restitution or recompense. An excuse is fitted to defuse the idea that such approaches are in order. An apology is fitted to defuse the idea that they are needed: the offender acknowledges the offense, and regrets it. Someone who, as we say, "takes something back" effects a kind of restitution.

I return now to the question of what a rebuke amounts to. I have observed that a rebuke is more than the noting of an error. In addition, it appears to have something punitive about it. The rebuking speaker, we may say, verbally chastises the hearer for a presumed wrong. One who issues a rebuke implicitly claims, then, to be entitled to chastise the rebuked person—verbally at least.

Perhaps not all rebukes imply that the rebuked person has somehow directly offended against the person issuing the rebuke. It may be that one's standing to issue a rebuke can sometimes derive from other sources. I shall not pursue that issue here. In the case with which I am concerned, there appears to be a rebuke in the minimal sense just noted, coupled with a sense of offense on the part of the person who rebukes. Presumably it is this sense of offense that justifies the rebuke in his or her own eyes. In case there are other sorts of rebuke, we may reserve for a rebuke which stems from a sense of offense the label "offended rebuke."

Talk of offenders, entitlements, and the like may call to mind the law and serious harms. Yet it seems to me that if we are to do justice to what is going on in the kinds of informal interchanges with which I am concerned, we need to bring in such concepts, or we cannot begin to see what is going on.

An offended rebuke clearly constitutes a form of pressure on the offender. The offender is called to account, and put on notice that any similar behavior may provoke further chastisement. The kinds of contexts at issue here tend to call out other kinds of pressure also, such as attempts to silence a speaker before the offending words are altogether spoken, attempts to shout them down, and so on.

In sum, the shocked surprise response in question here involves a sense of offense such that the surprised person will feel justified in uttering an offended rebuke. The recipient of an offended rebuke may be expected to understand its basis. It will be understood at some levels to be in order. These observations require explanation.

We now have a number of questions. On what grounds are people critical of certain expressions of belief when their criticism does not (as it seems) have epistemic grounds? In particular, it is neither a matter of the presumed epistemic unacceptability of what is believed nor some presumed epistemic flaw in the speaker. On what grounds do people feel entitled to communicate their sense of error to the person concerned? In particular, on what grounds do they feel entitled to issue a rebuke, where to rebuke is to chastise verbally for a presumed error? Given that the rebuke is an offended rebuke, whence comes the sense of offense?

These are questions of great practical relevance. An offended rebuke is both penalty and pressure. Such pressure (and its anticipation) can have grave consequences for the growth of knowledge in society, not to speak of the effects of self-repression on individual people.[5] One might indeed wonder how such practices of criticism and pressure could ever be defended.

II. Approaching Collective Belief

Allusions to What *We Believe* in the Context of the Shocked Surprise Response

What might explain the complex shocked surprise response at issue here? Let us look back at the examples presented in the previous section. We had various speakers saying something that evoked the shocked surprise response.

In the first example, the offending utterance was, "Jake Robins is so *nice*." As I have noted, the shocked surprise response might prod a listener to comment starkly, "*What*?" or "What do you *mean*?" and so on. There is, however, another familiar type of comment to which this response may give rise. In the Jake Robins case, someone might object, "But we decided that Jake was *unpleasant*!" In the case of the class discussing science, one can imagine someone responding, "But we know there is a masculine bias in science!" In the case of the apparently skeptical string theorist, one of the group might burst out, "But *we* don't think that!"

In short, sentences beginning "But we think that . . . ," "But we know that . . . ," "But we decided that . . . ," and the like might well be uttered in such contexts. Here beliefs, conclusions, knowledge, and so on are ascribed to "us." I shall call statements that do this *collective belief* statements.[6] The question of their interpretation, of course, remains.

Since utterances beginning "But we think . . ." and the like are liable to occur in the context of the shocked surprise response, it is a reasonable conjecture that at least some occasions of that response are situations in which, according to those who are shocked, one of "us" has denied the truth of one of "our" beliefs, either explicitly or implicitly. In other words, they are situations involving a collective belief.

More, it appears that in at least some of these situations the existence of a particular collective belief, as such, is taken to merit an offended rebuke. The implication is that the original speakers erred in saying what they said simply by virtue of the fact that they expressed a belief contrary to "our" belief. The form of words used—"But we think . . ." and so on—suggests this. That is, it suggests that the simple fact of our thinking that such and such is enough to ground a rebuke, the rebuke itself being signaled by the "But . . . ."

In interpreting collective belief statements it is reasonable, therefore, to raise again the question raised earlier of the shocked surprise response. What could justify the response? What rational basis could it have?

It could, of course, have no justifying basis. It could be a response which occurs spontaneously in certain contexts without any rational warrant. This possibility is no reason to abandon the search for a rational basis. So let us ask: what could justify the shocked surprise response? In particular, on what account of collective belief would the expression of a belief contrary to the collective one justify this response?

Two Summative Accounts of Collective Belief and the Shocked Surprise Response

Before proceeding to my positive answer I return briefly to the two summative accounts of "our belief" mentioned earlier. Consider the more complex one. This invokes a belief that is widespread in a certain population, where it is common knowledge that the belief is indeed widespread. Now suppose that it is common knowledge in a certain small community that most members believe that it is desirable to leave home on vacation in summer. One member, Claire, says to another, Dan, "You know, there is really little point in going out of town in summer." Is this enough to justify an offended rebuke on Dan's part, all else being equal?

Someone may argue that Dan is likely to be *surprised* at Claire's statement, knowing that most of their number think differently. Dan will then have some reason to be upset by it, since surprise can be seen as a reflection on the quality or efficacy of one's reasoning capacities. It is reasonable to assume that all this is common knowledge in the community in question. Claire will then have known that she was liable to upset Dan to some degree when she spoke as she did, and Dan will know this.

Suppose that for the sake of argument we accept these points. It is by no means obvious that both Dan and Claire will immediately understand that Dan is now justified in approaching Claire with an offended rebuke. The basis for the rebuke, given this argument, would presumably be that Claire did something she knew was liable to upset Dan to some degree. But to what degree? Suppose it were common knowledge between Dan and Claire that Dan was extremely sensitive to the epistemic implications of surprise: surprising him was always on a par with inflicting severe mental distress. An offended rebuke from Dan might then be in order. But in the world as we know it, most people are not like this.

In any case it appears that the appropriateness of the offended rebuke stemming from the existence of a collective belief is not a matter of sensitivities or evaluations that may vary from person to person or culture to culture. The simple fact that *we have a certain belief* provides a basis for rebuking one of our number who says something contrary to the belief.

If it is observed that one who expresses a minority view in a community is doing something *unusual* or *uncommon*, this does not in itself support the idea that Claire is in any way in error in saying what she said, let alone that an offended rebuke from Dan is appropriate. Highly conventional people may think that uncommon behavior is bad, but those who thrive on variety will find it delightful.

To say that a given belief is widespread in a particular community, then, or to say that this is so and that it is common knowledge in the community, is not in any obvious way to show that members of that community will have grounds for an offended rebuke if one member gainsays the belief in question. So, if this particular type of response is sometimes based on the existence of a collective belief, as there is reason to think, it is not based on collective belief according to the complex summative account, nor according to the simple summative account. This of course suggests that these accounts do not adequately describe what people mean when they refer to what *we* believe. If they sometimes intend these phrases in a summative sense, it appears that this is at least not *always* so.

Plural Subjects

In common parlance one hears frequent references not only to what we believe, but also to what we like, what we prefer, what we are doing, what we intend, to our principles and our purposes, and so on. My book *On Social Facts* (1989) constitutes a lengthy argument to the effect that analysis of such references discovers for us an important family of everyday concepts. I have labeled these concepts the "plural subject" concepts.

If the concept of collective belief is construed as a plural subject concept, the existence of a collective belief will be enough to justify the shocked surprise response, as I shall show. I first say something about the plural subject concepts in general, before focusing on the case of belief.

I should stress that the phrase "plural subject" is a technical one: it applies (as I use it) only to those who are connected in a way I shall specify. Meanwhile the phrase itself is intended to convey the underlying perspective of these concepts: the idea that a plurality of persons may in certain special contexts be seen as constituting the subject (as opposed to the subjects) of a certain psychological attribute.

For present purposes, I shall focus on the following account of plural subjecthood:

> For persons *A* and *B* and psychological attribute *X*, *A* and *B* form a *plural subject* of *X*-ing if and only if *A* and *B* are jointly committed to *X*-ing as a body, or, if you like, as a single person.

Some explanation of the terms of this account follow.

(i) What is the idea behind the alternative formulations "*X*-ing as a body" or "*X*-ing as a single person"? The way to convey this idea that is perhaps most entrenched in English is "*X*-ing together." However, this has its own ambiguity. "*X*-ing together" can be interpreted as "*X*-ing side by side" or "in close proximity." It can also connote the "*X*-ing as a body" or "as a single person" idea. Thus, "Jane and Sally are traveling together" could mean that they are traveling on the same train or whatever (though perhaps even unaware of each other). It could also mean that they are traveling "as a single body" ("as a single person").[7]

An important aspect of the idea of *X*-ing as a body is this: from the mere understanding that for some psychological attribute *X*, *A* and *B* are *X*-ing as a body, we cannot infer that *A* personally *X*-es or that *B* personally *X*-es. Consider the case of *A* and *B* building a house together. Normally when people build a house together there is some division of labor. One person installs the windows, say, and another lays the roof. Thus people may succeed in building a house together without any one of them doing anything that would count, on its own, as building a house.

There are, of course, more positive aspects of X-ing as a body. I shall not attempt to specify what these are for the general case here, but will rely on intuitive understandings. I will leave discussion of specific cases until I turn to the case of collective belief.

(ii) Membership in a plural subject of psychological attributes clearly requires an understanding of the nature of the attribute in question. I do not say that it requires the concept of an individual human being who X-es. There is no need here to preempt an answer to the question whether plural subject concepts are in some way parasitic upon or secondary to our conceptions of the psychological attributes of individual human beings. In any case, one must have the concept of X-ing in order to enter a joint commitment to X as a body.

(iii) The key concept in my account of plural subjects is the concept of *joint commitment*.[8] I use "joint commitment" as a technical phrase—though, of course, one chosen for its appropriateness to its intended content.[9]

The existence of any joint commitment is a function of the participants' conception of their situation. Roughly speaking, people become jointly committed by mutually expressing their willingness *to be jointly committed*, in conditions of common knowledge. One cannot be a party to a joint commitment, then, without having the concept of a joint commitment.

The basic idea of a *joint commitment* can be introduced as follows. A joint commitment is not an aggregate of independent personal commitments. It is not, for instance, Alan's commitment, plus Ben's commitment, plus Cecily's commitment, and so on. Rather, it is the commitment "of" *Alan and Ben and Cecily* and any relevant others.

More can be said about the nature and structure of joint commitment. Suppose that the parties to a given joint commitment are Alan and Ben. Both are then committed, but their "individual commitments" are understood to flow from a joint commitment. This way of understanding things has two central aspects.

First, the so-called "individual commitments" of Ben and Alan cannot exist on their own. These commitments are not independent commitments but depend on the existence of the joint commitment. Thus "Alan's" commitment and "Ben's" commitment are interdependent in the sense that neither can pre-exist the other or exist after the other ceases.

Second, the mutual consent of Alan and Ben is required to rescind their joint commitment. One does not hold sway over one's "individual commitment" here as one does over one's personal decisions. Given a decision of my own, if I want to change my mind, I can. I can rescind my own decision. I may be unwise or capricious or unstable to do so, but I have that option: my own decision is mine to change. A joint commitment in which I take part is understood not to be mine to change. It is ours, rather, and only we together can rescind it.

It is true that one party can deliberately violate or break a joint commitment. But the constraints the commitment creates exist in full force right up to the break. There is indeed a *violation*.

I have sometimes referred to the entry into a joint commitment as involving the expression of a "conditional commitment." This phrase is open to various interpretations. The rather delicate point I have intended should by now be fairly clear. One must evidently be "ready for joint commitment" as far as one's own will is concerned, yet (as one understands) only if a certain condition is fulfilled *can* one be committed as a function of a joint commitment. This is what each party must express to the relevant others. Each individual's participation in the joint commitment requires a similar expression of willingness on every other individual's part. Thus, a man who says "Shall we dance?" indicates that, in effect, he will be committed to dancing if (and only if) his question is answered appropriately. His ensuing commitment to dance will be a function of the joint commitment then, and only then created.

I have now elaborated up to a certain point the general nature of the plural subject concepts that I take to inform much of our everyday discourse. I take such concepts to be implicit, that is, in much if not most talk of what we prefer, what we think, what our goal is, and so on. More could be said, but for present purposes this should be sufficient.[10]

Joint Commitment and Obligation

Before focusing particularly on the topic of *our belief*, I want to connect the concept of joint commitment with the concepts of obligation and entitlement. I believe that understanding the concept of joint commitment helps us, indeed, to understand better what obligation is. I propose that joint commitments, given what they are, generate a special and central form of obligation. I have argued this at some length elsewhere, but since it is highly relevant to my present concerns, I must say something about it here.[11]

Suppose that June is party to a joint commitment. As she understands, the source of the commitment she is now personally subject to is not an act of her own mind or will alone, and she is not in a position to rescind that commitment by an act of her own mind or will alone. For it takes at least two to make or rescind a joint commitment.

Now, June's commitment gives her a reason for acting.[12] This is a reason that she is not in a position to remove by simply changing her mind. Nor, indeed, will a change in her external circumstances remove it. However justified she is from one point of view or another in acting against the commitment, she cannot remove it without the concurrence of the other parties to the commitment. We can thus pointfully say that the parties to a joint commitment are *bound or obligated to one another*. They have a reason for acting that will press upon them unless and until the parties decide otherwise as a body.

My hypothesis about obligation, then, is that a central use of the term "obligation" is to refer to a reason for acting such that the person who has it (the "obligor") is beholden to another or others (the "obligees") for its eradication by virtue of the participation of both obligor and obligees in a joint commitment.[13]

Apparently we can talk of rights and entitlements here, also. It seems natural to say that, unless they have consented otherwise, the obligees are entitled to certain behaviors from the obligors. If these behaviors do not occur, the rights of the obligees have been violated.

It is important to note that what I shall now refer to as the *obligations* of joint commitment have certain special features that distinguish them from at least one other familiar form of (so-called) obligation. In other words, the obligations of joint commitment are obligations of a special kind or in a special sense.[14]

First, in order to establish these obligations, each party must be willing to be jointly committed. The "willingness" at issue here might also be referred to as "readiness" or "preparedness." There is no obvious necessity for coercion to be absent from the situation. In other words, it looks as if it is possible to enter a joint commitment in coercive conditions. "So we're traveling together?" Doris says, threatening Al with a gun. Al might well say "Sure" in such circumstances, and do so sincerely. He may not mind traveling with Doris, but he would not have said he would do so unless Doris had threatened him. He has been coerced into traveling with Doris.

Now, if he has indeed entered into a joint commitment, he has the ensuing obligations, for these flow as a matter of logic from the joint commitment. One cannot be party to a joint commitment without having obligations of joint commitment.

According to many people, there is a sense in which Al "has no obligation" to go through the motions of traveling with Doris if Doris coerced him into agreeing to travel with her. If there is a sense in which this is so, then it corresponds to a type of obligation that is distinct from the obligations of joint commitment. Now, many would say that what Al does not have here is a "moral" obligation to go along with Doris. In that case, the obligations of joint commitment are not moral obligations.

It is not necessary here to debate the best way to delimit morality or moral obligation. One practically relevant aspect of the point about coercion is that joint commitments and their obligations can flourish in a wide variety of conditions, including conditions of intimidation and coercion. Someone who is coerced into a joint commitment experiences a double constraint: coerced into the commitment, Al understands that he will have a reason to do what he committed himself to do unless Doris releases him from the commitment.

A second aspect of the obligations of joint commitment is that they persist whatever the countervailing factors. Given a joint commitment to travel with Doris, even if Al subsequently has good reason to default on his commitment, his obligations to Doris will persist. For only with Doris's concurrence can the joint commitment be dissolved. If he does default, it would be appropriate for him to apologize to Doris for failing to fulfill an obligation he has to her. Given that Doris coerced him in the first place, he may of course decide not to apologize.

A final aspect of the obligations of joint commitment is that we can expect parties to a joint commitment to understand that they are obligated and entitled accordingly.

Rather than press the relatively obscure proposal that the obligations of joint commitment are not moral obligations, I shall rest with these three points about them: (1) they can arise in coercive conditions; (2) they persist in the presence of facts that justify not fulfilling them; and (3) they can be expected to be known to those who have them.

III. Collective Belief

Plural Subjects of Belief

If we follow the schema for analyzing plural subject concepts presented above, we get the following result for believing that *p:*

A and *B* form *a plural subject of believing* that *p* if and only if *A* and *B* are jointly committed to believing that *p* as a body.

Some comments are in order. First, let me spell out some implications of this account, which should be clear given the discussion in the previous section. Given this account, if Anne and Betty form a plural subject of believing that *p, each of them is obligated to the other* to do her part in believing that *p* as a body. Should Anne or Betty not act accordingly, she has defaulted on an obligation to the other, and the other's corresponding right to her performance has been violated. Both Anne and Betty will understand this. We see, then, that if they form a plural subject of believing that *p*, Anne and Betty will understand that *they have a basis for rebuking one another should the appropriate behavior not occur.*

Second, what precisely is the behavior appropriate to members of a plural subject of belief? What are their obligations? In this connection it must be noted that plural subjecthood, both in the case of belief and more generally, appears to admit of various forms of contextualization. This has implications for the extent of the obligations generated in a given case. A few rough pointers must suffice here on a topic of some interest, importance, and delicacy.

Suppose that George and Mary have to decide how late their son Johnnie can stay out tonight. Mary thinks he should be home by ten; George thinks that he should stay out as long as he pleases. They discuss the matter for a while, and can't agree. George: "Look, we've got to tell the boy something!" Mary: "Suppose we say midnight?" George: "Well, that's better than ten, anyhow!" At this point George might well go to Johnnie and say to him quite sincerely, "We think you should be home by midnight."

It appears at this juncture that George and Mary will understand themselves to be jointly committed to believing as a body that Johnnie should be home by midnight *at least insofar as they are dealing with Johnnie.* Now suppose that, in the privacy of their bedroom, George says, "I still don't see why the boy shouldn't be home at three if he wants to." Given that their joint commitment had the contextualized content suggested, we can expect Mary to hear this without any sense that an obligation to herself has been violated.

Things would be different if their discussion had proceeded as follows. Mary: "I think Johnnie should be home by ten." George: "Really? That's a bit early! He is sixteen, you know! I don't see why he shouldn't stay out as long as he pleases!" Mary: "Oh really,

George, be reasonable! He has to go to school!'' George: "Hmm. That's true. . . . Midnight's a bit more like it, though!'' Mary: "That's okay, I suppose." At this point George might go and talk to Johnnie as before. However, back in the bedroom, it would surely be harder now for George to sit down and say, "I still don't see why the boy shouldn't stay out til three if he wants to." For, among other things, the dialogue in this instance suggests a closure of discussion of the subject *between George and Mary*. For George to say this to Mary "without preamble" is for him to take their previous discussion in vain, so to speak.[15]

The latter hypothetical situation represents perhaps the simplest and purest type of plural subjecthood. It might be dubbed the "simple interpersonal" type. Two or more people have had a conversation and reached a conclusion. Their dominant sense of the proceedings is that they are these individuals discussing this issue. In such cases, it appears that if in personal conversation immediately after the close of the conversation one of the parties bluntly denies the conclusion to the others, he or she is not keeping to their bargain.

What would *keeping faith* with the joint commitment amount to in this case? I shall not attempt to explore all aspects of this here. One can at least say that, all else being equal, it would be appropriate for George and Mary to conduct their own subsequent conversations as if it were true that Johnnie should be home by midnight. They do not, of course, have to keep expressing this view. It will, rather, "go without saying." But if it is to go without saying, then it must not be gainsaid—or not without some delicate preamble. (I say more about this shortly.)[16]

Quite generally, the precise understandings between the parties is what determines the extent of their obligations in each case. Sometimes what understandings there are may be relatively vague, with perhaps a clear core. These understandings can, of course, change over time. They may become more or less definite; they may change radically. Sometimes, violation of the relevant obligations, as currently understood, may lead to settling on a different understanding.

Third, there are ways of talking that appear to allow people to affirm that not *p* although they are members of a plural subject of believing that *p* in a situation where the blunt denial of *p* is out of order. One may say, for instance, "Look, *I personally do not believe that p.*" Or, "Speaking personally, . . .".

One seems to differentiate oneself as *an individual* from—what? Oneself as a member of the relevant plural subject, perhaps. The fact that we have this way of speaking suggests that, in general, participating in *believing that p as a body* does not require *personally believing that p*. This accords, of course, with what was said earlier about the general idea of several persons "*X*-ing as a body": this does not entail, for every *X*, that each of the parties individually *X*.[17]

That is perhaps a surprising result, since it suggests that the summative views discussed earlier are completely on the wrong track. It is not even *a necessary condition* of our believing that *p* that each or most of us believe that *p* personally.

But perhaps I get ahead of myself. Is what people refer to when they speak of what "we believe" the belief of a plural subject constituted by each of "us"? There is reason to think that, at least sometimes, references to what we believe do have this meaning.

Collective Belief

Recall my discussion of the shocked surprise response. I noted that this might well be expressed in terms of what *we believe* or what *we think* and so on: "But we know that science has a masculine bias!"; "But we concluded Jake was quite unpleasant!"; "But we don't think string theory isn't going anywhere. On the contrary!"

If our believing something is a matter of our being the parties to a joint commitment to believe as a body, we have an explanation of how our believing something can lead to the shocked surprise response and of why that response should issue in "But we think . . ." and so on. For the speaker who provokes the response violates an obligation to his hearers. The three example cases can be interpreted along these lines, given the amount of description already provided. That gives us some reason to accept the following account of collective belief:

> There is a *collective belief* that *p* if some persons constitute the plural subject of a belief that *p*. Such persons *collectively believe* that *p*.

I write "if," rather than "if and only if": I have argued elsewhere that the type of collective belief characterized here may be the basic type, from our understanding of which other types attract the same label.[18]

I regard this account as essentially the same as a variety of rather different formulations I have used in other places. A note should be added here on one aspect of these other formulations, given that I have elsewhere referred to my account of collective belief as the "joint acceptance" account (in *On Social Facts* and Chapter 7, this volume).

I have written, in this connection, of a joint commitment to "accept that *p* as a body" or to "jointly accept that *p*." This was something that I did spontaneously, without questioning why I did not, rather, write of a commitment to "believe that *p* . . . ."

A number of philosophers have recently made distinctions between "belief" and "acceptance" such that there is a real distinction between the two (Stalnaker [1984], p. 74ff.; Van Fraassen [1980], p. 88). However, a look through a number of dictionaries suggests that there is a sense of "accepts that *p*" and "believes that *p*" such that these are virtually synonymous. I think it likely that when I originally wrote of "joint acceptance" I was not consciously meaning to introduce a concept distinct from that of belief, and that my spontaneous use of "accepts that *p*" may have been guided as much by my sense of euphony as anything else. There is no need to pursue this issue at length here. The following points may be noted, however.

The general schema introduced here for the plural subject concepts seems to me auspicious. It proposes that the plural subject of a psychological predicate "*X*" involves a joint commitment precisely to *X*-ing as a body. Nearly if "*X*" and "*Y*" are synonymous, it will be correct to say that (using the terms in the relevant senses) a plural subject of *X* involves a joint commitment to *Y*-ing as a body. Meanwhile, things will be clearer if we use the same term in both places. Then, if we define collective belief in terms of plural subjecthood, we will define it in terms of joint commitment to *believe* as a body (rather than using the putatively synonymous "accept").

Now it could be that you can only believe that *p* as a body if you also accept that *p* as a body, in some nonsynonymous sense of "accept" such that accepting entails believing. This could be a reason for proposing an account of collectively *X*-ing in terms of a joint commitment to *Y* as a body. I shall not pursue this, or related ideas, here.[19]

What I want to stress is that, as I understand it, the behavior that results from collective belief is driven by *the concept of belief* and *the concept X-ing-as-a-body*. It is as if the participants ask themselves, "What do I need to do to make it the case—as best I can—that I and these others together believe that *p* as a body?"—and then act accordingly. I have suggested that the answer given by our everyday understanding for the simple interpersonal case is that, among other things, in reasoning together we say things that entail *p* rather than not-*p*, we do not deny that *p* without preamble, and so on. More briefly, we attempt as best we can to make it true that the body we constitute relates to *p* the way any *individual* who believes that *p* relates to *p*.[20]

Concluding Remarks

Is there a moral here, a practical conclusion? It may well appear that collective beliefs in the sense delineated here are unsavory phenomena. They justify the infliction of pressure by one person on another in the service of beliefs that may be false, and which, indeed, may not be personally accepted by any of the parties. Thus we may well be moved to ask whether collective beliefs are avoidable.

In practice I think they are not. If you are taking part in a conversation you are liable to be faced with expressions of opinion you have to respond to in some way. You will have to accept or reject the opinions, or to express indecision on the matter. If you nod agreement, a collective belief will result, and you are, and know you are, now liable to evoke the shocked surprise response if you deviate from the obligations of the newly formed joint commitment.[21]

If collective beliefs arise so easily in our situation as interacting, conversing beings, then we may suspect that they have their uses, as of course they do. Apart from the general function of providing individuals with a sense of unity or community with others—a function all joint commitment helps to some degree to fulfill—the collective beliefs evidently provide points from which people can go forward, not forever locked in the back-and-forth of argumentative conflict.[22]

It will be hard to avoid the repressiveness of collective beliefs. Perhaps the best we can do is attempt to assure that the beliefs that become collective among us are beliefs we can live with. For, once they are set, they are powerful forces.[23]

Notes

1. See, for instance, Quinton (1975–1976).
2. The term "common knowledge" was introduced into the philosophical literature by Lewis (1969). There is by now a large literature on the subject in both philosophy and economics. To put things in familiar terms, one might say that it is common knowledge (in the relevant sense) that *p* in a certain population if and only if the fact that *p* is completely out in the open in that population. For further discussion of how common knowledge is best defined, see Lewis (1969), Schiffer (1972), Heal (1978), and Gilbert (1989a).

3. Chapter 7 in this volume discusses these two accounts. *On Social Facts*, Chapter 5, discusses these two accounts as well as a third summative account.

4. The main references are *On Social Facts*, Chapters 5 and 7, and Chapter 7 in this volume. Though this essay is intended to be self-contained, it is not intended as a substitute for these earlier discussions.

There is of course no question that when all or most members of a certain population have a certain belief, this will often be a matter with important consequences. If we all believe that Jones is the best candidate, Jones may be elected as a result. That a general belief is common knowledge will often have its own consequences. If it is common knowledge that we all prefer Jones, we will not waste time arguing in Jones's favor. The consequences in the case I have in mind are, in any case, rather different. See below in the text.

5. Cf. John Stuart Mill's classic text in political philosophy, *On Liberty* (1978).

6. For some purposes one might want to say that only "We believe that . . ." is properly labeled a collective *belief* statement. However, there is clearly quite a large number of other sentences that are understood to ascribe belief or something involving belief, including "We decided that . . . ," "We know that . . . ," "We are convinced that . . . ," "We think that . . . ," "Our opinion is that . . ." and "We concluded that . . . ," among others. For present purposes the category of collective belief statements may be taken to encompass all of these. In focused discussion I shall generally concentrate on "We believe . . ." specifically as an example. An approach to understanding each member of this family individually will be provided. This approach will also apply to related ascriptions such as "We are inclined to think that . . . ," "For present purposes we are assuming that . . . ," and so on.

7. If one pauses to think about it, these ways of describing things have their picturesque side. They bring to mind the well-known figure on the engraved title page to the first edition of Hobbes's *Leviathan*: a vast number of persons making up a vast person. A less picturesque alternative might be "as a unit." This may risk missing something useful in the connotations of the other phrases: the idea of a single "source of action." I have in mind the joint commitment that constitutes a given plural subject, and that has the power to motivate those involved to act appropriately. Joint commitment is discussed in some detail below in the text.

8. See *On Social Facts*, Chapters 4ff. The rest of this section differs slightly from the original.

9. In Chapter 7, this volume, I wrote of being "committed as a body." Either phrase could be used to convey the general idea.

10. For discussion of the resemblance between everyday *agreements* and joint commitment phenomena in general, see Chapter 13, this volume.

11. See in particular Chapter 12, this volume.

12. On this, see Chapter 12, including note 13.

13. It is clear from this that, strictly speaking, the obligation one is subject

to through a joint commitment is an obligation one has to the parties to the commitment in that capacity. Thus "obligor" June will be obligated to "obligee" Joe in his capacity as party to their joint commitment. She will not, one might say, be obligated to Joe "considered as an individual." She herself, of course, is a member of the group to which she is beholden for release. For present purposes the main point is that she is understood not to be in a position unilaterally to remove the relevant constraint on her behavior. Others—or at least one other—must be called into play.

14. The following discussion draws on that in Gilbert (1993ms).

15. Cf. N. Shakespeare (1993), on overhearing his parents in private conversation: "never before had I heard them converse unencumbered by the knowledge and presence of children. Nothing that passed between them was remotely embarrassing or distressing, or even particularly interesting, but, as if for the first time, I was hearing the two of them as man and woman rather than as parents." For some related discussion, see *On Social Facts*, pp. 219–21, 302, 374–75). I thank Fred Schmitt for discussion of the contrast illustrated in the preceding three paragraphs of the text.

16. David Lewis has suggested (written personal communication, 3 January 1989) that such ideas fit together well with those of Robert Stalnaker (1973, 1974) on presupposition. As Lewis observed, Stalnaker is primarily interested in the interaction of presupposition and language rather than in the analysis of presupposition itself. See also Lewis (1983).

17. Thus being part of a plural subject of belief allows in principle for one's "freedom of thought" (cf. Cohen 1967). But see Chapter 7, this volume, and *On Social Facts*, pp. 304–6, on the likely influence on individuals of membership in a plural subject of belief. See also Mill (1861, Chapter 2). Mill proposes that freedom of thought is closely tied to freedom of expression of opinion.

18. See, for instance, Chapter 7, this volume, and *On Social Facts*, pp. 311–12, 239–40). See also Gilbert (1994a, section 2).

19. This paragraph was prompted by comments from Fred Schmitt.

20. It may be suggested that what we in fact do *individually* in constituting a collective belief that *p* is *accept that p* in a sense in which this is not equivalent to *believe that p*. Rather, each uses the proposition that *p* as a premise in his or her reasoning, without necessarily believing it. (Tuomela [1992] appears to suggest this or something similar.) This would be relevant to my account of collective belief as an attempt to give a general account of what it is to do one's part in believing as a body in terms of a specific propositional attitude taken up by the individuals involved. I shall not attempt to evaluate it from this point of view here.

21. See *On Social Facts*, Chapter 5, section 7.3, which suggests that a conversation can be viewed as the "negotiation" of a jointly accepted view.

22. On the sense of unity aspect of joint commitment see *On Social Facts*, pp. 223–25; Chapter 8, this volume). Schmitt (1994) discusses uses of collective belief in the sense discussed here.

23. This accords with Emile Durkheim's insistence on the "coercive power" of collective beliefs in *The Rules of Sociological Method* (1982); see especially Chapter 1 and the prefaces. See also Gilbert (1989a, pp. 243–54; 1994a).

An earlier version of this essay was read to the Department of Philosophy, Hamburg University, June 1993. I thank those present for a lively discussion. Thanks also to Fred Schmitt for useful written comments on that version, and to Michael Cook and Saul Kripke for related discussion. The paper is already long enough, but I regret not having been able to address certain queries that have come my way regarding my account of collective belief. I hope to do that in another place.

15

Group Membership and Political Obligation

Many people feel, I think, that they are tied in a special way to their government, not just by "bonds of affection," but by *moral* bonds. While they complain loudly and often, and not without justification, of the shortcomings of government, they feel that they are nonetheless bound to support their country's political institutions . . . in ways that they are not bound to the corresponding institutions of *other* countries. Yet it is difficult to give any substance to this feeling of a special moral bond. It seems to me that the problem of political obligation is precisely the problem of explaining the nature and scope of such special moral bonds (if any such exist) and of determining who, if anyone, is constrained by them. [A. J. Simmons, 1979, pp. 3–4][1]

I. Political Bonds?

In the above passage A. John Simmons sets the scene for his discussion of political obligation in his book *Moral Principles and Political Obligations,* one of the best known contemporary philosophical treatments of the subject.

At the end of his book, Simmons concludes that, in his own words, "most citizens do not have political obligations." He is not alone in holding a view that could be so expressed. Yet there is something awkward about this conclusion in the context of his opening remarks.

As we have seen, Simmons begins his exposition by drawing attention to the fact that many people believe (or "feel") that they are bound to support their country's political institutions. He suggests that

361

he is about to explicate and justify this belief. He concludes, about two hundred pages later, that the belief is false. Thus he has not delivered what he encouraged us to expect.

Someone might respond that Simmons has delivered something better, from a philosophical point of view. He has delivered a sort of "skeptical paradox." He starts with an entrenched common belief, and concludes that it has no basis.

The problem with skeptical paradoxes in general is that they call into question beliefs that seem firm. They present not so much a point of quiescence, but a challenge. Can these common beliefs not after all find a satisfactory explication and defense? The more entrenched the beliefs, the more we "can't help having them," the more we are likely to have this reaction. We will think: something has gone wrong somewhere. I suggest that we *should* think this. We should go back to the beliefs and examine them again to see if something can be made of them after all.[2]

I start in this essay from Simmons's initial datum: many people feel that "they are bound to support their country's political institutions" (p. 3), or that they have "special political bonds which require that they . . . support the governments of their countries of residence" (p. 192). I shall focus on the explicatory question: what is the supposed nature of the bonds in question? What, in particular, is their presumed source? This question is, it seems, a necessary preliminary to any question of justification.

I do not mean to take it for granted at the outset that there is indeed a *single* presumed source of obligation. However, it is possible that there is indeed a "single thought" generally involved, and I shall be arguing in behalf of a single candidate thought, or type of thought. This, I shall argue, makes the common feeling Simmons is concerned with both less of a puzzle and more well-founded than Simmons's discussion as a whole would suggest.

A preliminary note before proceeding. In the opening passage quoted earlier Simmons wrote of "moral bonds." In other places he writes of "political bonds," or simply of *bonds* or *obligations,* but he appears everywhere to assume that the bonds in question are properly characterized as *moral* bonds with a certain content.

It is of course quite standard to interpret the problem of political obligation as a problem in moral philosophy, having to do with what is referred to as "moral obligation." In my own specification of my topic and in my further discussion, however, I shall drop the assumption that the bonds in question are "moral" bonds. Precisely how the *moral* realm is to be demarcated and defined is not altogether clear. In any case the crucial point, as I see it, is that we are supposedly talking about *actual* bonds or obligations, actual obligations with a certain content.

If I have what I am calling an "actual" bond, there is something that I am in some sense currently bound to do. In particular it is not a matter merely of what I would have to do if I wished to conform to some institutional practice, what may be referred to as an "institutional requirement" or "positional duty" (Simmons's phrase). It is a matter of what it is *now* incumbent upon *me* to do, all else being equal.

II. Analytic Membership Arguments

The common belief Simmons asked us to focus on had to do with (to quote his phrase) "our relationship to our government" (Preface, p. viii). He refers to people feeling that they are tied in a special way to "their" government, not to governments in general or to just governments in particular. They feel they are "bound to support their country's political institutions . . . in ways that they are not tied to the corresponding institutions of other countries" (p. 3).

If this is the feeling we are trying to understand, it would seem plausible to consider head-on what it is for a country to be "our" country. To put it somewhat more subjectively: when do people think of a country as *our* country? What do they believe the relevant relationship consists in?

Surprisingly, Simmons does not set out to explore this question. He does mention, however, a class of related arguments which I shall call "analytic membership arguments." The following quotation will serve to exemplify such arguments in general. It is from Thomas McPherson's book *Political Obligation*.

McPherson writes: "Belonging in society involves . . . rights and obligations. Understanding what it is to be social would be impossible unless we understood what it is to have rights and obligations—and *vice versa*. . . . That social man has obligations is an analytic, not a synthetic, proposition. . . . 'Why should I obey the government?' is an absurd question. We have not understood what it *means* to be a member of political society if we suppose that political obligation is something that we might not have had and that therefore needs to be *justified*" (p.64).

In his brief consideration of such arguments Simmons suggests that even if being a member of a political society logically entails having political obligations we can still quite reasonably ask "Why do we have such obligations? What is their ground?"

Simmons himself implicitly argues that the purported analytical connections do not in fact exist. Throughout his book he assumes a rather broad notion of membership in a political society, in which, roughly, one is a member if one falls within the "effective domain" of a society's laws. He ultimately argues, in effect, that there is no plausible way of supporting the idea that membership in a political society does carry with it political obligations. Presumably, then, if asked, he would say that the alleged conceptual connection between membership and obligation does not in fact exist.

Analytic membership arguments such as McPherson's do, indeed, raise *two* important issues. First, *is* there indeed some conceptual connection between societal membership (under some natural construal) and obligation? Second, what is the *ground* of the connection? Can the obligation be given *an articulate basis*?

Before leaving Simmons's discussion I want to draw attention to a place in his text where he comes close to acknowledging that there is in fact a familiar concept of group membership which is rich enough to provide a connection between membership and obligation. Here he refers to what is to be a "member [of an institution] *in the full sense of the word*" (p. 140: my emphasis). "I have given my express consent to be governed by its rules, or perhaps I have held office . . . or *accepted* . . . substantial benefits from the institution's workings. . . . In such a case . . . I have *done* things which seem to tie me to the [institution], rather than being a passive bystander" (p. 140, Simmons' emphasis).

Perhaps Simmons does not see a connection between this and the widespread sense of political bond because he believes that very few of us have ever "given our express consent" to the political institutions of our country, or held office, and so on. It would then be reasonable to assume that one cannot provide an account of the sense that *many* have that they are politically obligated by reference to their membership "in the full sense of the word." For they are *not* members in the sense in question.

III. Plural Subjects

I shall now produce my own analytic membership argument. I shall argue that *obligations* attach to group membership *according to a central vernacular concept of a social group* and I shall characterize *the ground of the obligation*. In this section I draw on previous discussions, summarizing to a large extent, though certain points are amplified.[3]

The first part of my discussion will aim to clarify some important features of an example. Recall that sociologists and others often include quite small and transient populations on their lists of social groups. I shall start with such a group.

I shall consider a small group comprising of two people who are going for a walk together. I assume that their going for a walk together makes them a social group, albeit a small and transitory one.

I take it that when people "go for a walk together" then, at the minimum, they walk along somewhere more or less side by side. Walking together, in other words, demands a certain physical proximity. Such proximity is a necessary but not a sufficient condition for walking together, as the following example shows.

Suppose that you and I are out on a walk. We are heading up Fifth Avenue in the direction of Central Park. Now imagine that without warning you suddenly turn away from me, without a word, and cross to the other side, disappearing down East 49th Street. Perhaps I will not be *disappointed*. But I will surely be *surprised*, and I will, more strongly, feel that you have done something "quite untoward." You have in some way *made a mistake*. We were out on a walk, and you suddenly disappeared without any "by your leave."

Your leaving would not have this effect in slightly altered circumstances. Suppose you had first clapped your hand to your brow and said to me in an upset tone "Look, I'm sorry but I've just remembered I have a doctor's appointment—I'm already late for it!—I've got to dash!" Such a speech is likely to elicit my acquiescence, at least if I believe you. Then you will have squared things with me before leaving.

This is a very humdrum story but it carries an important lesson. When two people are out on a walk together, *each is understood to be under a certain constraint*. This constraint can only be removed by mutual accord.

Without attempting a precise definition of "obligation," it is surely plausible to suggest that the concept of obligation applies here. If I am out on a walk with you, *I have certain obligations*.[4]

I shall now turn to the question of the ground of these obligations. How do people ever end up going for a walk together? This can happen in various ways. Usually there will be some kind of dialogue. Case I: I say: "Would you like to come for a walk up Fifth Avenue to Central

Park?'' You reply: ''Yes!—Let's go!'' Case II: I am already out on a walk. You see me and inquire as to my planned route. ''I'll come with you!'' you say. I am not altogether pleased about this but I don't demur. We set off. The first case involves an informal agreement between the parties. What happens in the second case may not amount to an agreement exactly. Nonetheless the relevant understanding can be thus established.

My suggestion about the ultimate basis for this understanding, in general terms, is this: each has expressed to the other his or her willingness to be parties to a *joint commitment* with a certain content. In Case I, we will be jointly committed at a minimum to walk up Fifth Avenue to Central Park in close proximity. It will not be acceptable for you suddenly to break away without checking with me first, nor will it be acceptable for you to walk five yards ahead of me, and so on, unless we establish a special understanding that that is how we shall proceed.

As I understand it, all that is necessary to *establish* what I call a ''joint commitment'' is that the relevant parties mutually express their readiness to be so committed, in conditions of common knowledge. The common knowledge condition means that the existence of these expressions must be ''out in the open'' between the parties. For instance, it is not enough for me to mutter my proposal so softly that you can't possibly hear.[5]

Once we have expressed ourselves in conditions of common knowledge, the joint commitment is in place. But what does this mean? Among other things, each of us is now subject to a commitment that he or she cannot unilaterally remove. More could be said about the nature of joint commitment but for the present purposes this should be enough.[6]

I believe that the concept of joint commitment is a fundamental social concept—perhaps *the* fundamental social concept. Its function, if you will, is to establish a set of obligations and entitlements between individual persons, to establish a special ''tie'' or ''bond'' between them.

I refer to those who are parties to joint commitments as members of a ''plural subject,'' for what the joint commitment creates is, in effect, a single center of action made up of a plurality of persons. Their commitment binds them together in the service of a single ''cause,'' such as walking up to Central Park in close proximity to one another. (As I shall explain, ''action'' and ''cause'' here have to be understood in a wide sense.)

Let me now make a few further points about the concept of a *plural subject* in my sense. This will make it clear that the range of this concept is quite wide: there can be plural subjects of many different kinds.

First, though people can apparently end up going on a walk together without exactly agreeing to do so, it may seem that they can only do so if they go through a "datable" process *much like* the making of an explicit agreement. If joint commitments (and hence plural subjects) can only be formed in this way, it may seem that they cannot underpin such things as social practices or institutions, whose beginnings are not plausibly thought of in this manner.

In order to defuse this concern, I shall appeal to another humdrum imaginary story. Suppose that you and I find ourselves standing together on the sidewalk after a meeting of the Society for Philosophy and Public Affairs. We decide to go out for coffee, which we do, before going our separate ways. After the next meeting, you ask if I'd like to go for a coffee. Though you don't explicitly allude to the previous occasion, you clearly do not feel presumptuous and suppose that I might well accept. In the event, I do. If this happens one or more times, one can expect a tacit understanding to emerge to the effect that "we are jointly committed to our going out for a coffee together after the Philosophy and Public Affairs meetings." If on the fifth occasion you come up to me and say "I'm afraid I won't be able to have coffee tonight, . . ." expecting my sympathetic concurrence, you indicate to me that you understand there is a joint commitment, so you need to come to me and reach a mutual accord about your nonconformity. Otherwise you violate an obligation. My responding appropriately would confirm this understanding.

This example was intended to show how joint commitments and their attendant obligations can become established as a result of a process that is considerably extended in time, and in such a way that it may be hard for the participants or for anyone else to "date" their establishment. That is not to say that there is in fact no single point in time at which the joint commitment in question was finally established. But the subtle kinds of communication that may be involved are quite likely not to be consciously noted by the participants. They will probably think of their practice as just having "grown up somehow."

It is worth observing that the *content* of a joint commitment may be quite vague. It may become more precise—or more vague—with time. Thus we may agree to "go for a walk" and only gradually clarify how long we will walk for or where we will go.

Change may be explicitly negotiated or it may "just happen" in accordance with the sorts of subtle communications just mentioned. Thus I may begin to feel that I would rather stop having coffee with you after the meetings. After I have brought a number of excuses to you on successive occasions, you wave me good-bye at the end of a meeting and I wave back heartily. At this point our joint commitment may be deemed to have ended. We may still constitute a plural subject—we may still be friends—but the character of that plural subject will have changed.

Two further points about plural subjects are relevant here. There is reason to suppose that the first person plural pronoun, "we," has a *central sense* in which its referent is a (presumed) plural subject. One way of arguing this is to see that certain rather striking inference patterns involving "we" premises like "We are looking for Jack" are made intelligible if we understand there to be an implicit reference to a joint commitment.[7]

One aspect of this sense of "we" that is of considerable practical importance is that "we" can be used in an *initiatory* fashion, as in the utterance "Shall we dance?" said by one stranger to another. If the second person "accepts," then a plural subject of a new kind is formed: the plural subject of dancing together or being ready to dance.

A final important point about plural subjects is this. People can form plural subjects not only of acts and practices involving regularly doing certain things together, but also of beliefs and attitudes, of principles of action, and so on.

In relation to *belief,* people may form a joint commitment to uphold some proposition *as a body.* They can then speak meaningfully of what "we" believe, in contrast to what "I" believe and even in contrast to what "you and I both personally believe." It is this phenomenon that, as I have argued elsewhere, underlies much of our talk of groups believing things, of their having attitudes of their own, and so on.[8]

If our vernacular concept of a social group is the concept of a plural subject then it has quite a wide range. The members of a group do not have to be "doing things together" all the time or even prepared to "do things together" in the normal, narrow sense. The group could be sustained essentially by a single belief or credo: "We shall overcome," for instance, or "We shall win the war."

My own analytic membership argument, then, is this: social groups are plural subjects; plural subjects are constituted by joint commitments, which immediately generate obligations.

IV. Social Groups

It is, I believe, quite plausible to argue that at least one vernacular concept of a social group is well analyzed in terms of plural subjecthood. Three reasons for thinking this are, in summary, as follows: First, if we consider the lists sociologists give, typical cases of standard members of these lists do seem to constitute plural subjects of one kind or another. Second, people often describe what it is like to be in a group using such terms as "union," "unity," "communion," and "community," and, indeed, in terms of constraints and claustrophobia. Clearly, group membership is experienced as something consequential, something that has its effects on the individual psyche, something involving a special tie or constraint. Third, the pronoun "we" is very comfortably used by their members to refer to "identified" social groups such as families, tribes, and so on, and it can be argued to refer, in one central sense at least, to plural subjects in general.[9]

Doubtless different people use the phrase "social group" in different ways. Thus people occasionally refer to various populations that are not plural subjects in my sense as social groups, and to their members as group members. Some may speak of the population of women in this way, for instance. Some may bring economic classes into their lists of social groups or refer to them in giving examples of groups and group properties. (Anthony Quinton does this in his article "Social Objects," for instance.)

Then there is the assumption I attributed to Simmons, that those who live within the "effective domain" of a government are members of a social group. Clearly such people may not form a plural subject. Some of them may be unaware of the very existence of the government (a point that Simmons seems to stress). As Simmons puts it, these are "passive" as opposed to "active" members, but he apparently regards them as members in any case—if not "fully-fledged" ones.

Nonetheless, as I have indicated, there is reason to associate a central concept of a social group with that of a plural subject, and hence to associate group membership in the relevant sense with obligation.

Now, at the end of the day, what is most important for my own approach to the problem of political obligation is the concept of a plural subject itself. What is important is that *this* concept is apparently a common one. We operate with it at the humdrum (but basic) levels of going for walks, engaging in conversation, living through department meetings, and so on. It is a concept that pervades our daily lives.

With this lengthy preamble I shall now return to Simmons' and my own concern about political obligation.

V. Group Membership and Political Obligation

My general line on the problem of political obligation with which I am concerned should already be apparent. Recall that the problem was this: many people apparently have a sense that they have "political bonds," that they are "tied in a special way to their governments" or "bound to support their country's political institutions and obey its laws." (These descriptions all come from Simmons.) What is the presumed source of the supposed political bonds?

I mentioned earlier that it seemed to me best to drop from our inquiry any special restriction to "moral" bonds, whatever precisely these are. It is enough that many people feel that they are tied, bound, or obligated in the relevant ways. What might be the presumed source of the obligation? It is in any case natural enough to express the thoughts at issue without using the term "moral"—in his discussion Simmons does this many times. If we drop this concern with specifically moral bonds, it leaves us freer to look around and see where and why we actually sense *ties* and *obligations* in our lives.

Clearly I am going to suggest that when someone refers to a certain country as "our country" or to a government as "our government" she may well be speaking *in the "plural subject" mode*: that is, there may well be a sense of joint commitment behind her use of such language. If she is indeed speaking in this mode, then we will expect her to have an accompanying sense of obligation. Whether or not all membership in social groups or membership "in the full sense" is always a matter of plural subjecthood and joint commitment is therefore ultimately not crucial here. The main thing is that *the plural subject concept could be in play, and, by the look of things, it is.*

As I have already indicated, it may be a mistake to press for too precise an answer to the question "What is the content of the relevant commitment?" One fairly minimal candidate with respect to the phrase "our government" would presumably be something like this: "we jointly accept that *that body* may make and enforce edicts throughout this territory."[10]

Suppose, then, that generally speaking when people refer to "our government," "our country," and the like, they do take themselves to be party to a joint commitment of the relevant sort, and hence to be obligated in the appropriate ways. There does of course remain a relevant question of justification: could their taking themselves to be jointly committed in this way be well-founded? Could the people concerned have reason to believe that they are indeed parties to a joint commitment of the kind in question?

The following brief remarks must suffice in discussion of this question here. The widespread observed use of such phrases as "our government" and "our country," alongside any relevant behavior, would itself appear to provide a basis for common knowledge in a population that a substantial portion of its members has openly expressed its willingness jointly to commit in the relevant way.

In such a context it may be reasonable for those who use these phrases to see themselves as jointly committed with all those others who also use such language—whoever precisely they are. This could be the reason people do believe or "feel" that they have a special tie to their own government or their own country: they are indeed aware of the proliferation of the relevant speech and action in the relevant population. If this is so, then contrary to Simmons's conclusion in his book, there will be about as much political obligation as there would appear to be from the way people talk.

VI. Concluding Remarks

There is nothing in what I have said so far that implies that there are any governments or political institutions that *deserve* communal support. That question lies beyond the scope of this essay. So do many of the questions to be found in the literature under the rubric of the problem of political obligation. Does one have some sort of obligation or duty to support all just governments? Does receipt of benefits obligate in some way? Do I owe whichever government it was a debt of gratitude for educating me and providing various forms of welfare services? Is there always something to be said for shoring up the present government, given that anarchy is the likely alternative? I shall not address these questions here.

One thing is clear, however. It is very easy to slip into the "plural subject" mode of endorsement of governments and other institutions in the countries in which we are long-term residents. It is very easy to go along with others who think in this mode, given a natural tendency to constitute some kind of group, and, of course, given the pressure from others to do so. Insofar as bonds or ties inevitably ensue, we could do well to make the details of our joint commitments as conscious as possible.

Thus we would do well to ask ourselves individually and collectively such questions as: is it good to be ready to defend with these others the Constitution of the United States? Is it good to be ready to support the duly elected government in this country? Is it good to commit to abiding by every single law on all occasions? How much free play is it good to reserve for ourselves?

In matters of state politics as in matters of personal relationships, such issues require serious attention. Thus I in no way urge unreflective commitment. On the contrary, that is all too easy to come by, and should be challenged, and become—if we were being reasonable all along—reflective commitment.

I have argued that to be a member of a plural subject of a certain sort is to have "political bonds." Plural subjects, as I define these, are constituted by joint commitments. The obligations that flow from such commitments are analogous to those that flow from common or garden agreements.[11] Thus I have given a sort of "actual contract" theory of (a certain type of) political obligation.

Now such theories have been much criticized. Simmons, for instance, rejects any such theory on the grounds that few people anywhere have a consent-based obligation to support a government. There are other writers more sympathetic to actual contract theory. One such theorist is Michael Walzer, and there are passages in Walzer's book *Obligations*, for instance, in which he says things that sound quite similar to what I say here. He sees a form of commitment as basic. And he implies that what he refers to as "consent" can be given in subtle ways, without the need for explicit agreements datable by the participants.

In any case, both those who endorse some form of actual contract theory and those who do not assume that the obligations in question only arise or have any real force when the commitment is entered into *freely* in a strong sense: coercive circumstances preclude genuine consent, and hence preclude political obligations. Thus, summarizing his position Walzer writes "Civil liberty of the most extensive sort is, therefore, the necessary condition of political obligation" (p. xiv).

I would put my own position quite differently. As far as I can see, coercive circumstances do not preclude political obligations *in the sense delineated here*. Coercive circumstances need not prevent me from entering into a joint commitment. If I am a party to such a commitment I am obligated and that is that. That is not to say that I may not subsequently have good reason to break my commitment and violate my obligation. I may or I may not. But the obligation is as real as the commitment is, and commitment can be full and complete in coercive conditions. I have argued that at length elsewhere. Here I must perforce close with that bald pronouncement.[12]

Notes

1. All quotations from Simmons in this essay are to Simmons (1979).

2. I discuss the skeptical paradox that Saul Kripke attributes to Wittgenstein in *On Social Facts*, Chapter 3.

3. The example of walking together is discussed in detail in Chapter 6, this volume.

4. I argue that there are two radically different types of obligation in Chapter 12, this volume.

5. In some contexts the mutual expressions of willingness can be made in a quite subtle manner. For example, suppose four of my colleagues are intently discussing a philosophical problem in the corridor. I come up to them, listen, and then interject a remark. They need do little more than unquestioningly treat my comment as part of the conversation in order that I become party to their joint commitment to converse. This observation was prompted by a comment from Roger Lee. See also the coffee-after-the-talk story below.

6. See also Chapter 12 and elsewhere, this volume.

7. I have in mind the fact that it seems I can make an inference from, say, (1) "We are trying to stop Harry crying" and (2) "I can stop Harry crying by putting on some rock music" to (3) "I have reason to put on some rock music." What is important about this is that there appears to be no suppressed or implicit premise to the effect that I personally want Harry to stop crying. Perhaps I personally would rather that he went on crying. Nonetheless I seem already to have reason to put on the music just because of what we are trying to do. One way the apparent acceptability of this inference can be explained is by reference to my being jointly committed to whatever we are trying to do. If such a commitment is assumed, the inference proceeds appropriately. Wilfrid Sellars noted this special type of inference in the early 1960s (see for instance Sellars, 1963a). I put forward the hypothesis that a joint commitment is presupposed in *On Social Facts*, Chapter 7.

8. See Chapter 7, this volume.

9. For a fuller discussion see Gilbert, *On Social Facts*, Chapter 4.

10. This particular joint commitment has one rather interesting aspect. Given that I am party to the commitment, I have not obviously committed myself to *obey* the edicts of the body in question.

11. For more on the relationship between agreements and joint commitment see Chapters 12 and 13, this volume.

12. For a detailed discussion see ''Agreements, Coercion, and Obligation'' (Chapter 12, this volume). That esssay and the present one constitute studies toward a projected monograph on political obligation. An earlier version of this essay was presented as an invited talk to the Society for Philosophy and Public Affairs at New York University, 12 February 1992.

16

On Feeling Guilt for What One's Group Has Done

Introduction

Can it be appropriate to feel guilt just because one's group has acted badly?[1] It may be thought that it cannot.[2] Appeal may be made to common claims relating both to the appropriate object of guilt feelings, and to what it is to feel guilt in particular.[3]

The appropriate object of a feeling of guilt, it may be said, is an action of one's own.[4] One can, after all, *bear* guilt only for one's own wrongdoing.[5] It has been said that to feel guilt is, at a minimum, to assess oneself negatively.[6] Why should one do this on account of one's *group's* bad action? One might well be *personally guiltless* with regard to that action!

In this essay I sketch an argument to the effect that it can be appropriate to feel guilt just because one's group has acted badly. My argument will put in question a number of standard assumptions about guilt feelings.

The argument invokes a particular understanding of what a group is. It therefore concerns cases that are assumed to meet specified conditions. I do not argue for any judgments on actual groups or particular people. The validity of such judgments depends on concrete historical facts. The determination of any such facts goes beyond the scope of this essay.

The feeling of guilt is unpleasant. Most people wish only to be rid of it, or never to experience it. One who seems to argue for an expansion of the territory of appropriate guilt feelings is likely to provoke resistance. I see myself not as expanding that territory, but as helping to map it.

I. Some Cases

Can one's group's action of itself make a feeling of guilt appropriate? Description of some possible cases can sharpen the question. In each of the following situations, my group has acted badly but it may seem that I cannot appropriately feel guilt as a result.

1. I knew of the action and attempted to prevent or curtail it. I did as much as I could reasonably be expected to do, given my situation and capacities.[7] I may have organized a large public protest against the action. I may have participated in such a protest. Unable to participate, I may have spoken warmly of the protest, encouraged others to go on it, loudly condemned the action, and so on. Unable to move or speak, but knowing of the action, I may have condemned it roundly in my heart.[8] Can it be appropriate for me to feel guilt about the group's action?

2. Though a member of the group when it performed the action, I did not learn of the action until it was too late to do anything to prevent or curtail it. I am in no way culpable for my lack of information about the action at the time it occurred.[9] Had I learned of the action in time to do something, I would have tried to prevent it. I would have done as much as I could reasonably have been expected to do. Perhaps I would have succeeded in preventing the action. Can it be appropriate for me to feel guilt about the group's action?[10]

II. The Problem

It seems that people do feel guilt over their group's actions even in circumstances such as these.[11] If this is so, that is in itself a reason for considering whether an appropriate basis can be found for the feeling. At the same time, it may be tempting to write it off as irrational, as going too far.[12]

The feeling of guilt has been characterized as, at a minimum, a form of negative self-assessment. It has been held, further, to suggest the appropriateness of reparative action.[13] It may already incorporate an element of self-punishment.[14] These characterizations of the feeling of guilt do not go so far as to say that a feeling of guilt over something presumes that one is oneself to blame for it. But each of these characterizations suggests the problem. The people in question here appear to be personally blameless with respect to their group's action:

they tried as best they could to prevent it, they knew nothing of it, and so on.

Let us assume that we can amplify their position further: they are blameless in the matter of being and remaining group members at the time in question. How, then, could the action of the group justify a negative self-assessment or, if feeling guilt comes to that, a form of self-punishment? In a word, why should they tell themselves off? How could that conceivably be appropriate?

There is no need to deny the possibility of guilt feelings which are irrational or ill-founded. Insofar as irrationality and ill-foundedness are flaws, however, respect for a response and the people who have it demands that we search quite seriously for an account that avoids irrationality.

III. The Appeal to Identification

In this context some authors appeal to what they refer to as "identification."[15] I am not sure that the bare appeal to "identification" advances our understanding of the phenomenon we are considering, or adequately addresses our concern about its appropriateness.

In discussions of guilt it is standard to assume that "feelings of guilt . . . cannot arise from the deeds or omissions of others."[16] Given that this is so—and I shall not dispute it here—to feel guilt in relation to the acts of one's country is already in some sense to *identify* with one's country. More tentatively, it is to reject the idea that one's country is something other than oneself.

The question immediately arising from the reference to "identification" is this: how is the relevant identification possible? How could identification be intelligible, let alone appropriate? Louis XIV notoriously claimed *"L'Etat, c'est moi."* Whatever precisely he had in mind, most citizens would not claim that, literally speaking, their country is no more than "me." What, then, is at issue here? When is the relevant way of perceiving one's relation to one's country—identification—legitimate? Can we go beyond the metaphor of identification to a more precise account of what is, or may be, going on?[17]

IV. The Intuitive Picture

At a simple intuitive level, first, there is a difference between accepting that "They did it" and accepting that "We did it." I am not one of them, but I am "one of us." I cannot detach myself from "us" while I regard "us" precisely as "us."

The intuitive picture goes further than this, somewhat as follows. If I am one of us, and we did something, I am part of what did it. More precisely, I am part of the agent that did it, part of the subject of the action. Whereas I am the subject of my action, I am part of the subject of our action. In my capacity as a member of "us," I am on a par with every other member.

If we did this bad thing, as opposed to this or that person doing it, we may bear moral guilt with respect to the doing of it.[18] If we bear guilt, the guilt in question is, precisely, ours. Not mine, nor mine and yours, but ours, ours together. Perhaps then it may be referred to as *collective* guilt. This guilt will be participated in, or shared, by all of us, in our capacity as members of "us."

It is important to note that, given this picture, different members can still bear different degrees of *personal* guilt in relation to what they understand to be "our" act. Some members might have done all they could to stop it, others may have been blamelessly ignorant of it, whereas some may have put all their efforts into its performance. It is clear enough where the personal guilt lies when this is so.

V. Plural Subject Theory and the Intuitive Picture

According to the intuitive picture, if we did something bad, and bear moral guilt for our bad action, there is a sense in which each one of us *shares in* the guilt as a member. It would seem that, if this is right, it can be appropriate for someone to feel guilt over, say, his country's starting a particular war when, by hypothesis, he was personally blameless in relation to this act of war-making. If the intuitive picture has this consequence, can it have any validity?

I believe that the theory of plural subjects I have been developing can make sense of this picture. Insofar as it is indeed the intuitive picture, this would help to confirm the theory of plural subjects as a theory of our everyday conceptual scheme. Let me now allude briefly to those parts of it that bear on the intuitive picture.[19]

Human beings form plural subjects, both large and small, in a variety of contexts.[20] The terms "social group" and "group" are, not surprisingly, standardly used in the sense of *plural subject*. Most to the present point, in a central sense, or standard use, the first person plural pronoun refers to a plural subject.[21] To say that "We did it," given this usage, is to say that "I am the member of a plural subject that did 'it.' "

"We did it" may sometimes be differently understood. Sometimes it seems to be used "distributively," to say that "We all did it." Perhaps it could even be used to mean "Some of our number did it." What I want to argue here is that the intuitive picture makes sense if we interpret "What we did" as referring to a plural subject.

If one's group membership is a matter of participation in plural subjecthood, then one is oneself, as an individual, genuinely involved in the group and in its actions (as one understands). This understanding comes from one's understanding of the nature of the underlying *joint commitment*.

To be the member of a plural subject is to be subject to a joint commitment together with the other members. Such a commitment is understood to be the commitment "of" all the members, as opposed to a "sum" of personal commitments. It is understood that it can only be rescinded jointly.

One can enter a joint commitment with a minimum of voluntariness. All that is necessary is that one indicate one's preparedness to be jointly committed in the relevant way.[22]

Joint commitment produces an involvement that is "deep" in two ways. First, one is personally affected in a "deep," psychological way. Second, as I explain below, the joint commitment in question here is foundational for a group's actions: it underpins these actions as it does the group itself. It is true that many have contributed to this foundation, but to say that is not to deny one's own contribution.

I take it that we can speak of a group acting when something like the following is the case: there is a plural subject of an intention, and, by virtue of its being the intention of that plural subject, the intention guides appropriate persons to act so as to fulfill it. People form the plural subject of an intention if they are jointly committed to accept that intention as a body.

Cases of group action fulfilling this condition can be more or less complex. In one important type of case, we may become the plural subject of an intention, by virtue of an underlying joint commitment to accept as a body that *some particular person or body may make decisions and forms intentions on our behalf*. We understand that when that person or body forms an intention in the appropriate circumstances, we will be jointly committed to uphold the intention as a body. We will, in short, constitute the plural subject of that intention.

We may jointly accept that some particular person or body is to ensure that our intentions are carried out. Thus it is possible in principle that we do something though some of us neither know of the existence of the guiding intention nor do anything personally to ensure that it be fulfilled.

To say that "We made war on Country X" when one sees "us" as a continuing plural subject of which one is a member is, then, to understand something like this: "I and other residents of this geographical area were jointly committed to intend as a body to make war on Country X, and this, our intention, was carried out accordingly by appropriate persons. . . ." One might add: "The action in question is no more any other member's than it is mine: it is *ours*, period."[23]

But suppose I did all I could reasonably be expected to do to prevent our going to war? Suppose, for instance, I organized a large protest march? Would the act of war still properly be said to be "*ours*, period" where I am one of us, on a par, qua member, with all the rest?

I take the question to amount to this: would a personal protest against the intended war somehow free me from the joint commitment to intend the war as a body? Would it somehow do away with my participation in the joint commitment?

Let us consider what I am supposed to do, given that we intend (according to the current construal) to make war on Country X. Does this mean that I am required personally to approve this war-making? That seems implausible, if only because approval and disapproval, like belief, are not clearly within our voluntary control. If the requirements imposed by the joint commitment do not go that far, am I perhaps required not to express any disapproval I may feel? There is reason to think that this, too, is not a requirement. More precisely, there is reason to think that I can express my personal disapproval of the war without violating the joint commitment.

We have at our disposal avowals of the following form: "Personally, I disapprove of our going to war" or "In my personal opinion, our going to war is a bad thing." Avowals of this sort, in particular, can be argued not to run counter to the joint commitment I am party to. The qualifiers "Personally," "In my personal opinion," and the like appear to put the avowal in a space not covered by that commitment: my personal space, so to speak. I am expressly not speaking qua group member here, but in my own voice.[24]

There is reason to suppose, then, that generally speaking I can express my personal disapproval, even my personal revulsion toward our act, without putting in question my participation in the relevant joint commitment. Something similar appears to be true of some of the more active forms of opposition to the group's act, such as organizing a protest march against the act. These may be, and be understood to be, expressions of one's personal attitudes.

It is possible, of course, that in some groups a rule of the group may forbid the expression of personal disapproval of the group's actions. According to the present argument, such a rule would be needed to supplement the understandings implicit in the joint commitment underlying the intention of a plural subject: it is not implicitly present.[25]

A joint act, like a protest march, may be understood as an expression of the attitude of a subgroup within the larger group. Such a statement as "In the view of this assembly, the country is wrong to embark on such a war" indicates that in their capacity as members of this assembly, as opposed to their capacity as members of the society as a whole, or, indeed, their personal capacity, these people oppose the war. A variety of forms of personal reaction and protest, then, appear not to go against the terms of the joint commitment under discussion.

Suppose now that all I could reasonably be expected to do was make some personal protest that does not violate our joint commitment to intend as a body to go to war, and that I made that protest. I could still accept what may be called the *participation argument* that begins from the assumption that *we* started the war. Insofar as this was a culpable act on our part, I can then accept that we did wrong and that we bear guilt for it.[26]

In short, I may be personally blameless in the matter of my group's act yet have a basis for feeling guilt in relation to that act. That basis is *our* guilt. As long as the group is my group, in the sense of being founded in a joint commitment in which I participate, I will have that basis.

VI. The Meaning of Default

I have focused so far on the question of when one will count as defaulting on a joint commitment, suggesting that one can go quite far by way of personal or subgroup protest without such default. There is also the question of what is achieved if one does default on a joint commitment.

We can assume that there are indeed ways of defaulting on a joint commitment such as the commitment to intend to make war on Country X. Refusal to comply with laws enjoining some act in connection with the war effort would presumably count, for instance, provided that no rules to excuse one were applicable. Though such refusal could express one's personal antipathy to the war, it is hard to see how it could fail to be an action one performs in one's capacity of group member. One is enjoined qua group member and must refuse in that capacity also.

Does default automatically rid one of the commitment? This would not mean that one had unilaterally *rescinded* it, since a joint commitment can only be rescinded jointly. Does default rid one of the commitment some other way? If so, the participation argument under discussion would no longer apply to the person who has defaulted.

The questions just put address the general case. Different things could be true, however, for different kinds of joint commitment, and for different forms of default. The issue is too large and too delicate for a full discussion here. The following points must suffice.

A joint commitment is not a sum of individual commitments, it is the commitment "of" a number of people. This would seem to imply that the commitment, if broken for one, is broken for all. In other words, if my default rids me of the joint commitment, it rids everyone of it.

Does one person's default rid all the parties of the relevant joint commitment? This seems credible enough in one important type of case, that of two people, each of whom is required to perform a single action, where one person willfully defaults.

There may seem to be a problem, however, in cases like the one with which we are concerned. Can the default of a single member, however willful, explode a commitment in which many people participate? This case has another feature that is not common to all cases of joint commitment. What is required is a continuing posture, roughly, a posture of support for our endeavor, given the qualifications noted. Many occasions are likely to call for a specific act or omission in the light of this requirement. If the requirements of the joint commitment on a given party are multiple and long-lasting, can a single default by that party explode the whole thing? One may feel that it could not, or, more cautiously, suppose that the answer may depend on various factors. What does the default in question amount to within the framework of the joint commitment as a whole, for example. Is it a peccadillo or a major crime?

Default in general clearly opens up the situation in important ways. For one thing, having violated a *joint* commitment I am now in some sense *answerable to* the other parties. I was not supposed to act that way, given that I did not have their permission. Certainly they now have a basis for rebuking me or, more generally, pursuing some form of recompense for the violation.

One possibility is that, to use legal jargon, default in at least some cases renders a joint commitment not void, but rather *voidable* by the other parties acting in concert. Should they not rescind it, the original joint commitment would remain. We can assume that often the other parties will prefer that the commitment remain, especially if the offending party will be subject to further obligations that he or she may (this time) be expected to fulfill.

Suppose now that in a particular case my doing what I can reasonably be expected to do to prevent a group wrong does count as defaulting on the relevant joint commitment. If the commitment is now voidable rather than void, then unless others take action, I am not yet "out of the group" on account of my actions. My feeling guilt over (subsequent) group wrongs would then still makes sense.

VII. Self and Other versus Group

Confusion as to the possibility of appropriately feeling guilt for the acts of one's group could be generated by the quite common claim that guilt itself cannot be "vicarious," in the sense that one cannot bear guilt for *another's* wrongdoing, and by the related claim that feelings of guilt are appropriate only to "*one's own* violations" (of moral obligations). Both of these claims appeal to the contrast between oneself and "others."[27]

This contrast, however, does not exhaust the possible objects of our reactive emotions, as might be thought—with one's group located on the "other" side. Even taking "group" quite widely, one is part of one's own group. In the case of groups as plural subjects, however, one is integrated with the others in one's group in a special way.

One's fellow group members, though individually other than oneself, create together with oneself a single joint commitment that functions as a motivating force for all.[28] It creates the conditions of appropriateness of the term "we," which refers to self and others only insofar as they are joined together through the medium of a single—supra-individual—thing, a joint commitment.

Reaction to the deeds of one's group is thus not best characterized as reaction to self, as reaction to others, or as even to self plus others, but rather as reaction to a distinct and distinctive entity—the plural subject—with a *sui generis* relation to both self and others. A feeling of guilt that arises out of one's group's bad action relates neither to one's own violations nor to those of "others."

If this is right, can feeling guilt be characterized quite generally as involving negative self-assessment or self-punishment? Certainly, if it hurts, it hurts the person who has it. But in the case on which I am focusing the feeling of guilt would most appropriately be expressed not by the words "I am guilty" but by the words "We are guilty." If it involves negative self-assessment of a sort, it involves negative assessment of the self-as-group-member or of the group-in-my-person, rather than of me personally. To give this kind of guilt feeling a special name we might call it a feeling of "membership guilt."

I have here argued, in effect, that certain widely held views, "truisms" even, about guilt feelings are either false or misleading as usually stated. The truisms are "Guilt is only appropriate to one's own moral violations"; "Guilt is an emotion of negative self-assessment"; "Guilt involves self-punishment." Thus I have challenged views about both the proper object of guilt and about what feeling guilt amounts to.

I have not challenged the claim that "Guilt itself cannot be vicarious" insofar as this is understood to mean that one cannot bear guilt for another's wrongdoing. This leads me to another important point, a point about who bears the guilt when the guilt is collective.

VIII. Collective Guilt Is Not a "Sum"

According to the intuitive picture, there is such a thing as collective guilt. This is the guilt of the group. According to the intuitive picture, if there is collective guilt it will be shared by members of the collective in question in their capacity as group members. My suggestion on behalf of the intuitive picture is that if groups are understood to be plural subjects, and the guilt of a particular group has been established, then it makes sense to say—as the intuitive picture has it—that each member shares or participates in this guilt in his or her capacity as a group member.

But what is it to share in collective guilt in one's capacity as a member? As I understand it, this is not in itself to bear guilt as an individual person: it is not to bear personal guilt. Let me explain. Collective guilt is not a kind of "sum" involving the personal guilt of many individuals. First, it is not built up of guilt independently accrued by particular members. A group can accrue guilt without all or most members being personally guilty. It may even be possible for a group to accrue guilt though none of the individual members are personally guilty. Second, the guilt of a group does not carry with it guilt personally born by its members.

If we think of all the members of a guilty group as bearing "membership guilt," we have to understand that membership guilt is not personal guilt. It neither derives from personal guilt nor results in it. In other words, sharing in collective guilt is not a matter of bearing personal guilt.

But how are we to understand such sharing? We might put things this way: members *share equally* in collective guilt, but they do not have *equal shares*. Nor do they have unequal shares. In short *there is no way of breaking collective guilt down into quantifiable shares.*

In case this situation seems hard to grasp, the following humdrum analogy bears some similarity to it. Two people may be said to "share equally" in their joint bank account—it is, after all, a joint account—but it is not clear that it makes sense to say that they have "equal shares" or, indeed, "unequal shares."[29]

IX. A Harsh Doctrine?

If we allow that mere membership in a group can be enough to involve one in guilt, whatever one does while remaining a member, is this not simply too harsh a doctrine?

One aspect of the matter that could help to spark such a question is that one's membership itself may not be a voluntary matter. This question may seem particularly apposite if we are considering families or whole societies.

Assume we have a large and enduring plural subject, a society, if you will. Presumably, many of the members had little real option about becoming members. They were "born into" the society, and pressured into membership by family, teachers, and peers. Again, it may be that few members have the means to leave the society. Perhaps this could be brought about by ceasing to be the residents of a particular territory. They may simply be too poor to travel the required distance.[30]

Is it not harsh, then, to suppose quite generally that such people share in the guilt of their group simply by being members? For many, their membership was in a sense forced upon them and is now in a sense inalienable.

Jean-Paul Sartre writes somewhere of two ways a soldier mobilized in a war could "always get out of it": "by suicide or desertion; these ultimate possibles are those which must always be present for us. . . ."

Not everyone has the option of suicide. Some people are carefully monitored so that they do not take their own lives. In any case, it certainly seems a little harsh if the perennial option of suicide is put forward as the reason why citizens generally "deserve" a war (as Sartre puts it) or "deserve" to share the guilt in a war.

I have not been arguing for the conclusion that members "deserve" the special guilt of membership, simply that they accrue it. Suicide can, I suppose, rid them of it, insofar as it rids them of membership itself. But they do not accrue it because they had the option of suicide, or any other option. They accrue it because they are members.

One can accrue membership guilt while being morally blameless *at the personal level.* But we social creatures exist, if you like, at more than one level.

We are group-forming creatures and our groups may act badly. If my group acts badly that means that I and my fellow members have some guilt to share. I'm not sure that that's a harsh doctrine. Perhaps, though, it is a tragic doctrine, incorporating a tragic truth. There has to be something tragic about group membership, if it can afflict people with a kind of guilt even though they are personally innocent.

In spite of this disturbing thought, the feeling of guilt over a collective action can play a very positive role. Since feeling guilt is unpleasant, and may have an inherently punishing character, it is liable to move one who feels it to act, and to act in an appropriate way. This will not (necessarily) be the personal undertaking of reparative action (such action may not be appropriate or feasible). In many cases, it will lead to political action, to attempting to stop the group action if it is in process, or to encouraging the group as a whole to do what it can for its victims. Collective guilt perceived as such by individual members can be the stimulus to improvement in group action and the moral quality of group life.

A less grim aspect of the argument of this paper is that it can apparently make sense to feel not only guilt, but pride, on behalf of what one's group has done, whatever one's precise role in the generation of the admirable action. As guilt is unpleasant, so pride is pleasant. Even someone of few achievements can legitimately (according to this argument) feel pride in the achievements of the relevant group.[31] The tendency of the literature has been to focus on collective wrongs and their relation to individual guilt, rather than on collective achievements and their relation to individual pride. But these appear to be two sides of the same coin.

Conclusion

Many people apparently feel guilt over their group's action, though we would judge them to be personally blameless. Prevalent understandings about what it is to feel guilt suggest that their feelings of guilt are inappropriate.

I have argued that if one's group is a plural subject and acts in a blameworthy way, a feeling of guilt over its bad action can be appropriate. There are two aspects of this. First, one's group's culpability is a proper object of guilt. Second, insofar as feeling guilt involves a negative assessment of something, it may not involve a negative assessment of the "self as such" but rather of "the self-as-group-member" or, "the group-in-this person."

If a plural subject acts badly and bears guilt for its action, then it makes sense for a member of the plural subject to feel guilt over the action.[32] That this is so does not touch the question of anyone's personal guilt or blameworthiness with respect to the action in question. The guilt it makes sense to feel is guilt of the group. It is guilt in which one shares, but does not own.[33]

Notes

1. In what follows, when I write of a group "acting badly" I should be taken to imply that the group acts in a blameworthy manner. The same goes for my references to a group's "wrongdoing."

2. See, for instance, May (1992), pp. 298–402; Wallace (1994), p. 244.

3. One feels guilt *over* something. That is what I mean by "the appropriate object of guilt."

4. See Wallace (1994), p. 66, note 22: "Guilt is appropriate to one's own violations [of moral obligation]." Taylor (1985), p. 91: "feelings of guilt . . . cannot arise from the deeds or omissions of others."

5. Cf. Taylor (1985): "Guilt itself cannot be vicarious"; Feinberg (1991): ". . . *there can be no such thing as vicarious guilt,*" p. 60, emphasis Feinberg's.

6. Cf. the subtitle of Taylor's *Pride, Shame, and Guilt* (1985): *"Emotions of Self-Assessment."*

7. Precisely what a given person could "reasonably have been expected to

do" in a given case may not be clear. This may be the occasion of serious moral debate. In what follows I shall simply take it that there are some relatively clear cases of doing what one reasonably could have been expected to do under the circumstances.

8. Perhaps this does not count as "doing everything I could to prevent the action," since it is not clear that unexpressed condemnation goes any way to prevent the action. On the other hand, in these special circumstances this is as far as I can go toward preventing the action. Condemnation is the first step to deliberate preventive action.

9. This point added in response to a conversation with David Luban, October 1995. Precisely when and why some ignorance is culpable is a matter of some delicacy into which I make no attempt to enter here. Evidently people sometimes experience guilt because they ignored signs that something bad was going on.

10. The simple ignorance of one's group's wrongful act may seem to be sufficient rebuttal, already, of the appropriateness of feeling guilt in its regard. The case in the text will, if anything, be even more persuasive.

11. Cf. Gray (1971), pp. 291–93; Horton (1992), p. 153; Greenspan (1995), p. 162. Greenspan gives the example of "white American guilt about slavery or guilt felt for various other misdeeds that occurred before the birth of those who felt guilty." I shall not here consider the case of guilt over "misdeeds" of one's group which occurred before one was a member. The story here may be at least somewhat different—though perhaps not wholly different—from that of those who were group members at the time the misdeed occurred.

12. As I read Karl Jaspers in his probing essay *The Question of German Guilt*, he takes this to be so. (He refers to "feeling coresponsible" as opposed to feeling guilt, but the basic issue appears to be the same.) Jaspers writes that " . . . in a way which is rationally not conceivable, which is even rationally refutable, I feel co-responsible for what Germans do and have done. . . . As a philosopher I now seem to have strayed completely into the realm of feeling and to have abandoned conception" (Jaspers, 1947, pp. 80–81). My argument in this essay suggests that he may not, after all, have "abandoned conception" or strayed from what is "rationally conceivable."

13. See Taylor (1985), pp. 91 and 93.

14. As argued by Greenspan (1995), p. 171 and elsewhere.

15. See, for instance, Horton (1992), pp. 151 ff.

16. Taylor (1985), p. 91.

17. Feinberg (1991) cites "solidarity" as a "necessary condition of the vicarious emotions" (he refers to pride and shame), p. 65. He gives a complex account of "solidarity," p. 62. Some elements of this (for instance "sharing a common cooperative purpose") have some affinity with the background conditions I describe in the text below. See also his brief allusion to "the plural possessive 'our,' " p. 63. It is not clear that he would allow that guilt, as opposed to shame, is a possible "vicarious emotion." I shall not attempt here any close comparison of my views with Feinberg's.

18. "We may bear moral guilt . . . ." I take it that according to the intuitive picture we do bear moral guilt for our bad actions in some circumstances. This does not mean that we will always do so. It could be that if we were forced to act badly, for instance, this would preclude our bearing moral guilt for our bad action. Or perhaps we did not and could not have been expected to believe that what we were doing was wrong.

19. Those unfamiliar with the theory are referred to *On Social Facts,* to the introduction, this volume, and to the relevant sections of Chapter 12, among others.

20. The question of large group plural subjects is particularly pertinent to the present topic, insofar as people often feel guilt over the acts of large nations, for instance. I cannot enter that discussion in this essay, but see Gilbert, forthcoming (b). See also Chapter 15, this volume.

21. *On Social Facts,* Chapter 4.

22. For more on joint commitment, see the introduction, this volume, and Chapter 12.

23. Gilbert, forthcoming (b), section I, includes a longer treatment of group intentions and actions, and of large groups as plural subjects. Gilbert (1993ms) is a self-contained discussion of what it is for "us" to intend to do something.

24. In Chapter 7, this volume, I discuss how the "Personally, I . . ." qualification may be used in the context of a group's belief. See also Chapter 14.

25. For a plural subject account of social conventions, a species of social rule, see Chapter 2, this volume, and *On Social Facts,* Chapter 6, section 8. The latter briefly presents an account of social rules in general, a discussion amplified in my essay "On Social Rules: Some Problems for Hart's Account and a New Proposal" (1995ms).

26. I shall not attempt to explore here the conditions under which it is appropriate to ascribe guilt or blameworthiness to a group in relation to a given action of the group.

27. Similarly, the idea of "egoism" (roughly, concern for self) finds its natural contrast in "altruism" (roughly, concern for "others"). For thoughts on this contrast that parallel those in the following paragraphs, see Gilbert (1994), pp. 621–22.

28. Here I consciously echo Rousseau's reference to people uniting so that "their forces are directed by means of a single moving power and made to act in concert" (Rousseau, 1792/1983). The passage in question has been translated rather variously, showing, I suspect, the difficulty people have in understanding it. Here I quote from—and echo—the translation of Donald A. Cress, p. 23.

29. Possibly my thought of this example was influenced by the reference to joint bank accounts in Feinberg (1991), p. 63.

30. I have in mind the possibility that one is committed qua resident in a particular part of the world, so that leaving that place would bring one's

commitment to an end without one's fellows having to agree to the rescinding of the joint commitment. On the topic of the "alienability" of membership see also the text, above.

31. Pride often concerns the achievements of those "representing" the group, and guilt may also. I will not be exploring this aspect of the question of collective guilt or glory here.

32. I do not go so far as to say that a member *should* feel guilt in such a case. This appears not to be true in general. If the wrong in question is very minor, for instance, a feeling of guilt may not be called for, because it would be too trivial (I owe this example to Joseph Raz, in discussion at Columbia University, 1995.)

Other cases may not be trivial, but it is still not obvious that members should feel guilt, in the sense that it is some sort of requirement that they do. It is not clear what it is to say of any *emotion* that one is required to have it. My main point in this essay is to argue that a feeling of membership guilt is *not ruled out* on the grounds of having an improper object (one's group's wrongdoing) or being an inappropriate form of response to that object (a feeling of guilt). This note was prompted by questions from several people in discussion.

33. The original version of this essay, entitled "Group Wrongs and Guilt Feelings," appears in *The Journal of Ethics,* vol.1, number 1, 1997. It was written while I was a Visiting Scholar at New York University, spring semester 1995. This shorter version omits several sections of the original. It also includes some additional material. I thank Angelo Corlett for the conference invitation that prompted my extended consideration of this topic. I am grateful for comments from audiences to whom this material has been presented: at Georgia State University ("Freedom and Responsibility" conference); the University of Massachusetts at Amherst; the University of Connecticut, Storrs; and Columbia University (all in 1995). Conversations with Donald Baxter and Angelo Corlett have been particularly helpful. I have yet to reply in print to a question from both Stephen Schiffer and Samuel Wheeler. I hope to address that and some other questions, elsewhere.

Bibliography

[Articles that appear as chapters in this book are so labeled.]

Albritton, R. (1959) "On Wittgenstein's Use of the Term 'Criterion'," *Journal of Philosophy*, vol. 56.

Atiyah, P. (1971) *An Introduction to the Law of Contract*, New York: Oxford University Press, 2d ed.

Atiyah, P. (1981) *Promises, Morals and the Law*, New York: Oxford University Press.

Aumann, R. (1976) "Agreeing to Disagree," *Annals of Statistics*, vol. 4.

Aumann, R. (1987) "Correlated Equilibrium as an Expression of Bayesian Rationality," *Econometrica*, vol. 55.

Ayer, A. J. (1968) "Can There Be a Private Language?" in G. Pitcher, ed., *Wittgenstein: The Philosophical Investigations*, London: MacMillan.

Bach, K., and R. M. Harnish (1979) *Linguistic Communication and Speech Acts*, Cambridge, Mass.: MIT Press.

Baier, A. (1985) "Promises, Promises, Promises," in A. Baier, *Postures of the Mind*, Minneapolis: Minnesota University Press.

Barzun, J. (1968) *The American University*, New York: Harper and Row.

Becker, L. C. (1981) "Hard Choices Are Not Enough," *Virginia Law Review*, vol. 67.

Bennett, J. (1973) "The Meaning-Nominalist Strategy," *Foundations of Language*, vol. 10.

Bennett, J. (1976) *Linguistic Behavior*, Cambridge: Cambridge University Press.

Beran, H. (1977) "In Defense of the Consent Theory of Political Obligation and Authority," *Ethics*, vol. 87.

Bowen, M. (1965) "Family Psychotherapy with Schizophrenia in the Hospital and in Private Practice," in I. Boszormenyi-Nagy and J. Framo, eds., *Intensive Family Therapy: Theoretical and Practical Aspects*, New York: Hoeber Medical Division, Harper and Row.

Brandt, R. B. (1965) "The Concepts of Obligation and Duty," *Mind*, vol. 73.

Bratman, M. (1987) *Intention, Plans, and Practical Reason*, Cambridge, Mass.: Harvard University Press.

Burge, T. (1975) "On Knowledge and Convention," *Philosophical Review*, vol. 84.

Cohen, G. A. (1967) "Beliefs and Roles," *Proceedings of the Aristotelian Society*, vol. 67.

Davidson, D. (1969) "How is Weakness of the Will Possible?" in J. Feinberg, ed., *Moral Concepts*, London: Oxford University Press.

De Moor, A. (1987) "Are Contracts Promises?" in J. Eekelaar and J. Bell, eds., *Oxford Essays in Jurisprudence*, New York: Oxford University Press.

Dostoevsky, F. M. (1943) *The Brothers Karamazov*, tr. Constance Garnett, New York: Random House.

Dummett, M. (1973) *Frege*, London: Duckworth.

Dummett, M. (1978) *Truth and Other Enigmas*, Cambridge, Mass.: Harvard University Press.

Durkheim, E. (1968) *Les Regles de la Methode Sociologique*, Paris: Presses Universitaires de France.

Durkheim, E. (1895/1982) *The Rules of Sociological Method*, tr. W. D. Halls, New York: Free Press.

Durkheim, E., and M. Mauss (1963) *Primitive Classification*, tr. Rodney Needham, Chicago: University of Chicago Press.

Fann, K. T. (1969) *Wittgenstein's Conception of Philosophy*, Oxford: Blackwell.

Feinberg, J. (1991) "Collective Responsibility," in L. May and S. Hoffman, eds., *Collective Responsibility: Five Decades of Debate in Theoretical and Applied Ethics*, Savage, Md.: Rowman and Littlefield.

Finnis, J. (1980) *Natural Law and Natural Rights*, Oxford: Clarendon Press.

Fried, C. (1981) *Contract as Promise: A Theory of Contractual Obligation*, Cambridge, Mass.: Harvard University Press.

Fuller, L. (1969) *The Morality of Law*, revised ed., New Haven, Conn.: Yale University Press.

Gauthier, D. (1975) "Coordination," *Dialogue,* vol. 14.

Gaylin, W. (1987) *Rediscovering Love,* New York: Penguin Books.

Geertz, C. (1975) "Thick Description: Toward an Interpretative Theory of Culture," in C. Geertz, *The Interpretation of Cultures*, New York: Basic Books.

Gibbs, P. J. (1965) "Norms: The Problem of Definition and Classification," *American Journal of Sociology*, vol. 70.

Gilbert, M. (1974) "About Conventions" *Second-Order*, vol. 3.

Gilbert, M (1978ms) *On Social Facts*, D. Phil. thesis, Oxford University (Bodleian Library Collection).

Gilbert, M. (1981) "Game Theory and *Convention,*" *Synthese,* vol. 46. [Chapter 5]

Gilbert, M. (1983abs) "Some Limitations of Rationality" (abstract), *Journal of Philosophy*, vol. 53.

Gilbert, M. (1983ms) "Some Limitations of Rationality," paper presented at the meetings of the American Philosophical Association, December 1983.

Gilbert, M. (1983a) "Notes on the Concept of a Social Convention," *New Literary History,* vol. 14. [Chapter 3]

Gilbert, M. (1983b) "Agreements, Conventions, and Language," *Synthese,* vol. 54. [Chapter 12]

Gilbert, M. (1983c) "On the Question Whether Language Has a Social Nature: Some Aspects of Winch and Others on Wittgenstein," *Synthese,* vol. 56. [Chapter 9]

Gilbert, M. (1987) "Modelling Collective Belief," *Synthese,* vol. 73. [Chapter 7]

Gilbert, M. (1989a) [1992] *On Social Facts,* London and New York: Routledge [2d printing, Princeton: Princeton University Press]

Gilbert, M. (1989b) "Rationality and Salience," *Philosophical Studies* 57. [Chapter 1]

Gilbert, M. (1989c) "Folk Psychology Takes Sociality Seriously," *Behavioral and Brain Sciences,* vol. 12.

Gilbert, M. (1990a) "Walking Together: A Paradigmatic Social Phenomenon," *Midwest Studies in Philosophy,* vol. 15; University of Notre Dame Press: Notre Dame. [Chapter 6]

Gilbert, M. (1990b) "Fusion: Sketch of a 'Contractual' Model", in R. C. L. Moffat, J. Grcic, and M. Bayles, eds., *Perspectives on the Family,* Lewiston: Edwin Mellen Press. [Chapter 8]

Gilbert, M. (1990c) "Rationality, Coordination and Convention," *Synthese,* vol. 84. [Chapter 2]

Gilbert, M. (1993a) "Agreements, Coercion, and Obligation," *Ethics,* vol. 103. [Chapter 12]

Gilbert, M. (1993b) "Is an Agreement an Exchange of Promises?" *Journal of Philosophy,* vol. 54. [Chapter 13]

Gilbert, M. (1994a) "Durkheim and Social Facts" in W. Pickering and H. Martins, eds., *Debating Durkheim,* London: Routledge.

Gilbert, M. (1994b) "Me, You, and Us: Distinguishing 'Egoism,' 'Altruism,' and 'Groupism,' " in *Behavioral and Brain Sciences,* vol. 17.

Gilbert, M. (1993ms) "Shared Intention," invited symposium paper, American Philosophical Association, San Francisco, 1993.

Gilbert, M. (1995ms) "On Social Rules: Some Problems for Hart's Account and a New Proposal."

Gilbert, M. (forthcoming, a) "Concerning Sociality: The Plural Subject as Paradigm," in J. Greenwood, ed., *The Mark of the Social,* Lanham, Md.: Rowman and Littlefield.

Gilbert, M. (forthcoming, b) "Group Wrongs and Guilt Feelings," in *Journal of Ethics,* vol. 1.

Gilbert, M. (forthcoming, c) "Social Norms," entry in E. Craig, ed., *Routledge Encyclopedia of Philosophy,* London: Routledge.

Grandy, R. (1977) "Review of Lewis's *Convention*," *Journal of Philosophy*, vol. 74.

Gray, J. G. (1971) "The Stains of War," in R. W. Smith, ed., *Guilt: Man and Society*, Garden City, N. Y.: Anchor Books.

Greenspan, P. (1995) *Practical Guilt: Moral Dilemmas, Emotions, and Social Norms*, New York: Oxford University Press.

Greenwood, J. (1990) "The Mark of the Social," *Social Epistemology*, vol. 5.

Guest, A. G., ed. (1984) *Anson's Law of Contract*, 26th ed., Oxford: Clarendon Press.

Hacker, P. (1971) *Insight and Illusion*, Oxford: Oxford University Press.

Hare, R. M. (1989) "Political Obligation," *Essays in Political Morality*, Oxford: Oxford University Press.

Harsanyi, J. (1977) *Rational Behavior and Bargaining Equilibria in Games and Social Situations*, New York: Cambridge University Press.

Hart, H. L. A. (1961) *The Concept of Law*, Oxford: Oxford University Press.

Heal, J. (1978) "Common Knowledge," *Philosophical Quarterly*, vol. 28.

Hobbes, T. (1651/1982) *Leviathan*, Harmondsworth: Penguin Books.

Hollis, M. (1977) *Models for Man*, Cambridge: Cambridge University Press.

Horton, J. (1992) *Political Obligation*, Atlantic Highlands, N.J.: Humanities Press International.

Hume, D. (1739/1978) *A Treatise of Human Nature*, London: Oxford University Press.

Hume, D. (1758/1957) *An Enquiry Concerning the Principles of Morals*, Indianapolis: Liberal Arts Press.

Jaspers, K. (1947) *The Question of German Guilt*, tr. E. B. Ashton, New York: Capricorn Books.

Karpel, M. (1976) "Individuation: From Fusion to Dialogue," *Family Process*, vol. 15.

Kavka, G. (1986) *Hobbes*, Princeton: Princeton University Press.

Kripke, S. (1982) *Wittgenstein on Rules and Private Language: An Elementary Exposition*, Cambridge, Mass.: Harvard University Press.

Kuhn, H. (1961) "An Algorithm for Equilibrium Points in Bimatrix Games," *Proceedings of the National Academy of Sciences*, vol. 47.

Kuflik, A. (1982) "Coordination, Equilibrium, and Rational Choice," *Philosophical Studies*, vol. 42.

Lawrence, D. H. (1949) *The Rainbow*, New York: Penguin Books.

Lewis, D. (1969) *Convention: A Philosophic Study*, Cambridge, Mass.: Harvard University Press.

Lewis, D. (1975) "Languages and Language," in K. Gunderson, ed., *Minnesota Studies in the Philosophy of Science*, vol. 7, Minneapolis: University of Minnesota Press.

Lewis, D. (1976) "Reply to Jamieson," *Canadian Journal of Philosophy*, vol. 6.

Lewis, D. (1983) "Scorekeeping in a Language Game," in D. Lewis, *Philosophical Papers*, vol. 1, Oxford: Oxford University Press.

Lindgren, R. (1988ms) "Models of Marriage and the Privacy Decision," paper prepared for AMINTAPHIL Conference, Pace University, 1988.

Linsky, L. (1957) "Wittgenstein on Language and Some Problems of Philosophy," in K. T. Fann, ed., *Ludwig Wittgenstein, The Man and His Philosophy*, New York: Dell.

Luce, R. D., and H. Raiffa (1957) *Games and Decisions*, New York: John Wiley Press.

Lukes, S. (1973) *Emile Durkheim*, London: Allen Lane.

Lurie, A. (1985) *Foreign Affairs*, London: Michael Joseph.

MacIntyre, A. (1967) "The Idea of a Social Science," *Aristotelian Society Supplement*, vol. 41.

Malcolm, N. (1957) "Wittgenstein's Philosophical Investigations," in K. T. Fann, ed., *Ludwig Wittgenstein, The Man and His Philosophy*, New York: Dell.

Maslow, A. H. (1953) "Love and Healthy People," in A. Montagu, ed., *The Meaning of Love*, New York: Julian Press.

May, L. (1992) *Sharing Responsibility*, Chicago: University of Chicago Press.

May, L., and S. Hoffman, eds. (1991) *Collective Responsibility: Five Decades of Debate in Theoretical and Applied Ethics*, Savage, Md.: Rowman and Littlefield.

McCullers, C. (1985) *The Member of the Wedding*, London: Penguin Books.

McDowell, J. (1979) "Virtue and Reason," *Monist*, vol. 62.

McGinn, C. (1984) *Wittgenstein on Meaning: An Interpretation and Evaluation*, Oxford: Blackwell.

McPherson, T. (1967) *Political Obligation*, London: Routledge and Kegan Paul.

Mill, J. S. (1861/1978) *On Liberty*, Indianapolis: Hackett.

Peacocke, C. (1976) "Truth Definitions and Actual Languages," in G. Evans and J. McDowell, eds., *Truth and Meaning*, Oxford: Oxford University Press.

Pitcher, G. (1964) *The Philosophy of Wittgenstein*, Englewood Cliffs, N.J.: Prentice Hall.

Pitcher, G., ed. (1968) *Wittgenstein: The Philosophical Investigations*, London: MacMillan.

Plato, (B.C./1925) *Symposium*, tr. W. R. M. Lamb, in *Plato*, vol. 3, Loeb Classical Library, Cambridge, Mass.: Harvard University Press.

Pollock, F. (1955) "*Gruppenexperiment—Ein Studienbericht*," in T. W. Adorno and W. Dirks, eds., *Frankfurter Beiträge zur Sociologie*, Bd. 2, Europäische Verlaganstalt, Frankfurt.

Postema, G. J. (1982) "Coordination and Convention at the Foundations of Law," *Journal of Legal Studies*, vol. 11.

Prichard, H. A. (1949) "Exchanging," in H. Prichard, *Moral Obligation*, New York: Oxford University Press.

Quine, W. V. O. (1969) "Foreword," in Lewis, *Convention*, Cambridge, Mass.: Harvard University Press.

Quinton, A. (1975–1976) "Social Objects," *Proceedings of the Aristotelian Society*, vol. 76.

Radford, C. (1984) "I Will, If You Will," *Mind*, vol. 92.

Raz, J. (1981) "Authority and Consent," *Virginia Law Review*, vol. 67.

Raz, J. (1984) "On the Nature of Rights," *Mind*, vol. 92.

Robins, M. (1984) *Promising, Intending, and Moral Autonomy*, Cambridge: Cambridge University Press.

Rousseau, J. (1792/1983) *The Social Contract*, tr. D. A. Cress, Indianapolis: Hackett.

Ryan, A. (1970) *The Philosophy of the Social Sciences*, London: Macmillan.

Scanlon, T. (1990) "Promises and Practices," *Philosophy and Public Affairs*, vol. 19.

Schelling, T. (1960) *The Strategy of Conflict*, Oxford: Oxford University Press.

Schiffer, S. (1972) *Meaning*, Oxford: Oxford University Press.

Schmidtz, D. (1990) "Justifying the State," *Ethics*, vol. 101.

Schmitt, F. (1994) "The Justification of Group Beliefs," in F. Schmitt, ed., *Socializing Epistemology: The Social Dimensions of Knowledge*, Lanham, Md.: Rowman and Littlefield.

Schotter, A. (1981) *An Economic Theory of Social Institutions*, Cambridge: Cambridge University Press.

Sellars, W. (1963a) "Imperatives, Intentions, and the Logic of 'Ought,' " in G. Nakhnikian and H. N. Castaneda, eds., *Morality and the Language of Conduct*, Detroit: Wayne State University Press.

Sellars, W. (1963b) *Science, Perception, and Reality*, London: Routledge.

Sen, A. (1970) *Collective Choice and Social Welfare*, New York: Holden-Day.

Sen, A. (1974) "Choice, Ordering, and Morality," in S. Korner, ed., *Practical Reason*, New Haven: Yale University Press.

Shakespeare, N. (1993) "Diary," *Telegraph Magazine*, July 10.

Simmel, G. (1908/1971) in D. N. Levine, ed., *Georg Simmel: On Individuality and Social Forms*, Chicago: University of Chicago Press.

Simmons, A. J. (1979) *Moral Principles and Political Obligations*, Princeton: Princeton University Press.

Simmons, A. J. (1984) "Consent, Free Choice, and Democratic Government," *Georgia Law Review*, vol. 18.

Sorokin, P. (1947) *Society, Culture, and Personality*, New York: Harper.

Stalnaker, R. (1973) "Presuppositions," *Journal of Philosophical Logic*, vol. 2.

Stalnaker, R. (1974) "Pragmatic Presuppositions," in M. Munitz and P. Unger, eds., *Semantics and Philosophy*, New York: New York University Press.

Stalnaker, R. (1984) *Inquiry*, Cambridge, Mass.: MIT Press.

Strawson, P. F. (1954) Review of *Philosophical Investigations*, *Mind*, vol. 62.

Taylor, G. (1985) *Pride, Shame, and Guilt: Emotions of Self-Assessment*, Oxford: Clarendon Press.

Thomson, J. J. (1971) "The Verification Principle and the Private Language

Argument," in O. R. Jones, ed., *The Private Language Argument*, New York: Macmillan.

Tuomela, R. (1984) *A Theory of Social Action,* Dordrecht: Kluwer.

Tuomela, R. (1985) "Social Action," in G. Seebass and R. Tuomela, eds., *Social Action*, Dordrecht: Kluwer.

Tuomela, R. (1992) "Group Beliefs," *Synthese*, vol. 91.

Ullman-Margalit, E. (1977) *The Emergence of Norms,* Oxford: Oxford University Press.

Updike, J. (1981) *Problems and Other Stories*, New York: Fawcett Crest.

Van Fraassen, B. (1980) *The Scientific Image*, New York: Oxford University Press.

Von Neumann, J., and D. Morgenstern (1953) *Theory of Games and Economic Behavior,* Princeton: Princeton University Press.

Wallace, R. J. (1994) *Responsibility and the Moral Sentiments*, Cambridge, Mass.: Harvard University Press.

Wallace, W. (1983) *Principles of Scientific Sociology*, New York: Aldine.

Wallace, W. (1988) "Towards a Disciplanary Matrix in Sociology," in Neil J. Smelser, ed., *Handbook of Sociology*, Newbury Park, Calif.: Sage.

Walzer, M. (1970) *Obligations: Essays on Disobedience, War, and Citizenship,* Cambridge, Mass.: Cambridge University Press.

Watkins, J. W. N. (1970) "Imperfect Rationality," in R. Borger and F. Cioffi, eds., *Explanation in the Behavioural Sciences,* Cambridge, Mass.: Cambridge University Press.

Weber, M. (1922/1964) *The Theory of Social and Economic Organization*, tr. A. M. Henderson and T. Parsons, New York: Free Press.

Weber, M. (1922/1978) in G. Roth and C. Wittich, eds., *Economy and Society*, Berkeley: University of California Press.

Winch, P. (1958) *The Idea of a Social Science and its Relation to Philosophy*, London: Routledge and Kegan Paul.

Wittgenstein, L. (1953/1958) *Philosophical Investigations*, 3d. ed., London: Blackwell.

Wolff, K. H., ed. (1969) *The Sociology of Georg Simmel*, tr. and ed. K. H. Wolff, Glencoe, Ill.: Free Press.

Woozley, A. D. (1979) *Law and Obedience: The Arguments of Plato's Crito*, Chapel Hill: University of North Carolina Press.

Index

Note: **bold type** indicates that an index entry is a technical term or phrase of the author.

399

About the Author

Margaret Gilbert is professor of philosophy at the University of Connecticut, Storrs. She is the author of *On Social Facts* (1989) and numerous articles. She has been a member of the School of Historical Studies at the Institute for Advanced Study, Princeton, and has held other distinguished research posts. She has taught at several universities in the United States and Great Britain, including Princeton University and the University of California at Los Angeles, and has lectured widely to audiences in a range of disciplines, including philosophy, sociology, and political theory.